GROWING CONCERNS

HARVARD BUSINESS REVIEW EXECUTIVE BOOK SERIES

GROWING CONCERNS
BUILDING AND MANAGING THE SMALLER BUSINESS

DAVID E. GUMPERT
Editor

JOHN WILEY & SONS
New York · Chichester · Brisbane · Toronto · Singapore

Library of Congress Cataloging in Publication Data:

Main entry under title:
Growing concerns.

  (Harvard business review executive book series)
  Includes index.
  1. Small business—Management—Addresses, essays,
lectures.   I. Harvard business review.

HD62.7.G76 1983   658′.002   83-17034
ISBN 0-471-88677-7

Printed in the United States of America

10 9 8 7 6 5 4 3 2 1

Foreword

For sixty years the *Harvard Business Review* has been the farthest reaching executive program of the Harvard Business School. It is devoted to the continuing education of executives and aspiring managers primarily in business organizations, but also in not-for-profit institutions, in government, and in the professions. Through its publishing partners, reprints, and translation programs it finds an audience in many languages in most countries in the world, occasionally even penetrating the barrier between East and West.

The *Harvard Business Review* draws on the talents of the most creative people in modern business and management education. About half its content comes from practicing managers, the rest from professional people and university researchers. Everything *HBR* publishes has something to do with the skills, attitudes, and knowledge essential to the competent and ethical practice of management.

This book consists of 36 articles addressed to the management problems of smaller companies. Under the direction of David Gumpert, HBR has encouraged contributions by the hard-pressed entrepreneurs who contribute an essential vitality to our business system. We have tried also to encourage academic research into small business and to develop a framework for understanding it better.

In the words of two of the contributors to this volume, a small business is certainly not a little big business. I hope that readers will better understand the full truth of this statement. Managers of smaller companies should be able to find specific support in the interesting experience analyzed here.

KENNETH R. ANDREWS, Editor
Harvard Business Review

Contents

Part Three   Effective Financial Management

Part Four   Best Use of Outside Resources

Part Five   Planning for Tomorrow

GROWING CONCERNS

Introduction

DAVID E. GUMPERT

Not too many years ago, a volume such as this would have been difficult to assemble, whether from articles in *Harvard Business Review* or elsewhere. Not only were far fewer articles about small business being published than is now the case, but those that did appear tended to view smaller companies as merely miniaturized versions of large corporations, rather than as entities with distinct problems of their own.

Since 1979, *Harvard Business Review* has been publishing in each issue at least one or two articles directed toward the special management needs of smaller businesses, under the feature title "Growing Concerns." We rather arbitrarily define small businesses as those with between $1 million and $30 million annual sales, though we have published articles in the feature about starting ventures and about managing companies with more than $30 million of annual sales. Of course, *HBR* before 1979 published a number of valuable articles about the managerial problems of small enterprises, and several are included in this edition.

HBR has not been alone in devoting more attention to small business. Several new publications directed specifically toward owners of small companies have sprung up in recent years; among them are *Venture*, *INC.*, and *In Business*. Established publications such as *The Wall Street Journal* and *Forbes* have started special sections about small businesses. Dozens of books about starting and managing small ventures have been published in recent years.

The increasing volume of printed material about small business is indicative of spreading interest in entrepreneurship. Each of the Big Eight accounting firms and many large banks have in recent years started special departments to seek out and effectively service small business customers. Lately, variety of commercial institutions and academicians have surveyed owners of small businesses about their attitudes and behavior related to a wide variety of subjects ranging from the impact of the recession to the level of owners' salaries.

Why all the interest in small business? How has this heightened interest—particularly as expressed through the articles in this volume—contributed to our knowledge of small business management? Which areas of small business management are in need of further exploration?

The answers to these questions, however tentative they may be, can assist entrepreneurs in better understanding their roles in today's society, in solving vexing management problems, and in appreciating which managerial areas warrant additional research.

In my view, the growing interest in entrepreneurship and small business management is the result of several independent but simultaneously occurring national developments. These trends are of a social, political, technological, and economic nature. The effect of these trends has been to create a climate increasingly favorable for new venture start-ups; since 1971 the number of new business incorporations has more than doubled to nearly 600,000 in 1982.

This new interest in entrepreneurship is not without its ironies. It has been occurring during a period of economic stagnation and recession in the United States. Indeed, 1982 saw more business failures than any year since the Great Depression. And many more small companies have teetered on the edge, struggling to avoid bankruptcy. But as disturbing as these economic problems are, they have also helped stimulate interest in entrepreneurship, as we will explore later in this analysis.

The favorable trends for business start-ups have had the additional effect of creating an identifiable new market—the small business market—for educational, financial, technical, and other goods and services. The products, which include the assorted publications and accounting banking services referred to previously, make available to owners of small businesses valuable assistance that either wasn't available or wasn't easily obtainable a decade ago.

New Stature

Socially, entrepreneurship is now more accepted, and indeed popular, than at any time in many years. During the Vietnam War years it was quite acceptable among academics, university students, and even some of the more popular politicians of the day, to view business disdainfully. Young people who talked openly about starting ventures were fair game for extensive ridicule. Today, popular attitudes toward entrepreneurship and small business are much different. Many daily newspapers have expanded their business sections to include glowing profiles of local entrepreneurs making good. The newsweekly and other mass circulation magazines make much of young fast-growing high-technology companies and the engineering wizards who have started them.

The new social acceptance of entrepreneurship has led to the creation of important nongovernmental resources for owners of small businesses.

The number of colleges and universities offering courses on starting and operating small businesses has grown to several hundred from only a handful in 1970. Organizations established by women to advance the interests of female entrepreneurs—nearly nonexistent in the early 1970s—have proliferated in recent years. Women seeking to start businesses or who already own businesses can thus turn to other women for management assistance and moral support. Similarly, hundreds of local chambers of commerce have established small business groups in the last few years to provide lobbying, technical, and other assistance to entrepreneurs.

A Role in Policy Making

Among the political powers that be there is an increasing awareness that small businesses offer hope for reversing this country's deteriorating competitive position versus the Japanese and Europeans in the areas of productivity and industrial innovation. Perhaps even more important in the eyes of politicians, evidence has accumulated suggesting that small businesses provide many more new jobs than large corporations. (Studies out of Massachusetts Institute of Technology indicate that businesses with fewer than 100 employees were responsible for about 70% of the new jobs created during the 1970s.)

Lawmakers have taken some specific steps to improve the overall climate for small businesses. For instance, the move to deregulate the transportation, financial service, and telecommunications industries, among others, has improved the competitive climate for new ventures in those areas. As a consequence, young, upstart companies in the airline, stock brokerage, and telephone service areas are providing significant competition to well-established giant corporations.

Among the most significant legislative steps of recent years from the viewpoint of stimulating financing for promising start-up and early-stage businesses has been the two-stage reduction of the capital gains tax to a maximum of 20% from the maximum of 49% reached in 1978. The lowering of the tax has provided a significant incentive to wealthy individuals to place funds in private venture capital firms, which then invest the money in small companies judged to have the greatest likelihood of achieving sales and profit growth of 50% or more compounded annually for five to seven years. Venture capital companies during each of the last two years have had more than $1 billion available for investments, versus less than $50 million in 1977.

At federal, state, and city levels, government agencies have in recent years begun taking a direct hand in making loans and management assistance available to small companies. Prior to the Reagan Administration, federal loan programs for small businesses had grown by billions of dollars. Some of those programs have been cut back or eliminated, but the overall scope of the programs is still greater than it was a decade ago. The Reagan Administration has also continued and upgraded educational and consulting programs funded by the Small Business Administration and Commerce Department through business departments of universities around the country. More than half the states now have financing, managerial assistance, procurement, or ombudsman-information programs specifically designed for small business owners. Nearly all of the nation's 50 largest cities have economic and financial specialists trained to put together private and public financing programs for smaller companies.

Effects of Technology and Economics

The plummeting costs of computers in recent years—which is fueling a worldwide technological revolution—has made possible the formation of new businesses that possess sophisticated modeling and records systems. For only a few thousand dollars, entrepreneurs can obtain computer systems that not too many years ago cost hundreds of thousands of dollars. The owners can then do sophisticated financial projections to understand the effects of changes in prices and costs as well as set up efficient accounting, payroll, inventory, and other systems. The effect of all this is to enable new businesses to plan more effectively and to operate more efficiently at an earlier stage and a lower cost than was ever before possible.

The current technological revolution also means that small companies now have access to important marketing information that was once the domain of large companies. For relatively nominal fees, small companies can plug into extensive computerized data banks and learn about complex demographic, competitive, and other trends they might otherwise be unaware of.

Finally, the sluggish, recessionary economy of recent years has helped spur interest in entrepreneurship. The well-publicized financial difficulties of many of the nation's largest corporations—and the layoffs that have resulted—have shaken people's confidence in the prospects of big business. Probably those most shaken are individuals who have lost their jobs. Being in business for themselves, with its accompanying sense of independence, is suddenly an attractive notion for at least some of these people.

The fact that the economy is moving away from manufacturing and toward services is also a boon to entrepreneurship. Because they require little or nothing in the way of equipment and inventory, service businesses can usually be started with much smaller financial investments than manufacturing businesses. They can also most quickly and easily make use of the low-cost computers now available.

In addition, owning your own business stands out as one of the last remaining investment opportunities with the real possibility of yielding returns far in excess of the inflation rate. Common stocks, collectibles, precious metals, and even single-family homes, by contrast, have mostly been disappointing investments over the last few years. Various commercial loan sources, among them insurance and factoring companies, have signaled their recognition of the economic importance of small businesses by significantly increasing the amounts they loan to small companies.

Managerial Lessons

If nothing else, the new attention being paid to small business management has taught us, in the words of an article in this volume by John A. Welsh and Jerry F. White, that "A Small Business Is Not a Little Big Business." That is, successfully starting and running a small business is not simply a matter of adapting principles developed over the years in the areas of finance, marketing, organizational behavior, and production-manufacturing and applying them on a smaller scale to new ventures.

Young companies are usually not in a position, if they need financing, to tap the public marketplace. Or if they want to develop a new product, they can't simply commission extensive market surveys, complete with focus groups and hundreds of individual interviews, to try the idea out. Similarly, small companies typically do not have extensive personnel departments to test the latest human-resource management techniques; nor can they offer fancy benefits to lure and keep employees.

Small companies don't implement all the options available to large corporations mainly because they can't afford such approaches. But that isn't the only reason. The argument can also be made, and indeed is made in many of the articles in this volume, that small companies face issues sufficiently different in nature from those confronting large corporations as to require quite different managerial approaches. In addition, even when the issues small and large companies face are the same, there is the question of whether small ventures aren't perhaps better off exploiting certain special attributes that their size allows them.

No occurrence is more unique in the business world than a new venture start-up. The birth of a new business requires generous amounts of creativity, energy, and money. It can be argued that large companies go through a similar process when they launch new products or start new divisions; certainly the creativity and energy required are at least somewhat similar. But in large companies, there is usually more than an ample amount of money to carry the new product or division comfortably for several years to test its profit potential. The financial risk to the corporate managers involved is much less than for entrepreneurs; corporate managers risk their jobs while entrepreneurs often risk all they own.

It's important to keep in mind, though, as several of the authors in the first section of this book remind us, that starting a new business is more than a matter of obtaining adequate financing. It is a matter of entrepreneurs objectively assessing their own business expertise, their personal aspirations, their partners' strengths and weaknesses, and broad-based marketing trends.

Equally important for entrepreneurs to keep in mind is that either starting out in business or diversifying an existing business doesn't have to be done from scratch. There is always the acquisition route. Several articles in the first section make that point, suggesting that acquisitions have some advantages over starting from scratch—notably, evidence of market interest and an existing organization. For entrepreneurs confident of their managerial and financial analysis abilities, the acquisition approach offers the prospect of reaching a profitable stage more quickly than via starting a new business.

Growth and Maturation

Just because a business makes it beyond the precarious start-up or acquisition stage doesn't mean that its problems are over. Indeed, the effects of the personal, partnership, and market planning done in the initial stages become increasingly apparent. Entrepreneurs who haven't done the hard analysis of their own goals as well as those of their partners invite the kind of difficulties Derek du Toit so graphically describes in "Confessions of a Successful Entrepreneur."

While the dream of most entrepreneurs when they start out is to have an avalanche of orders pour in, skyrocketing growth can create as many problems as not having enough business. The small business unprepared for fast growth can find itself unable to keep up with the financial demands of marketing products before being paid for them. There are also the problems of finding the right managers to handle the new responsibilities constantly arising in a fast-growth situation. And there are always big corporations on the prowl for new opportunities carved out and tested by enterprising small companies.

As a number of authors in this volume point out, though, small companies have certain advantages over large companies for coping with the problems of motivating employees and keeping up with changes in the marketplace. Perhaps the most significant advantage for dealing with both sets of challenges is a function of size—because the companies are small the owners can more easily identify problems and opportunities.

The advantages of size aren't always readily apparent to entrepreneurs. Probably the most frequent and vocal complaint of owners of small businesses is that nobody seems to want to work any more. Subordinates seem not to care as much about the quality of their work as they once did, the owners claim. Employees are too easily enticed to job-hop, it's argued.

The complaint is understandable. In many small companies, labor costs are the largest single expense. Moreover, the quality of people is directly related to the quality of the product or service that the company is ultimately able to produce. In other words, employee care and motivation can make or break a small company. (Probably more than in large companies, which have well-established marketplace reputations and are often extensively automated.)

Despite the recessionary economy, the competition for effective and loyal employees is quite keen among many small companies. In the area of high-technology, for instance, electrical engineers and managers with technological expertise are chronically in short supply. Similarly, the many new service businesses springing up frequently require specialized sales and service people to help ensure success.

But, as both Lore Harp in "The Entrepreneur Sees Herself as Manager" and Thomas Melohn in "How to Build Employee Trust and Productivity" suggest, the problem is far from hopeless. By virtue of their size, small companies can take certain steps to stimulate employee involvement that large corporations are unable to try. For instance, owners of small companies can be out on the plant floor, inquiring into workers' frustrations and inviting suggestions for improving productivity. Small companies can also retain the trappings of informality, such as flexible hours, casual dress, and few lines of authority, that many employees welcome and thrive on.

Small companies often can't provide the sophisticated profit sharing and comprehensive insurance programs of large corporations, but they can give employees tangible benefits unavailable elsewhere. For instance, small companies are able to reward employees who come up with productivity-improving ideas with immediate bonuses. And owners can provide detailed and realistic employee evaluations that workers appreciate, and which large companies typically can't or won't supply. That allows employees who are doing well to obtain feedback, and raises, based on performance.

In the area of marketing, too, small companies have more advantages than owners often realize. There's a tendency by owners to assume that corporations, by virtue of their financial resources, can do all the sophisticated research necessary to make effective marketing decisions. What owners forget is that large corporations are lumbering giants, with burdensome bureaucracies. True, they can and usually do carry out extensive marketing research before launching a new product, but they tend to spend much time evaluating their research and hemming-and-hawing before making a final decision.

Owners of small companies, for one thing, are usually much more aware of changes taking place in the marketplace than senior executives of large companies. The owners are talking to customers, visiting trade shows, and doing all the other tasks that, mundane as they might seem, keep the entrepreneurs in touch with marketing trends. Corporate executives must usually rely on reports of underlings for such on-the-spot assessments, and those secondhand reports may be inaccurate or out of date, if they come at all.

Once they note significant trends, small business owners can quickly start implementing fundamental changes to adapt. The changes might involve altering product design, using new distribution channels, or trying alternative methods of promotion. The changes might even be more fundamental—introducing new products or withdrawing existing ones. Whatever the changes are, though, smaller companies can usually not only see the need for the changes, but make them more quickly than their corporate counterparts.

Financial Considerations

Anyone who reads the financial press on a regular basis—including *The Wall Street Journal, Business Week,* and *Forbes*—can easily come to believe that any company's main financial yardstick is its year-end profit and the change from the prior year.

What's wrong with using profitability as the main criteria of financial health? Nothing, as long as that criteria is applied to well-established large companies. But using profitability to measure a young growing business's financial health can be misleading, and even dangerous, as John A. Welsh and Jerry F. White argue so persuasively in their article, "A Small Business Is Not a Little Big Business."

For small companies, especially if they are fairly new and fast growing, a more important consideration than profitability is cash flow. Because they rarely have the financial reserves or easily salable assets of large corporations, small companies tend to be operating very much on a hand-to-mouth basis. Business may appear to be great, with tremendous profits off in the distance. But the immediate concerns are to meet the payroll, pay for raw materials, buy new equipment to keep up with the orders, and so forth. Coming up with the cash—despite the promise of eventual high profits— can be difficult, especially for companies that have underestimated their financial needs or have fallen behind in their collection of receivables.

Owners of small companies, then, must devote much attention to anticipating their cash flow situations, planning at least a year ahead. They must also, at least in the early years, seek to temper their worries about profitability. In too many cases, companies within sight of profitability fail for lack of cash.

Another easy trap for entrepreneurs to fall into is to leave management of their financial statements entirely in the hands of their accountants. Business owners do that because, more often than not, they have primarily marketing or engineering backgrounds instead of financial backgrounds and are easily intimidated by the financial technicalities of management.

But, as several authors, including James McNeill Stancill in "Managing Financial Statements—Image and Effect" and Neil Churchill in "Don't Let Inflation Get the Best of You", suggest, a company's financial statements and results serve a larger purpose than merely satisfying the Internal Revenue Service. They are also used to plan growth, and to convince bankers, potential investors, and possible acquirers to get involved with the company. To sophisticated financial types, a company's operating statements and the ratios that are derived from them convey important messages.

Moreover, the authors point out, entrepreneurs can exert control over how these statements are presented. In some cases, the timing of purchases and collections, and the labeling of various transactions can affect the statements. In addition, owners must decide whether they are primarily concerned with minimizing taxes or maximizing performance; the decision can have a significant effect on the statements. The key point, though, is that entrepreneurs have more control than they may realize over the outcome and presentation of their financial results.

Using Outsiders

The advent of new resources for small businesses has important implications beyond what it says about the popularity of entrepreneurship. Traditionally, an important difference between large and small businesses has been the availability of resources. When senior executives in Fortune 500 companies need specialized expertise about a new approach to financial planning or data on competitors, they can call on various experts within their companies who either have the answers or will find them very quickly. Small businesses, of course, tend not to have anything approaching that array of internal resources.

The new small business resources make available to young companies managerial expertise that corporations once had a monopoly on. The effect is to make small companies potentially more competitive with their larger counterparts.

The availability of new financing resources has a similar effect. Whereas public companies can always seek to raise funds in the public bond and stock markets, private businesses have traditionally been almost entirely dependent on banks for loans. In recent years, though, small businesses have increasingly been able to tap into venture capital, federal and state financing programs, and various commercial lending options. Once again, the effect is presenting small businesses with additional options that can help make them more competitive.

Making use of the new array of outside resources is, for many entre- preneurs, easier said than done. For one thing, business owners tend to be an independent bunch, not easily given to admitting they need assistance of any sort. After all, they've usually started their businesses from scratch, often ignoring the advice of friends and relatives who argued that the odds were hopeless. When one swims against such a tide for very long, one understandably becomes wary of outsiders.

Business owners also have a tendency, when they do seek outside assistance, of going to extremes—either they hand over total responsibility for the task at hand, or they hand over very little real responsibility. When they deal with accountants and bankers, for instance, owners may let them- selves be intimidated, as several authors in this volume suggest. Figuring they have nothing worthwhile to add to decisions, owners tend to place total authority for their financial statements in the hands of their accountants. Similarly, owners view bankers as people in a position to extend favors, rather than seeing themselves as customers in a position to make choices and demands.

Yet when it comes to making use of the expertise of outside directors, owners tend to be much more reticent about supplying information and incorporating the advice they receive. In this case, say authors of articles in this book, entrepreneurs appear to be wary of possible encroachments on their authority.

Whoever the outsiders are, suggest the authors, owners must seek to keep the relationships flexible and open. The outsiders obviously have specialized expertise, and the owners have broad business experience. Each group can learn from the other; the relationships appear to work best when approached from this perspective.

The Planning Challenge

Given all the tasks and opportunities previously discussed, it's not difficult to appreciate why busines owners typically fail to do much personal or business planning. There are simply too many fires to put out to keep the business surviving and prospering for the time being. Who's got time to look a few years down the road? And even if owners have the time, how can they anticipate the future?

While those are certainly legitimate obstacles to planning, they probably should be viewed as merely symptoms of deeper inhibitions. As the article, "Coping with Entrepreneurial Stress," suggests, business ownership is one of the most satisfying career experiences available in American life, providing both substantial psychological and financial rewards to those who succeed. It's so enjoyable, in fact, that owners tend to ignore or simply accept extremely high levels of stress. Their acceptance of the future health dangers associated with stress, and their simultaneous avoidance of planning ahead, are understandable; since running a company is so much fun, why risk rocking the boat by being introspective?

Planning, of course, involves not only being introspective, but confronting possibly unpleasant issues. Foremost among these unpleasant issues are the owner's mortality and the business's future without the owner in charge. Even for owners who are young, planning frequently involves such potentially painful issues as delegating authority, resolving conflicts with partners, and phasing out old products in favor of new ones. And young owners who do a thorough job of planning do indeed consider such mortality-related issues as estate planning and selling the company.

The issue of divesting the company, in particular, is one of the most wrenching that the owner will ever confront. On the one hand, many owners fantasize about the day they can cash in their chips, as it were, and pursue unrelated business or nonbusiness interests. The day-to-day pressure of putting out fires would be gone, replaced by a more tranquil existence, they imagine. Yet, as Michael Berolzheimer in "The Financial and Emotional Sides of Selling Your Company" and Donald Grisanti in "The Agony of Selling Out to Relatives" so graphically describe, the experience of separating oneself from the company is extremely painful emotionally, even if one has made a mental commitment to do it.

Unexplored Issues

The literature on starting and managing small businesses has exploded in quantity and quality during the last few years. But because it started from so far back compared with other areas of business management, it still has a long way to go before it begins to be comprehensive.

Part of the problem has been the attitudes of academia; the subject of entrepreneurship hasn't been highly regarded in America's top business schools. As a consequence, the best professors have avoided doing research or developing courses in the area, knowing that advancement based on their work would not be forthcoming.

As the articles in this volume attest, academia's attitudes have begun to change. Many of the articles are authored by professors who have established reputations at business scbools on the basis of their exploration of small business management issues.

Still, the exploration has tended to focus most heavily on the financial aspects of entrepreneurship—negotiating loans, obtaining venture capital, managing cash flow, presenting financial results, and dealing with accountants and bankers. Little consideration has been given to the less quantitative aspects of small business management, including such areas as marketing issues for small companies, managing subordinates, and the personal-emotional aspects of being an entrepreneur.

For instance, what are the best advertising and distribution strategies for small companies in competition with large corporations? Which benefit and incentive plans work best for small companies seeking to attract and keep key managers? What keeps entrepreneurs plugging away, in the face of endless headaches and obstacles as well as difficult odds, at their managerial tasks?

Thus, the articles in this issue might be viewed as an impressive initial phase in the development of management approaches for small business. But much still remains to be done.

PART ONE

STARTING AND ACQUIRING VENTURES

AN OVERVIEW

Individuals who want to own businesses and owners of existing companies looking to get into new business areas can take either of two approaches: they can start a business from scratch or acquire an existing business.

Those who start from scratch must seek to temper the natural tendency of entrepreneurs to be overly optimistic and even romantic in planning a new venture. This tendency leads entrepreneurs to overlook or make light of potential problems that can plague the new business. It also leads them to focus too extensively on raising the necessary start-up funds.

In "Realistic Criteria for Judging New Ventures," James McNeill Stancill points out a number of personal, marketing, financial, and investment considerations that would-be entrepreneurs should take into account in evaluating start-up situations. These considerations require the entrepreneur to consider, for instance, what type and size of business is envisioned five or ten years in the future and whether the business is economically more attractive than other career options.

Similarly, the next four articles encourage the would-be entrepreneur to consider additional nonfinancing factors. Karl Vesper in "New-Venture Ideas: Do Not Overlook Experience Factor" contends that entrepreneurs who succeed appear in many instances to have drawn on their prior educational, hobby, and work experience rather than on ideas outside their realm of experience.

The importance of partners in a start-up venture negotiating such issues as compensation and future ownership is clearly demonstrated by John H. Hand, William P. Lloyd, and Robert B. Rogow in "Use Advance Agreements to Minimize Owner Discord." Jeffry A. Timmons in "Careful Self-Analysis and Team Assessment Can Aid Entrepreneurs" contends that partners in a new venture must not only have similar goals, but must also have complementary skills and experience. And in "A Business Plan Is More Than a Financing Device," Mr. Timmons argues that the plan new owners use to obtain financing should also be viewed as a serious blueprint of where the business will be headed in its early years.

Going the acquisition route to get into business or expand an existing business means that much of the uncertainty of starting from scratch can be avoided. But picking the most appropriate industry, finding the most promising candidates, and negotiating acceptable deals are tricky matters.

In "Finding the Best Acquisition Candidates," Herbert E. Kierulff offers criteria for identifying promising markets and companies within those markets that take into account not only future financial results, but ease of management. Once entrepreneurs have started their search, they can make use of Peter Mailandt's approach for screening candidates according to the most attractive prices and terms, as described in his article, "Simplifying the Search for Four-Leaf Clovers." James Howard has suggestions for preventing emotional issues from taking precedence once negotiations are started in "Defuse the Hostility Factor in Acquisition Talks."

1
Realistic Criteria for Judging New Ventures

JAMES McNEILL STANCILL

New ventures are extremely prone to failure in their early years. What can entrepreneurs do to reduce this likelihood? Perhaps the most important thing they can do is be more hard-nosed in evaluating their ideas than they are prone to be. Doing that effectively involves using objective criteria to assess the advantages and disadvantages of proposed businesses. In this article, the author describes a number of criteria in the areas of marketing, new product viability, and projected profitability that entrepreneurs can use to evaluate a new venture.

The notion of starting a business can be quite alluring, conjuring up images of independence, glory, fame and riches. Such emotionally uplifting images make it quite easy to be overly optimistic or even totally unrealistic in assessing markets, products, profits, and other aspects of a new venture.

This article is not meant to discourage budding entrepreneurs, but rather to identify the factors necessary for new business success that need objective assessment the most. These factors, in my experience, tend to get short shrift from would-be and even experienced entrepreneurs. Potential owners can evaluate these factors by considering certain basic questions:

1 What kind of business, in an economic sense, will be created?
2 What will be the size of the business's market?

Author's Note: I wish to thank the following people for their helpful comments and suggestions: Brent Rider, Union Venture Corp., Trudy M. Self, University of Southern California; and Marty J. Fegley, ARCO Solar Industries.

15

3   How marketable is the product that will be sold?

4   Are the start-up costs commensurate with the long-term prospects of the business?

5   What will be the relationship between profitability and price in the new business?

6   Can the business be easily explained to potential investors?

7   What mechanism exists for investors to cash in their chips and get out of the business?

The "Mom and Pop" Business

A new business can evolve into one of two essential types: the "Mom and Pop" variety or the "other" type, which has functional management. This distinction is particularly important in screening an idea for a new business because you devote all your time and energy to that business, irrespective of whether it is the first or second type.

A Mom and Pop type of business does not have to be the familiar example of a hardware store or gas station; it could be any type of business in which, as the bankers say, "When the president goes home, the business goes home."

Such a business frequently starts as an effort by the entrepreneur to "buy" a job. More often than not, the entrepreneur uses his or her own money to start the venture. How rational is this approach? It depends on the size of the salary from the job that is bought. If all the future owner gets out of the business is a salary comparable to what he or she could earn in an alternative situation, then an *opportunity cost* may be involved in terms of what the investment could return if placed in another business or investment medium.

For instance, an entrepreneur might invest $300,000 in a start-up business permitting a salary of $80,000 a year. A salary of $80,000 for the president of a manufacturing company with $1 million to $3 million in annual sales—which is what one might expect in a start-up funded by $300,000 of equity (plus other debt and spontaneous credit)—is not unusual. So if the entrepreneur could make about this amount by being president of a manufacturing company owned by someone else, what return would be obtained on the $300,000 equity?

Now, if this person's salary is $200,000 when the next best opportunity is to earn $80,000 as president of another business, then there is clearly a gain of $120,000 per year directly as a result of the $300,000 investment. (Remember that this income is subject to ordinary income tax as opposed to capital gains tax rates of invested funds.) In short, rationally speaking, the yearly income from a Mom and Pop type of business should be really substantial or the owner will suffer an opportunity cost by starting such a business.

Also, what happens when the owner wants to sell the business, such as when he or she is retiring? What is the venture worth without the entrepreneur? To be sure, the owner might sell the company for the value of its tangible assets or some knockdown value of the assets.

Even if he negotiates a better price, what does the entrepreneur have after spending 20 years operating his pride and joy? Maybe he has made a very good living from the business over the years, but unless he invested that after tax salary wisely, the entrepreneur may not end up with much in net worth.

Take the case of a custom plastics molding company with sales of about $1 million a year. The president and the bookkeeper-secretary-treasurer were equal owners. They were each earning a salary of $36,000 a year, but a review of the income statement revealed that the company had earned only $5,000 the previous year. Yes, you say, but salary doesn't really indicate what they were taking out of the business. What about the "goodies"? Unfortunately for these owners, the only goody was a modest car expense. The company was paying the owners' salaries— noticeably low salaries— and that was all.

When the president wanted to sell out and retire, he was unable to find a buyer. The owners expressed a willingness to take a large part of the purchase price in the form of a note, but the cash flow was such that the business could not service *any* debt. And why would anyone with presidential abilities want to "buy" this job when the current president was making only $36,000 a year?

Even if some of the funds for salaries could be reallocated to bolster profits, the situation was bleak. Apparently, the only way this man was going to get out of the business he had helped start 16 years earlier was to liquidate it.

Why, then, should an entrepreneur seek to start a business that has no profit above personal income, since selling the business may be difficult or impossible?

The Growth Business

Then there is the "other type" of venture. Consider the career of the individual who starts a business, works like a dog to get it through the lean and hungry years, sees sales go to $10 million, to $25 million, to $100 million, and after 23 years decides to retire when sales are at $150 million. If the company is privately held, consider what its worth might be. If this were a manufacturing company, even its book value would be substantial, in an absolute sense. The president-owner of this company would also have made a good salary over the years. Thus the balance sheet net worth of this other type of business would go up much more than that of a Mom and Pop type venture.

Of course, enjoying what you do is, in itself, rewarding. But for many people, there isn't just one— and only one—rewarding career, especially for business executives. Economically speaking, the issue boils down to making the best use of your time. If you choose the Mom and Pop route, both monetary and psychic income should be especially significant, or you will suffer an opportunity cost during your career.

The start-up that represents a 24-karat Mom and Pop opportunity for one entrepreneur could represent the successful start of a growth business to a second entrepreneur. Consider a new restaurant. If you want to start one restaurant, your wealth-building potential is considerably less than it would be from a chain of 100 restaurants. A similar difference exists between a specialized bookkeeping or tax preparation firm and an H & R Block-type chain of outlets.

Whether the type of business is a state of mind or a restrictive fact is conjectural. What is important is that the entrepreneur carefully consider the issue of business type and long-run returns when starting a venture. When thinking about your income statement, don't forget your balance sheet.

Potential Customers

At first glance, the issue of market size seems fairly simple: Are there enough potential buyers of the product or service to make a new business feasible? But when considered carefully, potential market size often poses problems of extremes—a market may be too small to be economically viable or a market may be potentially so large that a little fish would have trouble surviving. A few examples illustrate the difficulties.

In one instance, an individual wanted to start a company to distribute a product made overseas that would have particular interest to "one telephone" businesses. When I asked how many such businesses there were in the United States, he enthusiastically reported that there were about 200,000. When we started talking about the percentage of companies that might buy this wonderful invention, the numbers shrank in a hurry.

The real clincher came when we multiplied the selling price (to the new company) by this aggregate market. We were now talking about total potential sales of about $4 million to $5 million. These were not just sales for the first year, but total sales of the product. The entrepreneur's bubbling enthusiasm quickly turned to dismay. Clearly the market size was insufficient to warrant starting a new venture.

At the other extreme is what I will call the "1% syndrome." In this situation, a prospective business owner starts a venture on the premise that, "If we sell only 1% of the potential market, we'll be a big success." How inviting this sounds! Why waste time doing fundamental market research when, to be a success, all the business has to do is sell to this tiny percentage of possible buyers? But what if even this 1% of potential customers won't buy the product or service?

Take the case of a person who wanted to start a magazine to be sold at professional sports arenas. He pleaded earnestly, "Surely at least 1% of the people going to the games would buy this magazine." But that depended on how the magazine was sold (or perhaps not sold) at the stadium. The point is that it is unreasonable to *assume* any percentage of the potential market will buy without doing some research first.

Potential market size can also be *too* big. In this situation, if an entrepreneur starts a venture and thus leads the way into a substantial new market, much larger competitors can then quickly move in and swamp the upstart business.

For example, an inventor wanted to start her own company, producing a device that would allow a typewriter to transmit data over telephone lines. The product, as discussed, did not seem to have any special patent protection. When I asked the inventor about the market, she replied that it was "huge." When I asked about current or future competition, she named the corporate giants in the business equipment industry. But if this were the case, what chance would this little company have?

Before the reader takes me to task on this point, I am quite aware of the success that Digital Equipment Corporation and Amdahl Corporation have had competing head-to-head with IBM. But in each case, the companies had done sound research to clearly delineate the market niche or were aware of a managerial "lag" that permitted the new venture to obtain a special place in the market.

Thus the aspiring entrepreneur should not brush aside market size; he or she should do some market research for any new business before making a major investment.

Is One Product Enough?

Along with attempting to determine potential market size, entrepreneurs must carefully evaluate the product or products that they propose to sell.

First and foremost, future business owners should give consideration to the number of products they intend to sell. One-product businesses usually get started to produce some invention and, possibly, to show the world how clever the inventor is. But one-product ventures tend to encounter technological problems— namely, they can be quickly rendered obsolete by competitors. Of course, if the product that represents a new company's entire line is of low technology, technological obsolescence is usually less likely than if the product is of high technology.

Preferable to trying to base a business on only one product is to sell several products. By multiple products I do not mean mere variations of the basic product. Instead, I mean products that can possibly be produced in the same manufacturing facility and probably by the same manufacturing process, but which are perceived as different products.

For example, a business that manufactures a novel line of lamps might have the facilities to make either a completely different type of lamp, in order to guard against both technological obsolescence and a shift in market taste, or a different product altogether that might fit in with the company's overall marketing strategy.

The would-be entrepreneur should consider the following three questions: First, what would happen to the new company if there were a technological breakthrough by the competition? Second, if being a one-product business seems to limit the potential sales and profits, what additional products could the venture produce to provide the hoped-for growth? Third, what sort of second-generation products would result from the first set of products?

Avoiding Single-Sale Products

I recall one venture that was founded to sell tapes and books to hospitals. Experts in both audio-visual materials and technological science produced the materials that were to be used to train hospital staffs in specific subjects. The product was first rate in every sense. The potential market included every hospital in the country and, perhaps, in the world.

The new company started amidst much fanfare and excitement. Unfortunately, the owners didn't realize that they had to make a substantial sales effort to sell each unit, and the price did not warrant the onerous effort involved.

As if this problem were not enough, another more devastating factor was at work: there were no repeat sales. It was not that the customers did not like the product, because they did; but each hospital needed only one item. If the product had been a computer or a sizable machine with a hefty selling price, then the lack of repeat orders would not have been a problem. But the total selling price—with all the frills and add-ons—was only several hundred dollars.

Much superior to a single-sale product is one that produces add-on or repeat sales. If the customer is a manufacturer, then repeat orders for hundreds or thousands of units could develop in the years to come. If the potential customer is a major retailer (a Sears or Penney's), distributor, or wholesaler, then one convincing sales talk might persuade it to take on the line of products and place endless future orders. (Be careful of the one-customer problem. Aside from possible marketing problems, a "concentration factor" in a company's accounts receivable might convince banks to avoid financing such receivables.)

The future owner should view the business as a distributive network for products, so that the branches of the network not only remain after the sale but also grow stronger as the number of customers grows. This outlook entails a different philosophical conceptualization of the business than that held by the typical ambitious inventor, who is most likely thinking of (1) the product and (2) how this marvelous product will make him or her rich.

Once a venture has a repeat customer, then it can sell additional products during the same sales call or broaden the catalog that the customer uses to make repeat orders. One of the most precious and valuable assets any business possesses is its customer list. A company that can keep the customers on that list happy and even expand the list will itself grow. The more products that can be pumped through that customer pipeline, the more the company will grow.

Too Simple a Product

How can a product or service be too elementary? Looking at the countless examples of product ideas, one frequently wonders, "Gee, that's so simple, why didn't I think of it?"

Simplicity becomes a negative only if a business idea is so basic that little management or marketing expertise is required for success. After all, what is to prevent every Tom, Dick, and Harriet from duplicating your business if your venture looks successful?

An illustration of this problem is a proposed business that would sell a computer program of a file-and-retrieve system to help car dealers find needed cars in dealerships throughout a particular state. While the idea made sense as a product, it was the kind of thing almost any programmer could have written in a day or so.

If the entrepreneur got going with this program as a product, what was to prevent another business, or the regional representative of the car manufacturer, from duplicating the service and underselling the initial venture? "Oh, we'll have such a head start, the others will never be able to catch us" is the typical reply. This usually is a gross overstatement or an error. Even if the head start lets the new business get a beachhead, what happens when the competition comes charging—or flooding—in?

In and Out of Vogue

Finally, no product is less marketable than last year's red hot idea. The list of once voguish ideas is long: athletic gyms, handheld calculators, certain computer software, recreational vehicles, and mobile home parks, to name a few. What matters, then, is that the current product idea is not out of vogue.

As simple as this principle seems to be, someone invariably comes along trying to sell last year's pet rock and then wonders why it seems so difficult. If the entrepreneur is going to attempt business's version of surfboarding, then he or she had better be up on the wave and not a little behind it.

Evaluating Capital Intensity

New businesses can vary widely in the amount of "sunk" costs that they might require. Starting certain businesses entails raising enormous sums of money to build a plant (such as John Z. de Lorean's sports car factory in Northern Ireland), or to launch a satellite (COMSAT), or to buy a fleet of jet airplanes (Federal Express). For many individuals with considerably shorter track records than the entrepreneurs who started those companies, large initial capital outlays might greatly increase the potential losses.

Once a product is proven in the market and in other ways, investing large amounts of capital can make sense. But if a new business requires a sizable investment *before* finding out if the product will sell and, in turn, make for a profitable venture, I think that the potential owner and his or her financial backers ought to reconsider whether the reward is worth the gamble.

Entrepreneurs might also ask themselves if some way exists to reduce sunk costs. For instance, can production be subcontracted to someone who already has the facilities to make the product? In this way, they can reasonably prove the market demand before the expensive facilities are added.

The point is not that a start-up should involve only small amounts of money—this might guarantee failure. Rather, entrepreneurs should screen out ideas that require sizable sunk investments before they can be justified by sales performance.

Setting Prices

The issue of basic profitability sinks many new ventures, either because the future owner failed to consider the issue or because he or she exaggerated potential profits to appear more attractive to venture capitalists. The most important aspect of basic profitability is gross profit, that is, sales minus the cost of goods sold.

If a business is entering a new field, the profit expectations are likely to be quite different from the profit expectations of a business entering an established industry. The rule of thumb that some successful managers use for a venture making an innovative new product is a selling price of at least four to five times the cost of goods sold—in other words, a gross profit of 75% to 80% of sales.

The logic of pricing a product to attain this level of gross profits is rather clear. In the early going, the new venture will presumably not be able to supply the same quantity of product or service as later when capacity is larger. Therefore, a "skimming" pricing policy may be in order early on, while "penetration" pricing can be used when much larger sales are desired. After all, if a pricing structure results in a skinny gross profit *before* competition jumps in, what will happen to the gross profit *after* competing businesses invade the marketplace?

But how do you set the price of the product so as to return a minimum of 75% to 80% gross profits? Theoretically, both the price and production volume are based on market research. But with many start-up businesses, little or no money is usually available for market research to determine the optimal pricing structure.

Typically, a great amount of pure guesswork goes into the pricing strategy, which can lead to a fatal mistake—misleading yourself or others. When you make the pro forma financial projections and the gross profits from the predetermined price-quantity expectations look a "little skinny," the temptation is to say, "Oh, I'm sure we can sell just as many at a higher price."

Selling price should have little or nothing to do with the cost of the product. Price should be the result of potential buyers' perception that the product's intrinsic value is equal to or greater than the asking price. It simply does not matter how much something costs to make (or, if a service, to deliver); the question is, how much will a customer pay, in the quantities specified? (Government contracts might be an exception.)

Many examples exist of products that are truly creative—but for which buyers are unwilling to pay the price that would make the product (and venture) an economic success. A superb stereo system for cars was so good that the quality actually went beyond the range of normal hearing. "Sure it costs more," the management of the struggling stereo manufacturer said, "but it's worth so much more!" Worth so much more to whom? The buyers didn't perceive the product as worth "so much more"; in fact, they were unaware just how superior the product really was.

Another pricing pitfall to avoid is the "Cadillac syndrome." Some aspiring entrepreneurs brush aside the vital price-volume problem and its relation to gross profit with the explanation that, "We're the Cadillac of the field." Building a business on a profitability structure that implies unreasonably high pricing may imply a market so small that the *total* dollar gross profit—even if a good percentage—sinks the business.

For many inventors who fall in love with their inventions, financial failure is often of secondary importance to artistic success (unless it is their money at stake). The fact that *their* product is on the market is, in itself, sufficient success.

Of Profits Squeezed

A venture need not be a producer of a new or innovative product to be a successful start-up. Many entrepreneurs start businesses to produce products or deliver services in established markets. But what about the profit structure existing in that market before the entry of the new venture?

In economics we speak of a *normal profit* as being the price-quantity structure that allows for sufficient profits to prevent companies in an industry from leaving but not high enough to induce businesses to enter the field. How many entrepreneurs are bright enough to know the difference, privy to the actual economic facts about this, or, frankly, even concerned enough to care?

The problems of trying to enter certain established markets are illustrated by a new business started several years ago in a specialty branch of the pump industry. The successful manager who started the venture unfortunately chose an industrial segment so competitive that typical gross profits in the industry were 18% to 20%. It's hard enough to have a profitable manufacturing business with a skinny gross profit, but consider what would happen to the gross profit of the established companies when an additional venture squeezed into the marketplace. But hope springs eternal. "Our company will be different," the manager said.

The restaurant business in southern California further illustrates this situation. Restaurant owners lament that the marketplace is so competitive that menus cannot be priced high enough to provide realistic profit levels. If someone has an idea for a new restaurant, the romance of the new idea is all too likely to overcome objectivity about future profitability.

Role of Future Profitability

Profitability is also important as it relates to the percentage of the venture that the future owner will have to give to investors who will supply the start-up capital. How much of the new business should investors get if they put up all the money and the entrepreneur contributes his or her time and talents and the basic idea (product) for the venture? This is an age-old question for which there is no perfect answer.

Professional venture capitalists typically seek five to ten times their investment in five years. The following procedure might be used to divide the new company's stock ownership:

First, agree on some sort of multiple (price–earnings ratio) of the company's earnings for five years hence. This might seem questionable to some, but the way it is done in practice is to use the current price–earnings ratio for a comparable business. (For example, both businesses make dental equipment and related products.) If this multiple is say, 15 times earnings and the fifth year earnings are projected at $500,000 after tax, then the firm should be worth $7.5 million.

Now, if it takes $400,000 from the investors to start the business, then five to ten times this investment would be $2 million to $4 million. Now if we compare the $2 million to the $7.5 million, then about 27% of the stock would be given to the investors so that they can realize their five times investment profit. But if the investors demand ten times their money, then about 53% of the stock would have to be given.

(I would discourage anything over 49%, but the potential owner should not delude himself or herself into thinking that 51% guarantees control. It does not. If things go wrong, professional venture capitalists have ways of taking control even if they own less than a majority of stock.)

Thus, the more profitable the projected business, the smaller the percentage of ownership that will have to be given up to investors. When the aspiring entrepreneur analyzes the future profitability of a start-up proposal, he or she ought to ask these questions, "Will this idea result in higher future profits than all my other new venture ideas? Do I really want to spend years of my life developing a company with anemic profitability—especially if it means giving the lion's share to the financial backers?"

Making the Deal Understandable

Failing to make an idea for a new venture comprehensible to potential investors, creditors, and customers can doom the venture before it begins.

I recall trying to assist two friends, who had impressive educational and work backgrounds, in a real estate deal. But their idea entailed an extraordinarily complicated financial scheme. We took the proposal to another friend who was quite knowledgeable about real estate. After nearly three hours of explanation, we finally said, "Well, what do you think?" "Brilliant," he said, "but it will never fly. How are you going to raise the money from a group of unsophisticated people when it took me several hours to figure out what you are doing?"

In another instance, a man in his late twenties came to see me about starting a specialized type of garage for repairing cars. The idea seemed all right for a Mom and Pop type of business, but he was proposing a limited partnership with a corporation as the general partner.

While there's nothing intrinsically wrong with his approach, it's probably not appropriate for a small garage. Not surprisingly, he had been trying to put together his new company for well over a year. I suggested he get a relative to borrow about $40,000 on his or her home and loan it to him on a *subordinated* basis and, for the balance, apply for a Small Business Administration loan.

Giving Investors an Out

Finally, entrepreneurs forming a new venture must deal with the issue of how investors are going to realize their profits from the company.

From the mid-1950s through mid-1971, public stock offerings provided a frequent solution. In the typical case, the company would make a *combination* initial public offering that included some stock sold by the business (the *primary* portion) and some stock sold by the existing shareholders (the *secondary* portion). It was through this secondary portion that the initial investors could recover their original investment plus some of their profit.

During the ten-year period from 1971 to 1980 when the market for initial public stock offerings was nearly nonexistent, giving investors an "out" became quite difficult. Some received convertible notes or notes with warrants, so that the investments could be repaid via the notes with the profits coming at some undetermined time in the future, when the company went public or after it was acquired by some large corporation.

Not only was this rather roundabout way of rewarding the initial investors annoying, but the profits yielded to investors were considerably less than in the prior decade.

The 1980s have certainly started differently. Now we have a rather active new issues market in which all manner of ventures are going public. The price-earnings ratios of these ventures vary considerably from industry to industry. Therefore, the aspiring entrepreneur ought to seriously consider the future prospects for his or her venture's price–earnings relationship. What kind of P–E ratio *might* the new business have in the future? Obviously, the higher the P–E ratio, the better off the owner will be.

Of course, the present new issues market may not exist three to five years hence. Nonetheless, the very existence of such a market when funding is being sought may help greatly in raising venture capital. The psychology of the situation seems to be that if there is a hot new issues market today, there will still be one three to five years from now. Conversely, if no such market exists today, the assumption is that there will not be one three to five years from now. As logical or illogical as this psychology might seem, the future owner should keep it in mind when timing the start of a new company.

Is Entrepreneurship the Best Way?

At this point in the screening process, the aspiring entrepreneur might consider an alternative approach: not starting a business at all. Instead, how about placing the great new idea with an established company and letting it manufacture and market the idea and pay a royalty? If pushed too far, this notion would preclude the start-up of just about all businesses.

Surely, this is not what I mean. If an inventor has a good product, but does not have all the requisite skills to successfully garner the venture capital and then manage a start-up venture, putting the product with another company—assuming he or she can negotiate adequate and minimum royalties— might spare much frustration and possible failure. Besides, if the product is economically successful, this success might very well constitute the track record that venture capitalists look for in a potential business owner. Then the inventor or entrepreneur can point with pride and say, ''Look how much money I have made for other people. Now I want to do that for myself and my backers.'' This is an argument that professional and other venture capital sources love to hear.

Still, I don't expect this argument to have a great deal of impact on potential entrepreneurs. A man once came to me with a pill counter he had invented—similar to ones that are in rather widespread use today. I went down the list of criteria previously discussed and found the product lacking on a number of points.

While the logic of putting this device with a major corporation that had the necessary marketing resources to sell to pharmacies seemed convincing, the inventor had it in his mind that he was going to have his own business with *his* name on it. And that was that. And when you come down to essentials, perhaps this is what makes the entrepreneurial world go around.

2
New-Venture Ideas
Do Not Overlook Experience Factor

KARL H. VESPER

What are the best sources of new-venture ideas? That tantalizing question is raised by Karl H. Vesper. He contends that the question has received inadequate attention from scholars and other writers. After studying about 100 successful enterprises, he attempts to offer guidance on where would-be entrepreneurs should look for new-venture ideas.

Discovering workable new-venture ideas is no easy feat. Many would-be entrepreneurs have unsuccessfully gambled huge sums testing seemingly profitable concepts.

Even a man as creative as Mark Twain came up a consistent loser when he bet on new business ideas. In his autobiography, he recalled the first in a series of failures he encountered backing the invention of a friend.

> At last, when I had lost $42,000 on that patent I gave it away to a man whom I had long detested and whose family I desired to ruin. Then I looked around for other adventures. That same friend was ready with another patent. I spent $10,000 on it in eight months. Then I tried to give that patent to the man whose family I was after. He was very grateful but he was also experienced by this time and was getting suspicious of benefactors. He wouldn't take it and I had to let it lapse.
>
> Meantime, another old friend arrived with a wonderful invention. It was an engine or a furnace or something of the kind. . .

The best of Twain's business attempts was an invention of his that he patented and characterized as "the only rational scrapbook the world has ever seen." On that enterprise, he invested $5,000 and managed to recover $2,000.

Unfortunately, sound guidance on where to find profitable venture ideas is nearly as sparse today as it was in Mark Twain's day. And the guidance that exists is of questionable quality because systematic research on the subject is almost nonexistent.

Many books on entrepreneurship completely neglect the subject of new-venture ideas. In the most widely used text in entrepreneurship courses, *New Ventures and the Entrepreneur,* Patrick R. Liles devotes eight chapters to various aspects of entrepreneurship but fails to examine the origination of venture ideas.[1]

A book by Charles B. Swayne and William R. Tucker, *The Effective Entrepreneur,* offers a "road map by means of which any venture can be formed" but does not indicate how to formulate venture ideas.[2] Robert S. Morrison's 558-page *Handbook for Manufacturing Entrepreneurs* presents guidance on whether to start a company, who should start one, and how to "select" a product but fails to offer advice on how to find alternatives from which to do the selecting.[3]

More popularized books on entrepreneurship typically recommend various mental exercises. In *How to Think Like a Millionaire and Get Rich,* Howard Hill recommends dreaming up ways to "add color or a new twist to commonplace products and services."[4] Russell Williams, author of *How to Wheel and Deal Your Way to a Fast Fortune,* advises the reader to "pick a product in your home and ask yourself, how is it marketed? How is it manufactured? Could you introduce a competitor?"[5]

In *The Poor Man's Road to Riches,* Duane Newcomb tells the reader:

> Ideas are everywhere. . . . To find them, you generally decide on an
> area of interest like the restaurant business. . .then as you go about your
> daily business you simply let anything that comes close to your interest
> area trigger your imagination.[6]

A composite list of recommended venture idea sources from these and other books on entrepreneurship appears in Exhibit 1. Of course, most items on the list are categories that could be further subdivided into many other lines of action. Thus it is clear that the number of possible activities for seeking venture ideas is enormous and could consume nearly endless amounts of time.

Is there a better way of formulating new-venture ideas? A study of the histories of approximately 100 highly successful entrepreneurs suggests that there is. The cases were drawn primarily from five books about entrepreneurship as well as from magazine articles and interviews with successful entrepreneurs.[7] The objective was not so much to obtain a scientifically representative sampling as to discover the range of sources prospective entrepreneurs can draw on to find promising venture ideas.

One key finding was that instead of searching randomly, as many popularized entrepreneurship books seem to suggest, the entrepreneur should closely examine his or her own education, work experience, and hobbies as

Exhibit 1. Idea Sources Advocated in Entrepreneurship Books

Mental Gymnastics	Personal Contacts with	Visits to	Reading of	Observation of Trends
Brainstorming	Potential customers	Trade shows	Trade publications	Materials shortages
Observation	Potential suppliers	Libraries	Trade directories	Energy shortage
Seeking new twists	Business brokers	Museums	Bankruptcy announcements	Waste disposal
	Business owners	Plants	*Business Opportunities*	New technology
	Successful entrepreneurs	Invention expositions	*Classified*	Nostalgia
	Property owners	Universities	Old books and magazines	Fads
	Professors	Research institutes	*Commerce Business Daily*	Legal changes
			Other commerce department publications	Pollution problems
	Graduate students		NASA's *Tech Briefs*	Health
	Patent attorneys		Patents and *Patent Gazette*	Self-development
	Product brokers		New product publications	Personal security
	Former employers		Doctoral dissertations	Foreign trade
	Prospective partners		Idea books and newsletters	Social movements
	Bankers		Best seller lists	
	Venture capitalists		New technology publications	
	Chambers of commerce		Licensing information services	
	Plastic molders			
	Corporate licensing departments			
	Editors			
	Management consultants			
	Technology transfer agencies			
	Regional development agencies			

idea sources. The large majority of the entrepreneurs studied primarily used their own expertise rather than that of others.

The pattern of close connection between prior work and new-venture ideas was common to a large majority of the successful start-ups—between 60% and 90%, depending on the industry—the correlation being highest in advanced technology areas like computers and medical instruments and lowest in enterprises of a relatively unspecialized nature, such as nursing homes, fast food franchises, and other consumer-oriented businesses.

Variations in Background

Not surprisingly, the entrepreneurs differed in how they acquired their expertise. Nearly all entrepreneurs involved in starting successful advanced technology companies had earned one or more college degrees and had had substantial work experience in scientific research or engineering design before formulating their venture concepts. Entrepreneurs who conceived successful machining businesses, however, usually had not attended college but had put in five years or more working for other people on shop floors.

A spectacular, fairly typical example of an advanced technology start-up was that of Intel Corporation: Robert N. Noyce, an M.I.T. physics Ph.D., and Gordon E. Moore, A Cal Tech chemistry Ph.D., had worked for Fairchild Semiconductor since its inception in 1956. By 1968, Noyce was general manager, Moore was director of research, and Fairchild's annual sales had grown to $150 million.

At about that time, the two men became aware of a promising related area of semiconductors that had been neglected by big companies. Their observation coincided with their own growing frustration with long commuting times and the difficulties of working within a corporate bureaucracy. They convinced a venture capitalist to invest $300,000 and raised another $2.2 million through private placements.

The entrepreneurs used the money to start a new semiconductor memory company with Noyce as president and Moore as executive vice-president. Seven years after the company's inception, sales had grown to $134 million and profits to $19.8 million.

Although it involved exceptionally large seed capital, this venture was not unusual for advanced technology start-ups. A team of technical specialists employed a clear product concept and sought fast growth—a classic pattern carried out, albeit on a smaller scale, by many such companies.

In contrast, consider the following more conventional manufacturing start-up: In 1961, Al Richards was fired as a machinist for a small cutting tool company. The dismissal was a shock, made more painful by the fact that he had only meager savings. He was not unaccustomed to adversity, though, for he had been raised in orphanages, employed in a shipyard at age 16 by falsifying his age, and battle-tested in the Seabees. Because he had worked in several machine shops while he was taking related evening courses, he was confident of his knowledge of the cutting tool business.

Against the advice of his lawyer, he sold his boat, car, and guns and took a second mortgage on his house to raise the $18,000 necessary to start his own shop. With rented space and used machinery, he began soliciting orders. He also moonlighted to cover his business and personal expenses. Orders came in slowly, and the company, after losing money the first year, moved into the black the second year. Eight years after start-up, the company's sales had reached an annual level of about $300,000.

Similarities Stand Out

Though different conditions inspired creation of these two ventures—Noyce and Moore were motivated by dissatisfaction with secure jobs and Richards by unexpected discharge from a job he liked—a basic similarity stands out. Both enterprises represented activities similar to those performed for years in the entrepreneurs' prior jobs.

Working for Fairchild had given Noyce and Moore very special know-how, both in dealing with a particular advanced technology and in identifying and exploiting the technical frontier. The leap to the new-venture idea thus appears not to have been particularly difficult or surprising but rather a natural outgrowth of their work. Richards similarly did not have to search far for his new-venture idea.

Another important source of venture ideas can be hobbies, as the following example illustrates: Bill Nicolai dropped out of college in the late 1960s and hitchhiked to Yosemite to climb mountains. For several years he worked sporadically, supplementing his income with food stamps and spending much of his time climbing mountains in Yosemite and elsewhere.

Then one night a mountain blizzard blew his tent apart, bringing death too close for comfort and setting Nicolai to thinking about alternative tent constructions. He designed a tent made from a tube of fabric held open by circular metal hoops and borrowed a sewing machine to make it a reality. It worked, and he began to imagine an enterprise to fabricate and sell a product he would call "the omnipotent."

He then rented a booth at an annual Seattle street fair and put several tents on display. "I don't think we actually sold any at the fair," he recalled, "but we did sell a few a short while later after people had had a chance to look the flyer over." Sales began to drift in, and Nicolai moved the fledgling business from a friend's basement to a storefront with manufacturing space in the back. After two years, he was employing four of his friends, and annual sales were $60,000. "It wasn't much of a living," he said, "but we were surviving and enjoying the work."

At this point, we might note the source of the business idea and where it led. Nicolai used his substantial hobby experience to conceive his product and enterprise. In a sense, his hobby had been his job because it had been a relatively full-time commitment for several years. It had given him knowledge of the market and available technology. The tent collapse revealed a need, which in turn led to discovery of a product and creation of a business. Again, the moral for successful venture discovery seems to be to work from what one is familiar with—from a hobby if not from one's occupation.

Importance of Subsequent Events

Nicolai's venture was not particularly successful at this point. The meager $60,000 gross sales did not allow him to escape food stamps. By the usual standards for wages and profits, the business was, after two years, a loser with no salvation in sight.

Then things changed: A salesman tried to interest Nicolai in using a new tent fabric that boasted the unique property of venting vapor without leaking water, so that breath moisture could escape the tent but rain could not enter. Producers of the new fabric "went to all the big companies first, because we were nobody," Nicolai recalled, "but each big company assumed the material was no good because none of the other big companies used it."

Seeing little to lose, Nicolai introduced a tent made of the new material and threw all his resources into advertising it. Within a month, sales leaped from $5,000 a month to $6,000 a day. Over the next three years, sales rose to $2 million annually, at substantial margins.

This shift from a modest enterprise with little promise to a fast-growing, highly profitable business was another important characteristic common to a large proportion of other extremely successful ventures. Except for the advanced technology enterprises, which virtually all started with high expectations, roughly 40% of the ventures studied began as relatively small-time enterprises. Some event occurred later that induced fast growth. Thus another reasonable conclusion to draw from the cases studied is that highly successful venture ideas can easily emerge from apparently small-time businesses as entrepreneurs gain experience, expertise, and business exposure.

The successful entrepreneurs' experience thus contrasts sharply with advice offered in the how-to-succeed books. Jobs, the main idea source, are not stressed at all. Though some of the books suggest hobbies, they neglect to emphasize the importance of accompanying experience. What the books mostly suggest—daydreaming, visiting museums, browsing in libraries, and studying world trends—produced few ideas used to start the businesses studied.

This is not to say that following the advice in the popularized books is likely to cause failure. It is just difficult to find examples of successful entrepreneurs who have systematically used those approaches. While it seems plausible to expect that hopeful entrepreneurs who deliberately use such advice should achieve some success, this question might benefit from academic research.

Other Idea Sources

Occasionally, winning ideas are discovered the way the popularized entrepreneurship books say they should be. Ole Evinrude thought up the outboard
motor when ice cream melted in a boat he was rowing to a summer picnic.
King Gillette conceived the safety razor when his straight razor dulled. Such
incidents are extremely rare, however, and nobody has demonstrated that
a skill for creating them can be deliberately learned.

But there are some systematic approaches besides background and
experience that sometimes work, as the following three examples illustrate:

☐ E. Joseph Cossman, author of *How I Made a Million Dollars in
Mail Order,* tells of finding unexploited products by visiting trade shows,
reading classified advertisements, and seeking unused tooling from
products previously judged unsuccessful at plastic molding companies.[8]

☐ One entrepreneur adopted a strategy of calling or visiting at least
one person daily who might be able to help her find an opportunity,
any opportunity, After a year, she had located a partner. After two
years, they had a product—a blood-testing device produced under a
licensing agreement. And after three years, their company was profitable and nearing $1 million in annual sales.

☐ A prospective electronics manufacturer discovered a successful
product by asking purchasing agents what items they were having trouble obtaining. He identified the need for a certain sophisticated electronic component, got it designed and into production, and wound up
with a multi-million-dollar publicly held company.

Each of these entrepreneurs unearthed a venture opportunity through
someone else. Cossman bought products other people had developed and
then applied his merchandising talents to sell them. The medical product
manufacturer obtained a license (some entrepreneurs form partnerships with
inventors). The electronics maker obtained information about a need and
then developed a product.

But they all made use of others who had the specific idea they needed.
Thus the idea search process was largely one of making personal contacts
until one paid off in a usable concept. For the prospective entrepreneur in
search of a venture concept, the message is to seek new contacts for ideas.

A further possibility is to look to others not only for venture concepts
but also for complete ongoing ventures—that is, for acquisitions. This approach comprised about one-fifth of the cases examined in this study. What
is striking about this approach is that more than half of those who used it
had no prior experience in the business areas they suddenly adopted through
acquisition. Yet all emerged extremely successful.

Thus the acquisition approach seems well suited to those who either
cannot or prefer not to find new-venture ideas based on their own work or

hobby experience and who are not content to wait and hope someone else will come to them with a venture proposition.

Where do these findings leave the generalist manager? Does the view widely held among business schools that a good manager can manage any type of business also hold for entrepreneurs? Or can only a specialist start a particular type of business? No general answer has been demonstrated, but it can be observed that technical expertise must be brought into the new enterprise *somehow,* whether by the entrepreneur or by those he recruits.

One way to recruit needed talent is to buy a going concern in which the specialists are already employed. Another is to buy a franchise that comes with the opportunity for special training and guidance. A third is to hire or become partners with someone who has the needed special know-how.

In conclusion, it seems significant that none of the entrepreneurs in the cases examined discovered winning ideas through random mental reflection or even concentrated brainstorming. Those who scouted ideas out applied action, not just thinking, to find them. Hence, some final advice for the person desiring a venture who hasn't yet identified a suitable concept: don't just sit and think; move around, contact people, and act.

Notes

1. Homewood, Ill.: Irwin, 1974.

2. Morristown, N.J.: General Learning Press, 1973.

3. Cleveland, Ohio: Western Reserve Press, 1973.

4. West Nyack, N.Y.: Parker Publishing Co., 1968.

5. Parker, 1977.

6. Parker, 1976.

7. The five books used were: Orvis Collins and David G. Moore, *The Organization Makers* (New York: Appleton-Century-Crofts, 1970); Richard Lynn, *The Entrepreneur* (London: George Allen and Unwin, 1974); Harry Miller, *The Way of Enterprise* (London: Andre Deutsch, 1963); Lawrence A. Armour, *The Young Millionaires* (Chicago: Playboy Press, 1973); and Gene Bylinsky, *The Innovative Millionaires* (New York: Scribner, 1976).

8. Englewood Cliffs, N.J.: Prentice-Hall, 1963.

3
Use Advance Agreements to Minimize Owner Discord

JOHN H. HAND, WILLIAM P. LLOYD, and ROBERT B. ROGOW

In the euphoria of starting a new business or adding partners to an existing business, it's usually assumed that all the principals are working toward the same goal: success of the venture. Not surprisingly, much is frequently left unsaid in such upbeat circumstances about possible changes in employment and compensation, ownership proportions, and other related matters. The authors discuss the importance of agreeing in advance on key areas affecting the ownership and management of small companies.

The elderly owner of a prosperous farm-implement dealership invited the husband of his only child to join him in the business as a minority partner. The younger man enjoyed a good relationship with his father-in-law and was instrumental in significantly expanding the business. After several years, though, the senior partner, a widower, married a woman with children of her own.

The older man's affections shifted to his new family, and the son-in-law was reduced to the status of an employee. Finally, when the older man died, the son-in-law was forced by the widow to resign. Since then, the late owner's daughter has had strained relations with her stepmother, and the dealership has struggled for survival under the stepmother's uncertain leadership.

What is especially significant about this case is the absence of the usual factors that precipitate the breakup of a partnership. There was no takeover attempt, no irreconcilable difference of opinion about management policy, no sign of incompetence, and no significant change in the business that one or the other could not handle. All that happened was an unremarkable change in the personal circumstances of one of the principals.

Obviously, neither partner gave much thought to the possibility that something like this might happen; both failed to take any early steps that might have prevented damage to the business, to themselves, and to their family relationships. It never occurred to them that they should agree on their respective duties, responsibilities, and rights and put the agreement into writing.

All this points up the need for a clear and early definition of each participant's rights and responsibilities in order to avoid subsequent conflict. Among the many areas subject to agreement are access to business information, the right to sell or mortgage a company's assets, the right to restrict the growth of a business (for the purpose of limiting its need for funds), and the conditions under which a company should be dissolved and its net assets distributed.

The most important rights and responsibilities might best be grouped into four categories:

1　Employment and compensation.
2　Changes in ownership or ownership proportions.
3　Relationships between participants and outside interests.
4　Changes in the business's charter.

This article explores each of these four areas and then offers some general advice for working with lawyers to put together legal agreements among partners in small business enterprises.

Disputes Over Pay and Worth

Disagreements over employment and compensation probably cause more disruption in small businesses than any other conflicts. Compensation is the measure of the value of an employee to a business, and many individuals take it to be the measure of themselves as human beings. This is why keeping discussions of these matters objective and professional is so difficult.

A salary review can easily degenerate into an emotional battle over someone's value. The danger is especially great after the initial optimism accompanying a new venture has faded under the pressures of managing costs, sales, cash flow, and other realities.

Employment and compensation are matters in which an ounce of prevention is worth several tons of cure. Entrepreneurs can save themselves untold amounts of money and grief by working out in advance the terms of their association with a new venture.

Such an agreement must balance the legitimate interests of the principals and the business. A person expects to be protected against arbitrary and unjust dismissal like that experienced by the young man who had been a partner in the farm-implement dealership.

At the same time, the business must have the power to dismiss incompetent employees. Failure to retain that power can bankrupt a company, as the four brothers who owned a small foundry in the Midwest discovered. Unfortunately, one of the brothers did all the work because the others were lazy or incompetent. The three nonproducers drew high salaries, had the power to commit the foundry to agreements, and could not be terminated.

After several years of carrying the workload of the others, the ablest of the four got another job and left. The foundry soon staggered toward bankruptcy, and the three remaining owners pressed their brother to return. He agreed to do so because their mother depended on the business for her income, but he insisted that this time they draw up a detailed agreement specifying the rights and responsibilities of each.

Two of the brothers were assigned duties and paid salaries commensurate with their abilities. The third was dismissed from the company but was guaranteed a dividend for his share of the the stock.

An employment arrangement must prevent the dominant figure in a company from appropriating most of its resources through excessive salary and bonus payments. The chief executive officer of a small venture may well be the majority stockholder and in the latter capacity may vote himself benefits beyond those justified by his contribution. Situations like this frequently result in court action because minority holders have no alternative but to sue if they want redress. A written stipulation can limit salary and bonus payments but still allow highly productive executives to earn incomes commensurate with their contribution to a company's earnings.

If a small business is organized as a corporation, a compensation agreement covering its executives must also include dividend payments. In a small corporation, the top managers are usually the major shareholders as well. These people can pay out the corporation's earnings either as salaries and bonuses or as dividends. This choice allows management to manipulate the distribution of payments to its advantage. Usually, the dominant factor in the decision is the federal income tax law, which allows corporations to deduct employees' salaries, but not dividends, from corporate income.

Sometimes, though, the decision is controlled by other factors, as in the case of a building supply company in a small southern town. One man owned a 36% share of the business and was employed as its senior manager. He became an alcoholic and a disruptive influence in the business. He had difficulty performing simple tasks, his public appearances embarrassed the company, and he interfered with the productivity of its other employees.

The employment agreement drawn up when the company was formed allowed for dismissal for cause, so the man was fired for gross neglect of duty. The agreement, however, did not cover dividend payments; once the manager lost his salary, he was unable to compel payment of any cash return on his invested capital. The company had never paid cash dividends, and the remaining owners saw no reason to be generous to their fallen comrade.

A well-conceived agreement would have distinguished between labor income and capital income and provided for continued payment of capital income if an owner-manager were to become unfit for continued employment.

Who Owns What?

Changes in ownership or ownership proportions can create havoc among principals if not carefully controlled. Agreements should restrict or prohibit changes in the proportion of the stock held by each participant.

Changes in proportion can be achieved by the sale of new stock to selected insiders, the purchase of existing stock, reverse stock splits, mergers, and the formation of holding companies. These techniques are frequently used to extinguish small minority interests.

A particularly nasty application of the reverse stock split involved an auto supply store started by four individuals, each of whom received 25 shares of stock. When one of the four was killed in an automobile accident, his shares were divided among his three small children. The surviving owners declared a 1-for-5 reverse stock split, with fractional interests retired for cash.

The three original investors ended up with 5 shares each, but the children's shares ($8\frac{1}{3}$ each) were not divisible by five. Therefore, they received one new share each, and their $3\frac{1}{3}$ old shares were retired for cash. The children's combined interest fell from one-fourth to one-sixth.

The most obvious method to prevent dilution of an owner's interest is to provide him or her by stipulation with veto power over any action by the business that would result in dilution of ownership interest. The difficulty is that sometimes changes in ownership proportions are legitimate and desirable. A company's owners may want to dilute their ownership to attract otherwise unavailable financial resources. An active owner-manager may wish to reduce his or her responsibilities and for that reason want to reduce or extinguish his or her share of the stock. Death, incapacity, or retirement of an active owner may require redistribution of ownership proportions.

In the example just described, it may well have been better for the business not to have one-fourth of the stock controlled by children. All parties concerned would have been better off if an agreement covering this turn of events had been drawn up.

A closely related issue is the sale of stock to outsiders. Because owners of a small corporation are usually active in its management, each shareholder has an interest in the ability of fellow shareholders to contribute to earnings. This leads to two opposing dangers. On the one hand, shareholders have a legitimate interest in keeping incompetent or undersirable people out of a business. On the other hand, all shareholders want the right to sell their stock to the highest bidder in the event that they resign or retire.

These problems affected a dental supply company when one of its founders decided to retire due to ill health. He asked his partners to buy him out, but in the absence of an agreement establishing a value for the shares, the partners offered only a pittance. He retaliated by threatening to sell out to a rather unsavory character who, in the opinion of some, had ties to organized crime. Without an agreement to the contrary, the retiring partner could have done so. The ensuing stalemate brought both sides to their senses, but much tension and expense could have been saved by planning.

Owners and Their Pet Projects

The third major area of possible conflict in a small business is the relationship of participants to their outside interests. It is not unusual for participants in a company to have interests in other businesses that can be suppliers, customers, or competitors. A manager can easily be tempted to divert business from a company in which is is part owner to one in which he is sole owner. Favorable contracts with supplying or purchasing companies in which one has an interest can usually be arranged without much difficulty.

Though such arrangements occur in companies of all sizes, large public companies are more easily deterred because they are under the scrutiny of the Securities and Exchange Commission and other watchdog agencies. The opportunities for questionable transactions are thus greater for small private companies since they operate free from such observation. Franchise holders in particular encounter problems in their dealings with outsiders because they are often forced by agreement to purchase supplies or advertising from businesses controlled by their franchisors.

Unscrupulous managers or owners can divert resources in several other ways from the businesses they're operating to outside interests that they control. For example, they can force their main business to pay excessively high prices for supplies provided by the outside interest or to receive excessively low prices for output sold to the outside venture. The main business may pay exorbitant rates to lease space in a building owned by the outside interest. Also, a manager or owner operating a competing business can make prices, marketing strategy, finances, customer lists, and technology available to the competitor.

This isn't to say that all relations between one business and related outside business interests are questionable. It may be desirable for a company to purchase supplies from, sell products to, or lease space from a noncompeting business controlled by one of its officers. The only danger is that the price may be unfair. A company may be protected against unfairness through an accord to set prices by prevailing market prices, by bona fide outside offers, or by independent appraisal.

Changing the Rules

Even if the other dirty tricks mentioned previously are prevented by agreement, trouble can ensue when unwary shareholders assent to, or are unable to prevent, a simple amendment to the company's charter or to the original document that they signed.

One of the most common and most dangerous changes is conversion of a partnership into a corporation. Because tax and other considerations make incorporation advantageous, an unwary partner can be persuaded to make a change that is disastrous to his or her interests. In a typical case, an individual was convinced by his three partners to incorporate their business, with each former partner holding 25% of the stock. The three conspirators then controlled three-fourths of the stock and, under the rules of corporate governance, voted to dismiss the other man from his job.

Obviously, the victim was unaware of all the differences between a partnership and a corporation. Otherwise, he could have prevented a simple change in the structure of the business from effecting such a major change in employment policy.

Mentioning the Unmentionable

The dangers that await an uninformed participant in a small business are potentially so costly that many people shy away from involvement in a venture. Lawyers have been known to avoid mentioning these pitfalls to clients for fear of discouraging formation of the business in the first place.

We believe nothing can be gained by withholding information from intelligent people. If potential investors are aware of the traps that exist for the unwary, they can prepare to meet them, thereby building stronger relationships with business associates at the outset. It seems inappropriate to talk of employment agreements, dividends, sale of stock to outsiders, self-dealing, and other unpleasantries to optimistic young business people, just as it seems untoward to speak of sickness, death and financial difficulties to newlyweds. But all parties are better off if such possibilities are acknowledged and anticipated.

The appropriate vehicle for preparing for difficulties is a written, binding agreement. The stipulation should cover employment and compensation, actions that might change ownership or the proportion of ownership, relationships with outside interests, and ways amendments can be made. (See Exhibit 1 for a more detailed list.) It is not a simple document, for it involves conflicting rights and values that cannot be resolved by a simple list of "thou shalt nots."

Investors should consult a lawyer who is familiar with such agreements (not all are) and discuss their needs and circumstances fully and frankly. All investors should realize that planning does not imply that they cannot trust one another.

Exhibit 1. Items That Should Be Covered by a Formal Agreement

---

1 Employment and compensation

1. Duties and terms of employment of each participant
2. Salaries and bonuses
3. Dividend policy

---

2 Changes in ownership and ownership proportions

1. Sale of new stock to insiders
2. Purchase of existing stock
3. Stock splits or reverse splits
4. Sale of stock to outsiders
5. Disposition of shares of deceased, incapacitated, or retired owners
6. Mergers
7. Formation of holding companies

---

3 Relations between principals and their outside interests

1. Purchase of supplies
2. Sale of output
3. Lease of space
4. Competing businesses
5. Use of brokers and agents

---

4 Amendments to the corporate charter or partnership agreement

1. Conversion from partnership to corporation
2. Any amendment affecting items above

Once business associates recognize the dangers of having no agreement, they may be tempted to go to the opposite extreme and attempt to write a contract that anticipates and resolves every possible contingency. Lawyers sometimes have excessively fertile imaginations when it comes to uncovering grounds for litigation, and their clients can be left wondering if they will have any room for discretion. A good agreement adopts some of the genius of the U.S. Constitution: it avoids excessive detail and provides procedures for amending the document if necessary.

Finally, one word of caution: don't offer to compensate the lawyer with a few shares of stock. Two people did this a few years ago, expecting to save cash and still retain a controlling interest. The lawyer then formed a coalition with one of the principal owners and ran the other out of the company.

4
Careful Self-Analysis and Team Assessment Can Aid Entrepreneurs

JEFFRY A. TIMMONS

Successful entrepreneurship has long been viewed as a set of elusive qualities that one either does or does not possess. Jeffry A. Timmons disputes that notion. He argues that, by paying attention to their own strengths and weaknesses as well as their team's, entrepreneurs can substantially improve their chances of being successful.

To General Georges F. Doriot, elder statesman of the U.S. venture capital industry, a grade A entrepreneur with a grade B idea is much preferable to a grade B entrepreneur with a grade A idea. Surveys of venture capitalists indicate that the industry generally accepts his view.

That guiding principle for selecting entrepreneurs to support has apparently served venture capitalists quite well. Research carried out during the late 1960s and early 1970s on companies started with the aid of venture capital suggests that anywhere from 65% to 80% of such start-ups avoid failure.[1] Economists and government officials generally believe that only 20% to 40% of all new businesses last beyond the first five years.

Venture capitalists have the obvious advantages of contact with entrepreneurs who are more sophisticated than average and the experience to know how to weed out the most obviously poor investment risks. Nonetheless, their own ability to reduce the chances of failure is worth noting.

Opposite conclusions can be drawn from the venture capitalists' successful emphasis on the quality of the entrepreneur over the quality of the business idea. On the one hand, one can assume that successful entrepreneurs, much like successful baseball sluggers, are born, not made. On the other hand, one can infer that entrepreneurship can be learned and that entrepreneurs should concentrate on improving themselves in certain essential areas, not only to improve their chances of acquiring venture capital or other investment backing but also to heighten their overall chances of success.

Research and consulting that have put me in contact with nearly 1,200 entrepreneurs during the past dozen years convince me to support the second notion. I have seen entrepreneurs benefit from a systematic learn-by-doing approach to venture creation. Such an approach also helps to remove the mystique that pervades the world of venture capital. In this article, I shall share what I have learned from my experience in working with entrepreneurs to develop their ventures as well as some helpful sources of information. (See Exhibit 1) and the Appendix.

Key Requirements

Two areas in which entrepreneurs can exert control and improve their prospects stand out in my mind:

First, lead entrepreneurs must have a keen, realistic awareness of his own or her own entrepreneurial strengths *and* weaknesses; they must also know exactly what skills and experiences they already have and which ones they need to acquire in the future to make a particular venture succeed.

Second, the lead entrepreneur must have a highly committed and motivated team. These partners should be chosen for reasons other than friendship; their management skills, decision-making style, and experience should complement the founder's.

What Qualities to Assess?

The most successful entrepreneurs seem to have several characteristics in common:

☐ A high level of drive and energy.

☐ The self-confidence to take carefully calculated, moderate risks.

☐ A conception that money is a way of keeping score and a tool for growth.

☐ Unusual skill in motivating and eliciting productive collaboration from other people.

☐ High but realistic and achievable goals.

☐ The belief that they can control their own destinies.

☐ The ability to learn from their own failures.

☐ A long-term vision of the future of the enterprise.

☐ Intense competition with self-imposed standards.

You as an entrepreneur should, of course, realize that even the most talented entrepreneurs have weaknesses in some of these areas. But they clearly see their own shortcomings and aggressively tap their own strengths.

Exhibit 1. Sources of Assistance for Growth-Oriented Entrepreneurs

Some private sector organizations
Center for Entrepreneurial
Management
311 Main Street
Worcester, Massachusetts 01608
Joseph Mancuso, founder

Kentucky Highlands Investment
Corporation
Main Street
London, Kentucky 40741
Joseph Frye, vice-president

The School for Entrepreneurs
Tarrytown Conference Center
Tarrytown, New York 10591
Robert L. Schwartz, founder

Venture Founders Corporation
385 Concord Avenue
Belmont, Massachusetts 02178
Alex Dingee, president

**Some schools with entrepreneurship
courses or programs**
Babson College[a]
Babson Park
Wellesley, Massachusetts 02181
Professors Robert Ronstadt and John
Hornaday

School of Business[b]
University of California
Berkeley, California 94720
Professor Richard H. Holton

Cleveland State University[a]
Cleveland, Ohio 41115
Professor Jeffrey Susbauer

School of Business[b]
Columbia University
New York, New York 10027
Professor Ian C. MacMillan

School of Business[b]
University of Southern California
Los Angeles, California 90024
Professor Robert E. Coffey

School of Business and Public
Administration[b]
Cornell University
Ithaca, New York 14850
Professor Clifford S. Orloff

Harvard Business School[b]
Smaller Company Management
Program
Soldiers Field
Boston, Massachusetts 02163
William Presley, administrative
director

School of Business—304HA[ab]
Northeastern University
Boston, Massachusetts 02115
Professor Jeffry A. Timmons

School of Business[ab]
Ohio State University
Columbus, Ohio 43210
Professor Albert Shapero

Exhibit 1. *(Continued)*

Caruth Institute[b]
Southern Methodist University
Dallas, Texas 75275
Professor John Welsh

Keller Graduate School of
Management[b]
10 South Riverside Plaza, Suite 2124
Chicago, Illinois
Professor Dennis C. MacFarlaine

**Some schools with entreprensurship
courses or programs**
School of Business[ab]
University of Washington
Seattle, Washington 98195
Professor Karl Vesper

Wharton School[b]
University of Pennsylvania
Philadelphia, Pennsylvania 19104
Professor Edward Shils

National Science Foundation
Innovation Centers([ab]) at
Carnegie-Mellon University
Pittsburgh, Pennsylvania 15213
Professor Dwight Baumann

Krannert School[ab]
Purdue University
West Lafayette, Indiana 47907
Professor Arnold Cooper

School of Business[ab]
University of California at Los
Angeles
Los Angeles, California 90024
Professor Hans Schollhammer

Massachusetts Institute of Technology
Cambridge, Massachusetts 02139
Professor David G. Jansson

School of Business
University of Oregon
Eugene, Oregon 97403
Professor Gerald G. Udell

University of Utah
Salt Lake City, Utah 84112
Professor Wayne Brown

[a]Undergraduate program
[b]Graduate program

The Assessment Process

Deciding what your strengths and weaknesses are, however, is easier said than done. A good way to start is with a personal inventory of your own track record—your successes and failures, likes and dislikes. Questions such as what causes your satisfactions and frustrations, which activities excite you, what your short- and long-term goals are, and which personal values and needs are most important to you are especially worthy of consideration at this point.

More important, your insights need to be tested and augmented by input from peers who are entrepreneurs, work associates, or others who know you well and whose opinions you must trust and value. An hour or two spent discussing their evaluations against the qualities suggested previously can be extremely revealing. The key to this process lies in their being candid and specific. A general "Will I make it?" will simply not yield the subtlety and insight that you need to understand your risks and how to deal with them.

Interestingly enough, this process of self-assessment and open criticism from peers is something the best entrepreneurs seem to thrive on. They do not feel threatened or vulnerable but rather see the process as a unique opportunity for getting feedback from highly credible sources. Further, they readily see the implications for team building and partner selection. For instance, the realization that one is cautious about taking risks suggests the need for a partner who is more aggressive about risks. Similarly, a doer should be balanced with a thinker.

Most of the entrepreneurs I have worked with report that their efforts to assess themselves in these more intangible aspects of entrepreneurship are important. One entrepreneur, a man in his early thirties who graduated from a prestigious business school, made these comments about the role of assessment before he launched an import business:

> What it really did was give me confidence. I know the nuts-and-bolts things, but I wasn't at all certain I had some of the personal traits needed or exactly what I would be getting into. The peer feedback and my own assessments clarified a lot of fuzzy issues for me; and once I got going, I was ready for the inevitable pain and agony of cash crunches, huge uncertainty, and occasional chaos. Before, I probably would've been floored by some of these crises and would've given up.

Pitfalls in Feedback

Simply getting up the courage to seek feedback from others is only half the battle. The other half is prodding those from whom feedback is sought to be candid and objective and also interpreting less than forthright assessments realistically. Be wary of judgments like these:

☐ "You'll make a great entrepreneur." If the feedback you receive does not indicate areas of weakness or questions to think about, you have probably been too selective about the people you have talked with and listened to, or else you have not insisted on candor.

☐ "You can make it." Such generalities miss the entire point of the exercise. Insist on an appraisal with specific examples and illustrations based on your behavior rather than a pep talk.

☐ "You'll never make it." Equally simplistic and unreliable.

☐ "You quit school and got fired from a big company—you won't have enough persistence." Research on entrepreneurs suggests that *both* of these experiences can be assets instead of liabilities. The important issue is why you had such experiences. Entrepreneurs frequently take action to pursue their own goals and do not fit others' setups.

☐ "Your first venture failed. Why not become a manager?" How the initial venture was handled, what you learned, and how you bounced back are what count most. Early failures are quite common and important to learning the venturing ropes.

☐ "Look, don't bother with all this assessment and feedback business; just go do it." A perfectly tolerable strategy *if* you do not care about downside losses, your track record and reputation, the psychological impact if you fail, and your time.

The Importance of a Team

While I have thus far focused on the entrepreneur as the critical ingredient in a venture's success, evidence is accumulating that a team is a key to building a high-growth venture. For example, a recent study of 104 high-technology companies launched in the 1960s reported that 83.3% of the high-growth companies (those achieving $5 million or more in sales) were launched by teams, while only 53.8% of the 73 discontinued companies had several founders.[2] Other studies have shown that lone founders are much less likely to build million-dollar-plus ventures.

The systematic effort involved in assessing entrepreneurial potential applies also to assessing prospective partners. Analyzing the skills and capabilities of the founder and other members of the team is particularly important. Asking the following questions helps:

☐ Does the lead founder have key marketing and financial skills and a thorough knowledge of the business area?

☐ What skills and capabilities do team members need to complement the founder's skills and operating style?

☐ How is the leader perceived as an entrepreneur and as a team leader?

☐ Does the lead entrepreneur confront team members of differing opinions and use the weight of evidence and logic rather than superiority to arrive at decisions?

☐ Does the lead entrepreneur recognize and skillfully deal with the subtle but potentially disruptive interpersonal issues that inevitably arise on any team?

☐ Are the team members aware of each other's ethical stances and personal values and how these may affect the team?

Obviously, the team members will avoid many problems if they work together and deal with these questions prior to start-up.

Team-Building Problems

New venture teams usually evolve because of friendships or working associations and are further glued together by enthusiasm for a new product or idea. Substantial disaffection, however, usually becomes a problem for the founding partners within five years of launching a venture. Indeed, the breakup percentage of founding teams probably far exceeds the national divorce rate, thanks to problems that become evident during the early going.

One frequent team problem is the existence of similar rather than complementary experience and capabilities among the founding partners. In high-technology ventures particularly, three or four engineers, technicians, or scientists who have been working together on a project may join forces to start a business. They may have come from the same school, may be about the same age, or may have worked on the same product or technology. They may possess tremendous expertise, but they probably lack skill and experience in other areas and fail to appreciate how crucial general management, marketing, and finance are to the long-term success of a venture. Most of these teams do not survive, or, if they do, have only marginal success. Such a founding team must usually be reorganized or reconstituted if it is to attract outside venture capital and become commercially successful.

The desire for equality among partners frequently accompanies the previous pattern. Team members who have much in common in background and experience may faithfully adhere to their peer status when it comes to distribution of stock and salary levels; they may insist that all of them receive the same amount. They unrealistically assume that equality is best and make little effort to address the complex implications for motivating and rewarding contributions to the budding company. Nor do partners seem to appreciate that such an approach is a convenient way to avoid real differences that must be confronted.

The fact that the partners are avoiding these issues means that they are likely to ignore more serious problems later. Extremely rare is the new venture in which each team member's contribution is equal to the others'. The most successful ventures, in contrast, intuitively or by design, more realistically recognize the role and importance of the lead entrepreneur-president and the marketing talent and do not treat everyone equally. Nor do they avoid the very difficult, often painful, and time-consuming effort required to come to agreement.

In addition, the goals and values of the founders are often unclear or unarticulated. They may not be aware of why they are so intent on starting their own business. They may have started it for the wrong reasons. One researcher on entrepreneurship has found that about two-thirds of the people who start new companies do so because of dislocating or external events: they are fired, they are leapfrogged by the president's son, or their employer goes out of business.[3] Becoming an unemployed aerospace engineer is not necessarily a good reason for launching your own venture.

Unfortunately, entrepreneurs and investors are often embroiled in the heat of start-up before they discover that they have conflicting goals and values. If they work together on preparing a business plan, for instance, before they formally start up, they can clarify and resolve some of these problems. This demanding work can force prospective partners to make a realistic examination of the founders' goals and values before they become locked into a formal incorporation or partnership agreement.

Ethical conflicts, while less common, can also terminate partnerships. Because ethical values are deeply rooted, taken for granted, and infrequently tested, they can become an explosive issue when partners find that they do not share the same idea of what is ethical and what is not. Furthermore, most partners have very little basis by which to determine if their values are well matched. Ethical conflicts usually occur during a crisis for the business, when there is simply not enough time to talk out and resolve the differences.

In one instance, two young MBAs formed a business that enjoyed unusually early profit. Eager to grow, they formed a second venture, which, unfortunately, was unprofitable and drained resources from their original venture. Unable to raise additional outside capital, they faced severe cash flow problems. Partner A, who was responsible for trade payables, stretched many to the breaking point; some dependable creditors were not paid at all, even though they had been assured of payment.

Then partner B accidentally discovered that partner A was, to prevent the lapse of his own life insurance policy, at the same time making sizable, unauthorized payments to an insurance salesman who was one of his relatives. At first, A denied making the payments and then any wrongdoing. An unresolvable dispute developed between the partners, and within days their lawyers were their only mode of communication. A few months later the partners had to sell the business at a loss.

A final pitfall that new-venture teams usually face at the beginning is the entrepreneur's failure to assess himself vis-à-vis the requirements of the venture. A thorough awareness of one's entrepreneurial and managerial strengths and weaknesses is a prerequisite for forming a team. Difficulty in putting together a sound team may lie in the lead entrepreneur's unwillingness or inability to identify his own deficiencies and to choose team members with complementary strengths.

Difficulty may also arise from the lead entrepreneur's not understanding what is really needed to make the new venture grow beyond being a million-dollar business. This fault is especially true of technically oriented people and those with experience limited to a business other than the one they wish to launch.

In short, these and other team-building problems merit the serious attention of founders and investors alike. Clearly, anticipating all such problems in advance is extremely difficult. Problems no one expects will invariably occur. Yet, repeatedly, entrepreneurs report how valuable grappling with these issues prior to start-up is. Four hundred hours or more may go into putting together a complete business plan. Yet working together on the plan and even moonlighting together during the embryonic phase of a venture can be an excellent way to assess the balance of the team and its vulnerability.

The skills for entrepreneurial success can be learned. The art of teaching new venture management is in its infancy, but it has gained a foothold in U.S. business schools and other organizations aimed at helping entrepreneurs. In addition, we have the most promising climate for entrepreneurs in years, which should foster widespread acceptance of the notion of teaching entrepreneurship.

Notes

1. Among the research sources are the following: Russell B. Faucett, "The Management of Venture Capital Investment Companies," M.A. thesis for the Sloan School of Management, Massachusetts Institute of Technology, Cambridge, Mass., 1971.

Edward B. Roberts, "How To Succeed in a New Technology Enterprise," *Technology Review,* December 1970, p. 23.

Clint Taylor, "Starting Up in the High Technology Industries in California," a study commissioned by the Wells Fargo Investment Company, 1969.

Personal communication with the late S. M. Rubel, administrator from the National Venture Capital Association, Chicago, August 1975.

2. Arnold C. Cooper and A. V. Bruno, "Success Among High-Technology Firms," *Business Horizons,* April 1977, p. 20.

3. See Albert Shapero, "The Displaced, Uncomfortable Entrepreneur," *Psychology Today.* November 1975, p. 83.

Appendix

Help for Entrepreneurs

Aspiring entrepreneurs can get assistance in developing entrepreneurial skills from the organizations and programs listed in Exhibit 1. The following discussion may help you find a program for entrepreneurs that suits your needs.

What to Look for

A program with these characteristics will give you an overall sense of what the entrepreneurial process is and some idea of how successful you may be at it:

Content—Actual cases, business plans, and profiles of entrepreneurs; exercises that involve you with other entrepreneurs; focus on start-up and the early stages of ventures.

Methods—A learn-by-doing approach based on interactive methods rather than on lectures alone that includes an opportunity for you to develop your own business plan.

Instructors—A variety of people with experience in business, consulting, teaching, research, and capital investment and with the skill to lead a group of individuals through a careful assessment of their entrepreneurial abilities.

Management skills—Discussion and analysis of debt and equity, cash flow, and break-even analysis.

The role of the team and the business plan—In-depth consideration of the importance these factors have to a new venture and coverage of sources for seed and expansion capital.

Results and feedback—Information on managing new ventures from entrepreneurs who have already gone through the program themselves.

What to Avoid
The following claims are usually signs of a program with questionable quality:

"We have a battery of psychological tests that will predict whether you are an entrepreneur and whether you will succeed or fail." Such tests have never been validated; in fact, they may be misleading.

"We'll package and prepare your business plan." This is a route to avoid at all costs. It is easy, convenient, and fast, but it misses the entire point of the exercise, which is to help you yourself gain command of the intricacies and interrelationships of the components of your plan.

"We can raise the capital you need fast." Again, carts perform best behind horses; there are no 90-day wonders that last.

"We'll structure the deal so that you'll be liquid in three or four years." Such promises are clues to naiveté and greed on behalf of the "helpers." Successful ventures usually take eight years or so to become solid businesses.

"First, let's incorporate so that you'll be protected." This reasoning is faulty. Prematurely locking into roles, stock ownership, and legal boundaries can seriously cripple your ability to form a realistic, motivating structure for your team.

5

A Business Plan Is More than a Financing Device

JEFFRY A. TIMMONS

Jeffry A. Timmons emphasizes the importance of viewing the business plan as more than a means for raising capital. He points out its usefulness as an operations plan for running a new venture. And he offers guidance for putting together such a plan.

You are enthusiastic about an idea for a new business. You think the business has excellent market prospects and fits well with your skills, experience, personal values, and aspirations.

But what are the most significant risks and problems involved in launching the enterprise? What are its long-term profit prospects? What are its future financing and cash flow requirements? What will be the demands of operating lead times, seasonality, and facility location? What is your marketing and pricing strategy?

Once you have convinced yourself and your partners that the answers to such questions are favorable, can you also convince prospective investors? If you seek out investment capital or loans, you will face much skepticism from venture capital firms, banks, insurance companies, and other financing sources. For example, only 3% to 7% of proposals to venture-capital sources for start-up or ongoing financing are actually funded.

An effective business plan will convince the investor that you have identified a high-growth opportunity, that you have the entrepreneurial and

---

Author's Note: I wish to thank my colleagues, Leonard E. Smollen and Brian Haslett of Venture Founders Corporation, for their help in researching this article.

management talent to effectively exploit that opportunity and that you have a rational, coherent, and believable program for doing so.

The development of such a business plan is neither quick nor easy. Properly preparing a business plan can easily take 200 to 300 hours. Squeezing that amount of time into evenings and weekends can make the process stretch out to between 6 and 12 months. One might ask if such a time-consuming effort is really worth the trouble.

Wouldn't a more effective approach be to have an outside professional quickly prepare the business plan and then have the founders use their time to obtain financing and start the business?

Rewards of Preparation

Keep in mind that the careful preparation of a business plan represents a unique opportunity to think through all facets of a new venture. You can examine the consequences of different strategies and tactics and determine the human and financial requirements for launching and building the venture, all at no risk or cost.

One entrepreneur with whom I worked discovered while preparing a business plan that the major market for his biomedical product was in nursing homes rather than in hospital emergency rooms as she and her physician partner had previously assumed. This realization changed the focus of her marketing effort.

The business plan is thus another way to evaluate the start-up venture in addition to the two ways I described in an earlier article.[1] That article explained how the process of self-assessment and team assessment can aid entrepreneurs in exerting control over the new venture and improve their prospects for eventual success.

For the investor, the business plan is the single most important screening device. Once the plan has passed initial screening, the investor may request the entrepreneur to make an oral presentation describing key features of the venture. If the investor is still interested, the plan will be given a more detailed evaluation and will become a prime measure of the founders' ability to define and analyze opportunities and problems and to identify and plan actions to deal with them.

A Plan's Long-Term Value

Most founders find the business plan to be even more helpful after start-up. As the founder-president of one venture that grew to sales of $14 million in seven years put it:

> Once you are in the business, you realize that everyone, including the
> founders, is learning his or her job. If you have a thoughtful and complete

business plan, you have a lot more confidence in your decisions. You have a reference already there to say, "Well, I have already run the numbers on inventory, or cost of goods, and this is what will happen."

If an outsider prepares the plan, you probably won't have the same sense of confidence and commitment.

The business plan can be especially valuable in the important area of product pricing. In one instance, the initial strategy of the founders of a rotary-drill venture was to price its products below the competition, even though the venture had a superior product innovation in a growing market. When the founders consulted outside experts, they were persuaded to price 10% over the competition.

By its second year, the new company enjoyed pretax profits of $850,000 based on about $9 million in sales. The revised pricing strategy made a significant difference. Without the detailed analysis of the industry and competition that is central to the marketing section of the business plan, it is unlikely that outsiders would have seen the basis for a different pricing strategy.

Feedback on your business plan by trusted and knowledgeable outsiders can help in refining strategy and making difficult decisions. A Nova Scotia entrepreneur who builds commercial fishing boats recently decided to raise his prices more than 40% based on an outside analysis and critique of his business plan. He knew he would lose two orders, but he also knew he would make more profit on the remaining three than all five at the old price. His delivery time would be cut in half as well. He's convinced that the shortened delivery time will lead to additional sales at the higher margins. And with upfront progress payments, he won't have to raise outside equity capital.

The process can also clarify the venture's financial requirements. Another entrepreneur with a three-year-old $1 million business erecting coal-loading sites believed he needed about $350,000 in expansion capital. After reflecting on a detailed critique of his business plan presentation, he concluded:

"The worst thing I could do right now is put more money into the business. The first thing I should do is get my own backyard more in order. But I will be back in two or three years."

True to his prediction, he returned two-and-a-half years later. His company was now approaching $3 million in sales and had a business plan for expansion that resulted in $400,000 debt capital investment, without relinquishing any ownership.

Common Misconceptions

Entrepreneurs tend to downgrade the business plan because of certain false notions they hold about it. Technical and scientific entrepreneurs share one misconception I call the *better mousetrap fallacy*. They frequently place unwarranted faith in a product or invention, especially if it is patented. Indeed, technological ideas must be sound, but marketability and marketing know-how generally outweigh technical elegance in the success equation. The rotary-drill venture discussed earlier reached $40 million in sales last year, yet has no patents on its products.

To further illustrate, less than one-half of one percent of the best ideas contained in the *Patent Gazette* five years ago have returned a dime to the inventors. In essence, the patent is usually a useful marketing tool, but not much else, and may be worth 15% or considerably less of the founding equity.

A second misconception new entrepreneurs often have is that the business plan is essentially a negotiating and selling tool for raising money. It isn't considered relevant or useful beyond that. Indeed, I have heard more than one entrepreneur comment that the plan is "destined for the circular file" once the funds are in the bank.

Such a view is dangerous for several reasons. To prospective partners, investors, or suppliers, it communicates a shallow understanding of the requirements for creating a successful business. It can also signal a promoting quality—a search for fast money and a hope for an early sellout—that creates mistrust of the entrepreneur. If the plan isn't a serious promise of what the team can deliver, should investors believe anything the founders assert?

A third misconception some entrepreneurs have is a belief that the primary and most important task in the start-up process is to determine if they can raise money as an indication that their idea is sound. This "cart before the horse" approach usually results in a hastily prepared business plan and exuberant shopping around among prospective investors.

Because most venture capital firms are quite small—often no more than two or three partners—they generally cannot take the time needed to get to know each entrepreneur and to explain the details for rejection. They use the business plan for initial screening as well as for making investment decisions. I have met many entrepreneurs who, as long as two years later, still do not understand that they were unable to raise capital because their business plans were deficient.

A fourth misconception is a belief among some entrepreneurs that their particular plan has no fatal flaws. These entrepreneurs ignore the need to test the plan's soundness with knowledgeable outside sources. Entrepreneurs must search for flaws in the market analysis that would make further consideration of the venture unnecessary

One potential flaw is excessive dependence on outside suppliers for important state-of-the-art components that materially affect product development and prices. Suppliers of Viatron, a computer leasing company that obtained substantial public and private financing in the late 1960s, helped drive the company into bankruptcy in large part because they were unable to produce several semiconductors at low enough prices to enable Viatron to meet its own heavily promoted inexpensive prices.

A final misconception among some start-up and early-stage entrepreneurs seeking venture capital is the belief that retaining a minimum 51% control of the company is essential. This view seems to assume that control depends on legal percentage ownership rather than on management's behavior. In short, 51% of nothing is nothing. Compare this with the 20% ownership retained by the four founders of Digital Equipment Corporation.

Sound investment partners do not want to run your company—they invest in you and your team. More than anything else in the early going, the founders' actions are the ultimate controlling influence on the venture.

Putting Together a Business Plan

What format should the business plan take? The outline in Exhibit 1 suggests one commonly used organizational approach. Entrepreneurs should also keep in mind some important general guidelines for preparing such plans:

1. Keep the business plan as short as possible without compromising the description of your venture and its potential. Cover the key issues that will interest an investor and leave secondary details for a meeting with the investor. Remember that venture capital investors are not patient readers.

2. Don't overdiversify your venture. Focus your attention on one or two services or product lines and markets. A new or young business does not have the management depth to pursue too many opportunities.

3. Don't have unnamed, mysterious people on your management team, such as the Mr. G. who will join you later as a financial vice-president. The investor will want to know early on exactly who Mr. G. is and what his commitment to your venture is.

4. Don't describe technical products or manufacturing processes in terms that only an expert can understand. Most venture capitalists do not like to invest in what they don't understand or think you don't understand.

5. Don't estimate your sales on the basis of plant capacity. Estimate your potential sales carefully on the basis of your marketing study, and from these estimates determine the production facility you need.

6. Don't make ambiguous, vague, or unsubstantiated statements. They make you look like a shallow and fuzzy thinker. For example, don't merely say that your markets are growing rapidly. Analyze past, present, and projected future growth rates and market size, an be able to substantiate your data.

7. Disclose and discuss any current or potential problems in your venture. If you fail to do this and the venture capitalist discovers them, your credibility will be badly damaged.

8. Involve all of your management team, as well as any special legal, accounting, or financial help, in the preparation of the business plan.

9. Don't overstate or inflate revenue and accomplishments; be rigorously realistic and objective in making estimates and discussing risks.

Exhibit 1. Outline for Preparing a Business Plan

Introduction

Summary of business plan and strategy

The company and its industry

The company
Discussion of industry
Strategy

Products or services

Description
Proprietary position
Potential
Technologies and skills

Market research and evaluation

Customers
Market size, trends, and segments
Competition—strengths and
weaknesses
Estimated market share and sales
Ongoing market evaluation
Economics—margins, costs

Marketing plan

Overall marketing strategy
Pricing
Sales tactics and distribution
Service and warranty policies
Advertising and promotion
Profitability and break-even analysis

Design and development plans

Development status and tasks
Difficulties and risks
Product improvement and new
products
Costs

Manfacturing and operations plan

Geographical location
Facilities and improvements
Strategy and plans
Labor force

Management team

Organization— roles and
responsibilities
Key management personnel
Management compensation and
ownership
Board of directors
Management assistant or training
needs
Supporting outside professional
services

Overall schedule (monthly)

**Important risks, assumptions, and
problems**

Community impact

Economic
Human development
Community development
Environmental

**Financial plan (monthly for first year;
quarterly for next two to three years)**

Profit and loss forecast
Pro forma cash flow analysis
Pro forma balance sheet
Break-even charts

Proposed company offering

Desired financing
Securities offering
Capitalization
Use of funds

Source: Jeffry A. Timmons, Leonard E. Smollen, and Alexander L. M. Dingee, *New Venture Creation: A Guide to Small Business Development* (Homewood, Ill.: Richard D. Irwin, Inc., 1977), p. 426.

The search for seed and expansion capital is usually time consuming and exhausting. Failure under such circumstances can leave the founders illiquid and demoralized. A carefully prepared business plan can aid substantially in planning a new venture, screening would-be partners, evolving winning strategies, and joining with a sound investment source, before actually launching the venture. In other words, it can mean the difference between success and failure.

Notes

1. "Careful Self-Analysis and Team Assessment Can Aid Entrepreneurs" (*Growing Concerns*), *HBR* November-December 1979, p. 198.

6
Finding the Best Acquisition Candidates

HERBERT E. KIERULFF

Herbert E. Kierulff examines in introductory fashion the factors small companies should consider when hunting for acquisition candidates. He also offers advice for identifying and approaching potential candidates.

Expansion by acquisition is an attractive option for many small companies whose leadership is bright, aggressive, and unawed by the complexity of the task. Plying the acquisition waters can be hazardous, though. Even large, sophisticated corporations report that about half of their acquisitions are unsatisfactory. A recent study I conducted of 91 large companies showed that only 46% of their smaller company acquisitions were rated "good" or "excellent" by the acquirer; the rest were rated "fair" or "poor."

How can hazards be avoided? Primarily by identifying as acquisition candidates those companies which show promise on their own and which best complement the acquiring business. This article offers guidance for translating that goal into practice.

Best Candidates

The more closely the proposed acquisition matches the following criteria, the greater the likelihood of a successful marriage:

Well-Defined Market Niche.   The candidate's products or services should clearly differ from those of close competition. Going head-to-head with competitors is difficult under normal conditions; it becomes dangerous when the competitors are large and well financed or small and well entrenched. Differences in products or services can include such factors as geography (e.g., a hardware store with little competition in its market area), price, quality, service, or technology.

Growing Industry.   It is rarely worthwhile to invest in a company that is in a declining industry or does a significant amount of business with companies in a declining industry. There are more than enough companies in growth industries to keep acquisition-minded smaller companies busy. Why purchase a company and end up fighting a holding action which will only become increasingly desperate over time?

Cyclical Stability.   In general, companies that are relatively insensitive to the business cycle are superior acquisition candidates. Smaller companies in cyclical industries tend to fail when demand dries up during recessions, usually because such companies are less well capitalized than their larger counterparts. Similarly, when demand is extremely strong and inflation serious, smaller companies tend to fail because too rapid growth exhausts their working capital.

Seasonal Stability.   Nonseasonal industries are usually the most attractive ones for acquisitions unless the acquirer is in a seasonal business and is seeking a business counter-seasonal to its own. One such example I encountered several years ago was a maker of snowmobile parts that acquired a supplier of lawn mower parts.

Essential Products.   Entrepreneurs tend to be attracted to fad, fashion, and luxury items because of the short response time associated with their promotion and sale. Most entrepreneurs should avoid companies built around such products, though, since these companies have many of the high-risk attributes associated with new ventures.

Several small companies I know of produce fashion clothing or personal accessories and have run into financial difficulties from sudden market shifts. CEOs who do well in such companies seem to have a special knack for reading the market. Buying in from outside such an industry and hoping you have or can get the knack entails too much risk.

An essential product is less vulnerable to political, social, and economic forces. The market is assured and the need for large and sustained product promotion is minimized.

High Value Added.   A small company that assembles a few parts, supplied by others, into a finished product that is then shipped to a distributor is in danger of being squeezed out either by the supplier or the distributor. But a company which manufactures, assembles, *and* distributes a product to end-users or retailers has little to fear from its suppliers or distributors and is thus a better acquisition candidate for the small company.

Technical Know-How. A company that uses technical expertise is usually more attractive than one that does not because such know-how limits competition. Acquisition-minded CEOs of smaller companies may avoid such technically oriented businesses because they are uncomfortable with strange technical terms and would rather not take the time and trouble to acquaint themselves with an advanced technology. This can be a mistake if the technology is not too advanced for the acquiring company.

A technical product or service usually requires close interaction between the company and its customers. This interaction forms a tie that large competitors find difficult to break, even if they offer significantly lower prices. The customer is usually more interested in reliability and on-time delivery than price. A smaller company can excel at this and reap a handsome profit.

Short Production Cycle. A small company should acquire businesses with short production cycles and leave the long production runs to the larger companies. In this way, relatively less money is tied up in plant and equipment. More important, the smaller company is able to capitalize on its flexibility, which gives it an edge over large competitors.

Relation to Acquirer. It always makes sense that the industry or industries selected for acquisition be closely related to the acquirer's industry and areas of expertise. The buying company and its candidate should be linked in at least one of these areas: suppliers, production, or customers.

Proximity. Geography is often an important element in acquisitions because of the control problem. I have found it best to search first in an area that can be reached by automobile in less than two or three hours. If a company cannot be found in that area, the search should expand to cities with direct flight connections to the acquirer's home city.

Search Procedure

The small company CEO together with fellow officers and directors represent perhaps the best sources of leads in the acquisition search. Bankers, accountants, lawyers, and investment bankers familiar to the acquiring company are also valuable sources. These professionals may have personal contacts with good businesses not officially for sale.

In addition, advertisements in appropriate newspapers and trade journals can generate leads. Finally, it is possible to buy or develop from published sources a mailing list of smaller companies that meet the major requirements. A carefully worded letter of inquiry can be sent to these companies'

CEOs, inviting them to make contact. The person selected to make the initial visit to an acquisition candidate should obtain financial statements and product brochures beforehand. This information will prepare the visitor and permit more meaningful questions.

Most owners will provide financial information if they are impressed with the sincerity of the potential acquirer. I should note here that although it is not always obvious, negotiating for the sale of a company begins when the first contact is made. Seller is assessing buyer and forming opinions and strategies on the basis of any letters, advertisements, and telephone calls.

The practice of using commissioned business brokers is a controversial one. Some CEOs complain that brokers waste an inordinate amount of time showing companies that are of little interest. Other CEOs are quite satisfied with the help they have received.

Owners and executives of smaller companies often have unrealistic expectations about the worth of their companies, especially when they have been consistently profitable. For this reason, do not hesitate to ask during the first telephone conversation whether the potential candidate's CEO has established a selling price. You may not get a specific price, but you may get some indication of range.

Not long ago, for example, I encountered a president whose company had been earning in the neighborhood of $70,000 annually after taxes. The company had a long history of profits, but there was no expectation of rapid growth in the foreseeable future. Without hesitation, the president indicated that he expected at least $3 million for his company and was not interested in a lengthy payout.

Such experiences are not uncommon. Owners like to remember the late 1960s, when small companies traded hands at 10 to 30 times earnings and more. Furthermore, some large corporations are willing to pay inflated prices for small companies either because some of their executives are forced into weak negotiating positions by pressure from above or because the candidate company is well entrenched in an industry in which the large company plans to make a major strategic move.

The Best Fit

Once acquisition candidates have been identified and the field narrowed during the search procedure, acquiring companies must make some hard decisions on which candidates to be serious about. Those decisions should be based partly on how well the acquiring company and the candidates fit together from both marketing and financial perspectives.

But the key factor is the subsequent relationship of the management of the acquiring company to that of the acquired business. Should any or all of the acquired company's managers stay beyond the transition period? If so, what should their duties be, and how should they relate to each other and to the acquiring company?

How these questions are answered depends on the acquiring management's assessment of the quality and interest of the executives of the acquired company. In some cases, managers judged to be of high quality will prefer not to stay on long after the acquisition. In other cases, mediocre managers will seek long-term contracts to remain with the acquired company. Clearly, if arrangements satisfactory to the acquiring company cannot be worked out, the acquisition should be avoided.

In Conclusion

Expansion by acquisition has proved a rewarding route for smaller companies. As with most business endeavors, the factor which contributes most to a profitable voyage is careful planning.

Successful planning starts with the definition of desirable characteristics in the acquisition candidate. Planning continues on through the search, becoming more specific as more information is gained. The best candidate is the one that meets the search criteria and also fits the acquiring company's management needs.

7

Simplifying the Search for Four-Leaf Clovers

PETER MAILANDT

A convincing argument can be made that buying an existing business is preferable to starting a new venture. An established business already has a position in the market, its assets are in place, and managerial weaknesses are easy to spot and correct. But what is the best approach for identifying financially attractive targets? And once you have picked an acquisition candidate, how can you structure negotiations to minimize discord? Peter Mailandt offers guidance in finding those elusive acquisition candidates he refers to as four-leaf clovers.

Chief executives of smaller companies head down the acquisition path for various reasons. Some want to make their companies grow. Others hope to improve their returns. Still others seek to balance seasonal cycles in sales or earnings. Whatever the reason, most executives want to find an acquisition bargain—what I call the four-leaf clover—that will, for a reasonable price, add value to their own enterprises. Consequently, the acquisition process must take into account not only such considerations as the candidates' industries and markets but financial criteria as well.[1]

Several tested financial screening methods have evolved over time. For example, many acquisition specialists now believe that determining long-term increases in shareholder wealth—measured, say, by the present value of the expected future stream of cash flow or earnings per share (EPS)—is the best approach for evaluating the financial benefit from a prospective

---

Author's Note: I gratefully acknowledge Robert J. Donachie's contribution to developing the concept.

takeover. This approach, however, is time consuming and cumbersome and also yields results that typically are very sensitive to estimates of future performance.

While many big companies with large analytic resources can easily apply the long-term wealth concept (especially in selecting from among a few top candidates), others may find it less in tune with their needs or abilities to judge. The concept may be impractical for smaller companies, which may lack either the necessary analytic capabilities or must make quick decisions, as in the case of a company needing to acquire another business to prevent yet another company from acquiring it.

Managers of small companies need easily obtainable information to help them decide, first, whether a candidate is worth acquiring and, next, whether they can devise a financial package to entice shareholders of a target company to sell out. At the same time, a package must protect the interests of the acquirer's shareholders—that is, to avoid great leaps in financial leverage and to improve (or at least preserve) short-term EPS, the acquisition should pay for itself insofar as possible.

Assessing Leverage and EPS

This article presents an alternative financial screening process that helps identify acquisition targets most likely to meet the objectives just described. Small, busy staffs can use it to get a quick fix on many companies. By using both short-term EPS and financial risk as standards, the method presented here helps managers to evaluate risks and shareholders to measure performance.

To illustrate this financial screening process, let us assume that Company A, the buyer, has completed its evaluation of nonfinancial factors and is now ready to review the financial attractiveness of several acquisition candidates, beginning with Company X. Exhibit 1 shows the financial condition of both companies. The analysis proceeds in three steps:

1   For each candidate, determine the maximum price at which your shareholders' interests would still be easily protected.
2   Rank companies according to their acquirability and financial attractiveness.
3   Develop a financial package as part of a strategy for negotiating price and terms with the target company.

What's the Top Price?

Acquisitions are usually paid for with cash, debt, or equity—either separately or in some combination. In this discussion, I assume payment using all three: cash, to the extent that it can be squeezed from the candidate's operations;

Exhibit 1. Major Preacquisition Financial Data for Company A (Buyer) and Company X^a (Target) (in $ millions except per-share data and debt–equity ratio)

Statement of operations	Company A	Company X	Balance sheet	Company A	Company X
Revenues	$30.00	$ 3.60	Cash, marketable securities	$ 0.61	$0.12
Pretax profits	2.41	0.42	Other assets	11.90	1.58
Net income	1.30	0.225	Total assets	12.51	1.70
Shares outstanding	0.26	0.125	Long-term debt	3.76	0.40
Net income per share	5.00	1.80	Other liabilities	4.05	0.30
			Shareholder equity	4.70	1.00
Funds from operations	**1.65**	**0.27**	**Total liability and shareholder equity**	**12.51**	**1.70**
Cash dividends	0.375	0.04			
Capital expenditure	1.10	0.16	Debt/equity	0.80	0.40
Market value	10.40	1.375	Book value	4.70	1.00
Market value per share	40.00	11.00	Book value per share	18.08	8.00

^{a}Note that financial data of Company X should reflect "normal" operations; the impact of, for example, extraordinary items should be eliminated. If Company X is a very cyclical performer, some financial data (e.g., net income and capital expenditure) may have to be averaged over several years.

debt, to the extent that unused debt-service capacity exists in the target company; and stocks, to the extent that EPS is not diluted after earnings are adjusted to reflect increased interest charges and goodwill. The attractiveness of the resulting package of cash, debt, and equity to the individual target company is then analyzed, since it represents the top price the buyer could pay and still protect shareholder interests.

Squeezing Cash from Operations

You can determine sources of ready cash by studying the balance sheets of acquisition candidates. These sources include cash and marketable securities, sizable accounts receivable, contrasting low levels of payables, and high inventory levels or excess fixed assets relative to requirements. For the purpose of this analysis, assume that Company A can only withdraw 75% of cash and marketable securities ($90,000 in our example) from the operations of Company X to help finance its takeover.

Exploiting Unused Debt-Service Capacity

Raising such funds to help pay for an acquisition requires a certain amount of shrewdness, at least on paper. Company A can use a portion of Company

X's funds from operations to pay interest on new debt (see Exhibit 2). Half of the company's funds from operations—less dividend requirements and average capital spending—can be used to cover interest payments on a new loan from banks ($290,000, assuming a 12% interest rate). The remaining half of the funds can be used to cover interest on subordinated debt issued to the old owner ($350,000, assuming a 10% interest rate).

Issuing Stocks without EPS Dilution

In addition to the cash and debt raised, Company A can make payment with its stock—but only to the extent that EPS based on Company X's earnings, after adjustment for additional interest and goodwill charges, is equal to or better than Company A's EPS. If the calculation yields a negative number of shares, earnings of the company cannot support the additional debt load. Then one could classify the company as a poor acquisition choice from a short-range financial viewpoint.

Exhibit 3 illustrates the calculation of the number of shares that can be issued without EPS dilution. (The no-dilution condition is equivalent to the condition that the takeover has no impact on the price–earnings ratio of Company A.)

In our example, Company A could issue 31,420 shares with a market value of $1,250,000, together with $90,000 cash from internal sources and $640,000 in new debt. This would add up to a top price of $1,980,000 (see Exhibit 4). Thus, Company A could pay a 44% premium for Company X over its market value. The ratio of debt to equity of the combined companies—after the additional debt of $640,00 is taken out to pay top price—would be 0.81, slightly above Company A's ratio of 0.8.

Exhibit 2.   Sources of Cash and Debt Funds from Company X's Operations (in $ millions)

Cash	75% of cash and marketable securities	$0.09
Bank financing	Funds from operations	0.27
	Cash dividends	(0.04)
	Capital expenditure	(0.16)
	Available for new debt service	0.07
	Loan from bank (interest rate: 12%; expense: $0.035)	0.29
Note to old owner (interest rate: 10%; expense: $0.035)		0.35
Total cash and notes		**$0.73**

Exhibit 3. Calculation of "No EPS Dilution" Equity Financing (in $ millions, except per-share data)

Up to 31,420 new shares can be issued by Company A without causing EPS dilution as part of the finance package.

Abbreviations and values

A = Acquiring company
X = Target company
EPS = Earnings per share (A) = $5.00
NI = Net income (X) = 0.225
IE = Interest expense on new debt (X) = 0.07
GW = Annual goodwill charge = C^a
NS = New share to be issued (A) = C^a
TP = Top price (cash + debt + equity) = C^a
BV = Book value (X) = 1.00
MS = Market value per share (A) = 40.00
CN = Cash plus notes (X) (bank, old owner) = 0.73

Assumptions:
50% effective tax rate;
goodwill written off over
30 years

Note that EPS on newly issued shares must equal $5.00 EPS of Company A

Thus

$$EPS = \frac{NI - (IE/2) - GW}{NS} = \$5.00$$

$$GW = \frac{TP - BV}{30}$$

$$TP = NS \times MS + CN$$

or

$$NS = \frac{30NI - 15IE + BV - CN}{MS + 30EPS}$$

Inserting the values

$$NS = \frac{30 \times 0.225 - 15 \times 0.07 + 1.00 - 0.73}{40.00 + 30 \times 5.00}$$

$$= \frac{5.97}{190.00}$$

$$= 0.03142 \text{ or } 31,420 \text{ shares}$$

[a] Values to be calculated

69

Exhibit 4. Calculation of Top Price, Premium over Market, and Leverage of Combined Companies (in $ millions, except per-share data)

Top price	Cash			$0.09	
	Note to bank			0.29	
	Note to old owner			0.35	
	Equity			1.25	
	Number of shares	31,420			
	Market value per share	$40.00			
	Total value of finance package, or top price			1.98	
Premium over market value	Market value of Company X			1.375	
	Premium over market			44.0%	
Leverage	Debt: Old debt, Company A	3.76	Equity:	Old equity	4.70
				New equity	1.25
	Old debt, Company X	0.40		Total equity	5.95
	New debt(notes)	0.64			
	Total debt 4.80			**New leverage (D/E) = 0.81**	

Selecting Attractive Targets

With the top price calculated, buyers can compare various candidates on the basis of two important considerations: the premium over market that can be paid with no EPS dilution and the changes in financial risk or leverage, represented by the debt-to-equity ratio, that may result from the acquisition. Exhibit 5 illustrates a comparison of 29 companies in the course of such a search.

By mapping candidates on a matrix, you can easily separate the attractive from the unattractive companies. You can usually eliminate those that fall below the zero-premium line, since they can probably not be acquired for less than market price. Severe penalties to EPS may result if you pay more than their market value. Various studies of prices paid for companies indicate that, in most acquisitions, buyers pay a premium ranging from 20% to 80%.[2] Acquirers can tighten the noose a little more by shelving all companies for which they could pay no more than, say, a 20% premium. In general, the closer a company is to the upper right (Exhibit 6), the more financially attractive the company is. The chances are good that a buyer can acquire it for less than top price (which has positive implications for EPS) and also that unused debt capacity will exist even after partial financing with loans. In our example, the top price of almost $2 million—or a 44% premium over market—that could be paid for Company X may or may not be sufficient to buy that company.

Exhibit 5. Results of an Actual Acquisition Screening Analysis—Maximum Premium Overmarket Value Without EPS Dilution (and Resulting D–E Ratio)

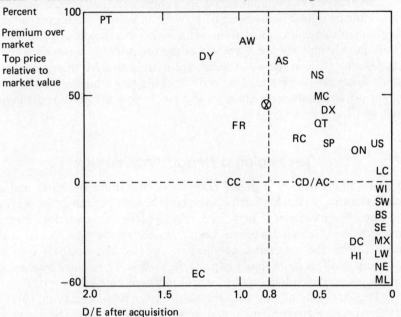

Exhibit 6. Relative Financial Attractiveness of Acquisition Candidates

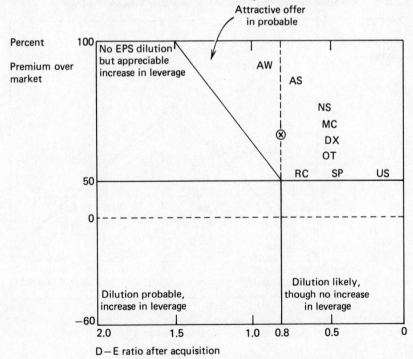

An analysis of premiums paid for comparably performing companies in the same or similar industry could provide an answer. Better yet, an initial offer and subsequent conversations with major shareholders of Company X would quickly indicate the adequacy of the top price. Companies AW, AS, NS, MX, or DX, on the other hand, are more attractive than Company X from a financial standpoint. Company A could pay a higher premium over market or, alternatively, reduce its leverage below the present debt-equity value of 0.8.

Developing a Negotiating Strategy

Exhibit 7 illustrates the possible range of combinations of shares and debt that Company A could offer for Company X and the impact on EPS and leverage. For example, if high EPS takes precedence over low leverage, Company A could put maximum cash and debt on the table before it adds shares (up to the maximum number) to sweeten the deal. Of course, if Company A offers more than top price, its EPS will be diluted and leverage may increase, depending on the form of payment beyond top price.

The strengths of this concept are its relative simplicity and the fact that the results answer many important financial questions. The assumption

Exhibit 7. Range of Shares and Debt for Acquisition Finance Package

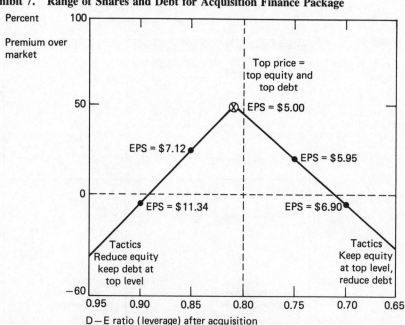

is that the market will likely reward a company paying less than top price for a purchase. Management has thus acted in the shareholders' best interests.

Notes

1. Malcolm S. Salter and Wolf A. Weinhold, "Choosing Compatible Acquisitions," *HBR* January–February 1981, p. 117.

2. The average premium over market price paid in 229 acquisitions of publicly owned companies in 1979 and 169 acquisitions in 1980 was about 50%; in more than 80% of the 1980 acquisitions, a premium of more than 20% was paid. For more details, see *1980 Mergers Summary* (Chicago, Ill.: W. T. Grimm & Co., January 1981), pp. 23–24.

Defuse the Hostility Factor in Acquisition Talks

JAMES HOWARD

James Howard describes a seven-step process that can eliminate much of the mistrust that tends to permeate acquisition discussions.

Buying or selling a small business is never easy. More often than not, both buyer and seller are more concerned with being taken advantage of than with finding a common ground. This suspicion breeds tension and, eventually, hostility.

How can the two groups allay their misgivings? Based on my experience brokering the sales of dozens of small companies (along with the experiences of other brokers, accountants, and attorneys), I suggest that buyers and sellers each shift their priorities. Instead of focusing on the dollar amount of an acquisition, they must concentrate on developing a mutually beneficial package.

For such a shift to occur, both parties need to understand each other's assumptions, definitions of company profits, and considerations of other factors in valuing assets. This article presents a seven-step method that the two sides can adopt for placing a dollar value on a business's earning power.

This approach uses a so-called evaluation trail, which allows for the review and debate of each assumption and judgment. The focus is thus where it should be—on the numbers and values reflected in the business rather than on the character and intentions of the parties involved. By making the whole matter more objective, the method that I discuss here reduces tensions and helps allay suspicions.

Some Ground Rules

This approach to acquisitions entails buyers and sellers arriving at certain preliminary understandings, as follows:

☐ Establish the business's profitability as of the proposed date of acquisition or evaluation to allow for the many distortions present in any owner's accounting approach. The idea is to develop a realistic financial statement.

☐ Appraise tangible assets like land, building, and equipment as to liquidation and going-concern value.

☐ Calculate the annual cost of ownership of the tangible assets, based on a market-determined substitute investment return, using clear-cut guidelines.

☐ Allocate the indicated earnings of the business according to a formula, to reflect varying levels of risk in the different types of assets being acquired.

☐ Develop a precise and realistic price–earnings multiple to reflect a variety of considerations, if the earning power is sufficient to justify payment of goodwill. Risk has the greatest weight, but other factors such as desirability of the business are also important.

☐ Prepare all valuations to determine selling price on the basis of an asset sale, not a stock sale. If both parties desire a stock sale, adjust the value to reflect all corporate liabilities (such as assumable debt) and include a penalty to compensate for depreciation opportunities that may be lost to the buyer.

Once such approaches are accepted, negotiating emphasis invariably shifts from the price to the package. For instance, a recent evaluation of a toy manufacturing company with no significant assets other than inventory but a record of consistently high earnings sparked the interest of several potential buyers. Three of them made offers at the appraised price level but with substantially different terms. The successful bidder developed the most innovative package, offering tax benefits to both buyer and seller.

The Seven Steps

Prior agreement to this approach enables the seven-step valuation process to proceed.

1. *Develop a stabilized income account.* This shows the earning power of the business for one or more years into the future. The stabilized income account eliminates the effects of a seller's special financial accounting. For example, many owners of small corporations devise elaborate strat-

egies to legally minimize taxes, such as switching from FIFO to LIFO inventory valuation. In privately held businesses, such tax-avoidance schemes usually understate the company's true earning power.

Similarly, buyers must adjust many corporate accounts to reflect expenses realistically—and more important, to give a clear picture of real earning power. Companies frequently overstate interest expenses, executive salaries, owners' perquisites, and depreciation expenses to hold down taxes.

Exhibit 1 summarizes an actual income account and the adjustments made to reflect real earning power during the 12-month period following the anticipated date of closing. A clearly stated assumption or reason must accompany each change from actual to stabilized earnings. In the case of the accounts summarized in Exhibit 1, the changes in sales reflect a planned price increase. Cost of goods and operating labor reflect stable variable-cost experience, as the unchanged percentages indicate. Changes in overhead expense bring executive salaries and various benefits into line with other companies of comparable size in the same industry. A fund to replace worn-out equipment with new equipment takes the place of an unrealistic book depreciation expense.

The net effect of these changes is to increase indicated earning power from $377,000 to $585,600.

Exhibit 1.   Private Company, Inc. Stabilized Income Account

	Actual, 1981		(Stabilized 12 months)	
Sales	$3,820,000	100%	$4,200,000	100%
Cost of goods	(1,160,000)	30.4	(1,276,800)	30.4
Operating labor	(1,100,000)	28.8	(1,209,600)	28.8
Gross profit	**$1,560,000**	**0.8%**	**$1,713,600**	**40.8%**
Sales expense	(621,000)	6.3	(556,000)	13.2
Administrative expense	(311,000)	8.1	(254,000)	6.0
Executive salaries	(120,000)	3.1	(84,000)	2.0
Replacement fund or depreciation	(70,000)	1.8	(150,000)	3.6
Maintenance and repairs	(32,000)	.8	(42,000)	1.0
Unclassified	(29,000)	.8	(42,000)	1.0
Total overhead expense	**($1,183,000)**	**31.0%**	**($1,128,000)**	**26.9%**
Indicated pretax profit	**$ 377,000**	**9.9%**	**$ 585,600**	**13.9%**

2. *Determine market value of fixed assets.* This is generally a straightforward job for a professional commercial real estate appraiser. A separate appraisal of fixed assets is necessary because their value, which is usually subject to lower risk than intangible assets, tends to exceed that of intangible assets.

3. *Agree on the capitalization rate.* Buyer and seller must reach a consensus as appropriate to the company and assets being evaluated on the interest rate, so that the annual cost of owning the tangible assets of the business can be calculated. The best approach is to use the prevailing lending rate at local commercial banks for companies of comparable size and risk. When interest rates are distorted, such as in recent years, modify the prevailing lending rate—otherwise estimated business value will fluctuate to the same extent as the money market.

But the market for companies doesn't work that way. To reach a realistic agreement, first determine an underlying lending rate, which is usually set at three to four percentage points above inflation. Then calculate a penalty on the selling price equal to the extra cost of interest for a period of time (usually one to three years), based on the assumption that prevailing rates will decline. The excess cost of $23,000 was treated as a deduction from value (see Exhibit 6).

4. *Figure the cost of ownership.* Given a good estimate of the fixed assets of a business and a defensible definition of the cost of money, determining the annual cost of owning the tangible assets is straightforward. Even if the prevailing rates are unstable, you can make and state assumptions as indicated in Exhibit 2. Such a method leads to an estimate of the dollar cost of owning the tangible asset portion of the business at temporarily higher

Exhibit 2.   Private Company, Inc. Interest Penalty Table

Current prevailing commercial rate		14%
Underlying rate		12%
Estimated time frame: will remain at	14% for 6 months	
will remain at	13% for 11 months	
will be	12% at end of 18 months	
Market value of tangible assets per appraisal		$1,200,000
Excess cost of money above underlying rate:		
2% × 1,200,000, 6 months		12,000
1% × 1,200,000, 11 months		11,000
Total		**$ 23,000**

rates for a specified period. Exhibit 3 shows this calculation using the underlying interest rate, estimated at 12%.

5. *Calculate earning power.* The next step is to determine the stabilized earning power of the company after deducting the annual cost of ownership of tangible assets, which leads to a figure described as excess earning power (see Exhibit 4).

6. *Determine the right multiple.* At this point—and not until this point—you can determine an appropriate multiple to estimate the value of the excess earnings of Private Company, Inc. A rating scale helps account for such factors as risk, growth, industry, track record, and desirability. Desirability is important, despite the difficulty of quantifying it; it boils down to the notion that the marketplace allows a higher price for a well-maintained suburban or rural business than for a junkyard in Hoboken, even though they may show identical earnings.

The rating scale in Exhibit 5 yields a bottom multiple of zero times excess pretax earnings and a top rating of six times excess earnings. With certain exceptions, this is consistent with the range in most transactions. For example, it is difficult to evaluate high-technology businesses with this or any other explicit method, since the marketplace tells us that, if they show any earnings at all, they frequently sell at enormous multiples. The method is also inappropriate for a recent start-up unless permanent earning power can be clearly established—an unlikely circumstance.

Note that excess earnings are stated on a pretax basis. (If you use aftertax earning power, you must alter the tables to reflect up to twice the indicated multiple.) Private Company, Inc. yields a multiple of 3.9 that, with the excess-earning figure of $441,000, values excess earnings at $1,719,100.

7. *Estimate the actual value.* Exhibit 6 shows the process of arriving at the final estimate of the value of Private Company, Inc. An alternative method is to project the income stream over a period of several years, determine an appropriate discount rate, and arrive at a net present value. While this method is sometimes appropriate, the single-year projections of earning power tend to be more accurate, more understandable—and hence more acceptable—to buyers and sellers.

Exhibit 3.   Private Company, Inc. Cost of Ownership of Tangible Assets

Value of real estate, buildings, and equipment, as determined by professional market value appraisal	$1,200,000
Underlying cost of money	12%
Indicated annual cost of ownership of tangible assets	$ 144,000

Exhibit 4. Private Company, Inc. Determining Excess Earning Power

Stabilized earnings	$585,600
(Exhibit 1)	
Cost of owning tangible assets	144,000
(Exhibit 3)	
Excess earnings	$441,600

Exhibit 5. Key to Rating-Scale Values Between 0 and 6

Risk rating
0 = Continuity of income at risk
3 = Steady income likely
6 = Growing income assured

Competitive rating
0 = Highly competitive in unstable market
3 = Normal competitive conditions
6 = Little competition in market, high cost of entry for new competition

Industry rating
0 = Declining industry
3 = Industry growing somewhat faster than inflation
6 = Dynamic industry, rapid growth likely

Company rating
0 = Recent start-up, not established
3 = Well established with satisfactory track record
6 = Long record of sound operation with outstanding reputation

Company growth rating
0 = Business has been declining
3 = Steady growth, slightly faster than inflation rate
6 = Dynamic growth rate

Desirability rating
0 = No status, rough or dirty work
3 = Respected business in satisfactory environment
6 = Challenging business in attractive environment

Rating formula (showing values used for Private Company, Inc.)

Risk	4.0
Competitive situation	3.0
Industry	3.5
Company	5.0
Company growth	4.0
Desirability	4.0
Total	23.5
Total ÷ 6	**3.9**

Exhibit 6.   Private Company, Inc. Summary of Value

Appraised value of tangible assets	$1,200,000
Value of excess earnings 3.9 × 441,000	1,719,100
Less penalty for temporary extra cost of money	(23,000)
Estimated value	**$2,896,100**

Several comments help explain the opinion of value of Private Company, Inc. expressed in Exhibit 6.

First, don't take the figure of $2,896,100 as an absolute statement of value. In fact, it is a beginning point for buyer and seller to check one another's assumptions, focusing the discussion on numerical judgments rather than on negotiating tactics.

Second, the actual selling price is often modified to reflect an entire package of money, securities, contracts, fees, perquisites, and intangible benefits. If skillful tax attorneys or accountants are available to each party to design the final package for maximum tax advantage, both parties will invariably benefit.

The importance of such strategic package design cannot be overemphasized. Only those who have worked with a skilled tax packager can appreciate the extent to which such an expert can satisfy the differing needs of an anxious seller and an eager buyer. Numbers are, of course, only abstractions of real benefits. When experts address the true needs of buyer and seller—emotional, symbolic, and monetary—mutual satisfaction is possible.

Third, no method can eliminate the need for the large number of individual judgments necessary to arrive at an opinion of value. Both parties must clearly state and debate the underlying assumptions.

Fourth, as previously stated, this technique is not appropriate for all acquisition situations—including start-ups, high-technology companies, and professional service or information companies.

Also such an explicit process helps narrow remarkably the high and low estimates of value in acquisition negotiations. In most cases, this method results in a range of 5% to 10% between high and low estimates—a far cry from the usual 50% to 100% range.

Finally, by focusing on objective rather than emotional factors, buyers and sellers are better able to put together an acquisition package that accomplishes both of their goals. Based on my experience, refocusing attention from gamesmanship to constructive packaging nearly always enables negotiations to proceed to closing—and the parties to the transaction almost always part as friends.

PART TWO
FORMULATING STRATEGIES

AN OVERVIEW

The concept of business strategy has different meanings to different people. Without attempting to offer a specific definition, suffice it to say that formulation of strategy implies anticipating major problems and opportunities in key business areas: organizational aspects, marketing, business policy, and so forth.

In a small, but rapidly growing company, formulating strategy is a major challenge. For one thing, the owners are more often than not managerial novices, learning as they go. For another, even assuming they had noteworthy management experience, there is no guarantee they would handle the job right simply because the problems associated with growth aren't entirely understood even by experts. The articles in this section begin to explore the difficulties and offer suggestions associated with formulating strategy in the rapidly growing company.

In "Confessions of a Successful Entrepreneur," Derek F. du Toit recounts his experience starting and managing a fast-growing company in South Africa, and how the venture nearly came apart because of internal dissension and miscalculations on his part. Among the lessons he draws is that owners must reconcile with both financial investors and key managers as early in the company's development as possible what each expects of the other. Even then, he warns, entrepreneurs must be prepared for resentment on the part of investors and incompetence on the part of managers as the business grows. He also cautions entrepreneurs to come to grips with their own limitations.

Thomas H. Melohn advocates direct, open, and sensitive treatment of subordinates as a key component of effective strategy in "How to Build

Employee Trust and Productivity." He argues that loyal and committed employees are such a decisive force in determining the success of any company, particularly a fast-growing one, that owners who avoid the issue are inviting disaster. He offers suggestions, based on his own experience managing a thriving electronic components company, for encouraging employee effectiveness; his prescription includes immediate bonuses for productivity-improving suggestions, serious employee reviews, and nonfinancial recognition of effective performance.

The next three articles concentrate on the marketing aspects of strategy. In "The Entrepreneur Sees Herself as a Manager," Lore Harp describes how she and her partner instinctively distinguished themselves from other makers of computer memory boards by emphasizing service—both in delivering the product and in the follow-up phase. That marketing oriented approach helped propel the company from a home-based business in 1976 to a $25 million microcomputer maker by 1981.

The authors of "Growing Ventures Can Anticipate Marketing Stages," Tyzoon T. Tyebjee, Albert V. Bruno, and Shelby H. McIntyre, provide an overview of the marketing function for growing companies. They conclude that rapidly developing companies pass through a four-stage process which, if the stages are anticipated, can be negotiated much more smoothly than otherwise. And Robert Hershey maintains that obtaining essential information about competitors need not be a costly undertaking in "Commercial Intelligence on a Shoestring."

The importance of keeping tabs on certain key investment and cost factors as a means of avoiding problems created by rapid growth is underscored by Herbert N. Woodward in "Management Strategies for Small Companies." He maintains that managers too often focus excessively on expanding sales, adding new products, and achieving profits, when they should be concentrating on controlling costs, cutting products, and upgrading key balance sheet items.

Finally, managers who want to reap the benefits of the ongoing computer revolution are discovering that the often-advocated advice of delegating responsibility may not be appropriate for selecting business computer systems. Richard Raysman maintains in his article, "Manager Involvement Needed in Computer Selection," that business owners must become direct participants in the process of finding and purchasing systems. He contends that to leave the decision to subordinates or vendors is to invite expensive repercussions.

9
Confessions of a Successful Entrepreneur

DEREK F. du TOIT

Entrepreneurial success is heady stuff. And therein may lie the greatest danger to owners and operators of fast-growing ventures. This article makes that point in chronicling the author's initial success and subsequent near failure in establishing a cookware company.

At the peak of the stock market euphoria in South Africa in June 1969, I resigned as a clerk in the marketing department of Mobil SA (Pty.) Ltd. to become the only employee of an investment syndicate I had helped start four years previously. Now, as I pause to reflect on my nearly 11 years as an entrepreneur, I can count some substantial successes and a number of lamentable failures.

My company, by any standards, has experienced explosive growth. Profits after taxes have increased at an average annual rate of 96% compounded for 12 consecutive years, and we now have volume well in excess of $15 million a year. However, I have irrevocably lost many valued friends and narrowly escaped business and personal bankruptcy—all because I disobeyed elementary rules that every entrepreneur wishing to retain control of a fast-growing company should follow.

Starting Out

Everything seemed much simpler 18 years ago when, at the age of 32, I was first exposed to the workings of the stock market by a superior at Mobil Oil.

Our interest coincided with the beginning of a period of growth and excitement in the South African stock market that continued almost unabated until June 1969.

At my enthusiastic prodding, we soon decided to form a syndicate of friends and business associates who would make monthly contributions of $12 each for investment; as more people joined the syndicate, an increasing monthly income could be invested in the market to make profits for everyone involved.

We felt we would do better than the various available mutual funds because each of us would contribute different abilities that would enable the syndicate to grow. Our syndicate would be unfettered by management costs since our efforts would be part-time and therefore unrewarded by the syndicate.

Differing Goals

It was only after we had encouraged 35 friends and associates to join the syndicate as equal shareholders that I began to realize the first of the human problems that were to beset us. Although several were energetic, not everyone was prepared to do the work required, because our reasons for joining were diverse.

Some, like me, saw the embryonic syndicate as a way of achieving eventual personal freedom by running their own company; others, in higher income brackets, saw the syndicate as a useful adjunct to their investment portfolios; and still others were essentially gambling relatively small sums because of the transparent enthusiasm of the founders.

Our common goal was making money. What I did not realize or allow for was that once we made money the divergence of motivating factors would create intense interpersonal problems. The first indication of such problems was that only a very few of us were doing the necessary work.

All the administrative tasks—writing up minutes, bookkeeping, buying and selling shares, and filling out the various forms that had to be submitted to regulatory authorities—were done by only a few people. This ran counter to the original intention of gathering together various skills so that all would contribute to the venture's success.

Initially, this was not an exceptionally difficult problem and was solved by creating a board of directors that administered the syndicate's affairs on behalf of all the shareholders. The board reported back to the shareholders on a quarterly basis and agreed to seek no more new shareholders.

Another problem was not so easily solvable. Our original intention was that the 36 of us who comprised the syndicate would share ownership equally, giving each holder nearly 3%. But because we were a small unquoted company, I had personally guaranteed to each of the shareholders I encouraged to join that—if they wished to sell stock in the company—I would be a buyer of last resort and pay the balance sheet value.

As various shareholders left Cape Town or wished to convert their investments into ready cash for the down payment on a house or a car, I occasionally fulfilled this obligation. By July 1969 we had reduced ourselves to approximately 13 shareholders; I held 25% of the shares of the company and another director held 24%, placing us in effective control. Thus instead of 36 equal holders we ended up a very disparate group of 13 shareholders, with holdings ranging from 0.5% of the total to my 25%.

Of Friendships Destroyed

In 1969 we were concentrating on three business areas: the stock market, land and property development, and door-to-door sales of cookware. Because direct selling is largely unaffected by the business cycle and we were successful in recruiting and motivating a growing sales organization, we achieved startling success in cookware sales and gradually phased out the stock market and property investments. This allowed us to concentrate effort on our most profitable area.

There seemed no limit to the successes we could achieve, and I proudly reported our results each month to the board of directors and each quarter to the shareholders. Because I was the only shareholder employed by the company, both the directors and the shareholders had to rely on me for their understanding of what, to them, was a novel and almost completely unknown business.

This did nothing to dampen their concern regarding their ever-growing investment. As the profitability and reserves of the company grew, their concerns kept pace—for nearly all the shareholders, their investment in the company represented their greatest single asset.

I argued very strongly for reinvesting the company's profits to finance greater growth, while the shareholders felt that dividends and large directors' fees should be paid out immediately. Because I did not realize or understand the shareholders' fears, we began arguing about trivialities. Eventually the pressure grew so great that I decided to resolve the problem by forcing a showdown.

Since the shareholders were personal friends (in some cases dating from school days), I wanted to be as fair and open as possible. I explained that I would resign as an employee and either sell my shares to the rest of the shareholders or purchase their shares from them, at a price they themselves would set. After a few weeks it was decided I would buy them out at a price of $63, tax free, for every 80 cents they had invested over a period of some 10 to 12 years.

Although the deal was consummated and everyone finally received full payment, the bonds of friendship from our previous relationships were irreparably broken. The shareholders discounted the financial reward they received because they felt I had virtually placed a shotgun at their heads to achieve my ambitions.

Struggling with Management Problems

When I took over the company from the previous shareholders, most of my time was taken up with the details inherent in such a transaction, like arranging financing, dealing with lawyers and accountants, and negotiating with the shareholders and all their professional people. After the arrangements were completed, I attempted to grapple with the task of managing my company.

I told my top management team—the sales director, manufacturing director, and administrative director—of the ownership change and arranged that all of them be sold shares in the new company for a nominal fee so they would have a stake in the organization.

Their employment package thus included the following: salaries above the industry averages for their positions; bonuses based on profits before taxes, which approximately equaled their salaries; and finally, their 2% shareholding in the new enterprise. This holding was such that the rate at which profits were being earned after taxes meant that their share of the annual retained earnings (we still paid no dividends) equaled their annual salary.

I later discovered that 2% of the shares was considered an insult as they, and other employees in the company, were expecting me to offer shares on a far greater scale. Indeed, when every individual's private expectations were added up, I would have had to part with well over 100% of the company's shares.

I also failed to address myself sufficiently to other problems regarding the top management team. I should have been more aware that two of the managers lacked the skills necessary to keep up with the very rapid growth rate of the company. It was evident that the increased money they were being paid and the stake that they had in the company were not sufficient to enable these executives to do a better job.

At about the time that I had finally and reluctantly concluded that I would somehow have to replace these two executives, they left to start a company in competition with mine.

The Difficulties Pile Up

Because no comparable company existed in South Africa at the time, the prospect of competition adversely affected morale within my company, especially as rumors about the new company assailed us from all sides. When, after nine months or so, the new company was turning out a product strikingly similar to ours, a significant number of our top sales personnel defected to the opposition. Once the new product got out into the market, the head-on clash of the two sales forces created even more difficulties.

Simultaneously, we were dealt several other body blows:

☐   The income tax authorities suddenly and without warning canceled a 12-year-old written arrangement we had for paying the company's taxes. This severely drained our cash flow.

☐   Our bankers adopted a much stricter lending policy and stopped allowing us to use an additional overdraft privilege.

☐   I was subjected to a thorough investigation by the foreign exchange authorities, and rumors began to circulate that I was selling the company and had arranged a Swiss bank account to sustain me when I left for an overseas destination. Such investigations are taken very seriously in South Africa, and these kinds of rumors are probably the most damaging that can be circulated about business people. The authorities eventually gave me a completely clean bill of health.

I am obviously unable to say how these problems originated, although it seems strange that they all occurred around this time and that each was an unusual action by the bodies involved.

These difficulties created another nearly disastrous problem: our cash flow suffered and I was unable to make the final two payments to the previous shareholders as arranged. When I endeavored to obtain additional time to make these payments, I encountered implacable hostility. Most of the previous shareholders refused to discuss anything except either full payment on the due dates or total bankruptcy.

What made the situation so frustrating was that our difficulty in meeting the payments stemmed from an inadequate cash flow; the company, however, was earning greater profits than ever before because of our sales efforts to counteract the new opposition.

I eventually arranged financing to bridge us over this difficult period— but at a steep cost. The interest rate was extremely high, and we had to agree to various financial and investment restrictions, all of which hampered our previously unfettered growth. The delay in paying the final installments to the shareholders also meant a total breakdown in whatever relationships still existed between them and me.

Another unpleasant side effect of the new competition was that several of our employees sent sensitive legal, sales, and production information— much of which came from my personal drawers—to our competitor. Once the competitor had grown sufficiently, these employees left to join it.

(Ironically, the competing company is now beset by many of the same problems that afflicted our syndicate in those difficult early years. There have been intense power struggles among directors, sabotage of machinery, and charges that private conversations have been secretly recorded.)

With Benefit of Hindsight

If I had correctly assessed various aspects of the situation at the start, I could have saved myself a great deal of heartache. My most significant miscalculation was of my own ability. The very success of the business gave me unwarranted confidence and blinded me to certain inescapable constraints on my freedom of movement.

When I wished to resolve the quarrels I was having with my previous coshareholders, I allowed them to set the price of the shares in the belief that I could pay whatever they asked. I wound up paying a premium of $35 a share over balance sheet value, which discounted nearly three years of future profits.

If I had been less anxious to obtain full control and so be master of my destiny, I would have thought about my coshareholders' tax positions. I would then have realized that after allowing for their tax situations and inflation, I was actually buying the company at balance sheet value plus about 10 years' future profits. If I had sought proper financial advice and also excluded personal relationships in my negotiations with the shareholders, I would not have landed myself in such a financial pickle.

Another problem area was my relationship with my wife and children. I have been blessed with a very supportive family, but the very real strain—spread over two years—that I went through left me with little time and a sensitive disposition. We were able to talk this over and arrest the difficulty almost before it began, but it could easily have grown out of control.

I had seen similar situations develop with other business associates, with disastrous results. Fortunately, however, I did not give up my regimen of many years' standing during that stressful period—I continued running up to 40 miles a week and so maintained my health and the ability to work the requisite long hours.

Some Lessons

Based on my experiences over the past dozen years, I offer the following six suggestions to other entrepreneurs:

1. First and foremost, you should understand yourself as an entrepreneur. The entrepreneur who starts his own business generally does so because he is a difficult employee. He does not take kindly to suggestions or orders from other people and aspires most of all to run his own shop.

When he goes into business on his own, facing all the risks inherent in a new operation, he is surrounded by people who advise him not to do it. If he succeeds, his self-confidence is reinforced: every time he succeeds in the face of all shades of experienced opinion advising him that he will not succeed, he becomes more sure of his ability to solve any problem.

His idiosyncrasies do not hurt anybody so long as the business is small, but once the business gets larger, requiring the support and active cooperation of more people, he is at risk if he does not change his approach. It has been correctly stated that the biggest burden a growing company faces is having a full-blooded entrepreneur as its owner.

2. Investors have different goals and will cause endless problems to

the entrepreneur if real growth is experienced, unless he has a controlling interest. We as a company did not have clearly defined goals at the beginning, and whatever private goals we had as individuals were not necessarily shared.

It would have been unwieldy and probably self-destructive to sit down and thrash out all our personal ambitions for the company once we had grown to a respectable size. The best answer would have been for me to have chosen my shareholders with greater care.

3. If you must bring friends and relatives in as shareholders, expect that the financial aspect will add a new, potentially destructive element to your relationships. The ideal—particularly if you wish to maintain your existing relationships—is not to include them in your financial enterprises. Your true-blue entrepreneur is not normally equipped with the tact and people-handling skills necessary to successfully cope with such complex relationships.

If you decide to go into business anyway with friends and relatives, be as certain as possible that everyone has similar understandings and expectations about every facet of the business. If the business is a real success, be prepared for differing monetary and psychological goals and rewards to make themselves apparent. If the business is a disaster, financial strains of a different sort will imperil your relationships.

4. Do not expect to be showered with praise if you succeed in your efforts to make others wealthy. In fact, any entrepreneur who feels he is entitled to praise should not really try to be one. It took a long time to learn this lesson. I somehow thought that if I did a good job as an employee of our fledgling company, my contribution to the success of the business would be recognized.

Some of my most exhausting battles with the board of directors concerned my remuneration. I could not get the directors to accept at first that my compensation as an employee had nothing to do with the size of my shareholding in the business. Their way of reacting to my growing confidence and dogmatic approach was to suggest that my salary should not be much above what I earned as a clerk at Mobil Oil.

This conflict was partially resolved when I proposed that I be paid what the average managing director of a company of our size was paid, established from an annual salary survey published in South Africa.

An entrepreneur generally gets his rewards from growing a business and solving problems of a physical kind. You should not be dependent on the plaudits of your peers, especially since the very nature of fast-track growth demands overcoming obstacles, some of which are human obstacles.

5. The Peter Principle will work quickly in a fast-growing company, so you must be especially aware of executive performance. This is not an area in which most entrepreneurs are particularly strong, because of their heady self-confidence.

6. If some of your top executives leave to go into competition with you, expect—and be prepared for—a drop in morale, raids on your key

employees, and a fair amount of internecine fighting. Change all your locks and bring in a firm of security consultants.

All this seems a lamentable catalog of human frailty, but growth of any kind provides many opportunities—good and bad. My opportunity to reassess the contribution I could make to the business resulted in the company being stronger than ever, with a professional management team to propel it through its next stage of growth.

10
How to Build Employee Trust and Productivity

THOMAS H. MELOHN

When the author and his partner acquired North American Tool & Die, Inc. six and a half years ago, it was not unlike many smaller manufacturers—marginally profitable, its work force unenthusiastic. Nor did the future look especially bright, since a number of long-time employees were exploring greener pastures. Today, the situation is much different. The company's sales are triple, and profits six times what they were three years ago. Moreover, turnover among its 70 employees has dropped sharply. A few employees told a visitor recently during a plant tour that they never imagined the company could become such a challenging and exciting place to work. The author argues that the connection between financial results and employee morale is far from casual. Indeed, he fully credits a carefully considered strategy of building trust between employees and owners for North American Tool's impressive earnings record.

Take a moment to ask yourself a few questions and consider some management problems. If you're at the top try these:

☐ Why is it I'm the only one to initiate new ideas?

☐ Why do our people avoid facing up to the tough situations affecting our business? All I hear or read are platitudes— "That's under constant review," "let's hold that in abeyance just for now," "perhaps we should appoint a task group to study it."

☐ Is our corporation any different from the government's bureaucracy? Middle managers always seem to resist innovation.

☐ Why are our employees cleaned up and ready to leave 15 minutes early, and why is our productivity failing to improve or even declining?

☐ Why is our sales force unwilling to make those extra calls? Is cutting prices the only way it knows how to sell?

☐ What's happened to company loyalty? For a few extra bucks, employees leave, after all we've done for them.

Now try the same quiz, but from the vantage point of the person looking up from lower down in the company hierarchy:

☐ Why won't they ever listen? After all that extra work, my new idea gets a brush-off or a put-down.

☐ Why won't they level with me? Meeting after meeting, and no real decisions made. Report after report, study on study.

☐ How is it that my job has become so boring, a means to an end rather than an end in itself? I can't wait till I'm out of here tonight so that I can work on my car, build that extra room, read that good book.

☐ What's company loyalty? For 30 years I've kept quiet and done my job, and for what? A watch, a phony ceremonial dinner, and out to the trash heap.

The Most Important Asset

The tragedy here is that both parties do care a great deal. Yet, these misunderstandings exist in company after company across the United States. Many are grasping at any possible solution to their problems—including reindustrialization, quality circles, protective import constraints, and government subsidies.

This article outlines a more old-fashioned philosophy that has worked for our company—the belief that a company's most important asset is its employees.

With the conviction that people make the difference between success and failure, my partner, Garner Beckett, Jr., and I set three objectives when we bought North American Tool & Die (NATD), a computer components contract manufacturer in San Leandro, California, in June 1978. First, we planned to steadily expand the company and raise profits. Our second goal was to share whatever wealth was created. Third, we wanted everyone to feel satisfaction and even have fun on the job. The only way to achieve these goals, we decided, was to create an atmosphere of complete trust between us, the owners, and *all* our employees.

To summarize the last three years, our sales have gone from $1.8 million to over $6 million, our pretax earnings have increased well over 600%, our stock appreciated 36% in 1980 and again in 1981, our customer reject rate has declined from 5% to 0.3%, our productivity has doubled, our turnover has dropped from 27% to 6%, and we've all had a good time.

To guide this kind of progress appears deceptively simple. We have no proprietary product, nor do we have any geographic advantage in our distribution pattern to add to our marketing ability. Instead, our primary strength is our employees.

Before I recount the steps Beckett and I took to create an atmosphere of trust, one admonition: you've got to really mean it when you say you want such an atmosphere. You truly have to believe in it. Then you've got to work at improving relations every day in every situation. Otherwise, your employees will sense the hypocrisy and all will be for naught.

Growth and Profits

In the analysis of our marketplace before we bought NATD, several marketing and competitive factors stood out. Total computer sales growth was quite impressive—up about 30% annually. With that growth rate and the inherent complexity of product design, we concluded that there had to be an ever-increasing customer need for quality and prompt delivery. Yet our assessment of potential competition suggested generally lax quality control and attention to delivery. Our competitive points of difference became apparent— quality and service.

Our potential competitors tended to be technically skilled entrepreneurs who were often only semiskilled as managers. Our business could then employ professional management skills and thereby position itself as a growth company rather than as just a two-person venture. That approach would be helpful as the big computer manufacturers got bigger. Their suppliers would also have to grow disproportionately. A cottage industry of regional suppliers will soon be an anachronism. The vendors who succeed over the long term will be those with the best organizational skills and employee motivation.

Such observations are relatively easy to come by. Making everything happen is tough.

We bought a job shop with a reputation for acceptable but not outstanding quality. The only way our quality would improve would be if our employees improved it—every day, on every job, on every part.

Ours is a highly technical business. We produce hundreds of different kinds of parts with a tolerance of ± 19.001 of an inch. That's about one-fourth the thickness of a human hair. Such minute tolerances require much skill and dedication. NATD manufactures each of those different parts by the thousands each year. Thus, the company's well-being depends entirely on employees caring a great deal about their performance.

Of course, truly good people want to do a good job. We spread the gospel of quality and repeatedly recognize their efforts to eliminate all rejects.

Each month, there's a plantwide meeting—on company time—with a threefold purpose. First, we recognize one employee (no supervisors allowed) who has done a super job of producing good quality during that month. A check for $50 is just a token of what we give. Of much greater import is the "Super Person of the Month" plaque. The employee's name is engraved on the plaque, and it is prominently and permanently displayed in the plant. Second, each employee is given a silver dollar for every year of service if his or her employment anniversary occurs during the month of the meeting. Finally, we share with our "family" where we've been, where we are, and where we're going—in percentages when appropriate. In that way, each employee knows firsthand what's going on at his or her company.

Every time we get a compliment from one of our customers, we tell our employees about it in detail at that meeting. Recently NATD won a supplier excellence award from one of our major customers. The morning after the awards banquet, we gave the plaque to our department heads because they had earned it. We conveyed our pride to all our employees at the next monthly Super Person meeting, and we put their plaque up on the wall of the plant. No, it's not in the office to impress other customers. It's in the plant to remind our employees each day—each shift—that they are good.

Sharing the Wealth

We share ownership primarily through our employee stock ownership plan (ESOP). We give each employee shares of NATD stock each year, according to three simple selection criteria. The employee must be at least 24 years old, work a minimum of 1,000 hours a year, and be on the payroll at year end. In our judgment, our people have earned the right to be given company stock without any cash outlay of their own. It's not a warrant, a reduced-price purchase plan, matching dollars, an option, or phantom stock. It's free.

By the way, my partner and I waived our rights to participate in this program. We wanted the number of shares allotted for our employees to be that much larger, that much more meaningful. The shares we grant annually are newly issued—we do not realize any gain by selling our own. NATD's ESOP program has also been instrumental in lowering our rejection rates from customers and improving our productivity and delivery time.

We also try to stress fair and equitable compensation as a motivational tool. We hold compensation reviews twice annually. This is not a rubber stamp operation. Each employee has a one-on-one performance review with his or her boss. Here's where you're doing well, and here's where you need to improve, and here's what the company can do to help.

Finally, we use cash bonuses to reward innovative employees. In recent months, several employees have taken action to help the company and win cash. In one instance, a young employee decided on his own to develop a means of both multiply riveting a very difficult part and automating the entire process. In another, a department foreman who saw that our labor cost for an important job was too high devised a new method of doing ten operations at one time. He challenged his young associate to "top this" and soon found the entire production step completely automated. Our labor costs were reduced 80%.

In a third instance, our chief engineer decided on his own to satisfy NATD's need for a much larger punch press than we had. After getting input from two other departments at NATD, he developed the specs, selected the top two choices of machines, arranged for demonstrations, identified additional required options, and purchased the entire package. My role was merely to sign the purchase order.

Satisfaction and Fun

With our strong belief in the importance of our employees, it's axiomatic that NATD hires only the best. We hire a certain kind of person— a decent person who cares about himself, his family, and his company. The person must be honest, willing to speak up, and curious, be it as a sweeper, machine operator, plant foreman, or office manager. That's why I interview each prospective employee myself. My purpose is to determine if the candidate will fit into the NATD family. Perhaps that concept seems old-fashioned, but to us it's pivotal. This process of lengthy evaluation and interviewing is a lot of work, but the results are well worth it.

Let's face it, the traditional adversary role between management and employees is not productive. In encouraging employee satisfaction at NATD, we follow the tenet that our employees deserve the same treatment we expect from them. They want to know about their future compensation, their potential career paths, how they are contributing, and what they can do to grow. To keep people involved and caring, we work at giving out real compliments—not just the perfunctory "Good job, Smith" but statements of sincere appreciation for each person's special efforts and accomplishments.

Compliments don't cost a company anything. We all need them and even crave them. Recognition—both personal and professional—is a major motivating factor. At least two or three times a week, we go through the plant chatting with each employee and complimenting those who've worked well.

Employees care deeply about their work. If you can tap this well of concern and mesh it with the goals of your corporation, the results will truly stun you.

Besides handing out compliments, we work at trying to promote our employees' best interests. Sounds out of place in today's cynical work environment, doesn't it? All we can say is that it works. At NATD we care about our people, not just as employees, but as human beings, as friends, and we try to help them in any way we can. Let me give you some examples:

☐ One outstanding Korean employee suffered a sudden weight loss but was having difficulty communicating this problem to his doctor. My partner searched the entire San Francisco area and finally found a Korean-speaking physician. The problem is now being resolved.

☐ NATD lends its employees company trucks on weekends for moving purposes— at no charge. Any employee can also borrow one week's pay—at no interest—in an emergency.

☐ We sometimes arrange flex hours, as we did for one employee who was going through some marital problems. Now they are happily resolved.

☐ Another employee didn't get all the maternity benefits to which she was entitled. NATD pestered our insurance carrier for over six months and finally rectified this oversight.

☐ NATD sends flowers to every employee or spouse who is in the hospital, and each employee gets a check from the company as a wedding present.

☐ Each month, the owners buy donuts for the entire plant to celebrate payday—Friday—and the end of the month. We also make four free season tickets to National Football League games available to our employees.

☐ We're even occasionally silly enough to send our employees home early on a beautiful day to enjoy it, but with a full day's pay.

By now, I'm sure you're thoroughly convinced my partner and I are deranged. I can almost hear the talk: "You're running nothing but a country club!" "You're squandering company assets!"

Well, perhaps, but the results outlined earlier seem to belie these observations. A happy employee is a productive employee. Output increases, rejects fall, attitude improves, and turnover drops. Besides, it's more fun to work in a happy shop.

Effective Implementation

My job as CEO is to outline the company's objectives and the strategies to attain those goals. To achieve them, we place heavy emphasis on true delegation of responsibility.

We believe that our managers really want to manage, but we realize that certain conditions must first be met. First, we work with managers to be sure the goals are clear and in fact attainable. Second, we give our employees the tools to reach our goals. Finally, we let our managers alone and allow them flexibility. The last thing any manager needs is a second-guessing or a preemptive superior.

Each foreman is responsible for on-time production with no rejects and at maximum efficiency. How he does it is totally up to him.

We then make sure our managers and employees get credit for their successful accomplishments—from us, from their peers, and in their paychecks.

Incidentally, we attach no blame to failure. If we have given a job "our best shot," there's no problem. If our people are inhibited by the fear of failure, they won't dare to try. If we don't try the unexplored and the untested, then our growth rate and profitability will suffer. And that's no fun.

Once your managers are truly managing, your job as CEO becomes much easier. Decisions stop drifting to the CEO, and you are able to concentrate on the issues that will affect the corporation's growth.

Von Clausewitz, the great Prussian military strategist (1780–1831) devised theories that were honed in battle and later brilliantly set forth in his book *On War*. One of his important concepts that's particularly applicable to business is to divide any problem into progressively smaller and thereby more manageable parts. To me, this reference to military strategy is frighteningly appropriate for American industry today because we're in a battle for long-term economic survival.

11

The Entrepreneur Sees Herself as Manager

LORE HARP

In 1976, at the age of 32, Lore Harp had two children, a nice home, a husband, and a growing dissatisfaction with her life. Wanting "to contribute something," she asked a friend, Carole Ely, to help her market a memory board that Harp's husband, then working at Hughes Research Laboratories, had designed. What happened then is absolute American dream. Harp and Ely (and later Bob Harp) turned their $6,000 investment into a $25 million company manufacturing eight desk-top microcomputer models selling in the $4,000 to $25,000 range. Located in Thousand Oaks, California, the company went public in 1981, and according to Harp, her goal is to hit $200 million in sales by 1985.

How has Harp, CEO of Vector Graphic Inc., done it? In this interview she discusses her background, her dissatisfaction with the role of housewife, the beginnings of Vector Graphic and the two women's nurturing of it, the rapid growth, and her attention to marketing, services, and support that distinguished Vector from other microcomputer companies right from the start. This success has not been without sacrifice, however. Because of her driving interest in Vector, Harp suffered the loss of friends as well as the breakup of her marriage. Being an entrepreneur is not easy at the best of times, but being female brings with it a separate set of problems. Yet if Lore Harp is an example, the difficulties might be worth it.

This interview was conducted and edited by Eliza G. C. Collins, senior editor, planning, *HBR*.

HBR. *Can we begin by talking a little about your background? You came to this country from Germany when you were 20. What had your life in Germany been like?*

Lore Harp.   I'm the oldest and I have one younger brother. I had a very normal childhood, in what you would call "a very nice family." My father was a businessman; my grandfather, whom I respected greatly, was a very successful politician during the Weimar Republic; and my father's 75-year-old twin sister was an attorney. I respected her enormously and always admired her spontaneity, her interests in so many things, her contributions.

> *So you grew up with the idea that success was achievable. Did you have any sense of being different as a child?*

No, but I was always tremendously strong willed. I came to the United States when I was 20 to visit friends. But then I wanted to see if I could do something on my own, so I moved to the San Francisco area. At one point, my parents felt they could starve me out and get me to come back to Germany, but I stayed.

> *What did you want to do?*

I just wanted to see what else there was. All the people I had met and stayed with in the United States were white, Republican, and wealthy. This was 1966, and so many other things were going on that I wanted to experience. I wasn't running away, though. I never got into a drug culture or anything of that nature; I was just terribly curious about life and what makes people tick. I had so much time ahead of me that it didn't seem a few more months out of my life would make that big a difference to what I did. I only had a visitor's visa, so I could neither go to school nor officially work. So I did all sorts of little diddly things, like babysitting.

> *Was it tough going?*

At one point I was down to $20, but I would just not call my parents and ask them to send me any money. Somehow I always made it. I had nothing to fall back on, but I suppose I knew that if things got too tough I could call my parents and have them send me a ticket. There was always that security factor.

> *The sense that you were ultimately acceptable somewhere allowed you to experiment?*

Yes, yes. Even though I really didn't think in those terms, probably having that little bit of a safety valve built in deep down made me dare a few more things than I otherwise would have. Eventually I met Bob Harp, got married, and started studying anthropology—probably because of the experiences I'd had during the prior months. And then I got pregnant; I have two daughters, 12 and 10.

Were you happy being a mother at home?

I cannot stand being at home; it absolutely drives me insane. I was always doing something outside, but I never once belonged to the PTA. When we moved to the suburbs, I felt obliged to join something like Children's Hospital, but I could just not believe the time the women would spend trying to analyze the "corporate environment." It was a waste, yet they thought it was so "important." I only joined because everybody thought I was strange anyway as I would not go to the bridge club or have my fingernails done. I enjoy cooking because it's creative, but I never could stand being at home.

It didn't occur to you that you were an oddball, that something might be wrong with you?

If you don't love scrubbing plates and making little knickknacks out of dough for the kid's Christmas trees? Not at all; it never crossed my mind. So I did a stint at law school, when the children were three and five.

How did you manage that?

I didn't. I just literally could not do the reading. It was such a massive amount, and my husband was not the kind of person who would say, "Okay, I'll take over half the chores; you go ahead and study," even though he was otherwise very supportive. I tried to do everything, but I just decided I could not finish school and keep my sanity. So I took a leave of absence with the idea of continuing later. But I got so bored again. That's when we started Vector.

In studying entrepreneurs, researchers have found that one of the things that characterizes them is that they hit a plateau and feel displaced, which they relieve by taking on a new activity. This sounds true of you.

I think it was, because I had quit law school and started to play a lot of tennis. I actually became quite good at it. But just playing tennis all the time was really not quite what I had in mind either. Bob Harp had designed this memory board that was supposed to be marketed almost a year earlier through another company he was involved with, but it never came off. So he said to me, "If you're really that antsy, how would you like to market it?" I said, "Sounds fantastic."

What did he mean you were antsy?

I felt very frustrated in that I wasn't really contributing to my own expansion. I wasn't doing anything except playing tennis and cooking meals. It was not so much the monetary reward: I'd had the children, but there was something *I* had to do that had a different meaning.

So there was still building you wanted to do for yourself?

You know, it's funny, I was 32 at the time, and I felt, "My God, suddenly I'll be 40, the children will be gone, and where am I going to be?" That may have been the subconscious reason. See, I'm always trying something new. Now that things will be settling down here a bit, I'm going to take a class in sculpture. I want to do something unrelated to anything I've ever done.

Was it important to start Vector on your own?

Oh, yes. What it really boils down to is that I don't like to be dependent on anybody. And that has been part of the problem with my marriage—why Bob Harp and I are divorcing. I'm independent, and I think many men have a problem with that. I like going to the airport in Tokyo or someplace where you can't read anything and still get on the plane without asking a husband, "How do I get there?"

So Vector was a result of your being antsy?

That and a combination of factors. Bob Harp had designed the computer memory board, which wasn't going anywhere, so I called my friend Carole Ely and asked if she wanted to join me in this venture. Carole was very involved with her children at the time, even though she had been a bond trader before. She thought the idea was great.

With no idea of computers except what you'd picked up at home and no formal business experience, how did you begin? I've read that two days after Bob Harp suggested you market the memory board, you went down to the southern California computer show and incorporated.

That's more or less what happened. I decided to market the memory board, called the attorney to incorporate, told Bob to finish designing the board, called the chip supplier, and we were off.

Did you have trouble with suppliers?

Initially. I remember calling the western regional sales manager for one of the chip manufacturers to discuss buying a large number of memory chips. He said, "Fine. How about if we have an appointment at your office tomorrow?" I was calling from my kitchen phone. I said, "That sounds great, but we're in the process of moving right now." Really, I meant moving into the downstairs bedroom, which I was cleaning out. So I said, "Could we meet maybe over drinks at the WestLake Inn?" So we met at WestLake an hour after we had incorporated.

What happened?

He looked at Carole and me and I could just see the thought process going on in his head. "Oh, my God, what did I get myself into?" We sat down and discussed buying 50,000 chips, representing about a $75,000 purchase. We started the company with $6,000. As we sat there and talked about chips and pricing, he gave us outrageous prices. I finally said, "That's ludicrous. We need a price now, not a year from now, in order to have an impact. It has to make economic sense!" He just didn't trust us. I said to him, "If you don't sell to us, we'll find somebody else. This is a hot market. Our product is going to be in tremendous demand." But he didn't want to sell to us.

What really amuses me today, considering we started with $6,000, a lot of enthusiasm, and knowledge that we would succeed (which buys you practically nothing), is that we were able to negotiate 30-day credit terms with the vendors—with no assets.

How did you do it?

Power of persuasion. After a while, salesmen started coming to the house. As a matter of fact, I think our neighbors must have thought we had a sort of brothel going, because the salesmen would stay for half an hour and leave. They'd arrive with doughnuts in the morning, and then they'd put on a pot of coffee. And one fellow would deliver memory chips he'd picked up at the airport, and so forth, at night.

Who was doing the manufacturing?

Initially we sold kits: Carole and I sat on the floor and packed all the stuff, and UPS would come by every day to pick up and deliver the product.

Did you have difficulty getting retailers to stock Vector?

One of the reasons we were very successful initially was total instinct. Basically we treated dealers the way we would like to be treated. We wrote potential dealers whose names we had found in the various trade publications that were turning up all over the place. We started off, "Dear dealer— meet the 8K baby." That's what we called the memory board because it was attached to a mother board. We described all the merits of this particular memory board and then signed our letters—I'll never forget—"Very truly yours, Lore Harp, president; Carole Ely, vice president and secretary/treasurer," which was ridiculous because nobody signs letters secretary/treasurer. And then to be more official, I would type LH/mtf, meaning "my two fingers."

Did the letters work?

They usually resulted in dealers stocking between two and ten boards. We'd call the dealers about five days later to ask if they'd received our letter and brochure and if we could sell them a memory board. And they said, "Um, yes." Most people were so flabbergasted by the attention they got and the fact that we were women. We really capitalized on that. They all wanted to help "the girls."

How did you know that the follow-up would make the sale?

It was a question of nurturing the process along. You don't send the child off on a trip without later checking to find out if he or she got there. I'm sure there was something of a female innate protectiveness about it, wanting to take care of something we'd started. For instance, two weeks after we had sent out the memory boards COD, I would call up again and ask whether they had received the board, did they have a chance to put it together, and did they like it? And how many more did they want to order?

Were the dealers surprised?

Yes, because nobody did that. They were overwhelmed by the support. If they had a problem they would call us up, and we would sometimes call Bob at Hughes Research Laboratories, where he was working, and ask him to call a dealer. So we were troubleshooting over the phone and servicing right from the start.

So you attribute much of your success to a special concern for something down the line?

I think so. Most of our competitors were very technically oriented people who saw a tremendous opportunity and wanted the satisfaction of having little computers they could play with. But they really had no interest in following through, in marketing, in getting the word out to the world as to why the computer is great and what it can do for the customer. Not being either designers or technically oriented, we took the other road.

How did you keep up with the growth?

Well, what I would do is get bowls out of the kitchen and put all the little components in them, and my children and Carole's would put the kits together. We also hired a lot of high school kids, part-time. It was chaotic with children, dogs, cats, and neighbors' kids. By December 1976, five months after we had incorporated, we moved to a 1,200 square-foot facility. We hired our first assembler and a receptionist, who was also a salesperson, order taker, and everything else. She was my next-door neighbor, Jenine Steele. And in May 1977, because things had really taken off, we moved to another facility. It was all such fun then.

> *It was fun, it wasn't work?*

No question about it. It was really what I think I needed for my satisfaction, let's say, as a contributor of something beyond myself. For example, I remember giving my next-door neighbor her first paycheck; it was just great. Or doing some accounting. For example, we kept books and financial statements from day one.

> *How did you know how to do that?*

I'm not sure. That was instinct too. You have to know where your money goes. I guess it's a bit of my German nature too. Some of the companies that have gone out of business essentially kept their bills and invoices and everything else in one big box.

> *I don't know whether that's necessarily Germanic; it sounds more like good planning.*

You need a structure to keep control of the details while you're doing something else. And even though we were operating on such a small scale, we were very organized. Things went very well, and Bob decided to design some other products. Soon we had a full-fledged computer, eventually hired some more people, and moved into a larger place. Everyone was scared. At the time, it cost us almost $17,000 a year for rent. And then we moved into this big facility, which costs $60,000 to lease. I started to look for this space in March 1980, a year and a half before we moved in. We've invested $2.3 million into this little building. I knew we were going to grow very fast.

> *When you were talking about your background, you said it was important to have your family to fall back on. Do you think that having a husband who had a good job allowed you to take risks?*

No, because I knew I could always go out and do something. I think it was much more important for Bob Harp. He wanted to see that the company actually was off the ground before he quit Hughes. It took him a year. But we had real estate and stocks and so on, so there was other income. It was not as if we were totally dependent on the salary from Hughes. It could have helped subconsciously, though.

It sounds as if you'd have done it anyway.

Yes! We went public, and I'm a million and a half dollars richer, and it's totally unimportant. Isn't that weird? You can change your clothes only so many times. Money's really not the underlying criterion. What I really enjoy is growing the company, growing people within the company, accepting the challenge of being out there, competing against other companies, and making an impact. Power may have something to do with it as well. I won't deny that.

Why did you go public?

Capital is one reason, but almost more important, I thought we needed the discipline. Some people feel they can make a lot of decisions without looking at the company's total picture, and we just cannot afford to do that anymore because of our sheer size. We have to communicate among departments, and I thought that going public was one way of signaling to people that we had to be more responsible.

Some people say that female entrepreneurs need to learn to think bigger and take more risks. Was risk taking a problem for you?

Not at all, because one of the things I can do is make very fast decisions. I plan a lot, make decisions, and am risk oriented. If I make a mistake, I acknowledge it and try not to make the mistake again. But making any decision is better than no decision at all. What makes me so mad many times during staff meetings is when people come up with reasons why something can't be done. I say, "Why don't you give me just *one* reason why it *can* be done?"

People theorize about what makes most women hold back. Many feminists say it's job and sex discrimination; other people cite psychological forces. What would you say?

Basically I'm not a feminist, even though I guess I should be because of what I'm doing. But I'm not, because I feel that most women gain acceptance from peers, male or female, by proving integrity and intelligence—not by talking about job discrimination and all sorts of other complaints. I just don't have time for that.

You mean, if you can do it, why can't everybody else?

I'm very strong in my convictions. For example, I was very firm in negotiating the stock price with the underwriters. I stood my ground and said, "You have five more minutes. We must have a deal at the end of that time or else we're going to walk." When they looked shocked, I said, "OK, that's thirty seconds."

When you started, were supportive friends important to you? You had Carole Ely of course. What about other women friends?

Well, as a matter of fact, it was bad at first. My best friend was resentful because I was very enthused and talked a lot about what we were doing at Vector. For about a year and a half we really didn't speak to each other. And then on Christmas day we both had the same thought to call, and now we're good friends again. But she was jealous, which is one of the conventional pitfalls women fall into.

So there really are sacrifices independent women make in the real world—friends, husbands?

Yes, but there are men who really want that kind of woman—not very many—but a few.

And it sounds like if you want to maintain your female friends, you have to support the belief that women should only be housewives.

Once in a while I go to a traditional occasion, say, a cocktail party, where it's the husbands who do all the work and the wives stay home. They're all intelligent women and so on, but they're not doing what I'm doing and sometimes I really have a hard time talking to them because the conversation invariably ends up on tennis, or having their fingernails done, or on something I don't relate to well anymore. I'm in a different stream.

Did being a woman make it difficult to get backing, once you'd stopped being considered just a "helpless girl"?

One question I was afraid would come up during the road show before going public was how can you, not having had prior experience or having been groomed at IBM, take the company to the next level? And I think they only posed that question because I am a woman; they would never have asked that of a man.

But isn't it reasonable for underwriters to question how you're going to take a company to the next level when you've had no experience?

We were one of the pioneers of the microcomputer explosion. The buying, as well as the selling, process in this industry is different from what it had been before for computers. Buyers were much less sophisticated; they really didn't know what they wanted. So I think principles that I may have learned at IBM, DEC, or any other computer company would probably not have served me well at all. We were dealing with a totally new element.

So how did you answer the question?

I gave a reasonable answer as to our track record and where we had gone, looked in a flirtatious way at the person, and said, "But you're not *really* holding one silly little chromosome against me." When you talk to people on a one-to-one basis, you don't run into that problem. It's only when men, especially in the investment community, are in a group that being a woman can be a problem.

Do women's business networks help?

I get invited to speak or visit a lot of different feminist-oriented groups, and as I told one of them, I'm just not interested. I said if women want to get off their duffs, they've got to get off them on their own and not suddenly start leaning on strong women when before they were leaning on strong men. To succeed you have to do it for yourself and not because somebody else is telling you to. We come into the world alone and the decisions we make, we make ourselves.

> *But you had role models. You had your father who was in business, your grandfather who was a politician, and your aunt. Other women might not have had somebody like that in their own backgrounds to emulate.*

And that's when they become feminists. I remember being at a party three years ago where I met a woman and her husband. This woman was so aggressive; I've never seen anyone like her. She had just attended a feminist seminar, and she treated her husband so poorly, it really was appalling. She said to me, "Oh, you'd better go to this assertiveness seminar so you can do something with your life." And a friend of mine who was there said, "Well, Lore just started a company and is doing something." "Oh, then," said the aggressive one, "you should get up there and talk to other women." I said, "Listen, I have no interest in talking to a bunch of women if they come on like you. But I'm going to give you one piece of advice." I asked, "Have you gone out and gotten a job yet?" "No," she answered. "Well," I said, "if you haven't, I wouldn't treat my husband the way you do because you are still dependent on him." Two years later she is still in the same rut.

So you think the lady doth protest too much?

Many women are ranting and raving against men and taking a hard line, while I like being feminine. I like a man to push in my chair at the table. I like somebody to open the car door and bring me flowers and treat me as a woman. I think, *vive la différence*. I love it.

> *When you look at yourself in your role as CEO, what do you think you are especially good at?*

I've made decisions that have been good for the company. Also I'm very people oriented. I manage by not restraining and restricting employees but by giving them the responsibility and letting them carry the ball. And people respect me for those reasons. I hold very loose reins. For example, when I'm out of town, I rarely call the office. If people are not carrying out what they're hired for, they're the wrong people to have. I was very instrumental in maintaining discipline in terms of credit and collection, but it's your treatment and attitude toward people that really tells.

> *How does that show itself in practice?*

Well, for example, a year ago I started something called the friendship lunch, where every week we post a sign throughout the company and nine people can sign up to be taken to a restaurant for lunch with a different vice-president or myself. My turn is every fifth week. What prompted me to do that was when I was walking through a manufacturing floor one day; I just stood there and looked at all those people working and I thought, I really don't know any of them. I don't know what they think, what makes them tick. These people are between 18 and 30 years old, and I thought, my God, they are really much more representative of the United States than I am. And I wanted to hear what they have to say.

> *Did you think it was important for them to know you?*

It was reciprocal, but I wanted to hear more about them, and I found if we had this lunch they'd get to know me and I'd be able to listen to what they have to say. It's vital to know how people think and function.

> *Do the vice-presidents talk to you and tell you what was discussed at the lunch?*

We get together afterward, and if there's something really critical to discuss we take it on. It's a two-way communication process: what's important to us and what's important to them. For example, everybody has stock options in the company. When we went public, I said, "I want everybody who has been hired through May 31 of 1981 to have some options in Vector." I really argued with our attorneys and underwriters about this. I said I don't care if they're assembly workers, vice-presidents, directors, or other managers, I want to give options to people not according to position but according to length of stay with Vector. Some people in the assembly area have more options than a director. I tell you, we got flak for this.

You got flak from Shearson Loeb Rhoades?

Yes, our underwriters felt that stock options are reserved for motivating management. I said if the assembly workers do a terrible job for Vector, the upper managers might as well be dead. I found out at a lunch that people here are extremely pleased with having options in Vector.

As you grow, how do you keep the personal touches, the service and support, that characterized Vector in the beginning?

Well, for one thing, we have a very big dealer-training effort going on, which Carole is managing.

What is the program like?

We hold several classes in our training center here, which has both a lecture hall and a "hands-on" room where salespeople from various dealerships learn how to work the computer. One class is purely technical training and lasts about four days. The other is a marketing class, to teach our master method of selling.

With that amount of training, the stores people work in would be almost like franchises.

Exactly. Selling a computer is not like selling a car or a piece of hi-fi equipment. What is really vital in this business is not battling our competitors but educating the end user. To do that, you need very knowledgeable salespeople in the distribution network. So one of our requirements is that all dealers come here for training. We also maintain four training centers across the country—in New York, San Francisco, Chicago, and Atlanta.

So what you've done is to turn into an outside function what companies such as IBM do in-house.

Yes, essentially. But look at the cost structure of our equipment. It retails from $4,000 to about $25,000 without fringes. We could not afford to have a full sales force out there selling that kind of equipment. Look at IBM's marketing of its new entry. They try to sell through the same distribution outlets we do, and that's why it's so important to support our dealers by training and advertising—and to raise their own expectations.

Do you think it's paid off?

Absolutely. Number one, we have a breadth of products to answer almost any kind of need, and two, the dealers have become so well versed about the Vector equipment that it's not necessary for them to carry other lines. They know the machines so well that they can address many different worker segments, which is a tremendous plus. We have almost 100 Vector-only dealers out of 420. These are the most successful dealers, who many times have written software to fit Vector computers.

> *But won't you naturally have to get more formal as you grow? For instance, do you have business plans now?*

Yes, but not until last year. Making a formal business plan around our initial product, let's say a three-year or a five-year plan, would have been ludicrous. The technology, the sophistication of the outside world, and the buyers all changed very quickly, and we had to react to almost day-to-day changes. To have a formal business plan at that point would have been counterproductive, and we probably wouldn't have made it. Even now, I don't believe in more than three-year business plans—one-year detailed, three-year conceptual.

We're still in an embryonic stage in our industry, and we need to let that embryo grow; at the same time, we have a one-year detailed budget and really stick to it, because we're getting too big. But a five- or ten-year plan is an academic exercise. It's cramping, and in our kind of industry we're not about to milk the company yet. With those plans, you begin to sit back, and before you know it, you've lost your flexibility.

> *What about people? Can you keep the spirit alive with new employees?*

We've always hired people who were more qualified than we needed at the time and who wanted to grow with us. For instance, our first vice-president, Dick Tata, had run a $200 million division of Burroughs and came to Vector because he saw an opportunity as well as enthusiasm here.

Also, I want us to stay manageable. For instance, I never want to have a facility with more than 700 people in it. The business becomes too abstract past that point; you lose touch.

Hiring people with the right personality also helps.

> *What's a Vector personality?*

Someone has to have an individual style. People who aren't faddish, who don't follow a trend. And people who want to be entrepreneurs, who can be creative on their own, people who are full of energy and ideas. But we also have a lot of company activities that get everybody together, to keep the spirit we started with. For example, to celebrate our first $2 million month we hired buses and closed the company at 11 A.M. Nobody knew where we were going. We had T-shirts made up saying "Vector Computers for the Advancement of Society." I wrote a little thank-you letter telling everybody how pleased I was and how important everybody was and handed it out with champagne as people were getting on the buses. Then we went down to the beach and played baseball.

> *It sounds as if you owe so much to these people that you have to show you care for them in a special way.*

I feel a great sense of responsibility. When we had our company picnic and about 600 people showed up, I thought, "My God, these people all depend on the paycheck they get from Vector. What if I screw up?" I almost got depressed.

> *That doesn't give you pause?*

No, I know I'm doing the best I can, and I'm not stupid enough to think that I can run this company forever. I try to acquire the necessary tools, and up to this point I think I'm definitely in charge, but if I feel that for the good of the company I should step down, I'll do that and let somebody else carry the ball. Maybe I'll build another company.

> *Do you think you could let go that easily?*

It's like learning to delegate. I used to be very involved in the financial activities. First, I hired a bookkeeper, then a very good comptroller, and then a few months ago a vice-president of finance. I had some problem giving that up because I'd been very involved in negotiating credit lines and in doing a lot of things in the financial department, and now he has taken over. A couple of times I interfered, but I'm over that now. I'm taking off a million different hats.

> *In managing the company, have you found things you're just not good at?*

Oh, sure. All the time. But when I find a weakness, I usually fix it by bringing somebody in who can do what I can't. For example, that's why we hired the vice-president of finance. We needed stronger financial controls, somebody who understands taxes, the new laws, implications certain requirements may have on the bottom line, and so forth. I was pretty good at the beginning, but I know when I'm out of my depth in certain areas.

> *So you don't have to do it all.*

Oh, no. My strength is the strength of other people. Where I find weakness in others, besides myself, I bring in someone else to fill in.

Have you noticed at Vector that the men manage differently from the women?

You know, I'm basically a no-nonsense manager. I don't need a lot of frills. But there's a lot of politicking going on with the men. They are empire builders, very much in competition with each other. Yes, there is definitely a difference in style. I think there's not as much honesty among the men. When we moved into this facility, I had a "cut the crap" meeting where everybody had to talk about their projects. Just by listening to the various presentations you could tell the difference between men and women. The men all used big words and covered for each other. It was obvious. Don't get me wrong. These people are real doers, but they're maybe not quite as honest because that's how they have been bred from the word go.

It's hard to avoid stereotyping, isn't it?

Oh, yes. You know, it's really funny, talking about stereotypes. I got a letter from an employee a few weeks ago in which she congratulated me on how well Vector has done. She told me that she'd been talking to a guy about Vector, when he started on about "the awful bitch who's running the company." I sent a nice note back thanking her for the compliment and said I especially enjoyed the comment about this bitch running the company because that poor guy is either so jealous or he's so stupid that he doesn't have anything else to talk about, and I must be terribly important in his eyes.

I bet you do have a reputation for being cold.

Oh, you bet. In northern California they call me the Ice Maiden. When I heard that I said, well, if the Iron Lady is good enough for Margaret Thatcher, the Ice Maiden is good enough for me. But it really doesn't bother me because people in the company, friends, and those who are important to me know me for what I am. And that's what counts.

You and Bob Harp are getting a divorce now. Isn't that another sacrifice you've had to make?

In a sense, because what he could not cope with was my own change and growth. We always had a stormy marriage because of my very independent nature. And Bob, who's seven years older than I am, wanted to protect his little-girl wife. He didn't see that the little girl never really was a little girl. I have definitely grown up, and he has said he should have recognized that a lot earlier.

Has there been a price with your children?

Not at all. My kids are the most terrific, independent, self-sufficient little people. And I have tremendous rapport with them. The only problem is that, because of our going public, I've been traveling too much this year, about 100,000 miles. So they once said, "Mum, you're gone too much." And I said, "Sweeties, I know; I've been traveling a lot." But I'm including them where I can.

> *According to the literature, entrepreneurs are not supposed to make good managers, and yet you seem to be able to make that switch. I'm wondering whether it's because your original allegiance was not to the product but to the company?*

I never thought about it in those terms, but that's probably a very astute assessment. I was able to take a closer look at the company structure and organizational development. Right now the product is obviously very important to me, but the initial challenge, which was more important, was marketing and getting the product recognized. There has been a tremendous amount of stress lately around the company to keep both in tune because of the move to this building.

> *Why was the move so stressful?*

People felt out of place, two of the founders were getting a divorce, and we were going public. I didn't want to lose any of the momentum within the company in terms of sales. It was important to maintain our growth pattern.

> *What do you want to do for yourself?*

I want to take the company to be about a $200 million company by 1985.

> *You want to have that $200 million party.*

You better believe it!

> *Do you enjoy it as much as when you started?*

Even more, because I've gotten out of some of the operational things. I remember, for example, going out to shipping to pack boxes, writing checks, talking to vendors—all at the same time. Today I really enjoy the planning activities, the streamlining, bringing people in who can carry that next responsibility.

> *So you enjoy the shaping?*

Yes. I think that's why I want to take up sculpting. You mold and sculpt from your own conceptual sense of how things ought to be. That's really what I enjoy. As the company grows, I like the challenges, which are getting much bigger. Where once I made a decision for a $10,000 item, now I'm looking at hundreds of thousands, or millions, of dollars. And if you make a mistake you can really be in a lot of deep water. But I enjoy the molding, the strategy, the planning.

When you started, did you think you'd succeed to this degree?

Never gave it any thought that it couldn't be done. Maybe I *should* have a chromosome test.

12

Growing Ventures Can Anticipate Marketing Stages

TYZOON T. TYEBJEE, ALBERT V. BRUNO,
and SHELBY H. McINTYRE

One outstanding characteristic of many new fast-growing ventures is near chaos as they struggle with such matters as monitoring cash flow and setting production schedules. Because they are so busy putting out fires, owners of such companies can easily lose sight of developments in the outside world, where they must do their marketing. The authors conclude, as a result of interviews with top managers of several rapidly growing high-technology manufacturers, that each company passes through a four-stage marketing development process. In the initial stage, entrepreneurs sell customized products to friends and contacts. They must then exploit a larger marketplace, build appropriate internal communications, and diversify. Companies that successfully negotiate the subsequent stages wind up with well-organized marketing departments that effectively oversee sales, research, and other functions. The key to building an effective marketing organization, the authors conclude, is planning for all the stages rather than reacting to them haphazardly.

The theory of evolution suggests that an organism can flourish only if it adapts to environmental changes. No doubt, a business can expect to succeed only if it changes in response to altered external circumstances.

It is through the marketing function that companies must do the bulk of their adjusting to the outside world. Above all, the growing company's marketing apparatus must evolve in an orderly fashion if the company is to

Author's Note: This article is based on research funded by the Marketing Science Institute and the National Science Foundation.

115

avoid a traumatic transition from one growth stage to another. In this article, we identify the important marketing issues for businesses in transition and advise them how to cope with key problems. A premise of our analysis is that top management must not simply react to new situations created by growth but rather that while operating successfully in the present stage, management must take the initiative in planning for the next one. A marketing organization and strategy that are appropriate for one stage can become liabilities as the company passes into its next phase.

Rapidly growing businesses seem to pass through four evolutionary stages, as Exhibit 1 shows. The marketing effort in each stage takes some time to have an impact, and the growth rate during each stage eventually slows as that arrangement becomes constraining.

Exhibit 1. The Evolution of a Marketing Organization

Problem	Diagnosis	Prescription
Top management suddenly finds itself unable to provide needed attention to marketing.	Stage 1 business is ready for transition to Stage 2.	Hire a sales manager. Continue to hold top management responsible for product planning and pricing and for providing sales support in initial contact with new customers.
There are too many products or markets for top management to coordinate all business functions for each.	Stage 2 company is ready for transition to Stage 3.	Hire product managers and give them support in sales, advertising, and market intelligence. Delegate all marketing responsibility to product managers. Put top management in charge of strategic planning.
Growth opportunities are limited in current product-market scope.	Stage 3 business is ready for transition to Stage 4.	Decentralize marketing activities to divisional level. Establish a corporate marketing group that: Reviews division marketing plans. Furnishes specialized skills in planning and research. Manages corporate level marketing communication.

Stage 1:
Entrepreneurial Marketing

Fast-growing high-technology companies are often founded by people who have left larger companies to start their own businesses. These entrepreneurs frequently have a wealth of technical expertise and a fund of innovative ideas but little marketing experience.

During the earliest phase of the young ventures' operations, the founders usually rely on a network of personal relationships built up during their previous employment. Early marketing successes are often in the form of sales to friends and acquaintances, and the products specially designed for these customers.

For example, Robert Buzzard, president of the rapidly growing Lexel Corporation (it had $50 million in sales in its sixth year), recalls that "during the first few years we built hardware for a few specialized companies. Our first customer, Varian, where we knew several people, wanted a particular type of laser, and we supplied it. I did a lot of engineering on the laser head and the optics, and I also did most of the marketing."

The company in this stage is simply trying to get its foot in the door of the market. It tries to identify customers whose needs are not being met by established competitors—"the elephants." The low production volume at this point cannot support much overhead, so the venture can ill afford a formal marketing organization.

The entrepreneurial marketing approach does furnish the new business with at least one powerful selling point: buyers are assured the undivided attention of top management. Eventually, however, personal attention becomes a drag on the company's growth.

Thus, entrepreneurial marketing helps to establish the business and generate early growth, but its effectiveness diminishes with the overextension of key people. The customer base is too small, the company's product line is too customized, and the founding managers are spread too thin to meet all their responsibilities effectively.

Stage 2:
Opportunistic Marketing

The companies that continue to grow past Stage 1 do so by changing their operating objective from merely getting a foot in the door to seeking new customers. By the time they reach Stage 2, their credibility and products' technical feasibility have been established. A more standardized product line capable of appealing to a wider set of potential buyers replaces the customized product strategy of Stage 1. This expansion means that the business begins to compete directly with established companies. Successful Stage 2 businesses usually concentrate on introducing economies of scale and improving their internal reporting systems and financial controls. At the same time, an infant marketing department emerges that is often staffed exclusively by salespeople. Since it is tactical in orientation, product planning and pricing become the responsibility of top management.

The narrow tactical focus tends to create conflicts as new channels of distribution open to serve the broadening customer base. The case of Stoneware, a microcomputer software company, illustrates this point.

In its early days, Stoneware sold its products directly to retail dealers because of the more attractive profit margins available when it bypassed the wholesaler. It grew so rapidly (it had $2 million in sales in its first year) that it began to recruit wholesale distributors. It also continued to sell directly to the dealers with whom it had established relationships. Naturally, the company's new wholesale distributors objected, and since the broad distribution provided by wholesalers was important to Stoneware's growth goals, the company decided to stop selling directly to its original customers and to guarantee its wholesalers exclusive distribution rights. Thus, Stoneware eliminated the last vestige of Stage 1's entrepreneurial handholding so as to realize the high volume it needed to achieve economies of scale.

As a company such as Stoneware completes Stage 2, it should be poised for explosive growth. Its narrow customer base and specialized product line have been broadened and standardized, and its manufacturing capability is in place. Many companies at this point, however, fail to organize adequately for the next phase of marketing.

Stage 3:
Responsive Marketing

By Stage 3, the company is usually expanding so fast that managers face serious problems of poor organization and division of responsibility. Often they have to make the difficult decision to delegate day-to-day responsibility for key products that have been their pet projects. Relinquishing responsibility is inescapable, but it has a great benefit—it often initiates a process that ends with the creation of a sophisticated marketing department.

Naturally enough, the new product managers emerge as champions for the marketing needs of their wares. Their energetic efforts are rewarded with more people and larger budgets for promotion, customer service, and, ultimately, market research. When the company has integrated such functions, a modern marketing organization emerges.

At this point, effective internal communication is vital to rapidly growing businesses, whose various units risk losing touch with one another and whose customers are becoming so numerous that informal monitoring is unworkable. Successful businesses appear to rely largely on marketing research and their field sales forces for intelligence on customers.

Whereas marketing goals in previous stages are formulated in terms of the needs of the venture, Stage 3 marketing goals are driven by customer needs. One company requires key technical personnel to accompany sales personnel periodically on calls to customers. Another company, which sells diagnostic test kits to medical laboratories, has organized an in-house lab to simulate customer use of the products; any new product has to be "sold" to this internal group before it can be put onto the market.

Eventually, market saturation may slow growth, or competitive forces may make additional gains in market share economically infeasible, or the prospect of antitrust action may make further dominance in a single business unattractive. Thus, the Stage 3 company must seek other product–market positions to sustain growth.

Stage 4:
Diversified Marketing

As a business diversifies, it must reorganize, usually by creating divisions, to cope with increased complexity. As a company progresses into Stage 4, a marketing reorganization also takes place. Depending on the degree of decentralization, each division may operate as a quasi-independent Stage 3 unit within a larger portfolio. Each division has a group of product managers with total marketing responsibility for products in the line. Supporting marketing functions such as sales, advertising, and customer research provide the necessary resources to product managers.

The major marketing change in the transition to Stage 4 is the emergence of a marketing function at the corporate level. Regardless of the titles on the organizational chart, the marketing function has the responsibility for monitoring the company's divisions and for maintaining a favorable image of the company with customers and the general public. By providing specialized skills in market research and planning, the corporate-level marketing staff acts as an in-house consultant to the division's marketing staff. Marketing also plays a key role in setting the strategic direction for the company, particularly in identifying new growth opportunities.

Building a Marketing Organization

During Stage 1, management should carve out identifiable domains of responsibility that it can gradually delegate to the growing staff of specialists. This staff's control over day-to-day operations then expands to incorporate all duties the founding entrepreneurs once performed.

Toward the end of Stage 2, a mature marketing organization is needed to coordinate the product line and monitor the market. Finally, as a company outgrows the narrow focus of product–market coordination and evolves into Stage 4, each division spawns its own product organization. Supporting functions such as advertising and research are decentralized among the divisions into autonomous marketing groups. Exhibit 2 outlines the evolution of a marketing organization.

Exhibit 2.   The Evolution of the Marketing Function

	Stage 1 Entrepreneurial marketing	Stage 2 Opportunistic marketing	Stage 3 Responsive marketing	Stage 4 Diversified marketing
Marketing strategy	Market niche	Market penetration	Product-market development	New business development
Marketing organization	Informal, flexible	Sales management	Product-market management	Corporate and divisional levels
Marketing goals	Credibility in the marketplace	Sales volume	Customer satisfaction	Product life cycle and portfolio management
Critical success factors	A little help from your friends	Production economies	Functional coordination	Entrepreneurship and innovation

At the corporate level, a strategic marketing group reviews division plans, manages corporate-level marketing communications, and provides help in marketing research and planning.

What happens after Stage 4? Products and technologies eventually become obsolete, whereas basic market needs generally endure. A slide rule manufacturer will go out of business when the electronic calculator is invented unless it defines itself as a business to meet calculation needs, not to make slide rules.

The typical Stage 4 business has a highly bureaucratized organization that can easily encounter marketing problems. For the Stage 4 company, a key issue is whether it can continue to foster a spirit of seeking new venture opportunities, the same spirit that gave birth to the business.

13
Commercial Intelligence on a Shoestring

ROBERT HERSHEY

Every small company's market research effort should include gathering as much information about competitors as possible. This article explores ways in which small companies can start programs for monitoring their competitors' activities. The author maintains that some of the most effective methods for monitoring competitors cost little or nothing. He also describes approaches companies might take to organize their commercial intelligence programs. This feature's editor offers some additional observations and suggestions for gathering commercial intelligence, based on his research experience.

Small companies planning long-term strategy and goals should understand all aspects of the commercial environment in which they operate. One particularly important and frequently neglected aspect is commercial intelligence.

The term commercial intelligence evokes images of cloak-and-dagger efforts among corporate competitors to steal each others' secret marketing and new product plans. But viewing commercial intelligence in such a way confuses it with commercial espionage, which often involves unethical and sometimes illegal attempts to obtain information.

Commercial intelligence is essentially publicly available information about competitor capabilities and intentions that provides a basis for planning long-term strategy and goals. Most often, commercial intelligence consists of information about competitors that companies would like to be aware of but are not, because of limited resources.

Gathering commercial intelligence involves going beyond use of trade show gossip to using formal techniques to obtain specific kinds of information. As such, the practice involves one aspect of market research.

Commercial intelligence tends to come in fragments. Sometimes a competitor's capabilities, but not its intentions, can be determined. For example, a competitor may have filed a patent application, but still unknown is whether the patent will be exploited. Sometimes a competitor's intentions, but not its capabilities, can be determined. A competitor may have broken ground for a new plant, but can the announced production timetable for the plant be met? And sometimes both the intentions and capabilities of a competitor can be determined, while on other occasions, neither can.

Executives of small and medium-size companies who are in awe of their larger competitors' seemingly endless information-gathering tentacles should remember that even a conglomerate cannot exchange cost and price data with either a competitor or a trade association without risking legal action under antitrust legislation. Although some companies continue to make elaborate illegal efforts to learn about competitors' secret formulas, long-range plans, new products still on the drawing board, new operating techniques, and production capacity, they cannot engage in such industrial espionage without risking legal action and moral condemnation.

Managers of small and medium-size organizations frequently believe that their limited financial resources prevent them from doing much to determine their competitors' intentions or capabilities. They attribute a mystique to intelligence gathering that suppresses their curiosity about the competition.

Such executives should take note of three market research truisms:

☐ Some commercial intelligence activities cost nothing.

☐ Some commercial intelligence activities require only a very modest expenditure.

☐ Some commercial intelligence activities cannot be done at any price, even by large companies.

Making a Start

Small and moderate-size companies that wish to develop commercial intelligence programs can take some simple yet important steps at minimal cost:

☐ Continually buy competitors' products, tear them down, and evaluate them. (This is entirely legal and ethical.) A toy manufacturer which was able to sell a novelty item for less than a competitor by substituting plastic for some metal components, was chagrined to discover subsequently that another competitor replaced some of the plastic parts with specially processed cardboard and lowered its price below both the metal- and plastic-part competitors.

☐ Require field sales personnel to provide feedback on the activities of customers, suppliers, distributors, and competitors. (This is not a hard-and-fast recommendation. Some companies, because of the paperwork and commission pressures on their salespeople, might acquire higher-quality information from independent marketing companies.) Another approach is to call in all sales personnel for a discussion with key officers on competitive matters.

☐ Assign key officers to spend several days a year talking to customers. These contacts can provide valuable information about competitors' products and services. Of course, such brief exposure may provide a distorted picture of the competitive situation, but more often than not the benefits outweigh the drawbacks. When the officers of a small chemical specialty company decided to interview customers, the vice-president for marketing learned that several customers were buying only one highly specialized chemical rather than the various standard chemicals because they resented the neglectful attitude of a salesman. The salesman was very attentive to his biggest accounts, and when his commissions reached a level that was adequate for him, he stopped beating the bushes for other available business from smaller companies.

☐ Study internal security to ensure that competitors cannot gain access to company secrets. Don't ignore obvious leaks. Make certain, for example, that a competitor cannot obtain your price list from your printer; urge your key people to avoid loose talk at trade association meetings; and take care that by holding a sales meeting out of sequence, you don't tip off a competitor that a new product is being introduced.

☐ Stay abreast of what overseas competitors are doing. Since foreign competitors often have financial and regulatory support from their governments, they may be in a position to aggressively cut prices or offer other inducements to customers.

☐ Remember that giants are often clumsy. A smaller company's response time to customer needs can frequently offset a larger competitor's advantage in advertising power, distribution competence, or cash flow. A small market research firm recently courted away some major clients of a dominant company. The larger company had so many departments competing for computer time that it took more than two weeks to produce reports based on stored standard data. The smaller firm set up a manual sorting system and could deliver needed information in three days.

☐ Become familiar with the kinds of competitive information available to you under the Freedom of Information Act by asking your departments to compile a list of reports your company is required to submit to the federal government. By doing so, you not only become aware of what information you might obtain about your competitors, but you can also determine what they might learn about you. Of course, certain types of information, such as trade secrets or IRS submissions, are protected from examination by competitors.

Buying Information

Executives of small and medium-size companies are frequently unaware of the many small market research firms whose services are reasonably priced and who compete with large market research firms. These small firms can provide the small or medium-size company with continuous data about a given competitor for $3,000 to $5,000 annually.

As a whole, market research firms can provide a wealth of information about publicly held companies. The kinds of information include the following:

☐ Patents filed.

☐ Labor contract expiration dates and strikes.

☐ Research and development activities and personnel assigned to those activities.

☐ Overall and, in some cases, individual product sales data.

☐ Profit and loss statements.

☐ Biographical information on company executives.

☐ Number of employees by division.

☐ Acquisition or divestiture announcements.

☐ New plants or plant expansions and closings.

☐ Executive compensation practices.

☐ Credit arrangements.

☐ Advertising expenditures.

☐ Leasing commitments.

☐ New product announcements.

☐ Lawsuits.

☐ Stockholder actions.

☐ Antitrust actions.

☐ Regulatory compliance investigations.

☐ Changes in top personnel.

Collection of this information does not require secretive methods. Most of it is either in the public domain or regularly reported in the financial press. However, the value of retaining a research consultant for the small company lies in his or her systematic ability to free the CEO and key staff members from the burden of ferreting out the information. Subscriptions to trade publications and economic newsletters are appropriate for a general understanding of the marketplace, but zeroing in on specific competitive activity is the key to obtaining commercial intelligence that can be used to formulate sound strategic plans.

A case can be made for using such outside research as insurance alone, even if the small or medium-size company is doing some of its own competitive research. Top executives preoccupied with operating matters stand a good chance of missing important items. In addition, they cannot assume that they will always find out what is going on in the marketplace from their own people.

How a company uses the information from commercial intelligence efforts will depend on individual circumstances. However, some potential applications include:

☐ Changing pricing strategy.
☐ Changing product-response strategy.
☐ Reevaluating advertising or promotions.
☐ Changing distribution or packaging.
☐ Adjusting trade discounts.
☐ Altering sales techniques.
☐ Forestalling patent infringements.
☐ Avoiding legal entanglements.
☐ Changing marketing strategy.

Do-It-Yourself Approach

But where do moderate-size companies that wish to set up their own commercial intelligence groups start? Primarily by deciding how much of their financial resources they are prepared to commit. At first, a moderate-size company might be prepared to hire an experienced market researcher and an assistant; a smaller company can begin with a part-time clerk.

The difference between the two approaches is that the full-time researcher and assistant will not only be actively locating sources of information, they will probably also be interpreting the data collected; the part-time clerk, though, will only be collecting data from standard sources and passing it on to executives in the organization for evaluation.

A modestly budgeted operation would contain the following standard sources:

1. A subscription to a clipping service that scans newspapers, financial journals, trade journals, and business publications for articles concerning designated competitors. Make certain the service monitors the local newspapers where your competitors have facilities. A medium-size manufacturer of plastics responded immediately when it learned from its clipping service that its major competitor's plant had a fire that would adversely affect deliveries for several months. Sometimes an unobtrusive help-wanted advertisement or the announcement of executive changes can herald very impor-

tant competitive changes. Typical clipping service costs are $105 a month for the first competitor and $10 a month for each additional one, plus 55 cents a clipping.

2. A subscription to the *Wall Street Transcript,* which gives access to corporate presentations to the various financial analysts' societies as well as brokerage house assessments of listed companies. A New York manufacturer of security devices scrapped its entire marketing plan for the upcoming year when it learned from a speech by another company's president to financial analysts that the other company planned to enter the same business. The *Wall Street Transcript* reproduced the speech verbatim.

3. A subscription to the *Official Gazette* of the U.S. Patent and Trademark Office, which includes weekly abstracts of newly issued patents cross-indexed to their corporate owners. An office equipment company embarked on a research effort after learning that one of its products was threatened with obsolescence because a competitor had filed a patent for a display device.

4. The purchase of a small number of shares of a competitor's common stock. This brings quarterly earnings reports, prospectuses, annual reports, and 10Ks. Many companies will accommodate stockholders, on request, by adding their names to mailing lists for press releases and new product announcements.

Obviously, the skilled researcher will know of and be able to locate many more sources of information, particularly in the federal arena. He or she will know about the industry analysts of the Commerce Department, the commodity experts in the Agriculture Department, and the National Referral Center of the Library of Congress that will locate experts (frequently supported by foundations) who will provide information without charge.

For example, a small New England rubber-products company decided not to develop a new product after examining two competitors' labor agreements that it learned were available from the Labor Department. The salary structures of the competitor companies, contained in the contracts, convinced the New England company that it would be unable to price its existing product competitively.

I do not wish to understate the difficulties that even the experienced researcher may face when the competition is privately held. A case in point is the hydraulics-pneumatics industry. Along with publicly held giants like Parker Hannifin (1979 sales of $846.4 million from all divisions) and small over-the-counter companies such as Arkwin Industries (1979 sales of $10.5 million) are many privately held, even smaller companies—all competing for similar business.

Although some financial information concerning privately owned companies may be available from state offices, such as the uniform commercial code division of a secretary of state's office, most kinds of competitive information about private companies are almost impossible to obtain ethically.

Structuring Management

Once the decision to initiate a commercial intelligence program has been made, a number of questions must be answered: To whom will it report? Who will the recipients of the information be? Shall it be centralized or divisionalized?

If the practices of larger companies are an indication, there is no single correct answer. Each company decides such issues based on its understanding of what will work best for itself. Only one rule seems universal: keep permanent files on competitors. A piece of information that seems unimportant at the time of its collection might provide a valuable clue when linked with some future data.

For the small or moderate-size company, the competitive intelligence program will usually be best directed by the president or the vice-president of marketing. The president has a number of built-in advantages; he or she can, for example, fit data into a bigger picture, quickly incorporate information in policy decisions, avoid filtering or nondisclosure because of parochial interests, and remain objective in using information as an auditing tool of the sales department.

The executive in charge of marketing, though, has a few advantages over the president. This executive is likely to be more in touch with the day-to-day work of the researcher and is also closer than the president to the field sales force that collects much of the commercial intelligence data.

Benefits of Size

As previously noted, small companies possess certain competitive advantages by virtue of being small. Little information about them is available to the public, and they find it easier than large companies to protect trade secrets. Because they are generally not large enough to have public relations departments, they encounter no institutional pressures to generate press releases. Large companies must divulge trade secrets to more employees than smaller companies, and so the chances of information leaks are greater.

Because of their size, small companies can also determine the effectiveness of their own security measures more easily than larger companies. In a Conference Board study, the president of a precision instrument company stated, ". . . while the security practices of smaller companies are inclined to be more lax, this disadvantage is offset by the greater personnel turnover that is likely in larger companies."[1]

Many small company officers believe that their employees are keenly aware—more so than their corporate counterparts—of how vital a trade secret is to the survival of their organization. One company officer noted that an employee in a large company, who knows certain parts of a trade secret without being aware of the relationship of the parts to the whole, can quite innocently betray his employer.[2]

This is not to say that being small does not have drawbacks. Probably the major handicap of the smaller company is its lack of financial resources to support expensive litigation when its proprietary information has been infringed on. The very concentration of trade secrets with a small number of employees, which can be viewed as an advantage, could be disastrous if someone defected. Also, financial limits exist to the number of guards and security devices that the small organization can afford, even when prudence dictates their acquisition.

Then, too, small company presidents might be more inclined than large corporations to appear before financial analysts and answer probing questions in the hope of securing capital. Another risk for technically oriented small companies can be pressure from engineers and scientists to publish their latest discoveries so they can maintain their personal reputations.

In this vein, presidents of small or moderate-size companies that do not have in-house counsel might do well to explore with their attorneys the provisions of secrecy agreements and patent assignments. They should also ask their attorneys to acquaint them with the legal pitfalls of hiring a competitor's employee and whether their present practices of obtaining competitive information are proper.

Recently, a Massachusetts judge ordered a small company, Data Translation, Inc., to stop selling a device that Analogic Corp. claimed was a duplicate of its own. Two top officers of Data Translation were former Analogic employees. A few years ago, Fairchild Camera and Instrument Corp. had a temporary restraining order clamped on National Semiconductor Corp., alleging an attempt by National to hire away an engineer with knowledge of Fairchild's patented isoplanar process.[3]

Of overall importance for small and medium-size companies is that in their day-to-day involvement in corporate affairs, they may be missing out on an important game being played out there. The price of admission may not be as high as they think.

Editor's Observations

Hershey's article deals with one of the most important marketing issues facing small companies. Small company executives tend to be aware of basic information about competitors—who the top officials are and what new products they have on the market—to go along with unverifiable trade show gossip. But, as Hershey notes, they frequently shy away from seeking some of the more elusive competitive information available. As Hershey also notes, much of the information is fairly easy to obtain if one knows where to look for it.

Simply because commercial intelligence is at the same time important, intimidating, and relatively easy to obtain, I would argue that small business executives should be personally involved in the intelligence-gathering program, at least in its initial phases. From years of personal experience, I know that seeking out sensitive and important information and guiding others in that search requires a certain attitude that comes only from exposure to the process.

Such exposure helps one become aware of both the seemingly endless possibilities and definite limits for gathering commercial intelligence. Knowing these, executives can then evaluate the results they are getting from market research firms, subordinates, and their own efforts.

Hershey discusses a number of information-gathering techniques that, once described, seem fairly obvious. But many of them don't become obvious until they are mentioned or used. And additional techniques don't become apparent until one searches for data.

Of course, the techniques that are best remembered and most frequently used are those one discovers oneself. But specific suggestions can aid in the discovery process. With that in mind, I would add a few suggestions to the many helpful ones described by Hershey:

1.   Cultivate relationships with securities analysts and stockbrokers who keep tabs on companies in your industry. Securities analysts, in particular, follow specific industries and public companies within those industries quite closely so they can advise institutional clients on buying and selling stocks. Much like journalists, analysts are in the information-gathering business.

For them, obtaining information often involves trading information, and it is on that basis that small business owners can develop their contacts. Small business owners can tell knowledgeable and trustworthy securities analysts and brokers about trade show gossip or other information they judge is not required by their companies on an exclusive basis. Small business owners can then feel free to question the analysts and brokers for information about competitors. Such contacts, of course, take time to develop because they are based on reciprocity and trust, but they can be quit valuable.

2.   Use computerized information services. They can provide recent wire service, newspaper, and magazine articles about your industry and about specific companies in your industry and can thus complement the newspaper clipping services that Hershey suggests. The New York Times Information Bank subsidiary and Dow Jones News Service provide such services, as do smaller data collection services such as Information Data Search Inc. of Brookline, Mass. Big city and business school libraries can often provide information about using computerized data collection services.

3.   Play or have a subordinate play customer to find out how competitors are marketing their products. Usually this task can be carried out quite casually and innocently. Sometimes, though, it means being vague or perhaps even dishonest about one's identity; though not illegal, some might find this distasteful. A recent newspaper account of a national computer trade show noted that an official of a minicomputer vendor "attended the show posing as president of a phony company just to learn how his competitors were pitching their products."[4]

Assembling commercial intelligence can actually be fun something like putting together a puzzle. And, as Hershey observes, the importance of such information in long-term planning cannot be overemphasized.

Notes

1. *How Smaller Companies Protect Their Trade Secrets* (New York: The Conference Board, 1971).

2. Ibid.

3. "Business Sharpens Its Spying Techniques," *Business Week,* April 4, 1975, p. 62.

4. Ronald Rosenberg, "A Disneyland of Computers," *The Boston Globe,* May 25, 1980, p. 23.

14
Management Strategies for Small Companies

HERBERT N. WOODWARD

Numerous small businesses suffer from underlying weaknesses which lead to mistakes that can adversely affect their return on investment. These management problems tend to arise when the business is expanded beyond the limits a particular manager can cope with. In this article, the author offers lessons about operating small businesses, drawing from his own successful experience in acquiring and turning around sick companies.

After looking at hundreds of small businesses and working on a number of them, I have seen certain patterns of conduct recur again and again that lead to eventual failure. If a company is in difficulty, it is almost always a management problem, scarcely ever bad luck.

When a company survives for many years but finally comes upon hard times, it usually means (a) that there is a valuable core of talent and expertise somewhere in the corporate structure yet (b) some persistent management inadequacies have gradually eroded its strengths and left it vulnerable to whatever adverse fortune it encounters.

In a moment, I shall get into those areas that cause management the most trouble, but first permit me to clarify one point. While this article focuses on the lessons I have learned about operating small manufacturing businesses, much of what I discuss is applicable to the practical problems faced by operating units of sizable companies.

In my judgment, there are three principal areas of weakness in small businesses that cause trouble, all of them management centered:

1.   Growth of sales is commonly seen as the solution to all problems. There is an unawareness that, except in the short run, there is no such thing as fixed overhead. Managers, trapped by the concept of marginal income accounting, bring out additional products, believing that their overhead will not be affected.

2.   Inadequate product-cost analysis blinds managers to the losses incurred by adding new products willy-nilly. Usually, there are one or more products or product lines that should be dropped.

3.   Gearing operations to the income statement, while ignoring the balance sheet, is all too common. Lack of concern with cash flow and the productivity of capital employed can be fatal. Managers tend to seek new funds instead of making better use of those they already have.

Growth for Growth's Sake

The most common cause of trouble is the widely held belief that the only road to success is through growth. Many businessmen see growth of sales as the solution to all problems. It seldom is. Growth is not synonymous with capitalistic success. In fact, shrinking the number of products or product lines is usually the surest route to better profit and higher return on investment.

The mania for growth is commonly expressed in the battle to increase sales. Standard methods of accounting tend to encourage the belief that higher profits automatically follow from higher sales. Several standard accounting techniques tend to mislead those who accept standard cost allocations as gospel.

Marginal Income Accounting

Much has been written about the advantages of marginal income. The theory is that, for a short period, additional sales can be added to the normal sales volume profitably even at prices too low to cover a proportionate share of fixed overhead. Managers often do this because they presume that 100% of the fixed overhead of the company is borne by their regular business anyway.

However, pricing your product so that it does not cover a full share of overhead is dangerous. Except for rare and well-controlled exceptions, marginal business taken to keep the operation going incurs the same overhead costs as the regular business and, by adding to the complexity of the total operation, often requires more than normal overhead.

Recently, one company manager proudly mentioned that his leading accounting firm had advised him to price all products to obtain any profit margin over his direct material and direct labor costs. He had taken this advice to heart. No wonder his company was in trouble.

Yet, if the overhead really cannot be cut during a short period of overcapacity it may make sense to take added business at prices that will pay less than full ovehead expenses. Even a modest contribution to paying these expenses for that period may be better than none. However, the danger is that an emergency measure often becomes standard practice. It is a good way to go broke.

Break-Even Accounting

Another management tool that inadvertently encourages growth for growth's sake is break-even accounting. Like marginal income accounting, the theory is that certain elements of overhead cost vary with the volume of operations, while others, which are called *fixed costs,* do not. The sale price is set to provide for material and labor costs, plus variable overhead costs, plus an additional increment to allow for fixed overhead costs and profit. When the sales volume is high enough in a given period to absorb all variable costs as well as the lump of fixed overhead costs, you have reached the break-even point. The margin above variable costs on additional sales goes entirely to profit, because all the fixed overhead costs have already been taken care of.

No wonder a manufacturer gloats about a high-volume month, because, although he makes no money and actually loses until the volume reaches the break-even level, his profit on volume above the break-even point is disproportionately large.

The fallacy of break-even accounting is the assumption that expenses are easily divisible into fixed and variable. Overhead is rarely as fixed as accountants are inclined to think, except for very short periods. In any long-range analysis of a business, there is no such thing as fixed overhead—it is all variable to some degree, even such items as rent, heat, light and power, depreciation and amortization, professional services, and executive salaries. The terms *variable overhead* and *fixed overhead* would be better called "overhead that varies immediately with the level of activity" and "overhead that varies in the long run with the level of activity."

Except in the very short run, there really are few, if any, fixed expenses. If you lease a 100,000 square-foot plant for a ten-year term, cost accountants will normally treat your rent as a fixed expense. But is it really? If you don't have enough space, you can rent more and thus increase that expense. If you have too much space, you can sublet part of the space, or if that is impractical, you can even buy your way out of the lease and move to a smaller building. Thus rent expense can go up or down.

The danger is that some managers tend to pay no attention to so-called fixed expenses. Even worse, they assume that they are stuck with them and see an increase in volume as the only means to pay for them.

One able executive of a large merchandising company recently said: "Our biggest problem is sales. Our industry has high fixed costs, and we have to promote hard to maintain a rate of sales to cover these costs. Securing more sales is far and away our number one problem." This is a typical, mistaken business attitude: assuming that the cost structure is a given and that the company must grow to cover all the overhead.

Variation of Break-Even Costing

Manufacturers often take their profits only at the tail end of a run, absorbing all their fixed overhead before any profit is counted. In airplane manufacture, for instance, it is common to determine how many planes must be sold before the company breaks even. The danger of this variation of break-even accounting is that it may stimulate concern with volume of sales, not with margins.

As such, once the fixed costs have been absorbed, profits on the last increment of volume (either monthly or, if it is a one-shot product, by unit) are big, thus encouraging the attitude that more is automatically better.

It is understandable that accounting practices permit amortization of much of the special costs of a particular project (largely tooling and start-up costs) over the estimated number of units expected to be produced. Also, management may be wise to plan for low sales to avoid the unpleasant possibility of taking a big write-off on unamortized costs should the product not sell well. The result, however, is to put the major emphasis on marketing effectiveness rather than on cost effectiveness. It is not surprising, therefore, that increasing sales is the generally accepted prescription for all corporate ills.

Inadequate Cost Analysis

At best, cost accounting is an inexact study with limited goals. It is a method of looking at the direct costs attributable to a particular product or activity. However, it does a poor job of allocating indirect costs. Old and new product lines are normally charged the same proportionate amounts for overhead, although the more recently added lines cost far more to start up. The new product line that adds one more straw to the management load rarely gets charged as much as it should, while the well-established line that runs itself is expected to carry the load for the new line.

Research and development costs, for instance, are usually charged to current operations—which they don't benefit—rather than to the new lines that the R&D is supposed to develop. It is probably necessary to have the old products subsidize the introduction of the new ones. Many managements are scarcely aware, however, that they are doing this. Therefore, they undervalue the profits on the old line and understate the costs in bringing out the new one. The effect is to encourage costly new projects and downgrade current results.

Advantages of Simplification

Once a manager understands how to interpret his cost accounting information, however, he can see that shrinking is a good strategy. If the manager is willing to recognize that all overhead expenses are variable (although a few expenses take time and effort to change), it is easier for him to identify the costs which can be eliminated when his organization is trimmed down in size and complexity.

A few years ago, one of our operating companies disposed of a line of portable positive-displacement pneumatic machines that had an annual sales volume of about $500,000. Although the line was a natural companion to a much larger and long-established line of fan-operated equipment and a prodigious effort had been devoted to get it going, it had not made money and the prospects of success were poor. We finally made the painful decision to sell the line for a nominal amount. The buyer was one of our employees, who set it up as a separate business that later proved modestly successful.

The beneficial effects of that sale on the company's operation were substantial and almost instantaneous. Our balance sheet improved dramatically as we collected the remaining accounts receivable, worked off the inventory, and—by buying no more material—cut our accounts payable. Our earnings improved more than the elimination of this relatively minor line seemed to justify. Only then did top management realize how much this one activity had demanded in attention and effort from almost everyone in the parent company. The product line had had a disproportionately high overhead, but the figures didn't show it.

The advantages of simplification are hard to quantify, but they are real. Despite all that the computer can do to make possible a wide span of control, there is no better road to efficiency than to eliminate complexity entirely, usually by shrinking the business to a smaller and more manageable size.

The manager's job is to maximize the opportunities of the business, not to solve all its problems. He can do this best by focusing on a limited number of objectives to the exclusion of all the irrelevancies of much business activity. It is not easy. As E. F. Schumacher says, "Any third-rate engineer or researcher can increase complexity; but it takes a certain flair of real insight to make things simple again."[1]

In simplifying a business, the best place to start is usually with the products. This is where the ball game is really played. Take each product line and analyze it separately. In most companies with more than one product line or group of products, there are some that are contributing to its growth and success and some that are dragging it down; it takes a careful study to tell the difference.

If the company has adequate product-line cost information, so much the better. Learn how the information is developed and analyze whether the cost allocations between product lines are reasonable. Look for the low-margin product lines that represent a substantial part of the volume.

For example, if a line has been a company mainstay for a long time, your people are likely to tell you that, despite its low margins, it is absolutely necessary to keep this line because of the overhead it absorbs. You will probably also be told that it carries more than its share of overhead and that it really does better than the figures say. In my experience, this is usually not true. In fact, such a line may be doing worse than shown on the statement and may have more actual indirect expense than is charged to it on the accounting books.

Often one line is holding a company down. In one of our operating companies, we found a major product line that had been the backbone of the company for almost a generation. The line showed a minor loss year after year, while gradually declining in volume both absolutely and relatively in relation to a newer line marketed through other channels. This old line was being marketed to original equipment manufacturers (OEMs) in an industry where the smaller customer manufacturers were gradually being driven out by a few large survivors, who had become demanding buyers of components. The company's newer line of products, however, was sold to the consumer market through several thousand distributors. And it was growing profitably every year.

We were told that the company could not survive without the old OEM line because the overhead it carried made the profits on the distributor line possible. But that was not true. The OEM line required extensive engineering for annual model changes for each separate customer, had generally more stringent requirements for quality performance, and had a greater variety of more complicated mechanisms. Yet the customers demanded immediate response to up-and-down schedule changes that made production scheduling beyond a few days almost impossible to achieve.

We sold off the OEM line. And, by so doing, we were able (a) to cut the overhead more than proportionately, (b) to free funds tied up in a non-profit program, and (c) to turn the company from a big loss to a big profit in less than a year.

What You Need to Know

In studying product lines, management should ask some basic questions. In this section, I shall discuss seven of them:

1. *Is the sales volume of the product or product line rising or falling?* Most products have a life cycle of from 5 to 20 years (depending on how you define "product"). If sales are on the downtrend, spend little or nothing to keep it from dying a premature death.[2] If it is losing money and it is past its peak, let it die quietly. You should spend money on the product that is on its way up. Indeed, if this product already has a good margin, it probably can be increased even more.

2. *Is the product line making a profit?* If it is not profitable, as shown by the company's existing cost system, don't lightly accept the argument that it is really doing better than the figures show, that it doesn't use as much overhead as is allocated to it, and that, if only such and such were done, it would start making money. Particularly, don't listen to this argument for a product line the company has had for years which once made money. Better than revive it, let it die quietly.

3. *What are the gross margins of the different product lines?* There

is no fixed rule for a satisfactory gross margin (the difference between net sales price and the total cost of material, direct labor, and applicable factory overhead). One manufacturing company had a material cost alone that represented over 90% of sales price, but the product had a very satisfactory profit. The reasons: the material was expensive but not bulky, and the company made only a slight addition to the product before selling it to a few large users; in addition, operating expense was negligible and the company didn't pay for the raw material until after it had collected for the modified product from its own customers. Consequently, almost all the gross margin went directly to the owner's salary and profit.

In general, however, in the manufacturing business, if you are to have a profit of at least 10% on sales before federal income taxes, your gross margin should be no less than 35% and preferably well over 45%. If your gross margin is low, unless you can raise selling prices (the first place to look) you face a long struggle to improve operating efficiency. For, while you battle to reduce manufacturing costs, you can be sure that your competitors are plowing that field too. You may find later that your hard-won improvements have only kept you from losing more ground.

4. *What do your customers think of each product line, its price, its quality, and your company's service?* Most companies have their own definition of their products' quality and competitiveness, but the customer is the only person who is entitled to judge quality. He often has quite different ideas from you about what is important and what is not. Often products that managers or owners think are marvelous fail miserably in the marketplace, for reasons that are entirely unanticipated.

One maker of television sets claims that its product is better because the sets are handcrafted. The company does make a superior product, but handcrafting doesn't impress me. Personally, I trust machine manufacture more. The customer most likely doesn't care how difficult it is to make. If a product is as hard to make as some manufacturers advertise, it probably can't be very reliable. Quality is only what the customer says it is.

5. *Is the sales department determining the pricing?* If so, you can bet the prices are too low. Salesmen rarely believe that they can get a higher price for the product until they are told by management that they have no choice. (Overly marketing-oriented officers have the same failing.) It is amazing how often the customer will pay more with little or no complaint, despite all the salesmen's warnings that to raise the price is suicide.

6. *Is your sales department's pitch that "we have to have a full line"?* Only the "full line" approach justifies continuing to make and sell low-volume items which are expensive to tool and manufacture and which, per unit sold, cost a fortune to catalog and carry in stock. If your competitor carries a full line, your sales people will insist that they cannot compete unless they have all the items too, because the buyer wants to purchase from one supplier.

One-stop purchasing is a good sales gimmick but often is not good business. The Crane Company had the most complete line in the plumbing industry, but its losses mounted until Thomas Mellon Evans acquired it, eliminated the low-margin items, and thus put it back in the black.

7. *Does your sales program offer a wide variety of options, extras, and specials?* Custom products always cost more and, unless the volume is large enough so that some economies of scale can be realized, they are certain to lose far more money than the books show. Many companies gradually add more and more variations to their line to suit the particular specifications or whims of various customers. These specials are ordered as a matter of habit for years thereafter, even when the customer can do just as well with a standard product. If you rigorously cut out the specials, you can usually convert the customer to a standard item. If you can't, you are probably better off losing his account.

All of the foregoing should aid you in cutting out low-profit or unprofitable product lines. If you are lucky, you can sell off the line to a competitor or someone who wants to get into the business. If you are not able to do this, just stop making it. One way to stop is to put into effect a large, across-the-board price increase. If the line has been grossly underpriced, you may not lose much business and may have turned a bad line into a good one. But even if you lose most of the business, a few of your customers, although they may object noisily to the price, may continue to buy from you—at least for a while—so that you can favorably dispose of your inventory.

When you cut out a line entirely, several things happen. Because your sales volume is reduced, your accounts receivable in that line turn into cash. You stop buying inventory and stop putting in direct labor, and this saves you more cash. You terminate all personnel involved in the line except those necessary for the final salvage operation, saving still more cash. You simplify your total operation which makes even more savings happen. You will probably need less machinery and may be able to sell off the surplus for cash. Finally, even if you can't sell all the inventory, you can scrap the rest, thus freeing up space which you can put to better use or even no use at all.

Closing down a product line is usually recorded on the accounting books as a loss. However, you are merely recognizing losses that were actually incurred sometime ago but don't show on the books yet. You might as well bite the bullet now.

Lack of Balance Sheet Concern

Another common failing is gearing the operations to the income statement and ignoring the balance sheet. The management of one company International Science Industries purchased from a large conglomerate had never seen a balance sheet because the parent supplied all its cash needs automatically on request. Lack of concern with cash flow and the productivity of capital, however, can be fatal to the small company that is on its own.

Your best source of capital often is hidden in your balance sheet. I have become particularly aware of this because in most turnarounds the first concern is cash flow.

Accounts Receivable

Look through your assets to see what you can turn into cash. Often, the quickest and best source of cash is your accounts receivable. An intelligent analysis of accounts receivable can be made without knowing much about the details of the business. If the book figure for accounts receivable is higher than the equivalent of 40 to 50 days of company sales, you may be sure that there is work to be done.

Collecting amounts owed you by customers is a boring and unpleasant job. In poorly managed companies, the job is often neglected. If the company has not earned a profit, there has been no income tax incentive to write off uncollectible accounts. As a result, these uncollectibles continue to clutter up the balance sheet, making it harder to identify the accounts you should be working on.

Obtain a report showing all of the accounts by invoice number divided into categories by age of invoice (less than 30 days, 30 to 60 days, 60 to 90 days, over 90 days). Such a report will show you at a glance where the problems are; establish the procedure if you don't already have it. Decide who is to police the accounts receivable and then ensure that they are really worked on.

In many companies, the salesmen are not penalized when their customers have a poor payment record. Salesmen are naturally reluctant to irritate the people on whom they rely for business by insisting that the customer really should pay his bill. The result is that the only customers who make timely payments are those who do so automatically, without the needling that many companies expect before paying any bills. If you find that the salesmen are responsible for collection, reassign the responsibility to someone in the accounting department who has no compunction about being firm with a slow-paying customer. What good is it to make a sale if you don't get paid?

Once the salesman is freed from the responsibility of collection, he can sympathize with the customer about the demands of that "damn credit department" and spend his time selling, which he does well, instead of collecting, which he does ineffectively—if at all.

Study the accounts receivable records to see whether the financial department is doing a good job. If you find a host of small unpaid balances in the receivables, and, at the same time, many unmatched credit entries, then you know that procedures don't exist or aren't being followed for matching cash receipts with the appropriate invoices in order to straighten out any discrepancies. Examples of the latter are when the customer pays for the product but doesn't pay for the freight, or takes an unauthorized discount, or in any way pays less than what the invoice calls for.

If these discrepancies are ignored for long, it becomes almost impossible to straighten them out without writing off your loss. If an adequate job has been done, such a writeoff will never be necessary. I am particularly partial to nit-picking bookkeepers who keep tidy books and work at cleaning up all (and I do mean all) open items within a reasonable period.

If you can find time to be your own credit manager and to do some of the telephoning to delinquent accounts, you will be rewarded with new insights into your business. When you talk to a customer who hasn't paid his bill, you find out why he isn't paying. Often it is because your own company has made mistakes that no one has done anything to correct.

You also discover which salesmen are doing a poor job in handling difficult product and sales problems. If they aren't solving such problems as they arise, they are not helping to build your company. Instead, they are effectively tearing it down.

Inventory Items

If your company is operating in the black, you have every incentive to write down or write off any inventory that is no longer worth full value. Necessarily, all accountants and auditors have to rely on management judgment as to which inventory is still useful and which is obsolete. Their statistical analyses of inventory aging can be very helpful, but the manager is the one to decide which items are good and which are not.

Even when there are no favorable tax consequences, a physical housecleaning is good. Poor housekeeping generally goes with poor management. Some years ago when a company I ran first took on a turnaround, we trucked out 23 semitrailer loads of scrap inventory in the first three weeks, inventory that the previous management had been afraid to write off the books, although they (and we) knew that it was valueless.

Most of us hate to throw things away. Somehow the right time never seems to come. But never has anything turned up to make me thankful I had not thrown something out or to make me regret that I had. It is good for the soul to roll up your sleeves and to clean house physically. And it is good for the business, too.

Fixed Assets

Managers are likely to neglect looking into their fixed assets for hidden capital. Somehow land, buildings, machinery, and equipment seem sacred. If the company has been in existence many years, these assets are usually deeply depreciated on the books. However, because of inflation, these assets are likely to be worth far more than book value. (Land, although it is not depreciable, usually has inflated in price too.)

The capital you are actually employing in the business is not measured by the net book value of these assets, but by their current market value. Once you recognize this, you should seriously consider whether you need all of them and whether you are using them effectively. If you have a fully tooled machine shop to support your manufacturing effort, can you justify tying up that much capital in expensive equipment when there are competent subcontractors available to do your work? If not, you can close it down, sell off the equipment for cash, free up some space, and reduce your payroll.

My general rule is to subcontract whenever possible all work for which our company has only an intermittent need. If the work is a follow-up step in the production process that, if not properly done, can damage our products, we may make an exception and invest the money to do it ourselves. Heat treating of critical aerospace parts is a typical example of an exception.

Also, when we manufacture in high volume, it is advantageous to integrate backward as far as possible and to do it ourselves. Only in that way can we keep our unit costs down. But we still let outsiders make our tools.

One important management decision is whether to continue to operate at all in a given location. Years ago, it may have been necessary to have satellite plants in various cities to serve your customers. But is that still true, and, if so, what is it costing you to serve those customers? Several years ago, International Science Industries acquired a manufacturing company with plants in five cities around the country. Within a year, we closed and liquidated two of them. We were able to shift much of the business to the remaining three plants. Thus, while sales volume scarcely declined at all, costs plummeted. More important, this shift released a large chunk of capital for better use.

A Final Reminder

The name of the managerial game is return on investment. ROI is the ratio between the profit of the operation after tax and the assets employed. Management tends to look only at the former, neglecting the latter. In seeking to maximize profits, attention is often focused exclusively on sales. The stockholder, however, has no interest in sales; he looks at earnings per share, because they largely determine how much the stock sells for and what dividends are paid.

If assets employed can be sharply reduced, even if profits drop a little, ROI will increase and the stockholder will be better off. Is this a risky strategy? Not if the assets were previously employed inefficiently. Putting the company in a financially sound position is a first step.

Once the company is in a solid position, you can, if you desire, go after renewed growth. Or, if you get hooked on the beauties of simplicity, you may just keep on making money at that level.

Notes

1. E. F. Schumacher, *Small Is Beautiful* (New York: Harper & Row, 1973), p. 146.

2. See Joseph A. Morein, "Shift from Brand to Product Line Marketing," *HBR*, September–October 1975, p. 56.

15

Management Involvement Needed in Computer Selection

RICHARD RAYSMAN

There are many dangers small businesses face in selecting and ordering computer systems. The author cautions small business managers to become actively involved in arranging contract terms and timetables.

Richard Raysman is a New York attorney specializing in the legal aspects of computers. He is chairman of the New York State Bar Association Computer Law Subcommittee.

The president of a small real estate management company recently retained a computer consulting firm to represent his company in acquiring a computer system. He also directed the consultants to engage a lawyer familiar with the computer industry to negotiate and draw up the contract.

The president's actions were not those of a novice looking for guidance in buying a first computer system. Rather, the company was about to purchase its second computer system. The president's actions resulted from the failure of its first computer system to perform as promised. The failure cost his business about $100,000 for the unsuitable system and lost profits.

Even worse, it caused a two-year delay in installing a fully operational data processing system. In buying the first computer, the real estate company relied entirely on the promises and representations of the computer vendor, which for the most part turned out to be false.

Executives in small businesses in particular often do not realize until too late the expensive repercussions of a failed computer project. Too often they leave the planning and decision making to subordinates inexperienced in contract matters and to one or two vendors whom they trust. But managers do not recognize that failure of an initial computer installation or of a substantial addition to an existing installation can adversely affect a company's operations.

A data processing installation affects the heart of a company's systems—order entry, invoicing, accounts receivable, inventory control, sales analysis, market research, and other important functions. If a computer system fails, the company loses not only money but also valuable time and quite likely a competitive edge in the marketplace.

Expensive and Complex Considerations

Frequently, large sums of money are at stake in acquiring hardware and software. During recent years, the cost of hardware has dropped sharply, while personnel costs for software development have skyrocketed. It is in the area of software that small business managers often encounter their most serious selection and contract problems, because many software development efforts fail.

What makes the problems so potentially complex is that software is elusive to define. It comes in three forms. The first, custom software, is specially developed for a particular company's operations. The second, application software, is an existing program or series of programs—usually with a track record—that a company licenses from a software vendor. A third area of software development, which incorporates custom modifications in existing application packages, is evolving rapidly and being used with increasing frequency. Such software reduces the risk of failure since the programs already work, yet it can be adjusted to a company's individual needs.

Because software cannot be defined precisely, a legally binding contract covering its delivery does not always provide the necessary protection. After all, delivering software is not equivalent to delivering an automobile or other tangible finished goods. The skill in negotiating and drafting a computer contract lies in designing an agreement that acts as a blueprint and sets a firm foundation for the project's success.

Anticipating Difficulties

The key to a good contract is to catch problems—both real and potential— early so that they can be remedied before they grow unmanageable. While everyone wants an agreement that provides legal protection, the thrust of the contract should be to design a practical approach for developing and installing a system.

Managers should plan the acquisition and take the initiative in proposing contract terms to a computer vendor. Management should not simply rely on the primarily oral representation of the vendor's salesperson and on what it thinks to be certain technical expertise, which may or may not exist.

Potential Problems

The expensive repercussions of failure to plan and take the initiative are illustrated by a lawsuit, *Carl Beasley Ford, Inc.* v. *Burroughs Corp.*, filed in federal court in Pennsylvania. The *Beasley* case involved both hardware and software and has been relied on by numerous courts as a precedent for legal cases relating to computers.

Burroughs submitted a proposal to Beasley, a Ford dealer, to sell and deliver to Beasley a computer system. Beasley needed the system to comply with its franchise agreement with Ford Motor Company to furnish accounting records on a regular basis.

Representatives of Burroughs promised to furnish 13 programs that would produce the required accounting records. However, their oral agreement was not included in the written contract, and the cost of the programming service was included in the price of the equipment.

When the equipment was delivered, Burroughs assured Beasley that the programming would be completed in two months. So sure was Burroughs that it advised Beasley to cancel an arrangement with a service bureau that was processing Beasley's accounting records.

Despite all these assurances, Beasley was unable to get the programs to operate correctly. The result was that 14 months after installation, the computer was working improperly, and Beasley was having serious problems compiling a number of important accounting records and reports. In spite of continual reassurances from Burroughs that the programming problems would be corrected, Beasley finally rejected the system and sued Burroughs.

Beasley won its suit and was awarded a refund of the purchase price plus "consequential" damages that almost equaled the purchase price. Consequential damages are those resulting from breach of contract and, in this case, included interest on a loan taken to purchase the equipment and money spent for extra clerical help, accounting services, and other computer services.

The Ripple Effect

Beasley may have won the courtroom battle, but it nearly lost the business war. In addition to lost executive and clerical time, disruption of day-to-day operations, and legal fees, Beasley was set back almost two years in installing a computer system. During that time, it had not received the advanced sales analyses and inventory information necessary to remain competitive with other area auto dealers. Nor had it furnished certain required reports to Ford, thus jeopardizing its franchise.

Similar problems are often encountered when managements yield to the temptation to order turnkey systems, in which vendors perform all the development and install the operating systems. Users do little or nothing except to sign the contract and write the checks when payments are due. Since vendors do not usually understand fully how users' businesses operate, turnkey systems frequently fail.

Chatlos Systems Inc., a New Jersey designer and maker of cable equipment for the telecommunications industry, found that out the hard way when it purchased a turnkey system for $75,000 several years ago from NCR Corporation. The system was supposed to process Chatlos's accounts receivable, payroll, order entry, inventory control, state income taxes, and cash receipts, but after two years only the payroll part of the system was working, and Chatlos was pursuing a suit against NCR in federal court. In 1979, Chatlos won $120,000, which included a refund of the purchase price plus lost time and profits.

Improving the Odds

To avoid such problems, computer customers along with their employees should become involved in the formulation and performance of contracts with vendors. Customers should formalize in writing their participation in contract performance.

A customer's employees know the peculiarities and requirements of their organization. They can ensure that the vendor builds the right specifications into the system. Such input is particularly important in cases where noncomputer personnel such as clerical staff or salespeople will be using the system regularly. If they don't like the system, they can render it ineffective right at the start by either not using it at all or using it improperly.

Early user involvement does not, of course, ensure success, but it greatly reduces the chance of problems. When employees are involved, they can monitor the vendor's progress and alert management if time schedules deteriorate or if the project drifts off course. The user then can require the vendor to remedy any deficiencies early on or can even cancel the project. Timetables for software development projects, in particular, often deteriorate quickly.

Thus, the agreement should require the vendor's technical and development personnel to provide a progress report to the customer's technical representative twice a month. The agreement should also require a senior executive of the vendor to provide a summary of progress to a senior executive of the customer once a month. These reports and summaries can be compared with the supplier's timetable, which should be part of any contract.

Such a reporting system alerts the customer to potential problems at an early stage. It also encourages the vendor to attend to problems as they occur, instead of waiting until the situation deteriorates.

Three Key Elements

To prevent misunderstandings about what the vendor promised, the customer should seek the following three forms of definition of the finished product:

1. Clear, detailed design specifications that describe all system components.

2. A description of the customer's business functions that the system will perform. Otherwise, computer programs may meet the letter of the specifications but still be inadequate for the customer's needs.

3. A guarantee that once the system begins to process live daily transactions, it will run without significant error for a reasonable time, for example, 90 days. Sometimes a programming system will run for a few weeks or even months without difficulty and appear to be error free. Then, because of unusual circumstances, the system may break down. A promise of continual operation may offer protection against such an event.

As in any business relationship, the executive exercises great leverage by hinging payment to contract performance. The user should be careful to tie periodic payments to specific completed and proven tasks—a technique that maintains the vendor's interest during the entire system development process. A serious error small businesses make is to authorize large front-end payments to vendors. The businesses should also try to retain the final payment until after the system is installed and has been operational for a specified time so that the supplier will remain committed to implementing the system.

Changing technology clearly increases the financial risks that small business executives confront. If contracts covering computers and other high-technology equipment are not sound, managers risk substantial amounts of their companies' financial resources. Thus, managers must learn to be as creative and innovative in the technical areas as they have historically been in other business functions.

PART THREE
EFFECTIVE FINANCIAL MANAGEMENT
AN OVERVIEW

Managing the finances of a smaller company on a day-to-day basis is a much different proposition than managing the finances of a major corporation. For one thing, smaller companies are frequently operating close to the brink of disaster as they struggle to come up with the cash to pay pressing bills. For another, owners of small companies tend to be very concerned with minimizing taxes. Large companies, on the other hand, usually have ample financial reserves, elaborate controls, and sophisticated financial managers weighing the impact of results on the balance sheet and financial statement as well as on taxes.

Rather than attempt to emulate the financial practices of large companies, though, owners of small businesses should seek to cope with and make the most of their special situation. John A. Welsh and Jerry F. White argue persuasively that "A Small Business Is Not a Little Big Business" when it comes to financial management. Rather, small businesses are prone to a condition they call *resource poverty*, which necessitates focusing on such fundamentals as cash flow planning, break-even analysis, and liquidity.

The fact that small companies usually don't have in-house financial analysts monitoring balance sheets and financial statements doesn't mean owners must ignore the appearance of their results, leaving them in the hands of outside accountants. James McNeill Stancill contends in "Managing Financial Statements—Image and Effect" that small companies' results convey important messages to potential bankers, investors, and acquirers. Moreover, he argues, owners can, through sensible timing and management, affect the outcome of sales and earnings as well as various balance sheet ratios.

147

The underlying messages of Neil C. Churchill's "Don't Let Inflation Get the Best of You" and Steven D. Popell's "Effectively Manage Receivables to Cut Costs" are similar to Mr. Stancill's: that managers can and should exert control over the outcome of their financial statements. Mr. Churchill considers eight serious financial problems common during periods of inflation, including overstated operating profits and growth rates, and suggests ways of countering the difficulties. The aim is to provide owners with a more realistic picture than they might otherwise have of their companies' finances to aid in planning.

In the same vein, Steven D. Popell maintains in "Effectively Manage Receivables to Cut Costs" that managers of small companies can significantly better their financial situation by being tough in extending credit and persistent in collecting on receivables. He provides guidance for doing credit checks and tracking receivables and concludes that the most important ingredient is management commitment.

Those owners of small businesses attempting to do financial planning can easily feel that they're operating in a vacuum. After all, how do they know what's appropriate to plan for? In "Performance Measures for Small Businesses," Stahrl W. Edmunds provides guidance based on cash flow, profits, and capital productivity of various size companies in a number of industries.

Finally, business owners seeking to get more managerial benefits from their accounting statements, but who don't feel their companies need a full accounting audit, have a new choice. Jerry L. Arnold and Michael A. Diamond describe its benefits and drawbacks in "The Accounting Review: A Happy Compromise."

16

A Small Business Is Not a Little Big Business

JOHN A. WELSH and JERRY F. WHITE

How is managing a small business different from operating a big corporation? The authors of this article take on that question directly by arguing that, in the area of financial management at least, small business owners and managers must have a different outlook and must apply different principles than those ordinarily used by big companies. The authors examine such fundamental financial concepts as cash flow, break-even analysis, return on investment, and debt–equity ratio to demonstrate important differences in the financial management of small businesses and big businesses.

A traditional assumption among managers has been that small businesses should use essentially the same management principles as big businesses, only on a smaller scale. Underlying that assumption has been the notion that small companies are much like big companies, except that small businesses have lower sales, smaller assets, and fewer employees.

We would argue, though, that the very size of small businesses creates a special condition—which can be referred to as *resource poverty*—that distinguishes them from their larger counterparts and requires some very different management approaches.

Resource poverty results because of various conditions unique to smaller companies. For one thing, small businesses tend to be clustered in highly fragmented industries—wholesaling, retailing, services, job-shop manufacturing—that have many competitors which are prone to price-cutting as a way to build revenues. No matter that excessive price-cutting quickly destroys profits.

Also, the owner-manager's salary in a small business represents a much larger fraction of revenues than in a big company, often such a large fraction that little is left over to pay additional managers or to reward investors. Similarly, small businesses cannot usually afford to pay for the kind of accounting and bookkeeping services they need, nor can new employees be adequately tested and trained in advance.

In addition, external forces tend to have more impact on small businesses than on large businesses. Changes in government regulations, tax laws, and labor and interest rates usually affect a greater percentage of expenses for small businesses than they do for large corporations.

Such limitations mean that small businesses can seldom survive mistakes or misjudgments. For instance, a production unit of a New York Stock Exchange listed company not long ago installed an additional steam generating plant at a cost of $3 million. On the first day of operation, the Environmental Protection Agency closed the new generator plant because of a fundamental design fault. It took several months and a million dollars to correct the flaw, but production continued unabated and local management was not even scolded. Few small businesses could survive such an error.

What can small businesses do to overcome the problems posed by resource poverty? Certainly no magical solutions exist. But we believe there are some special financial management tools available to small companies that can enable them to make the most efficient and practical use of their meager resources.

Predicting Cash Flow

Small business owner-managers usually agree quite readily that growth requires investment. To them, however, the need for cash seems only temporary. Profitable growth will produce greater profits and hence, they conclude, more money. Nearly every owner-manager hears at some point the financial principle that cash flow equals net profit plus depreciation and other noncash expenses. Owner-managers of many fast-growing companies, however, cannot avoid the gnawing feeling that somehow the principle doesn't apply to them.

The following example may help explain the cash flow problem confronting many small companies. Exhibit 1 forecasts the operations of Intercity Assembly Company, Inc. for the first seven months of the coming fiscal year. The company's owner-manager, Mr. Smith, is quite confident he can attain the forecasted sales. The cost of materials for a unit, whatever it may be, is a dollar, including freight. They are delivered in lots of 5,000 units. Labor costs to assemble each unit average 10 cents, and the work force is fully employed at that task. Mr. Smith does not hesitate to send the workers home when they have produced sufficient units to meet orders.

The company is on good terms with its suppliers. It purchases materials, advertising, brochures, and other general and administrative services

Exhibit 1. Intercity Assembly Company, Inc. Pro Forma Income Statement

		Month 1	2	3	4	5	6	7
Revenue	Units sold	40,000	42,000	44,000	47,000	50,000	53,000	55,000
	Sales	$80,000	$84,000	$88,000	$94,000	$100,000	$106,000	$110,000
Expense	Direct materials	40,000	42,000	44,000	47,000	50,000	53,000	55,000
	Direct labor	4,000	4,200	4,400	4,700	5,000	5,300	5,500
	Overhead	4,000	4,000	4,000	4,000	4,000	4,000	4,000
	Cost of goods sold	48,000	50,200	52,400	55,700	59,000	62,300	64,500
	Gross profit	32,000	33,800	35,600	38,300	41,000	43,700	45,500
General and administrative	Salaries	6,900	7,450	7,500	8,350	8,350	9,000	9,000
	Rent	2,000	2,000	2,000	2,000	2,000	2,000	2,000
	Insurance	500	500	500	500	500	500	500
	Depreciation	170	170	170	170	170	170	170
	Other general and administrative	3,000	4,100	4,550	5,500	6,600	7,050	7,850
Marketing	Advertising	9,750	9,800	10,200	11,000	11,600	12,500	13,000
	Brochures	450	450	450	450	450	450	450
	Total expense	70,770	74,670	77,770	83,670	88,670	93,970	97,470
	Taxable income	9,230	9,330	10,230	10,330	11,330	12,030	12,530
Income taxes		2,769	2,799	3,069	3,099	3,399	3,609	3,759
	Net profit	$ 6,461	$ 6,531	$ 7,161	$ 7,231	$ 7,931	$ 8,421	$ 8,771

on net 30-day terms. It buys brochures, however, in quantity, receiving a one-year supply in Month 1.

The company makes income tax deposits in the month following each quarter in an amount equal to the accrued liability for that quarter. It uses an estimated average income tax rate of 30%, based on a rough forecast of the coming year's earnings.

The "overhead" item contains, among other things, the depreciation on expensive production equipment. The company will install this new equipment in Month 1 at a cost of $180,000. It depreciates the equipment at $2,700 per month by the straight-line method. The company's investors guarantee payment for the equipment and will provide most of the cash through a purchase of $175,000 worth of common stock in Month 2.

Customers of Intercity are quite reliable in their payment patterns. In the past, units shipped in any month were promptly paid for 45 days after the end of the month, plus or minus a few days. Intercity management confidently began the seven-month period knowing that it had reliable customers and strong, sympathetic investors to buy the new equipment. The minimal bank balance of $1,100 at the beginning of Month 1 was not a concern in view of the anticipated growth in profits.

Intercity's owner-manager realizes that it is important to know how the company's bank balance is doing. Management thus prepared an additional forecast showing when checks would have to be written and when deposits could be expected (see Exhibit 2). To determine when checks were to become due to the materials supplier, and in what amount, the company prepared a small subsidiary forecast, shown in Exhibit 3).

The Cash Flow Illusion

During the seven months, the bank balances caused dismay at Intercity. In only one month of the seven was there a positive bank balance. Cash flow was negative in four out of the seven months. Mr. Smith then decided to prepare a table comparing cash flow as it should have been, according to cash flow theory, and as it will appear at the bank. The comparison is shown in Exhibit 4. It only confirmed the owner-manager's gnawing feeling of doubts about the value of the theory.

Where did the money go? The owner-manager did not get it. The banker did not get it, as the company shows no loans. It is in the boxes in the warehouse and in little pieces of paper in the front office. At the end of Month 7, there are $14,000 worth of boxes in the warehouse filled with the company's product that weren't there at the beginning of Month 1. And in the front office, there is $65,000 in outstanding invoices, not cash. The problem is that not all of the cash has flowed yet. When the boxes and the little pieces of paper are converted to cash, it will flow.

The cash consumed by growth is even greater than depicted by Exhibit 2. The materials supplier, the advertising agent, and the other vendors of

Exhibit 2. Intercity Assembly Company, Inc. Pro Forma Statement of Receipts and Disbursements

		Month 1	2	3	4	5	6	7
Receipts	Sales	$74,000[a]	$ 77,000[a]	$80,000	$84,000	$88,000	$94,000	$100,000
	Common stock	—	175,000	—	—	—	—	—
	Total receipts	**74,000**	**252,000**	**80,000**	**84,000**	**88,000**	**94,000**	**100,000**
Disbursements								
	Direct materials	40,000[a]	40,000	45,000	45,000	50,000	55,000	55,000
	Direct labor	4,000	4,200	4,400	4,700	5,000	5,300	5,500
	Overhead	1,300	1,300	1,300	1,300	1,300	1,300	1,300
	Manufacturing equipment	—	180,000	—	—	—	—	—
	Salaries	6,900	7,450	7,500	8,350	8,350	9,000	9,000
	Rent	2,000	2,000	2,000	2,000	2,000	2,000	2,000
	Insurance	6,000	—	—	—	—	—	—
	Office equipment	—	3,000	—	—	—	—	—
	Other general and administrative	2,800[a]	3,000	4,100	4,550	5,500	6,600	7,050
	Advertising	9,000[a]	9,750	9,800	10,200	11,000	11,600	12,500
	Brochures	—	5,400	—	—	—	—	—
	Taxes	11,000[a]	—	—	8,637	—	—	10,107
	Total disbursed	**83,000**	**256,100**	**74,100**	**84,737**	**83,150**	**90,800**	**102,457**
Total cash flow		(9,000)	(4,100)	5,900	(737)	4,850	3,200	(2,457)
Beginning balance		1,100	(7,900)	(12,000)	(6,100)	(6,837)	(1,987)	1,213
Ending balance		$(7,900)	$(12,000)	$(6,100)	$(6,837)	$(1,987)	$ 1,213	$ (1,244)

[a]From operations during prior periods.

153

Exhibit 3. Materials Inventory Schedule (Calculated in Units) and Purchases Overview

	Month 1	2	3	4	5	6	7
Beginning inventory	43,500	43,500	46,500	47,500	50,500	55,500	57,500
− Shipments (out)	40,000	42,000	44,000	47,000	50,000	53,000	55,000
+ Purchases (received)	40,000	45,000	45,000	50,000	55,000	55,000	55,000
Ending inventory	43,500	46,500	47,500	50,500	55,500	57,500	57,500
Purchases overview							
Value of purchases (received)	$40,000	$45,000	$45,000	$50,000	$55,000	$55,000	$55,000
Cash disbursements (net 30)	$40,000[a]	$40,000	$45,000	$45,000	$50,000	$55,000	$55,000

[a]From a transaction in a prior period.

154

Exhibit 4.   Comparison of Estimated Cash Flow

Month	Net profit (from income statement)	Total depreciation (from income statement)	Estimated cash flow (net profit and depreciation)	Cash flow (from receipts and disbursements statement)
1	$6,461	$(2,700 + 170)	$ 9,331	$(9,000)
2	6,531	(2,700 + 170)	9,401	(4,100)
3	7,161	(2,700 + 170)	10,031	5,900
4	7,231	(2,700 + 170)	10,101	(737)
5	7,931	(2,700 + 170)	10,801	4,850
6	8,421	(2,700 + 170)	11,291	3,200
7	8,771	(2,700 + 170)	11,641	(2,457)
Cumulative			$72,597	$(2,344)

general and administrative services have increased their credit lines extended to the company by $24,050. Had they not done so, the bank balance at the end of Month 7 would have been overdrawn by $25,294 and the cash flow for the seven months would have been a negative $26,394 (ending balance minus beginning balance).

Suppose the investors purchase an additional $25,000 in common stock of the company. That would cover the negative cash flow for a while. But if whatever is happening in Intercity continues as it has been, will the company consume that additional $25,000? Of course it will, because growth requires cash. Adequate capitalization is momentary and fleeting. Exhibit 5 shows the normal relationships among sales, profits, and cash flow for a growing business.

Big and Small Company Differences

In big businesses the rates of change and annual growth are normally small; thus their financial statements describe a system in approximate equilibrium. The principle that cash flow equals net profit plus depreciation and amortization is correct for a system in perfect equilibrium. Small differences from equilibrium do not significantly distort the underlying principle.

Big business analysts usually apply the principle to long time periods. Short-term variances during the year are small compared to the overall result. A big company's short-term borrowing capacity can readily accommodate those variances.

Small businesses are seldom in equilibrium, or even near it. Even with uniform growth and earnings, Intercity Assembly Company's bank account

Exhibit 5.   The Relationships Among Sales, Profits, and Cash Flow for a Growing Business Under Normal Conditions

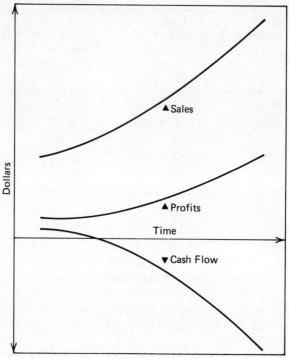

is subject to very significant short-term fluctuations compared with the over-all cash flow. Despite the excellent performance displayed in Exhibit 1 and the good quality accounts receivable, the banker will surely be pointing out that Intercity lacks an extensive track record. The owner-manager's sig-nature will have to be affixed to any short-term loans against either the receivables or the equipment.

Small businesses are also frequently subject to seasonal variations in sales, which lead to successive periods of rapid growth and contraction. During seasonal periods of high sales, small businesses consume cash, as Intercity did. During the off-season, they often find that cash flows into the bank since it is not consumed by growth. Unfortunately, many owner-man-agers see this cash build-up as spendable. All too often a new car or a vacation trip consumes this war chest, which will be sorely needed for the next period of high sales.

How can owner-managers cope with their cash flow problems? A small business must respond to large, often severe, short-term fluctuations in every aspect of the business. Cash in the bank is the foremost concern of the owner-manager. One of the most understandable ways to monitor cash needs and cash availability, from that person's perspective, is to show the future operations of the business in a simultaneous portrayal of the income statement and the statement of receipts and disbursements over successive short time intervals for the coming 6 to 12 months. (See Exhibits 1 and 2). A small business should update this forecast at the end of each time period, at least monthly.

The differences between cash and profit over short periods result from the many different cycles of payments. Salaries and wages may be paid weekly, biweekly, monthly, and semimonthly. Some tax deposits are made monthly, some quarterly. Only a few expenses fall into the uniform monthly cycle portrayed by the income statement.

The accrual presentation of the income statement was devised to resolve the problems created by the various cycles in the flow of cash. By ignoring when cash actually flows, the accrual method provides a more orderly picture of profit. Profit, by the accrual calculation, is a mathematical concept. You can't get a bagful of profit. Cash, as owner-managers perceive it, is tangible. For the small business manager, who must worry about this week's payroll, profit is not cash, and profit plus depreciation is not the available cash flow.

The Elusive Break-Even Point

A classical method for determining the sales needed to support a new business, a new product, a new sales outlet, or a new plant is break-even analysis. Conceptually it is easy to grasp. Sales rise in proportion to the number of units shipped or services performed. Expenses are of two kinds, fixed and variable.

The fixed expenses—like rent and the boss's salary–are, of course, those incurred whether there are sales or not. And variable expenses are the labor, materials, and other outlays connected with the product or service. They are very nearly in direct proportion to the units shipped. The sum of the fixed and variable expenses is the total expenses.

This information may be plotted on coordinates, with dollars on the vertical axis and the units shipped per accounting period (usually per month) on the horizontal axis. The result is two straight lines rising to the right with different slopes. Their intersection defines the necessary number of units shipped per accounting period to make the revenue equal the expenses.

We observed this break-even analysis in action. The first sales in a new business came in March, nine months after the business was founded. Then sales grew from $3,000 in April to $20,000 in September. Management calculated that by maintaining spartan facilities and a pittance in salaries it could establish $3,000 per month as the break-even level of sales. But the financial statement for April, received in mid-May, indicated a substantial loss.

The manager and a member of the founding team decided to determine the real break-even point. With quick strokes and a little calculation, they found that the fixed and variable expenses required $9,000 in sales. Then, in June, the company generated $9,000 worth of sales, with much work and even more luck.

During the first half of July, management waited confidently for the financial report describing June. When it arrived, the manager was astonished to discover that it showed a substantial loss. Apparently the break-even point had moved. By quickly changing the graph to include the previously nonexistent new expenses on the income statement, the manager determined that the break-even point was now $15,000.

Because the company had the good fortune to be selling a superior product against a weak competitor in a growing market, its sales for August exceeded $15,000. This time, management anxiously awaited the mid-September financial report.

Once again, the manager was disappointed: the company was still operating at a loss. The break-even point had grown to $18,000. Not until mid-October did the company learn that it had achieved break-even in September with sales of $20,000.

Behind the Problem

A subsequent examination of the detailed monthly income statement revealed the difficulty. The so-called fixed expenses were anything but fixed; they grew in a stair-step pattern. The variable expenses grew with the sales, but not in the smooth proportionality of the break-even graph. And sales did not follow a straight line, growing from zero in direct proportion to the units shipped.

The company achieved rapid sales growth in large part by offering discounts, making contract deals, providing bonuses, and supplying potential customers with impressive quantities of free samples. The actual plot of fixed and total expenses, along with sales, is characterized on the graph in Exhibit 6. It has multiple break-even points.

During the initial growth of this company, the production facility operated at capacity and the direct expense per unit held fairly steady. The front-office expense held constant except for the several additional people needed to process orders and issue invoices. The biggest growth occurred in expenses for warehousing and materials handling. For instance, quantities of corrugated boxes preprinted with the company logo occupied a surprisingly large space.

How does break-even analysis differ in big businesses? For one thing, in a big business, the additional break-even operation is usually small compared with the size of the whole business. When a big business starts a new project, it can draw on the services of planners, designers, and analysts with access to historical data on indirect expenses. When launched, the new project may be sized for ongoing operations well beyond the break-even.

Exhibit 6.   Break-Even Graph for a New or Small Business

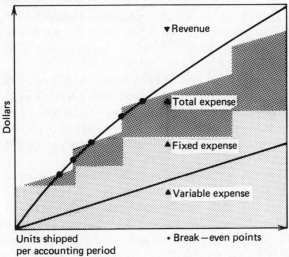

Because owner-managers of small businesses have few, if any, staff people to prepare plans and analyses, decisions to launch new projects are typically based more on hunch, necessity, or desire than on cold and extensive analysis. The company probably has little experience on which to draw for predictions of indirect expenses. Even if it does have experience, data are likely to be scarce.

Getting More from Break-Even Analysis

Small businesses seldom have large and stable operations from which to launch a new endeavor. Typically, financial troubles at the new operation threaten the existence of the basic business.

A break-even graph plotted on broad assumptions about fixed and variable expenses can be misleading. The accuracy of the break-even analysis depends on detailed and conservative planning.

Planning for growth by small businesses is often superficial. That the small business can afford little more is cold comfort when a new endeavor begins to go awry.

Owner-managers embarking on a new project or product can benefit from visualizing the future operations in great detail. They can portray operations in the income statement format of Exhibits 1 and 2, changing the numbers to reflect a variety of contingencies and deciding how to handle these various situations in advance.

The ROI Strategy Trap

A popular business premise is that the primary objective of management is to maximize the return on invested capital to the benefit of the owners. This seems a reasonable premise for a small business, since the owner-manager is one of the owner-beneficiaries.

Return on investment can be defined in a variety of ways. Most often, of course, ROI is expressed as a fraction with earnings as the numerator. The denominator varies according to what is considered to be the investment. While additional investment is hard to obtain and existing investment is hard to change, the numerator is subject to the manager's control. To increase ROI, you increase profits.

Exhibit 7 portrays four months in the life of a thriving small business. Sales, at $2.00 per unit, are growing, and pretax profits are a healthy 10% of sales. Labor expense is 40 cents per unit. The owner-manager has held the cost of materials to 80 cents per unit by taking advantage of a quantity price break for purchasing units in lots of 15,000 and for payment in the month the materials are received. It is the manager's policy to have enough on hand at the end of the month to take care of next month's anticipated sales.

Exhibit 8 shows what can be expected to happen at the bank. Balances are growing nicely, although an income tax deposit of more than $5,000— to accommodate the 30% tax rate—will reduce them somewhat. The materials purchasing schedule in Exhibit 9 is needed to determine the disbursements for materials.

The owner-manager concluded that the numerator of the ROI ratio could be improved by raising sales. It might be hard to increase cash sales, but if the product were offered on credit, sales could rise dramatically. The manager decided to change the forecast to reflect a best guess of what would happen if terms of net 30 days were offered. That forecast saw monthly sales increasing by an additional 4,000 units each month.

The revised forecast income statement is shown in Exhibit 10. Profit improved dramatically. The manager then changed Exhibits 8 and 9 to reflect this new performance. At the bank, things did not look very comfortable. The company forecasted negative cash flow and overdrafts in three of the four months, as shown in Exhibit 11. A quarterly income tax deposit of more than $7,000 at the 30% tax rate will make the overdrafts even worse.

The materials supplier offered what appeared to be a way out of this dilemma. The next quantity price break for purchase in multiples of 40,000 was an additional 10%. Since materials were the largest item of expense, this reduction would improve the operating results; instead of paying 80 cents per unit, the company would pay only 72 cents.

The owner-manager revised the forecast one more time. The results of the three forecasts are compared in Exhibit 12. Each move to improve ROI resulted in trading liquidity for profit. Thus, additional financing through debt or equity or a combination of the two was required.

Exhibit 7. Forecast Income Statement (in thousands)

		Month 1	2	3	4
Units shipped		20	22	24	26
Revenues	Sales (cash)	$40	$44	$48	$52
	Sales (credit)	—	—	—	—
	Total revenues	**40**	**44**	**48**	**52**
Expenses	Direct materials	16.0	17.6	19.2	20.8
	Direct labor	8.0	8.8	9.6	10.4
	Overhead, general and administrative, and marketing	Paid current 7.0	7.7	8.4	9.1
		Paid net 30 days 5.0	5.5	6.0	6.5
	Total expenses	**36.0**	**39.6**	**43.2**	**46.8**
Profit before income tax		4.0	4.4	4.8	5.2
	Cumulative profit	**$ 4.0**	**$ 8.4**	**$13.2**	**$18.4**

Exhibit 8. Forecast Receipts and Disbursements (in thousands)

		Month 1	2	3	4
Receipts	Sales (cash)	$40	$44	$48	$52
	Sales (credit)	—	—	—	—
	Total receipts	**40**	**44**	**48**	**52**
Disbursements	Direct materials	12.0	24.0	24.0	12.0
	Direct labor Paid current	8.0	8.8	9.6	10.4
	Overhead, general and administrative, and marketing	7.0	7.7	8.4	9.1
	Paid net 30 days	4.5^a	5.0	5.5	6.0
	Total disbursed	**31.5**	**45.5**	**47.5**	**37.5**
Cash flow		**8.5**	**(1.5)**	**0.5**	**14.5**
Beginning cash balance		5.0	13.5	12.0	12.5
Ending cash balance		$13.5	$12.0	$12.5	$27.0

^{a}From transactions in a prior period.

Exhibit 9. Materials Purchasing Schedule (in thousands)

	Month 1	2	3	4
Beginning inventory	30	25	33	39
Units shipped	20	22	24	26
Units received	15	30	30	15
Ending inventory	25	33	39	28
Disbursements for units received	$12	$24	$24	$12

Liquidity, Liquidity . . .

A small business can survive a surprisingly long time without a profit. It fails on the day it can't meet a critical payment. In a small company, the cash flow is more important than the magnitude of the profit or the ROI. Liquidity is a matter of life or death for the small business.

Owner-managers who are aware of the profit and cash flow relationships expressed in Exhibits 7 through 12 will recognize that the priority is to maintain liquidity. There must, of course, be some profit, but the efficiency with which profit is produced—the ROI—is secondary. To grow you must survive.

When it comes to ready access to external financing, big businesses have it and small businesses don't. Borrowing negotiations are very personal. The lender looks to the owner-manager for repayment and recalls past experience with small borrowers. Many commercial loan officers have observed that a client had record sales during the month that the company folded.

Businesses have a hierarchy of needs that are related to their sizes and their resources. At the lowest level, management is occupied with making a sale and producing the required product or service. As these events occur, the next needs arise—to generate profit and cash flow. Once these are accomplished with some regularity, management can devote time and energy to the next need, which is to improve the efficiency with which profit is generated. In most small businesses the manager is confined to the middle tier in this hierarchy.

The Debt—Equity Impasse

Lenders usually have a list of criteria for identifying good prospective clients. One of the criteria high on their list is a low debt-equity ratio. Typically, lenders want the total debt-equity ratio to be no more than 2 after the proceeds of the loan are incorporated into the balance sheet. Most successful big businesses have debt-equity ratios of 2 or less.

Exhibit 10. Forecast Income Statement with Addition of Credit Sales (in thousands)

		Month 1	2	3	4
Units shipped		20	26	32	38
Revenues	Sales (cash)	$40	$44	$48	$52
	Sales (credit)	—	8	16	24
	Total revenues	**40**	**52**	**64**	**76**
Expenses	Direct materials	16.0	20.8	25.6	30.4
	Direct labor	8.0	10.4	12.8	15.2
	Overhead, general and administrative, and marketing	7.0	9.4	11.8	14.2
	Paid current				
	Paid net 30 days	5.0	6.0	7.0	8.5
	Total expenses	**36.0**	**46.6**	**57.2**	**68.3**
Profit before income tax		**4.0**	**5.4**	**6.8**	**7.7**
	Cumulative profit	**$ 4.0**	**$ 9.4**	**$16.2**	**$23.9**

Exhibit 11. Forecast Receipts and Disbursements with Addition of Credit Sales (in thousands)

		Month 1	2	3	4
Receipts	Sales (cash)	$40	$44	$48	$52
	Sales (credit)	—	—	8	16
	Total receipts	**40**	**44**	**56**	**68**
Disbursements	Direct materials	24.0	24.0	24.0	36.0
	Direct labor	8.0	10.4	12.8	15.2
	Overhead, general and administrative, and marketing	7.0	9.4	11.8	14.2
	Paid current				
	Paid net 30 days	4.5[a]	5.0	6.0	7.0
	Total disbursed	**43.5**	**48.8**	**54.6**	**72.4**
Cash flow		(3.5)	(4.8)	1.4	(4.4)
Beginning cash balance		5.0	1.5	(3.3)	(1.9)
Ending cash balance		$1.5	$(3.3)	$(1.9)	$(6.3)

[a]From transactions in a prior period.

Exhibit 12.   Forecast Operating Results (in thousands)

| | Ending cash balance | | | | |
	Month 1	2	3	4	Total profit
Continue present operations	$13.5	$12.0	$12.5	$27.0	$18.4
With addition of credit sales	1.5	(3.3)	(1.9)	(6.3)	23.9
With credit sales and quantity purchasing	$ (3.3)	$(12.9)	$(16.3)	$(13.5)	$33.2

When the stockholder's equity, or net worth, is negative, the lender cannot form a debt–equity ratio. When the net worth is only a little more than zero, the ratio becomes incredibly large. One small business we know of turned the corner with sales of about $1 million per year, excellent profits, and net worth of about $5,000; it needed $300,000 to support the growth in hand. The banker calculated the debt–equity ratio at 60, not counting the short-term debt the company already had. Debt financing was out of the question.

This phenomenon occurs at some point in the lives of almost all small businesses. It is quite often a predictable phase on the road to success. Blind application of the debt–equity ratio criteria to a business in that phase can, and often does, threaten its survival.

The small business that survives start-up losses may have excellent capacity to service an additional debt burden. But the business must generate sales and earnings for a considerable period of time before its net equity on the balance sheet approaches a reasonable sum acceptable to most bankers and investors. It has to earn back the start-up losses.

Acquiring additional equity when the company is in this phase of growth is extremely difficult. The original investors have watched their holdings dwindle from the losses of the start-up period. Now they want their capital returned before allowing other investors to reap the benefits. Also, original investors have often paid steep prices for their ownership. The offering price to new investors will likely be lower since it must be based on the current financial statements.

It is during this phase that the original stockholders often develop investor fatigue. They have heard the glowing promises for too long. They want their money back with a reasonable return. The original investors may even act in ways that are detrimental to their stock; they have no patience left just at the time when patience is the only thing they need to see their investment objectives fulfilled.

Improving the Debt–Equity Ratio

Owner-managers can better their debt–equity ratio. Earnings help most, but achieving earnings growth takes time. Since improved earnings from sales growth consumes cash, the wisest course may be to increase the earnings by increasing the profit margin. This can be accomplished by constraining expenses, improving productivity, or increasing prices.

A company can constrain its growth rate by increasing prices or tightening sales terms. Increasing prices is fine, if the market will stand for it. Improving the terms of sale—such as by moving from net 30 to net 10 days—improves cash flow.

The denominator of the ratio can sometimes be improved by creatively rearranging liabilities. From a relative of the owner-manager, one company borrowed $25,000 on a one-year note with an annual rollover provision. The company's executive changed the loan to a personal obligation and wrote a new note with the company. Then, with the consent of the directors, he accepted common stock in payment of the company's obligation. This move reduced the company's debt by $25,000 and increased the equity by an equal amount, and had a dramatic effect on the debt–equity ratio.

In Conclusion

Owner-management of a small business is a distinct discipline characterized by severe constraints on financial resources, a lack of trained personnel, and a short-range management perspective imposed by a volatile competitive environment. Liquidity must be a prime objective. The analytical models applicable to big business are of limited use in this arena. Typically, they assume steady-state conditions subject to minor changes.

Most small companies seem to do best with conservative growth rates. The small business cannot afford much professional service. The owner-manager needs to have the broad thinking of a generalist and be able to tolerate disorder, endure switching from role to role, and stick to fundamentals. In big business management, the direction appears to be toward ever-increasing sophistication. For owner-managers, the direction must be just the opposite, back to basics.

17
Managing Financial Statements
Image and Effect

JAMES McNEILL STANCILL

It's tempting for small business owners and managers to leave to their accountants the full responsibility for composing financial statements. Such a practice may be risky, however, because financial statements can often be presented in more than one correct and legal way. Like so many other aspects of business operations, financial statements can be improved by appropriate management techniques. The images and impressions conveyed by financial statements can, of course, affect the attitudes and decisions of important outsiders, particularly lenders. The author describes some of the more common variations for presenting financial statements. He then advises small business managers to assist their accountants in putting together statements that work for their companies' short-term and long-term interests. This article's editor adds some concluding remarks.

The president of a growing young company that provides helicopter transportation was very upset and confused. He was running up against a brick wall in his attempts to obtain financing from banks, finance companies, and even the Small Business Administration. What made the loan rejections so difficult to comprehend was that the president thought his company was making money.

I met this company president, whom I'll call Frank, right after one of his rejections, and it didn't take me long to understand the reason for his difficulties. Nor would it have taken anyone with rudimentary understanding of financial statements long: his balance sheet showed a negative net worth.

Author's Note: For their helpful comments, I wish to thank William Smith and Jerry Arnold, both of the University of Southern California, and Jane Jalenko of Peat, Marwick, Mitchell & Co.

When I asked Frank about the accountant who prepared his company's financial statements, he had only complimentary things to say. Key investors in the company had recommended the accountant because, as Frank told me, "He's a really good tax accountant."

I then sent Frank to another CPA, who immediately discovered how the company could seem to be making money and yet still show a negative net worth. It turned out that the company's accountant was "expensing"— that is, writing off in one year—the entire cost of the major overhauls the company did on its helicopters. This second accountant suggested a simple expedient: Frank could capitalize this substantial expense and charge off the capitalized amount as the helicopters were used. This would produce an operating profit rather than a loss.

The new CPA redid the financial statements for the previous three years, and almost magically the retained earnings account turned positive. Even though this developing company became only marginally attractive, lenders would at least give it consideration.

How could a thoroughly experienced accounting firm have let such a situation develop in the first place? Why weren't *two* financial statements prepared—one for tax purposes and one for bankers, creditors, and stockholders?

One possible reason is that the company president never asked for a separate set of statements showing the capitalization election. In fact, he did not know that he *could* elect to capitalize this major overhaul expense.

(For further consideration of the propriety of two financial statements, see the Appendix.)

Misusing Accountants

The point is that small company managers are too inclined to delegate to outside accountants every decision about their companies' financial statements. Indeed, it is most unfair to suppose that accountants can produce— without management's advice and counsel—the perfect statement for a company. Instead, I contend, top managers of growing small companies must work with their independent accountants in preparing company financial statements to ensure that the right message is being conveyed.

If it sounds as if I am advocating playing around with companies' statements, I am not. I'm not even talking about what is sometimes referred to as "creative accounting." What I am saying is that top management has a responsibility to make sure that all legitimate accounting elections are at least considered before financial statements are struck. I hasten to emphasize the word *legitimate*, for I have never condoned any practice that is not in accordance with generally accepted accounting principles.

Accountants are the experts; but for decisions affecting the overall financial appearance of small companies, management should make the basic decisions once accountants have explained the options. What this means is that management must stay abreast of the more salient accounting principles, the statements of the Financial Accounting Standards Board (FASB) and other standard-setting bodies. It does not mean that corporate presidents of developing companies should study advanced accounting. Leave the details to the accountants. But the more top management knows the better; it has to be able to ask the right questions.

Even if management does not know whether such accounting options as expensing versus capitalizing are available, it is important for management to explain what it would most like to see in its statements—regardless of whether it's possible.

Managing the Income Statement

Managing an income statement really means managing a company's income. This rather obvious fact seems to elude some managers. Specifically, it involves a business's pattern of earnings. An earnings record that fluctuates radically is not as impressive to outsiders as one that shows more consistency and less volatility.

Currently there is a rather strong tendency in the accounting profession to let the chips fall where they may with respect to a company's earnings. The idea behind this thinking is that a company's management should not be allowed to "manage" earnings—in other words, that the facts alone will determine earnings. In short, this thinking advocates a narrowing of the alternatives available to management. Whatever the merits of such a philosophy, the application seems to be more clearly suitable to large corporations. The circumstances attendant to the developing venture are such that even small changes might materially affect net income or loss.

Management's Options

What, then, are the accounting elections that management of a developing business can make? Though certainly not complete the following are some of the key options.

Sales

To many managers sales recognition is the least complicated item on the income statement. But is it? Most businesses record a sale when an invoice is completed and goods are shipped to the customer. (Here *billings* would by synonymous with *sales*.)

But suppose the company makes or sells something that takes a while to deliver or install—a conveyer system or a computer software program, say. When is the sale recorded? Either of two elections could be made: the *completed-contract* method or the *percentage-of-completion* method.

With the first method, no sale is recorded on the income statement until the entire job is completed—regardless of how much money has been received in the form of progress payments. In fact, progress payments are recorded on the balance sheet as a current liability. Offsetting this is a build-up in "work in progress" under current assets. (Together these two items can produce a rather strange-looking balance sheet, especially if one is not aware of this accounting method for recording sales.) The advantage—if in fact it is an advantage—of this method is that it results in deferring taxes to a later period, perhaps next year. Thus, the business has use of money that would otherwise be used to pay for taxes, and the effective tax is somewhat less.

A business might also elect to use the completed-contract method for tax purposes and the percentage-of-completion method for published statement purposes. In this way, published profits tend to be increased in the short run. Conversely, a business might want to defer profits and thus use the completed-contract method for both financial statement and tax-reporting purposes.

For businesses selling their products or services on an installment basis, such as a franchise operation where all the money is received up front and service follows for a period of years, a "sale" might refer to the total contract amount instead of revenue over time. But, with the exception of retail land sales, this method is looked on so disdainfully today that it is improbable a business would use it. It dramatically overstates earnings and therefore endangers the credibility of a company's total statement.

Cost of Goods Sold

Three principal items comprise the cost of goods sold for a manufacturer: labor, cost of materials, and the so-called factory overhead (usually rent or depreciation of a building, or other fixed costs not directly traceable to the production of specific units). Cost of materials has the most accounting options.

Much has been written about FIFO versus LIFO methods of valuing inventory. In periods of rising prices, the FIFO (first-in, first-out) method tends to overstate gross profit relative to what would result if the LIFO (last-in, first-out) method were used. But while FIFO might result in a larger amount of taxes being paid, it also results in a higher net income, which goes to build up a company's retained earnings account on its balance sheet. The number for retained earnings is extremely important to the developing venture's appearance to lenders and investors.

The decision between LIFO and FIFO therefore involves a trade-off between paying more (or less) taxes versus increasing (or not increasing as much) the company's equity. For a business with pretty much level sales, the amount of equity already on its statement might be quite sufficient for its needs. In this case, minimizing taxes would be stressed. But for growth-oriented businesses that may need to borrow money, the amount of equity becomes quite important; in fact, it is a limiting factor on growth.

Research and Development Expense

The widely publicized accounting rule FASB Statement Number 2 prohibits capitalizing R & D expense, right? Well, several years ago a computer software company needed some additional equity on its balance sheet and turned its attention to the treatment of development of the software—which was the basis for forming the company.

Management asked its independent accountant if this item could be capitalized—that is, put on the balance sheet and then written off as an expense on the income statement over the next five years or so. "Of course not!" he snapped. Fortunately for this company, the CPA was removed as the company's auditor soon afterward for other, unrelated reasons.

When the new accountant was presented with the same question, his reply was, "Well, at first glance, I don't think so, but let me investigate the matter since it really makes a difference." After considerable research, he came back with the reply, "Yes, there is a provision of FASB 2 such that the company can capitalize this particular item and thus not expense it all at once." (A trade association has since published this information, but it was not readily available at the time.)

The point of this example is simply that elections or exceptions—which *are* publicized—apply to many general accounting rules. Sometimes, only a careful reading of the FASB statement (or prior Accounting Principles Board opinion or the *Accounting Research Bulletin*) enables a proper ruling to be made.

Will the company's independent accountant research important issues sufficiently? Will management ask the question in the first place? Not if the company turns over to the outside accounting firm all decisions regarding statement preparation.

Depreciation Expense

Here you have the option of either accelerated or straight-line depreciation. Many companies take accelerated depreciation on their tax statements and straight-line on their published statements. Although the tax payment is thereby postponed, the published statement recognizes the income sooner.

But these are not the only choices a company has with respect to depreciation. For example, it may be possible to depreciate equipment on a per-unit-produced basis. In this way, a slower (or faster) rate of depreciation might be charged off to current revenue than would otherwise be the case. This variation is possible, even for tax purposes, owing to the wording of a 1954 tax ruling that allows for other "consistent" depreciation methods.

An extremely important reason for using this per-unit-produced method of depreciation is that it converts depreciation expense from a fixed cost to a variable cost. When a venture is just starting or business is extremely slow, minimizing losses (or maximizing profits) can be quite helpful in protecting the venture's equity postion.

Another little-known depreciation option is decelerated depreciation which is simply the reverse of accelerated depreciation. Depending on the type of deceleration used, perhaps only a quarter or a third of the total depreciable amount would be written off in the first half of the depreciable life of the asset.

But while decelerated depreciation is a legitimate method, its use is so rare that it might raise eyebrows and call into question a whole set of financial statements. For this reason I am not advocating general use of decelerated depreciation for published statements. A particular business might elect decelerated depreciation for published statements if it has tax losses or some other reason for wishing to defer tax-deductible expenses.

Prepaid Expense

One of the most common ways of managing income is to exercise control over the treatment of such prepaid items as extraordinary legal expense or incorporation expense. With these items, management has to decide whether it wishes (a) to expense or (b) to capitalize the item and write it off on the income statement over some period of time. Sixty months is allowed for incorporation expense for tax purposes, but some businesses write this expense off over a longer time for published statement purposes.

Managing the Balance Sheet

While the election of various accounting options with regard to the company's income statement will modify its earnings—a dynamic measure of success—the "management" of the balance sheet involves portraying the business in a stop-action sense. While many managers give a lot of thought to their income statements, they may forget the appearance of their balance sheets. This fault could be serious if a company needs external financing; the helicopter service company described at the outset of this article is a good example.

What impression do people get of your business when they look at its balance sheet? What impression are you trying to convey?

Cash on the Balance Sheet

Consider first the treatment of cash on a company's balance sheet as shown in Exhibit 1. What is the first thing one notices about this balance sheet? Only $221 in cash! Here the company has $1.8 million in assets, but only $221 in cash. The impression conveyed is that this company is in a bind.

For statement purposes, the company's accountant lists the checkbook balance on the last day of the statement period for the cash balance—regardless of what the balance was the day before or the day after. What this means is that it behooves the company to check its *book* cash balance before the close of the fiscal period in order to estimate how much cash there will

Exhibit 1. Sample Balance Sheet

Cash	$ 221	Accounts payable	$ 450,655
Accounts receivable	402,695	Accrued taxes	105,750
Inventory	514,250	Due to bank	50,000
Other current assets	55,400		
		Total current liabilities	**$ 606,405**
Total current assets	**$ 972,566**	Long-term debt	**$ 450,000**
		Capital:	
		Common stock	$ 100,000
Plant, property and	$ 850,400	Paid-in surplus	50,000
equipment, net of		Retained earnings	616,561
reserve for depreciatio			
Total assets	**$1,822,966**	**Total liabilities and capital**	**$1,822,966**

be in the company's checkbook balance. If it appears to be too small an amount, then a hold might be placed on the checks to be written, or certain customers could be asked to pay their bills before the end of the statement period.

Another example of a business which might be short on cash is one that is borrowing from a bank with its accounts receivable as collateral. The bank might use what is called a cash collateral account. This means that whenever the company deposits the checks it receives (as payment for accounts receivable or for whatever reason), the bank uses those deposits to reduce the amount of the loan instead of to increase the cash balance. If this is your situation, you would be wise to talk to the company's bank officer and somehow arrange for a sufficient amount of cash to be in the account when the accountant makes his or her check of the company's books.

The petty cash account might also cause a bad impression. Quite frequently, accountants make up the balance sheet and other statements from the trial balance, which uses the company's chart of accounts as the source. Because petty cash usually appears ahead of other accounts, it may be listed ahead of the regular checking accounts. Thus, the company's cash position on the balance sheet might be shown as follows:

Petty cash	$ 14
Cash in central bank	19,413
Cash in savings account	2,500
Total	$21,927

For this company $21,927 might be a reasonable cash balance. But what figure catches the eye first? And what would an observer probably remember if he or she didn't have the statements in hand? True, a trained eye might completely skip over the trivial petty cash amount. But why take a chance?

Why not include petty cash with the general cash account? In fact, listing two, three, or four separate lines for cash might convey an impression of less cash than would just one line ("cash in banks" or "cash and marketable securities").

Reviewing the Basic Ratios

With the exception of cash, the sufficiency of the other balance sheet items is primarily a function of (a) the nature of the business and (b) the application of ratios.

Each industry—manufacturing, service, distribution—has its own characteristics; even within industries there are potentially wide variances in the typical balance sheet. But despite the fact that variation is natural, it behooves a manager to make sure the company looks acceptable not only according to typical ratios for that industry segment but also from an overall point of view.

Robert Morris Associates publishes typical ratios for many different types of companies in many diverse industries. But how do you know if your banker, for example, is using the right set of ratios to evaluate your company? I know of a major bank that once issued ratio guidelines for credit officers to follow which did *not* differentiate industry categories. Such an obvious goof did not go long without comment; but until the error was finally corrected, businesses were being judged by the most generic standards.

What, then, are the most important ratios that managers of developing businesses should worry about, and what can managers do about them? Virtually every analyst or loan officer looks at three balance sheet ratios: the debt–equity ratio, the current ratio, and the quick test.

The Debt–Equity Ratio

Like so many formulas, this ratio suffers from definitional problems. Does the numerator include all debt (current and long term) or just long term? Here it behooves managers to discover what their bankers (and others) use; but usually only long-term debt is included in the numerator.

A debt–equity ratio of 1:1 or less would tend to be viewed favorably for many developing ventures. But 2:1 or even 3:1 might be acceptable depending on other factors, including industry differences. (This discussion excludes real estate companies, in which debt–equity ratios are normally quite high.)

Bankers cannot make loans with complete independence. Each loan application is scrutinized by at least two or three review examiners to see if it appears to be questionable. One of the first things any bank analyst considers is the debt–equity ratio. So even if a banker would like to help a company, his or her hands may be tied by all the conventional ratio tests being applied by colleagues.

What can be done if the venture's debt–equity ratio seems too high? Well, the obvious solution is to decrease the debt and/or increase the equity. Decreasing the debt is certainly easier said than done, but it can be accomplished more often than you might think.

In one instance, a company purchased two major metalworking machines on an installment basis for approximately $500,000 each, paying 20% down with the balance due over five years. Shortly thereafter, the company's industry went into a pronounced slump and the company faced extremely tough times. When business was good, the company's manager didn't care about the debt–equity ratio; the cash was available to service the debt. But when adversity struck and the manager had to have help, the relatively high debt burden meant that no bank would come to his aid.

Finally the equipment manufacturer was contacted and, because a reasonable market still existed for these machines, he agreed to tear up the note for one of the machines and rent it to the company until it could be sold and moved. In one stroke, a material amount of debt was removed from the company's statement, and its bank suddenly became interested in discussing loan requests.

In the past, equipment leasing was a way for some companies to reduce balance-sheet debt. This arrangement was referred to as "off-balance-sheet financing." But FASB 13 now clearly distinguishes between financial and operating leases. Leases that are in effect financial leases must be entered on the balance sheet as a form of debt, with the value of the equipment placed as an asset.

This ruling has received widespread publicity. For many managers it put an end to off-balance-sheet financing. However, FASB 13 does not preclude a company from leasing equipment; instead it says that if the lease is in effect just a financing device, it should be shown as a type of debt.

But the company that needs more equipment yet shies away because it has too much debt on its balance sheet might still acquire the leased equipment and keep it off the balance sheet. The way to do this is to make sure the lease is not a financial lease—in other words, that it *is* an operating lease. The operating lease arrangement may mean that the company does not contract to acquire the equipment at the end of the lease for a bargain price but instead has an option to acquire the equipment. That way it can enjoy the earnings the equipment produces—earnings which would not be realized if the company's management felt its balance sheet couldn't afford more debt.

(FASB 13 provides four criteria that, if met, require the accountant to "capitalize" the lease and put it on the balance sheet. It would be beyond the scope of this article to get into even some of the subtleties of this rather complex accounting opinion; suffice it to say that there are ways of keeping certain leases off the balance sheet. It is incumbent on a manager to ask his or her accountant about a particular case.)

Another approach for reducing debt is to make subordinated debt serve as equity, since many banks and other lenders consider subordinated debt to be the equivalent of equity for purposes of loan analysis. But getting subordinated debt to be considered as equity involves presenting the item on the balance sheet in such a way that it does not get overlooked.

Consider, for instance, the computer software company of my previous example. While preparing its year-end balance sheet, it realized that there was once again a problem. Its equity, althougb growing steadily, wasn't keeping pace with the business's growth. The company needed a larger revolving line of bank credit.

The company's bank thought that a 1:1 debt–equity ratio was appropriate for such a company. Fortunately, some company debt was held by one of the stockholders, and in such circumstances banks usually ask for a subordination agreement from the debt holder-stockholder.

The way the external accountant had struck the draft of the balance sheet, readers of the financial statements had to read the notes to the financial statements to see that the debt was in fact subordinated. That's okay if you can be sure all the notes will be read but what if the loan officer didn't get that far? To solve the problem, the company's accountant inserted on the balance sheet a major subcategory entitled "subordinated long-term debt," under which to list the debt. This debt item immediately preceded the capital section and was obviously subordinated; when it was added to the equity, the total approximately equaled the line of credit requested.

Companies must exercise some caution about attempting to increase equity without the actual sale of stock or the realization of retained earnings. Some approaches are apt to be quite difficult from an accounting viewpoint; some are even disallowed.

Amateurish efforts might include adding some sort of goodwill or other intangible to the asset side of the balance sheet with an increase in stock and capital surplus as the offset. This maneuver depends on state laws; in some of the most populous states it is deemed an illegal consideration for the issuance of stock.

But even if you are able to issue stock for some intangible such as a patent, lenders will typically defeat the move by subtracting the amount of the intangible from the equity section. This subtraction not only hurts the company's debt–equity ratio but also casts suspicion on the entire set of financial statements—a most undesirable event.

Close contact between managers and their accountants can aid in avoiding such snafus, which sometimes irretrievably damage companies' reputations with borrowers.

The Current Ratio

Since the beginning of ratio analysis of financial statements in the late nineteenth century, the current ratio has been used and, I believe, misused for testing the financial health of companies.

Developed during a time when trade creditors predominated as unsecured creditors, the current ratio's purpose is to show the amount of *un-secured* assets a business possesses to pay its creditors. If a business with two dollars of assets for each dollar of liability gets into trouble, its asset value could shrink by half yet it could still pay off its general creditors. The origin of this system (with its magic 2:1 current ratio) is lost to history, but today 2:1 is definitely the rule of thumb for the current ratio.

Besides having some conceptual weaknesses, the current ratio is misleading. If a company's accounts receivable or inventory turnover is slowing down, the current ratio may be increasing even though the operating cash flow is decreasing. But whatever the conceptual and technical deficiencies of the current ratio, the fact remains that it must be watched and managed by developing businesses.

Consider this example: a company that had experienced considerable adversity was in the process of reversing its fortunes. It had trimmed costs and gotten production in line with sales. The business had reduced its long-term debt in part by conversion to a type of preferred stock.

When it came time to do the year-end financial statements, the company's external accountant was asked for a preliminary draft. As he handed it over, the accountant looked pleased; a lot of improvement had been made since the previous year-end statement. The financial manager of the company was chagrined, however. Among other things, the current ratio was only 0.95:1.

Realistically, this ratio represented a major improvement, but from both psychological and technical viewpoints it was unacceptable. The company's bank had a series of tests it applied to statements, tests which placed a high priority on current ratios of 1:1 or better.

The company's ratio was very close to 1:1. Could anything be done—legitimately—to move the ratio up? The company did not have any cash to speak of in its bank acount, so the owner personally borrowed $25,000 from a bank and loaned it to the company on a long-term subordinated note. This move had two advantages. First, it added nothing to current liabilities (the denominator of the current ratio). Second, it decreased the debt–equity ratio by increasing that denominator (or that's how the bank would see it).

Before you conclude that this was some underhanded technique, let it be noted that the entire transaction was completely documented in the notes to the financial statements. However, it is also true that in a rather perfunctory check of the current ratio, the notes to the financial statements are usually incidental.

Next management scrutinized the accounts payable closely. It then approached some of the oldest accounts-payable holders (several suppliers) and asked them to take a one-year note in exchange for a portion of their account payable. Several creditors agreed, perhaps because they wanted to help the company or perhaps because they felt more secure with a formal note. This arrangement removed some debt from the current debt section and replaced it in the long-term section. True, it increased the long-term debt, but the psychological advantage it produced with regard to the current ratio was overwhelmingly more important. The current ratio was now a shade better than 1:1. Admittedly only a *little* bit better than 1:1, but better nevertheless.

A trick, you say? Not really; instead, this example points out once again that management must stay on its toes when it comes to accounting. Arbitrary tests like the current ratio, when applied to a small business, may affect its growth and financial health.

The Quick Ratio

Also known as the "acid test," the quick ratio is thought by some credit managers to be a much better test of a business's financial strength and its ability to pay its suppliers than the current ratio. The ratio's numerator—which is obtained by subtracting the illiquid inventory—includes cash, marketable securities, accounts receivable, and prepaid expenses from the current assets. The denominator, as in the current ratio, is the business's current liabilities. Without going into detail, let me say that the adverse aspects of the current ratio are present here as well. Nevertheless, the quick ratio and variations of it have many adherents.

I remember a talk given by a veteran credit manager to a meeting of a nonfinancial trade association; after extolling the merits of the "acid test," this credit manager said: "If I really want to be tough, I not only take out the inventory, I take out the receivables as well. Then I might limit my line of credit to the amount of cash the company has." And with this statement, the credit manager rested his case.

Well, if a business owner knew that a very important supplier was using such a myopic and illogical test, the owner could adjust the company's year-end financial statement accordingly. Financial statement analysis is a tenuous game at best, and conclusions based on it should be guarded. So we have here yet another reason for managers of developing ventures to pay close attention to their financial statements.

In Conclusion

When a business grows to the point of having specialized functional management, the job of managing financial statements should be delegated to a financial officer. But until that point, it is incumbent upon the company's top management to be aware of the appearance of its balance sheet and income statement. Furthermore, management must see to it that the message the business conveys is in keeping with the overall goals the business has set forth. Management must consider the psychology of financial statements.

To retain an external CPA to produce financial statements that don't include discussion with management is an abdication of management's rights and responsibilities. Before the fiscal period is ended, management should address itself to the question of what income or loss the business will make for the period. Are results in line with the game plan the business has set out for itself? If projected income is above expectations, is this a good time to write off to expense certain items that have been capitalized? Or, conversely, do the projected earnings need a little help? Are there some items that could be capitalized yet still conform to generally accepted accounting principles? Does the balance sheet tell the good story it might tell?

A strong movement is brewing among accounting professionals and the SEC to get away from an acounting system that permits large publicly owned businesses to exercise the options discussed here. Although the merits of such efforts are beyond the scope of this article, it is important to point out that accounting for small developing ventures is so different as to remove it from the same considerations.

What conclusions can small-business people make about their role in accounting matters? First, although managers do not have to be accountants, they should be able to ask probing questions. Second, if the independent accountant is unwilling to discuss the options with managment or is otherwise intractable, get another accountant. Most accountants are perfectly willing to work with management in the final preparation of a company's statement— as long as this means exercising legitimate accounting elections without intending deception. All in all, the more management knows about its own statements, the better managed they will be.

Appendix

The Need for Two Statements

To many managers, the idea of keeping two sets of financial statements— one for the bank, creditors, and stockholders (the "published" statement) and one for tax purposes—seems like cheating.

"Don't you tell the truth to the Internal Revenue Service?" they might ask. Of course, but the rules—if we can call the maze of IRS regulations rules—were made for the purpose of effecting taxation and for politically or economically desirable ends. In some countries of the world, two statements would be tantamount to committing a crime, but this is not the case in the United States or in most Western countries.

For tax purposes, a company's income might be reduced to a minimum, but for published statement purposes, a higher income might well be shown. However, the extent to which taxes can be deferred or reduced varies with individual circumstances.

True, in many businesses it is possible to minimize taxes continually, but is that really desirable? Can you show on your published statement that you are making an appropriate net profit? Failure to adequately build up a company's net worth can result in limitations on its bank borrowing—with all the attendant drawbacks that presents. It might even impede growth.

In short, businesses must consider their objectives. Some businesses seem to have one thought in mind: minimize taxes—regardless of everything else! That's fine if businesses can continually show profits on the published statements without showing profits on the tax statements. But if they can't, isn't it worthwhile to pay some taxes to keep the published statements in good order?

18
Don't Let Inflation Get the Best of You

NEIL C. CHURCHILL

Much has been written and discussed about inflation as it affects the economy and consumers. But what effects does prolonged inflation have on the financial under-pinnings of small companies? How can managers of small companies counteract problems created by inflation and even turn them into opportunities? Mr. Churchill examines eight serious financial problems small companies face during periods of inflation. He notes, for instance, that profits can wind up being overstated when depreciation expenses associated with fixed assets are understated. Similarly, revenues may rise, giving the appearance of steady growth, while unit sales are unchanged. Among the solutions he offers are closely monitoring profit margins and considering interest on working capital in the gross profit calculation. By taking inflation into account in reporting financial results and planning strategy, he suggests, a serious problem can sometimes be turned into an opportunity.

Inflation in the United States and elsewhere has persisted at high enough rates for a long enough period of time to make many of its debilitating effects well known—such as rapidly rising prices and inducement to speculate. But inflation's potentially destructive impact is even more pervasive than many of us realize.

Beyond rising prices and speculation, inflation creates two essential problems for companies of all sizes. First, it distorts the financial yardsticks by which outsiders judge businesses and managers make decisions. Second, it leads to rapidly changing and dislocated financial markets, which create difficulties for companies seeking credit.

While these problems do affect all businesses, they frequently have a more pronounced and damaging effect on small companies. That is partly because small company managers are often in a position of trying to minimize or exaggerate their financial accomplishments, depending on whether they are preparing tax forms or seeking loans. With such important interests in mind, managers are likely to ignore the effects of inflation on financial results. Moreover, because small companies often depend on short-term loans in their financing, they suffer disproportionately from high interest rates caused by tight money policies used to combat inflation.

Inflation distorts financial results in these ways:

1   Overstated gross margins.
2   Overstated operating profits.
3   Overstated returns on investment.
4   Overstated growth rates.
5   Eroded owners' equity capital.

Among the adverse financial dislocations precipitated by long-term inflation are the following:

1   Excessively high interest rates.
2   Working capital requirements that may outstrip available lines of credit.
3   Rapidly rising asset costs.

In this article, I explore financial problems created by inflation and ways to mitigate their impact.

Effect

Gross Margins Overstated

Response

Manage Your Margins

One of the most important things for any company to do in an inflationary period is maintain its gross profit margin. A company cannot remain profitable very long if it sells an item for the customary 40% margin, based on its purchase price (historical cost), and then has to replace the item at a higher cost. Consider a manager who does the following:

Buys a case of item A	for $13.50
Sells the case of item A	for $22.50
Replaces the case of item A	for $15.00

Conventional accounting would show a profit o $9.00 ($22.50 − $13.50) and attainment of the target margin of 40% of sales. But a company does not make an operating profit until the merchandise it sells is replaced. The profit in this example is really only $7.50 ($22.50 − $15.00)—a gross margin of 33⅓%—since only $7.50 is available to cover salaries, pay bills, or finance expansions. To maintain a 40% profit margin, item A in this example would have to be sold for $25.00 a case. This would yield $10.00 profit over the $15.00 replacement cost, and $10.00 ÷ $25.00 is 40%.

LIFO accounting (last in, first out) is a major weapon against capital erosion. Applied to the same example, it generates a profit of $7.50 since the $15.00 replacement cost of the last item purchased is matched against the sales price of $22.50. And when used for tax purposes, LIFO shields the corporation from capital erosion brought about by the taxation of holding gains on inventory as operating profit. Indeed, rising prices and the *Thor Power Tool* decision make adoption of LIFO a matter worth serious consideration for all corporations.[1]

LIFO is not of much use for ongoing decision making, though, because it is calculated only at the end of the fiscal period. What many small companies need is a system in which the replacement cost of each item sold is immediately available for market pricing and profit accounting. Thus, a number of companies have adopted a replacement-cost method termed NIFO (next in, first out).

A NIFO system would insert the $15.00 replacement cost into the records (along with the $13.50 historical cost) and, if a 40% margin is desired, would trigger the $25.00 price. Companies on NIFO-type systems cannot always make the NIFO price stick in the face of competition, but even when they cannot, they know how far off target they are and which products, customer groups, lines of business, and so forth are producing the desired margins.

In summary, LIFO can protect cash flows from taxes, but replacement-cost accounting (NIFO) must be used to protect profit margins.

Effect

Operating Profits Overstated

Response

Inflation-Adjusted Accounting

Besides overstating gross margins, historical cost-based accounting overstates profits by understating other expenses, particularly depreciation expenses associated with fixed assets. Depreciation takes into account the prevailing belief that operating profits should be calculated only after deducting as an expense the value of the assets used in producing the revenues. Depreciation based on historical cost is far less than depreciation based on replacement cost, hence the overstatement of profits.

Consider the example in Exhibit 1 of a machine that cost $140,000, has a seven-year life, and has a replacement cost that increases 12% each year. Replacment cost will rise from $140,000 to $309,495 at the end of seven years (column 3 of Exhibit 1). While depreciation calculated on the replacement-cost basis totals $225,994 (column 5), depreciation calculated on a historical basis accumulates to only $140,000 (column 2). Indeed, in each of the last three years, historical-cost depreciation expense is only about one-half replacement-cost depreciation (columns 1 and 4). The result of historical-cost accounting is a profit and loss statement that inaccurately portrays the relationship of expenses to the revenues and increasingly overstates profit each year.

The accumulated effects of inflation on the replacement cost of long-term assets can be quite significant, sometimes turning profits into losses, such as in the steel industry, because the accumulated depreciation reserves are considerably less than those required to replace the assets.

Of course, high replacement costs of assets encourage companies to spend money to extend the useful life of old equipment by modifying and adapting it to new uses rather than to purchase new equipment. Such actions partly offset the understatement of depreciation expense, since such costs are usually expensed in the year incurred and deducted on the company's tax returns. Thus the accumulated effects are not quite as bad as the example in Exhibit 1 indicates. Yet they are pernicious enough to warrant management concern. The understatement of cost of goods sold and of depreciation are the two most important causes of overstated income.

Effect

Returns on Investments Are Overstated

Response

Use Inflation-Adjusted Returns and Market Value of Investments
The commonly used calculation of return on investment is profit returned per period divided by the investment that produced the profit. Inflation, as we have seen, overstates profits, or the numerator of this calculation. By increasing replacement value of the assets used or the market value of the investment, inflation can also have a significant impact on the denominator.

Return on investment became an issue in a small metal-plating manufacturer with 40% of a small market. The father-and-daughter management team disagreed about pricing. Believing that the company (which we shall refer to as Olson Metals) was not keeping up with inflation, the daughter wanted to raise prices significantly. The father believed that (a) an aftertax profit of $426,000 was sufficient, (b) a large price increase would encourage

Exhibit 1. Depreciation on a $140,000 Machine with a Seven-Year Life and a Replacement Cost That Increases at 12% Per Year

Year	Column 1 Depreciation expense	2 Accumulated depreciation	3 Replacement cost	4 Depreciation expense based on replacement cost	5 Accumulated depreciation on replacement cost	6 Accumulated depreciation plus 12% interest on beginning balance
1	$20,000	$ 20,000	$156,800	$22,400	$ 22,400	$ 22,400
2	20,000	40,000	175,616	25,088	47,488	50,176
3	20,000	60,000	196,690	28,099	75,587	84,296
4	20,000	80,000	220,293	31,470	107,057	125,882
5	20,000	100,000	246,728	35,247	142,304	176,234
6	20,000	120,000	276,335	39,476	181,780	236,859
7	20,000	140,000	309,495	44,214	225,994	309,495

competitors to come in and take a swing at Olson's market, and (c) if faced with such high prices, their customers might integrate backward.

The daughter restated the company's finances on a replacement-cost basis with the following results: (a) the aftertax profit went to $273,000, (b) the assets increased in value from $4,450,000 to $13,310,000, (c) the rate of return went from 10.2% to 2.1% and (d) there seemed to be far less chance of competition or backward integration since new producers wouldn't be attracted by this return.

This same striking difference in return on assets arises when different divisions or product lines of a company are examined on the basis of inflation-adjusted profits vis-à-vis the market value of the investments. Such calculations can pinpoint areas for expansion or for disinvestment. This may be an important first step in considering where to obtain or use capital in the face of sustained inflation.

Effect

Overstated Growth Rate

Response

Inflation-Adjusted Growth Rate

During periods of double-digit inflation, a company that looks good in dollar sales growth can be standing still in units sold per year. While the general price level can be a misleading indicator of the effects of inflation on a corporation, say, a petrochemical company (with a much higher than average level of inflation in its products) or a computer company (which has a deflationary, specific price index), it can be used in a "quick and dirty" way to squeeze inflation out of a series of sales and profit reports.

Accounting rules now require large publicly held companies to show performance for the past five years on such an inflation-adjusted basis. Allowing for the specific impact of inflation on a company's individual assets is most telling, but general price level adjustments of trend data are almost as useful. For example, the results of Schooner Press (the disguised name of a real company) for five years are shown on a pre- and post-inflation-adjusted basis in Exbibit 2. Note that historical-dollar sales and profits grew at 20.5% and 20.6%, respectively; on a deflated basis, sales grew at only 9.8% a year and profits at 12.5% a year (compounded)—a significant difference.

Effect

Erosion of Corporate Capital

Exhibit 2.   Inflation-Adjusted Sales and Net Profit Figures for the Schooner Press (in thousands of dollars)

		Compound growth rate	1980	1979	1978	1977	1976
Sales	in historical dollars	20.5%	$8,744.5	$6,166.6	$5,384.6	$4,425.6	$4,149.9
Net earnings	in historical dollars	20.6[a]	64.5	173.5	86.6	(2.2)	56.3
Sales	restated in 1980 dollars	9.8	8,744.5	7,000.5	6,801.0	6,017.8	6,007.0
Net earnings	restated in 1980 dollars	12.5*	64.5	197.0	109.4	(3.0)	81.5
Consumer price index	1967 = 100		246.8	217.4	195.4	181.5	170.5

Source: Annual reports.

[a]Average of 1979 and 1980 net earnings used in calculating the compound earnings growth rate

Response

Calculate the Impact; Change the Tax Laws

The effects of tax policies that ignore inflation are pernicious and significant for companies of all sizes. While LIFO can offset inflationary effects on inventory and cost of sales, there is no such relief for depreciation of capital assets.

Consider the example cited in Exhibit 1. At the end of seven years, accumulated historical depreciation is only $140,000, while the replacement cost of the machine is $309,495. Thus, less than half of the funds to replace the machine have been sheltered from taxes on the income the machine produced. If depreciation could be based on replacement cost, some $225,994 would have accumulated at the end of the period and have been deducted from taxable income (column 5). This amount is still less than that required for replacement.

If, however, the company can earn 12% interest tax free on the depreciation set aside, we can see by column 6 that the "invested depreciation" will accumulate to $309,495—the exact amount of replacement cost. Note that this requires that replacement-cost depreciation be deductible from taxes and that interest income on the depreciation be accumulated tax free (or on an aftertax rate of accumulation that equals the rate of price increase). Current tax laws do not allow companies to do either of these things.

There is, however, some tax relief on fixed investments. The Economic Recovery Act of 1981 allows an investment tax credit and accelerated depreciation. Exhibit 3 shows the results of these policies for the example we have been using. Column 1 shows the depreciation each year; column 3, the investment tax credit of 10%; and column 2, the accumulated depreciation. Column 4 shows the accumulated aftertax amount when depreciation expense and investment tax credit are put aside and invested at 12% and the results taxed. Note that this "depreciation fund" rises to $216,000 at the end of the seventh year. On the other hand, the replacement cost of the equipment rises from the initial $140,000 to some $310,000 at the end of the seventh year—44% more than accumulated replacement-cost depreciation.

This example makes clear that business could benefit from more protection against capital erosion, through either a change in the tax law or a reduction in inflation.

The General Electric Company graphically depicted its situation in the company's 1979 annual report Exhibit 4. Note that the effective tax rate rose from 41% to 51% of income, and earnings retained in the business

Exhibit 3. Depreciation and Accumulation of Interest on Machine

	Cost $140,000	Useful life seven years	Tax life five years	Investment tax credit of 10% and double declining balance depreciation	Replacement cost of machine increases at 12% per year
Year	Column 1 Depreciation expense	2 Accumulated depreciation	3 Investment tax credit	4 Accumulated depreciation and investment tax credit at 12% before tax of 40%	5 Replacement cost
1	$56,000	$ 56,000	$14,000	$ 70,000	$156,800
2	33,600	89,600	—	108,640	175,616
3	20,160	109,760	—	136,622	196,690
4	15,120	124,880	—	161,579	220,293
5	15,120	140,000	—	188,333	246,728
6	0	140,000	—	201,892	276,335
7	0	140,000	—	216,429	309,495

Exhibit 4.   General Electric Company and Olson Metals Profits

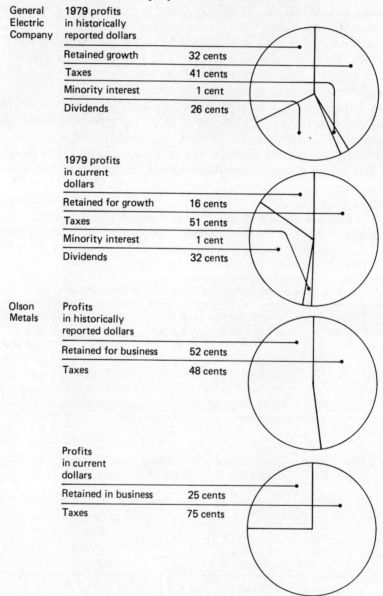

General Electric Company	1979 profits in historically reported dollars	
	Retained growth	32 cents
	Taxes	41 cents
	Minority interest	1 cent
	Dividends	26 cents

	1979 profits in current dollars	
	Retained for growth	16 cents
	Taxes	51 cents
	Minority interest	1 cent
	Dividends	32 cents

Olson Metals	Profits in historically reported dollars	
	Retained for business	52 cents
	Taxes	48 cents

	Profits in current dollars	
	Retained in business	25 cents
	Taxes	75 cents

decreased from 32% to 16% of profits before tax, in inflation-adjusted terms.

This tax on corporate capital applies equally to small companies. Olson Metals has been aggressively deducting improvements in its plant and equipment. Its effective tax rate rises from 48 cents to 75 cents on the pretax dollar (see Exhibit 4) and would go to 84 cents if the company changed to a regular, more balance-sheet-oriented capitalization approach.

This erosion of corporate capital is not unique to General Electric and Olson Metals. Using 1980 corporate annual reports, *Business Week* calculated that inflation-adjusted profits were 48% of historical-cost profits with a general inflation-level adjustment and 43% on a specific price-adjusted basis.[2]

Effect

Inflation and High Interest Rates

Response

Explicit Consideration of Financial Cost in Decisions
and Sales Transactions

At present, Federal Reserve policy seems to be the only weapon used to combat inflation. The result is interest rates that have risen faster than the rate of inflation in the past few years, with little chance of abatement in the near future to pre-1978 levels.

The burden of these interest rates falls on everyone, pressuring companies of all sizes to stretch their payables, manage their inventories carefully, and worry a great deal about their accounts receivable. But certain industries, such as construction and automobiles, and small businesses in general suffer disproportionately.

Large corporations raise capital through long-term issues of debt with fixed interest rates (bonds and negotiated loans with insurance companies) and through the equity market. Small businesses raise their initial capital from friends and relatives, but they raise their seasonal and expansion capital through short-term borrowing from banks with interest rates that move up and down with the prime rate—albeit a percentage point or two above it. Thus, periods of high interest rates affect small businesses immediately but affect large businesses only when they go to the money market.

One response to high interest rates is, of course, to avoid borrowing. Indeed, the purpose of a monetary policy is to slow spending. But most small companies don't borrow to spend; they borrow to "roll over" their short-term debt. The only way small companies can avoid borrowing is to convert their debt to equity or to contract (by selling or liquidating operations earning an inadequate inflation-adjusted return on the market value of assets). While these may be attractive options, they are not always feasible. The only option open to all is to explicitly consider financial costs in every decision and in every sales transaction and to cut back where profits are smallest.

Most accounting systems produce P&L statements that show revenues less costs of sales at the top of the statement and financial expenses at the bottom. Small companies can benefit by moving the financial costs up and associating them with each transaction. Consider three product lines (or customers, or channels of distribution) as shown in Exhibit 5. Conventional analysis shows that product A has the highest unit profitability and percentage return, but product C produces, at high volume, the most gross margin dollars—seemingly a "winner."

The lower half of that exhibit shows profits with financing costs included, assuming that the prime interest rate is 18% and the company finances at 2% over prime. Note that the comprehensive total gross profit on product B is the same as — instead of less than—that on A, and its margin on sales is greater. Product C, however, moves from the main profit contributor to becoming a financial disaster because the cost of financing a $30 unit for one year is $6, versus a $5, gross margin.

Exhibit 5. Product-Line Profitability Analysis

Product-line statistics

	Product A	Product B	Product C
Volume in units	500	500	1,600
Inventory level	180 days	60 days	240 days
Inventory turns	2 per year	6 per year	1½ per year
Accounts receivable	90 days	30 days	120 days
Net cash-to-cash holding period	270 days	90 days	360 days

Conventional product-line profitability

	Product A		Product B		Product C	
Sales price per unit	$45	100%	$42	100%	$35	100%
Cost of sales per unit	30	67	30	71	30	86
Unit gross profit	$15	33%	$12	29%	$ 5	14%
Total gross profit	$7,500		$6,000		$8,000	

Comprehensive product-line profitability
(the prime interest rate is 18% and the company finances at 2% over prime)

	Product A		Product B		Product C	
Sales price per unit	$45.00	100%	$42.00	100%	$35.00	100%
Cost of sales per unit	30.00	67	30.00	71	30.00	86
Unit gross profit	15.00	33	12.00	29	5.00	14
Financial costs	4.50	10	1.50	4	6.00	17
Comprehensive unit gross profit	$10.50	23%	$10.50	25%	($1.00)	(3%)
Comprehensive total gross profit	$5,250.00		$5,250.00		($1,600.00)	

Similar calculations could be made to determine the income lost versus the interest cost saved by inventory reductions, credit tightening policies, customer cutbacks, and the like. The point is that financial costs are now too large to be ignored in the day-to-day operating decisions or policies of your company. This goes against the instinct of many managers, who prefer to leave financial considerations to "bean counters" and to concentrate on the operations, "where the real money is." The real money, today, is the profit left after financing.

Effect

Working-Capital Requirements That Outstrip Available Credit Lines

Response

Plan Growth; Consider Asset Productivity

To demonstrate the impact of inflation on working capital and to explore what courses of action might be advisable, I will examine an imaginary corporation, let's call it Willow Corporation, under three sets of circumstances:

Scenario A
A four-year period with a 15% inflation rate but no growth in unit sales and no investment in productive assets beyond mere replacement.

Scenario B
A four-year period with real sales growth of 10%, a 15% inflation rate, and investment to replace assets as needed to support the sales growth.

Scenario C
A four-year period with no growth of unit sales, a 15% inflation rate, and an investment in productivity-producing assets instead of growth assets in a dollar amount equal to the expenditure in Scenario B.

The beginning financial statements are shown in Exhibit 6 and the balance sheets at the end of four years under each of the three scenarios are shown in Exhibit 7. The assumptions for each scenario appear in the Appendix.

Scenario B produced the highest profit over the four years: owner's equity increased by $1,074,000 ($1,574,000 less $500,000 at the start), compared with $954,000 and $766,000 for scenarios C and A, respectively. Sales in the fourth year (not shown in the exhibits) were $9,938,000 for scenario B (121% greater than at the beginning) and $7,388.000 for scenarios A and C (64% greater). Thus, scenario B, involving growth, appears on the surface to be the most desirable.

Exhibit 6. Willow Corporation's Financial Statements (year ended December 31, 1980)

Balance	Cash		$ 30,000	1.3%
sheet	Accounts receivable		750,000	31.2
	Inventory (turnover: three times per year		900,000	37.5
	Fixed assets		720,000	30.0
	Total assets		**$2,400,000**	**100.0%**
	Accounts payable		$ 450,000	18.8%
	Bank loan		910,000	37.9
	Long-term debt		540,000	22.5
	Owner's equity		500,000	20.8
	Total liabilities and net worth		**$2,400,000**	**100.0%**
Operating	Sales		$4,500,000	100.0%
statement	Operating expenses:			
	Cost of goods	$2,700,000	60.0%	
	Cash-based expenses	1,458,000	32.4	
	Depreciation	72,000	1.6	
	Total operating expense		4,230,000	94.0
	Operating profit		270,000	6.0
	Bank interest 5%	46,000		
	Mortgage interest 5%	26,000		
	Total interest		72,000	1.6
	Profit before taxes		$ 198,000	4.4%
	Taxes 40%		79,000	1.8

Scenario B has some drawbacks, however:

In spite of high profits, all three scenarios entailed increased bank borrowing— $680,000 in A; $838,000 in C; and $1,316,000 in B. If enough short-term bank credit is available, scenario B is profitable. If cash is short, scenario B can lead to extreme financial difficulties. Indeed, inflation alone leads to bank borrowings of 175% of those at the start.

While working capital increases and the debt–equity ratio improves in all three cases, the absolute amount of short-term financial exposure (cash plus accounts receivable less accounts payable and bank loan) rises in all three scenarios and doubles in scenario B.

Exhibit 7. Willow Corporation: Comparative Balance Sheets at the Beginning and End of Four Years of Operation (in thousands of dollars)

	Beginning balance sheet	Scenario A No growth; no investment	Scenario B Growth; investment in growth	Scenario C No growth; investment in productivity
Cash	$ 30	$ 46	$ 46	$ 46
Accounts receivable	750	1,848	2,484	1,848
Inventory	900	1,546	1,890	1,546
Fixed assets	720	848	1,194	1,194
Total assets	**$2,400**	**$4,288**	**$5,614**	**$4,634**
Accounts payable (60 days)	$ 450	$1,108	$1,490	$1,108
Bank loan	910	1,590	2,226	1,748
Long-term debt	540	324	324	324
Owner's equity	500	1,266	1,574	1,454
Total liabilities and net worth	**$2,400**	**$4,288**	**$5,614**	**$4,634**

An alternative scenario to growth involves investing in productivity rather than expansion, as in scenario C. The cash borrowing is some 50% less than B, the financial exposure increase is some 40% less, and given the assumptions, profits are also less—$954,000 versus $1,074,000, or a difference of 11%. Yet under cash rationing or uncertain economic conditions, investments to improve the quality of profits have a lot to offer compared with investments to increase the quantity.

Effect

Rapidly Rising Asset Costs

Response

Own Those Assets That Rise Fastest in Value

Inflation-adjusted profits are usually lower than historically reported profits because of the higher replacement costs of items sold and assets used. While managers might view that as a problem, it can also be an opportunity. Consider the hotel business, in which construction costs have escalated faster than the general price level. For the owner-operator of an older hotel, room rates, which are a function of the construction costs per room, rise at a similar pace as for newer hotels. The result for older hotels is cash flows that increase faster than refurbishing expenditures. In addition, a capital gain can result from holding the building.

In a period of inflation, then, managers should examine where their assets are deployed and consider redeployment or new investments based not only on projected profits and cash flows but also on the rate of inflation as it affects each different asset group. Since the rate of inflation of cash is zero, holding cash is a good strategy only if interest rates are expected to stay higher than specific inflation rates. This is a different way of thinking about investment decisions, but a relevant one today.

Looking Ahead

Inflation presents small company managers with a new set of problems. As one owner-manager said to me, "I have learned how to manage my company in depressions. I have learned how to manage it in periods of scarcity and war, but have not yet learned how to manage during the inflation we have now." I could reply only that the lessons learned in one problem period cannot always be applied in the next; one can profitably hold cash in expectation of a depression but not in expectation of inflation.

Looking to the near future—that is, at least the rest of 1982 and 1983— the following trends appear likely:

☐ A growth in worldwide population, particularly in Third World countries, with each new person requiring a share of world production.

☐ A resulting strain on capital supplies for modernization and industrialization here and abroad.

☐ A balance of $600 billion to $850 billion in dollars and investment held by foreigners attracted to the United States by economic and political stability along with high interest rates.

☐ Pressure on interest rates and the monetary supply that will continue to make borrowing expensive.

☐ A built-in cash flow from the federal government that will decline much more slowly than budget cuts, which are enacted only after much delay and then apply only to a small proportion of government expenditures.

☐ Political pressure to make tax cuts general rather than productivity oriented. Hence, a decrease in revenues.

☐ A "now" psychology that encourages consumption rather than saving. To quote a businessman and student of inflation from Argentina, "The general thinking by the majority in a democracy today is to look for an easy way out. We want to live now, spend now, and not bother with what happens in the long-range future. If somebody has to suffer, let it be the other person.''

The foregoing trends suggest that an annual inflation rate of more than 10% is quite likely in the foreseeable future. That represents a doubling of prices every seven and a quarter years. It also suggests annual interest rates of more than 13%.

To be sure, managers of small companies must learn to change their ways of thinking about finances. Among the steps they must take are the following:

☐ Look through their accounting systems at the true profits.

☐ Evaluate areas of business activity to see if they are profitable after financial costs and if they return an adequate profit on the value of the assets employed.

☐ Manage margins and assets to keep abreast of inflation.

☐ Plan activities with interest rates, inflation, and return rates on the market value of investments explicitly taken into account.

☐ Think of levels of activity and growth rates in terms of a common measure other than dollars—units, hours of equivalent work, and so on—because dollars can mislead.

☐ Be aware of industries in which inflation permits holding gains that offset operating losses or add to operating profits and do so at capital-gain rates.

In conclusion, inflation *is* a problem but an informed manager can turn the problem into opportunity.

Notes

1. The *Thor Power Tool* decision restricts the write-down of inventory to essentially those items physically segregated and offered for sale at reduced prices. *Thor Power Tool* v. *C.I.R.*, 439 U.S.522 S. Ct. 773,58 L.Ed.2d 785(1979).

2. "How 1980 Profits at 370 Companies Were Hit," *Business Week*, May 4, 1981, p.84.

Appendix

Assumptions in Projecting Balance Sheets for Four Years
Basic assumptions for all scenarios:
    1. Inflation increases evenly at 15% a year. This is 1.1715% compounded monthly.

2. Interest rates are three percentage points above inflation, that is 18%. Interest is paid on beginning loan balance to simplify calculations.

3. Accounts receivable and accounts payable stretch out from 60 days to 75 days in the first year and 90 days in the second year.

4. Accounts payable originate from the purchase of inventory; inventory is valued at FIFO and turnover is three times per year.

5. Cash in excess of $30,000 (in beginning dollars) is used to pay off any loans.

6. The long-term debt is paid off in the amount of $54,000 each year.

7. Profits are taxed at an annual 40% rate.

8. No dividends are declared or additional equity investments made.

9. Assets wear out over ten years. There are ten assets each worth $72 at the beginning. One wears out each year; it is replaced at the current cost, which rises with the inflation rate.

Scenario A:

No growth; no investments; 15% inflation.

1. Since inflation is uniform throughout the year, sales increase by 7.95% the first year and by 15% each year thereafter. Inventory increases 12.93% the first year and 15% per year thereafter.

Scenario B:

Ten percent real growth; investment 10% plus replacement at cumulative inflation rates; 15% inflation; inventory increased 5% in real terms.

1. The assets wear out as before—one unit per year for ten years. Two assets are purchased, one for growth and one for expansion.

2. Sales rise the first year by 13.08% and 25% per year thereafter.

3. Inventory increases by 5% in real terms plus 15% inflation. This is 17.5% the first year and 20% each year thereafter.

Scenario C:

No growth; investment 10% per year plus replacement at cumulative inflation rates that yield 40% reduction in operating costs; 15% inflation; inventory constant in real terms.

1. Assets wear out as in scenario A but an equal amount (same cost as in scenario B) is invested in assets that reduce operating cash costs by 45%.

19
Effectively Manage Receivables to Cut Costs

STEVEN D. POPELL

In their push to increase sales, small companies sometimes grant credit too liberally or fail to be diligent enough in collecting receivables. Such practices can result in unnecessary costs which, during recessions, can be the difference between survival and failure. This article prescribes specific actions that can aid in reducing receivables costs.

Ask 100 small company presidents what they see as the most serious threat to small companies during recessions, and probably 95 will respond, "Lost sales." Serious as lost sales can be, however, management can often compensate by scaling down inventories, payroll, and other expenses.

But if companies maintain healthy sales levels (and the cash outlays necessary to support those sales) and cannot collect their receivables, the companies' very survival can be jeopardized. At the least, high interest rates and slow collections can sorely strain the financial resources of most small businesses. During a recession, therefore, collection of accounts receivable must be upgraded from a necessary evil to a high priority. This article presents some practical, tested methods for improving collection procedures.

Tough Credit Policies

The best way to avoid collection problems is to avoid giving credit to potential deadbeats in the first place. While it is axiomatic that no sale, however large, is worth making if you cannot collect, most salespersons instinctively side with potential customers in credit matters. Therefore, management must retain responsibility for granting credit. Credit policy making should not be ceded to the sales force, because the risks are simply too great. What, then, should credit policies be?

First, make clear to all concerned that only the president can overrule the credit manager or accounting supervisor on credit matters. A number of years ago, a computer hardware manufacturer I know shipped $20,000 worth of merchandise to a new customer at the direction of the marketing vice-president, despite the strenuous objections of the credit manager. The company is still trying to collect on that account.

Second, and perhaps obviously, never make delivery of goods or services on credit until credit for the amount of the proposed sale has actually been cleared. When companies get in financial trouble, they often look for second sources to supplement suppliers which may be lost because of slow payment.

Any time you grant credit to an unknown, even on one initial order, you are taking unnecessary risks with your receivables. A percentage of these new accounts is bound to turn sour and, during a recession, that percentage will increase dramatically. Any and all deliveries prior to credit clearance should be made on a COD basis. Your salespeople may not like it, but they will not like a subsequent chargeback against commission, either, or worse, poor company cash flow jeopardizing their jobs.

Third, obtain an adequate number of credit references and check them thoroughly. While ratings can be helpful, they cannot replace first-hand credit information. There should be a minimum of three trade references, preferably local so they can be telephoned inexpensively.

Bank references can also be helpful, but they should not be used as substitutes for trade references. Many bankers are reluctant to provide the most helpful kind of financial information. This potential customer of yours is already a customer of the bank, so even a most scrupulous banker may use some rose coloring when portraying the condition of a borrower.

Evaluating References

When checking trade references, seek to answer the following question: How long has the company been a customer? What has been the high credit? Is there currently a credit limit? What has been the payment record, especially during the past six months? Does this company typically pay within terms? Does it pick up discounts with any frequency? Has the pattern of any of these behaviors changed significantly during the past six months? Finally, can the management be trusted to keep its promises? Most companies experience financial difficulty at some time but if management can be trusted, you will probably be paid eventually, despite the company's short-term problems.

If you use a trade reference checking service, be sure to spot-check the results. One company I worked with lost $2,000 because the customer set up phony references which had passed the checking service.

Few prospective customers would knowingly give out bad credit references. So anything less than a good reference should be considered a bad reference. Never settle for surface gloss, but probe for hidden weaknesses, such as a contractor without a state license, for example, and pursue any negative indication. If you have any doubts, however slight, you may want to impose a credit limit. Thus, even if your initial judgment is faulty or if your customer's financial condition suddenly deteriorates, you will limit your risk.

Other Considerations

While some argue for extending liberal credit terms to maximize market penetration at the expense of more financially strapped or conservative competitors, I contend that this argument is fundamentally weak. For one thing, high costs associated with carrying receivables require you either to raise prices or to lose profits. Worse, you inevitably attract an increasing percentage of new customers who could not deal with you were it not for the extra 30 or 60 days you are granting. The financial instability and insecurity inherent in such customer relations should be avoided, not encouraged.

Finally, do not be influenced by friendship when your judgment tells you a company is in financial trouble. A number of years ago, the head of a mailing company I was working with was reticent, for strictly personal reasons, to pressure a long overdue customer by holding up the Christmas mailing until the account was cleared. When the customer went bankrupt a few months later my client's thank you was ten cents on the dollar.

Maximizing Accounting Information

Your accounts receivable collection effort will be no better than the accuracy and timeliness of your accounting information. Whether you use ledger cards, a computer, or something else, information on shipments and payments must be posted as quickly as possible. How else, for example, can you be sure a customer has not exceeded the credit limit?

The most useful summary display of this information is the accounts receivable aging, normally pulled from accounting source records at the end of each month (see Exhibit 1).

This format seems quite straightforward. "Current" denotes the month just ended, "30 days" denotes the previous month, and so on. There is not much room for improvement here—or so it would seem. In reality, every heading between "Current" and "Prior" is terribly misleading. The truth is that all receivables in the 30-day column are *over* 30 days old. Assuming that the deliveries reflected in that column were made evenly over the course

Exhibit 1. Typical Format for Accounts Receivable Aging

Customer	Current	30 days	60 days	90 days	Prior	Total
A						
B						
C						
Total						

of the month, the average age of the receivables in the 30-day column is 45 days—a significant difference. Succeeding columns indicate an age of 75 and 105 days, respectively.

To turn this reporting problem into an opportunity, I recommend a simple format revision—dividing the Current column into the first and second halves of the month just concluded. Thus the first column of the January 30 aging would be headed "January 1–15" and the second column, "January 16–30." This provides two distinct advantages:

First, it allows you to get at least a half-month head start in running down overdues. For example, if your terms are net 30 days, you know positively that every receivable in the second column (first half of the month) is past due on the 16th of the month following delivery, since, by definition, all second-column receivables reflect deliveries made on the 15th of the previous month, or earlier. Therefore, you can start your follow-up procedure then, instead of waiting for the February 28 aging to be completed two or three weeks later. You can use that extra time to uncover problems of nondelivery, partial shipment, damaged merchandise, customer dissatisfaction, or any of the myriad of problems which make collections so much more difficult after 90 or 120 days.

The best way to keep a receivable out of the 90-day column is to keep it out of the 60-day column; and the best way to prevent that is to keep it out of the 30-day column. This format along with aggressive collection efforts during this extra two or three weeks can help you achieve that objective.

Second, this format allows you to calculate more accurately the average age of your receivables, which aids in comparing your accounts receivable status from one month to the next. The most common method for calculating average age is simply to divide total sales for the most recent fiscal year, or the most recent 12-month period, by the number of days in the year to get the average sales per day. Then divide total receivables by the result of the previous calculation to get the age of receivables in days.

The flaw in this method is that it makes no provision for the spread of the receivables among the various aging columns. Thus $200,000 in the 90-day column would have exactly the same average age as $200,000 in the Current column. Little help for management can be gleaned from such a superficial analysis. Compare, however, the weighted average calculation shown in Exhibit 2 for the period ending January 31, 1981.

Exhibit 2. Accounts Receivable Aging January 31, 1981 (In thousands)

Customer	January 16–31	January 1–15	December	November	October	Prior	Total
A	$10	$ 5					$15
B	15	10					25
C	8	15					23
D	7	10					17
E			$20	$10	$10		40
Total	**$40**	**$40**	**$20**	**$10**	**$10**	**$0**	**$120**
	× 7.5 days	× 22.5 days	× 45 days	× 75 days	× 105 days		
	$300 days	$900 days	$900 days	$750 days	$1,050 days		

900
900
750
+ 1,050

$3,900 days ÷ $120 = 32.5 days

By multiplying the total receivable dollars in the first column by the average age of that column (7.5 days) we get $300,000 days. We then perform this same calculation in each of the remaining columns, with a judgment factor for the average age in the Prior column. Next, the sum of the dollar-days column totals is divided by total receivables. The resulting weighted average is a far more accurate figure for the average age of the receivables, and one which is more readily comparable from month-to-month and year-to-year.

If your company is a general contractor or subcontractor, you are probably well aware of the impact of retentions on your overall collection status. (Retentions are the portion of the bill—often 10%—held back by the customer until all your work is deemed satisfactory.) Take, for example, the relative average age of receivables of a contractor client—with retentions both omitted and included (see Exhibit 3). Note that many more dollar-days are involved in retentions than in all other receivables combined. Also, retentions have increased the average age of receivables by more than a month, while tying up nearly $200,000 in cash.

In addition to being particularly aggressive in collecting retentions (and all other receivables if you have much money tied up in retentions), you

Exhibit 3.   Average Age of Receivables With and Without Retentions

Without retentions

Current	30–59 days	60–89 days	90–119 days	120 + days
$441,434	$118,912	$1,610	$9,712	$95,064
× 15	× 45	× 75	× 105	× 150
$ 6,621,510 days	$5,351,040	$120,750	$1,019,760	$14,259,600
5,351,040				
120,750				
1,019,760				
+ 14,259,600				

$27,372,660 days ÷ $666,732 (total accounts receivable without retentions)
= 41 days

With retentions

Average age of retentions = 180 days (conservative estimate)
Retentions $199,984
                       × 180 days

          $35,997,120 days
          + 27,372,660 days (total dollar-days without retentions)

          $63,369,780 days ÷ $866,715 (total accounts receivable) **= 73 days**

should control your percentage of new construction jobs, since these are where retentions tend to be most common and severe.

Improving Collection Procedures

When formulating your collection policies and procedures, remember that firmness and consistency are far more important than fairness. Let your competitors settle for an average age of 50 to 75 days. You should strive for 30 days and should settle for no more than 45 days. All it takes is an early start and dogged determination.

As receivables get older, you must get progressively tougher. The matrix in Exhibit 4 suggests a series of progressive measures you can employ. The essential element is consistent implementation of your collection policies. Once a receivable is past due according to your published terms, you have more right to the money than your customer does.

Be aggressive in your collection effort. Establish as personal a relationship as possible with those responsible for paying the bills. Among small company customers, those responsible will usually be the president, controller, or bookkeeper; thus they are easy to identify and locate. In larger companies, the accounts payable department processes payables, so it is important to find out specifically how bills are paid and by whom. Not infrequently, for example, payables in large companies are divided among payables clerks alphabetically by supplier. But these procedures and responsibilities vary from one company to another, so you should become acquainted with each system and use it to your advantage.

Get to know the individuals who can influence how quickly you will be paid. Let them know that yours is a small company and that quick turnover

Exhibit 4. Suggested Collection Procedures According to Age of Accounts Receivable

	30 days	45 days	60 days	75 days	90 days
Communication	Telephone & letter	Telephone & letter	Telephone & letter	Telephone & letter	Letter
Message	Overdue. Please pay.	Pay in 15 days or will stop shipments.	Have stopped shipments. Pay now.	Pay in 15 days or will turn over for collection, small claims court, etc.	Am taking action previously cited.
Action	None	None	Stop shipments.	None	Take action previously cited.

of money is critical for your success. You would be surprised how favorably many large company employees react.

When attempting to collect an overdue receivable, exact a specific and personal promise for payment. Write down the promise and who made it on a key receivables sheet. Not only will this procedure allow you to keep track of collections more easily, it will give you a greater feeling of confidence and controlled righteous indignation when following up on broken promises.

And do not believe someone in an accounts payable department who tells you that payments are computer controlled and that the process cannot be interrupted or circumvented. Any company, large or small, has the capability to handwrite checks.

Using Cash Discounts

In some industries, cash discounts are so deeply rooted that all suppliers must use them. If the practice does not prevail in your industry, the factors to consider in determining whether to offer cash discounts to your customers are similar to those for deciding whether to pick up supplier discounts. First, consider the availability of cash. If you are frequently in a cash bind and additional debt to alleviate the situation is not readily available, then cash discounts could improve cash flow.

Next, consider the cost, that is, the effective discount interest rate. The most common discount interest calculation shows, for example, that a cash discount of 2% to pay 30 days sooner (say, in 10 days rather than 40) reflects an annual interest rate of 24%—2% for 1 month times 12 months. Not so obvious is the fact that a large proportion of customers picking up this new cash discount may already be paying within terms. So, in effect, you may be paying much more than the 24% annual interest just cited to get your slow payers speeded up.

Thus, before starting something which may be difficult to stop, analyze carefully your mix of receivables to determine whether cash discounts will solve more problems than they create. As a rule, try to keep your effective discount interest rate no more than one percentage point higher than the rate at which you borrow, unless you are strapped for cash.

In Conclusion

This article has tried to accomplish three principal goals: (a) to point out the critical importance of fast collection of receivables, particularly during a recession; (b) to present some practical techniques for improving the availability of receivables information; and (c) to emphasize that the most important ingredient in effective collection of accounts receivable is management's desire and attention.

20
Performance Measures for Small Businesses

STAHRL W. EDMUNDS

Stahrl W. Edmunds explains how the early detection of venture success or failure can be improved by measures of profitabilty, cash flow, and capital productivity.

Large and small businesses have at least one thing in common. That is, both types of enterprise start small and must master successful venturing to survive and grow. Large businesses may do their venturing in the form of new product lines or new venture subsidiaries. Small businesses are usually entrepreneurial ventures by reason of their owner's purposes. Small companies have trouble surviving, and their failure rates are high. Large corporations have been singularly unsuccessful in starting new ventures, because the requirements of venturing differ markedly from the more highly structured regime of a large ongoing corporation.[1]

Therefore executives of large and small businesses alike have a common interest in devising some simplified schematic for planning and decision making that will help improve the probability of venturing success, or at least give an early indication of the probable lack of success.

Small as well as large businesses need benchmark planning data if they are to develop operating plans and policies that are effective in controlling performance of their enterprises. The literature suggests that small ventures have more difficulty in planning than do larger enterprises. The smaller the venture, the less time and staff available to search for planning data. Part of this difficulty may be due to lack of managerial skill or experience. Part of the planning problem, too, may be the greater difficulty of finding appropriate statistics by which small ventures can measure their performance, because small businesses are numerous and diverse, and the data base on the U.S. small business universe is poorly defined.

Statistical measures of planning performance can present insurmountable obstacles for small businesses. Data must be locally available or easily at hand to be usable in a simplified planning exercise. The following discussion attempts to provide some rough target data that may be useful for decision purposes, together with a simplified planning framework for their use.

The most comprehensive data on the business universe, including small business, are found in the tax returns of the Internal Revenue Service, the industry statistics of the U.S. Department of Commerce, and the credit data of Dun & Bradstreet, Inc. However, these data sets are frequently not current, reconciled, or tabulated in a form that reveals size, industry class, or performance characteristics; indeed, the special tabulation costs of the huge data bases are very high.

Fortunately, former Secretary of the Treasury William E. Simon had a special tabulation made in 1975 for his testimony to the Select Committee on Small Business of the U.S. Senate, which provides the basis for estimating several performance targets for businesses of all sizes.[2] This tabulation, together with interpolative data from the Commerce Department and the Federal Trade Commission, can be used effectively as the basis for rough estimates of *profitability, cash flow,* and *capital productivity*. Taken together, the use of these measures—whether these performance targets are exactly appropriate or not—imposes a tight planning discipline on managers of small ventures that forces them away from failure and toward at least average historical standards of performance.

Profitability Estimates

One measure of profitability is the amount of net earnings per dollar of assets employed in the business, which is the special tabulation Simon presented to the Select Committee on Small Business. Corporate earnings per dollar of assets were compiled by both industry class and size and included and excluded executive compensation.

Excluding officer compensation, the earnings per dollar of assets were somewhat lower for businesses having under $100,000 in assets than for larger enterprises. Including officer compensation, shown in Exhibit 1, the earnings per dollar of assets are seen to be higher for smaller business ventures of every size and of every industry class.

The earnings including officer compensation provide the most comparable data across size classes, because of differences in effective tax rates. The statutory income tax rate is lower for small companies than for larger ones; yet the effective tax rate is consistently higher for small businesses—

Exhibit 1.   Earnings, Including Compensation of Officers, Per Dollar of Assets for Corporations With and Without Net Income, by Asset Class, 1972

Asset class (in thousands of dollars)	Manufacturing	Services	Construction	Transportation	Wholesale and retail trade
Under $25	$.49	$2.42	$.85	$.42	$.49
$25–$49	.39	1.03	.53	.26	.34
$50–$99	.35	.53	.40	.26	.29
$100–$249	.28	.29	.30	.23	.24
$250–$499	.24	.19	.23	.18	.21
$500–$999	.22	.13	.19	.15	.20
$1,000–$2,499	.18	.11	.16	.13	.17
$2,500–$9,999	.16	.09	.13	.11	.15
$10,000–$24,999	.14	.09	.09	.10	.12
$25,000–$99,999	.12	.09	.08	.08	.12
$100,000 and over	.10	.07	.05	.05	.09

Income = total receipts − (total deductions + interest + officers' compensation + charitable contributions)

Source: The Office of the Secretary of the Treasury and the Office of Tax Analysis, November 12, 1975.

averaging 50% for those under $25 million in assets but only 35% for those over $1 billion in assets.

That is, the corporate income tax is regressive and declines with company size. Under these circumstances, a rational small business executive would withdraw earnings as personal income from his enterprise at least until his personal tax rate exceeded 51%. Of course, in small businesses, these withdrawals could constitute a large part of total earnings; hence the earnings per dollar of assets including officer compensation provide the most comparable data across size classes.

Exhibit 1 presents two significant sets of fact: the first concerns profit planning targets and the second, relative efficiency. For *profit planning,* a small business manager can use the data in this exhibit to set minimum profit goals for himself, on the assumption that if his enterprise cannot match the average earnings per dollar of assets for others in its industry class and size, then the funds might be better invested elsewhere. Consider that a venture with assets of $25,000 to $50,000 should be able to set planning targets for earnings (including officer compensation) of $1.03 per $1.00 of assets in a service industry, $0.53 per $1.00 in construction, and $0.34 per $1.00 in wholesale or retail trade. Those figures represent averages, of course, plus or minus what other deviations the manager may be able to ascertain regarding his own two- or three-digit standard industrial classification. Such deviations may be obtainable from comparative statistics within trade associations.

Similarly, a large corporation in manufacturing or retailing with assets from $25 million to $100 million could expect to set a profit target of $0.12 per $1.00 of assets.

For *relative efficiency,* this exhibit clearly shows that smaller companies have higher earnings in every industry group and size class. The smaller the company, the higher the earnings. That is, earnings are inversely related to size.

The data shown in Exhibit 1, far from demonstrating economies in scale, suggest that there are large diseconomies of organizational scale. The small companies (under $250,000 in assets) consistently show earnings rate from two to five (or more) times the largest corporations' ($100 million and over in assets). Such findings bely the common presumption that small businesses suffer from management inadequacies. Indeed, the management of smaller companies, by this performance standard, is superior to that of the large ones.

Cash-Flow Planning

Exhibit 1 also makes it possible to approximate some rough estimates of cash flow by industry group and size class. This may be done by using the Federal Trade Commission data on depreciation allowances by asset size and adding them back to earnings to obtain the average cash flow.[3] This cash flow by industry and size class is a useful planning target and tool, particularly since cash-flow planning is one of the more difficult and vulnerable areas in small business management. Exhibit 2 shows the average cash-flow estimates by size and industry class.

The advantage of cash-flow planning to businessmen, whether in large or small enterprises, is that it imposes the discipline of a cash budget, which is essential to survival. Because records, budgets, and cash flow closely interlink, it is scarcely possible to solve the cash-flow problem without dealing with the adequacy of financial records and budgets as well. Yet the techniques for cash-flow planning are relatively simple, and they may be summarized in the following nine steps:

1. Make a sales projection based on historical experience by week or month, broken down by cash and credit sales.
2. Analyze accounts receivable by adding projected credit sales weekly (or monthly) and subtracting the payment rate on accounts receivable to obtain a cash payments schedule.
3. Estimate the total cash inflows by combining the cash sales, the accounts receivable payments schedule, and the projected sale of any business assets.

Exhibit 2. Cash Flow of Corporations Per Dollar of Assets, by Asset Class

Asset class (in thousands of dollars)	Manufacturing	Services	Construction	Transportation	Wholesale and retail trade
Under $25	$.58	$2.44	$.88	$.45	$.53
$25–$49	.48	1.05	.56	.29	.36
$50–$99	.44	.55	.43	.29	.31
$100–$249	.37	.31	.33	.26	.26
$250–$499	.33	.20	.25	.20	.23
$500–$999	.31	.15	.21	.17	.22
$1,000–$2,499	.21	.12	.18	.15	.19
$2,500–$9,999	.18	.10	.15	.13	.16
$10,000–$24,999	.16	.10	.11	.12	.13
$25,000–$99,999	.14	.10	.10	.10	.13
$100,000 and over	.14	.08	.07	.07	.10

Source: The Office of the Secretary of the Treasury and the Federal Trade Commission.

4.   Test the reasonableness of the estimates by comparing the cash inflow with comparable standards for like companies in the same industry, such as data from Exhibit 2 (which is on an annual basis) or other more specific trade association data on cash flows within one's own industry. To use Exhibit 2, multiply the appropriate number in the exhibit by the business's assets to get the cash flow.

5.   Make a budget of all operating and capital expenditures with an estimate of the timing of payment to arrive at a cash-outflow schedule.

6.   Plan to pay fixed costs first (e.g., rent or interest), payrolls second, other operating expenses third, and capital items fourth to yield a priority schedule of cash outflows.

7.   Pay officer compensation last, if there is a net balance of cash remaining after all outflows, but do not overdraw the projected cash balance.

8.   If there is no cash balance, see an accountant and a banker about the possibilities of using float, accounts payable, or loans as temporary sources of cash inflow.

9.   If credit is needed to meet the cash requirements temporarily, go through the exercises of steps 1 through 7 a second time to see if cash balances are likely to materialize in the future by either strengthening sales or paring costs. If not, the projection implies impending failure, and consideration should be given to early termination to conserve the assets for the owner as well as for the creditors.

The management discipline in this process, of course, lies essentially in steps 3 and 6 where all cash inflows and outflows are scheduled and compared. To make this comparison, the manager must have adequate financial records, budgets, and cash-flow statements.

The reason a cash-flow statement is so important to a small business is that it forces a second kind of discipline—that is, combining the net effect of operations on the balance sheet as well as on the income statement. Herbert N. Woodward has shown that one of the weaknesses of small business is undue concentration on the income statement, particularly an attempt to achieve growth for growth's sake while reducing fixed costs per unit and trying to optimize net income on the income statement (which is on an accrual, not a cash, accounting basis).[4]

The fallacy of such strategy is that there are relatively few true fixed expenses, except in the very short run. Therefore, to concentrate attention on them (by trying to reduce fixed costs per unit on an accrual accounting basis) can cause a manager to overexpand operations beyond the capacity of his cash resources.

Thus the cash-flow statement provides a check and discipline on the manager, because it shows him how the balance sheet items such as cash, inventory, accounts receivable, accounts payable, and capital expenditures are likely to be affected by operating decisions reflected in the income statement. That is, the cash-flow statement keeps operations (as reflected in both the balance sheet and the income statement) within the cash resources of the business.

In short, the cash-flow statement is perhaps the single most important control that the manager of an enterprise has, particularly for small companies, which are inclined to be short of cash.

Capital Productivity

So far this discussion has treated profit estimates and cash-flow planning as though all or most of the expenditures were operating expenses; this is likely to be true, especially for the new companies in trade and services, where facilities requirements are relatively small and may often be rented. Even manufacturing organizations frequently start with low overhead in the owner's garage.

However, as an enterprise grows, particularly in manufacturing, capital equipment or buildings may be needed. Such capital expenditures should only be considered when the cash-flow statement indicates that the net cash balances are large enough either to buy the equipment outright or to pay the service costs on a loan to finance it. At that time, the entrepreneur or manager should have some historical standards by which to compare his own capital performance before making capital expenditures.

One such standard is to calculate the capital–output ratio of the capital investment—that is, to see how many dollars of new output (and sales) can be produced per dollar of investment input. The standard to be used might well be this: the capital budget item must be able to produce at least $0.30

in new added output for every $1.00 of new capital invested, and, after the addition, the net capital stock of the enterprise (i.e., all its capital assets less depreciation) should be able to produce at least $0.80 in total output per $1.00 of capital invested.

The reason that marginal productivity of new capital investment is lower than the average historical standards of performance is that the new capital additions are usually not used to full capacity immediately on installation, but rather they provide some excess capacity. If the proposed capital item does not meet this test, its inclusion in a capital budget should be gravely questioned, because this standard is about the average performance of business investments throughout the economy in the recent past, as shown in Exhibit 3.

In this exhibit, the average capital–output ratio, or average capital productivity, is the net output divided by the net capital stock. The marginal capital productivity is the net increase in output divided by the net increase in capital stock.

The indication is that the capital productivity of the United States has been falling gradually for the past three decades, for both proprietary and corporate business, and for both average and marginal capital productivity. These facts are cause for considerable concern because they indicate that the growth rate of the economy is falling and that the economy is in a state of diminishing returns on capital investment.

A variety of reasons may account for these diminishing returns on capital investment, such as (a) declining rates of technological advancement, (b) increasing marginal costs of new resources (e.g., deeper oil wells or less-concentrated mineral ores), (c) inflation of capital equipment prices, or (d) poorer management decisions regarding the company's capital budget expenditures.

Perhaps the entrepreneur or manager can do little about the first three items, other than encourage effective research in his own organization and encourage a more balanced fiscal policy on the part of the federal govern-

Exhibit 3. Capital–Output Ratios of Proprietary and Corporate Business, 1949–1975 (in constant 1972 dollars of sector income per dollar of net capital stock)

	Average capital–output ratios		Marginal capital–output ratios	
	Proprietary	Corporate	Proprietary	Corporate
1949–1953	1.34	.92	.37	1.05
1954–1960	1.12	.90	.30	.19
1961–1969	.92	.96	.40	.84
1970–1975	.75	.86	.01	.15

Source: U.S. Department of Commerce, Bureau of Economic Analysis.

ment. However, the manager can do something about the fourth item; he or she can make better capital budget decisions.

One criterion for better decision making in capital budgeting is that new expenditures must at least meet average historical standards in the economy for capital productivity. That is, a new investment should be able to produce at least $0.30 per $1.00 invested in marginal (net new) output and $0.80 per $1.00 invested in average output.

In the final analysis, better decisions are what management is all about. Improved decision making is especially vital when the standards and techniques are relatively simple to use and when the growth rate of the venture and the economy depends on it.

Notes

1. See, for example, Mack Hanan, "Venturing Corporations—Think Small to Stay Strong," *HBR*, May–June 1976, p. 139.

2. U.S. Senate Select Committee on Small Business, *The Role of Small Business in the Economy—Tax and Financial Problems, 94th Congress: 1st Session* (Washington, D.C.: Superintendent of Documents, November 21, 1975), p. 19.

3. U.S. Federal Trade Commission, *Quarterly Financial Report*, 4th Quarter (Washington, D.C., 1975).

4. Herbert N. Woodward, "Management Strategies for Small Companies," *HBR*, January–February 1976, p. 113.

21

The Accounting Review: A Happy Compromise

JERRY L. ARNOLD and MICHAEL A. DIAMOND

As small companies grow, their accounting statements assume more importance. If the companies decide to seek financing or to make acquisitions, outsiders want to examine their accounting statements. Moreover, the companies must rely on the statements to make managerial decisions. Until recently, companies could choose to have one of two very different sorts of statements prepared—a bare-bones disclaimer of opinion or a full-scale audit. The authors describe the advantages and disadvantages of a compromise approach that is becoming increasingly popular.

A growing electronic components manufacturer with $5 million in annual sales has for many years had its financial statements audited, primarily to assure the owners that the statements conform with generally accepted accounting principles (GAAP). But the owners now wonder if there isn't a way of obtaining the same assurance without the expensive analysis that an audit entails.

Another company, a family-run retailer of children's toys with average annual sales of slightly over $1 million, has always financed its needs internally and has never used an outside CPA. But because of planned expansion, the company will soon apply for a substantial bank loan. Officials of one bank the company has approached suggest that the bank's policy is to reject

Authors' Note: We wish to express our appreciation to James McNeill Stancill, associate professor of finance at the University of Southern California, for his comments and suggestions. This research was sponsroed by Fox & Co., certified public accountants.

internally prepared statements. Company officials don't know what type of accountant's report to get.

These situations are indicative of what numerous growing private companies face today. Until July 1979, these companies could have opted for either a full-scale audit or an unaudited disclaimer, in which the CPA would take no responsibility. (See Exhibits 1 and 2 for examples of each kind of accounting statement.) At that time, the American Institute of Certified Public Accountants (AICPA) endorsed a new service for accountants to make available to managements of nonpublic companies—the review. (See Exhibit 3 for a sample review statement.) It offers a compromise between a compilation and an audit. By doing a review, CPAs can for the first time provide some assurance about whether financial statements conform with generally accepted accounting principles.

The purposes of this article are to suggest, first, that growing companies should seek to ensure that their financial statements conform with GAAP and, second, that a review is often the best way of gaining such assurance. We have reached these conclusions by analyzing the results of a national survey we conducted in 1980 in which bankers and CPAs considered the propriety of compilations, reviews, and audits. In all, 138 bankers from 30 banks (representing a response of 58%) and 213 CPAs from 45 firms (representing a response of 61%) returned the questionnaire.

The Importance of Conformity

Prior to the stock market crash in 1929, less stringent ground rules existed for the preparation of financial statements. The crash and ensuing depression convinced the accounting profession and the Securities and Exchange Commission to formally develop the generally accepted accounting principles, now known as GAAP. Although not codified in one source, these principles provide an accepted and consistent framework for preparing financial state-

---

Exhibit 1.   A Sample Audit Statement

We have reviewed the balance sheet of ABC Company as of December 31, 19XX and the related statements of income, retained earnings, and changes in financial position for the year then ended. Our examination was made in accordance with generally accepted auditing standards and, accordingly, included tests of the accounting records and such other auditing procedures as we considered necessary in the circumstances.

In our opinion, such financial statements present fairly the financial position of the ABC Company at December 31, 19XX and the results of its operations and the changes in its financial position for the year then ended, in conformity with generally accepted accounting principles applied on a basis consistent with that of the preceding year.

Exhibit 2.   A Sample Compilation Statement

We have compiled the accompanying balance sheet of ABC Company as of
December 31, 19XX and the related statements of income, retained earnings, and
changes in financial position for the year then ended.

A compilation is limited to presenting in the form of financial statements
information that is the representation of management (the owners).

We have not audited or reviewed the accompanying financial statements and
accordingly do not express an opinion or give any other form of assurance about
them.

ments. The process of determining GAAP is ongoing and primarily the responsibility of the Financial Accounting Standards Board and the SEC.

While all financial statements carry management's implied warranty
that they conform with GAAP, it is clearly in management's interest to retain
a CPA to determine conformity. The data generated by the accounting system
must be accurate and reliable because the quality of managerial decisions is
directly related to the quality of the input on which they are based. Much
of a CPA's work consists of evaluating the accuracy and reliability of the
accounting system.

In addition, the standard CPA's report provides the growing company
with the comfort that its statements are, in fact, consistent with professional
standards. When the company's actions are inconsistent with those standards, the frequent result is overstatement of such items as assets, earnings,
or net worth. For example, an inflated value for inventory leads to understated cost of sales and overstated profit, which in turn can lead to misdi-
rected spending or investment.

As business owners are well aware, lenders require assurance that
financial statements conform with GAAP. Bankers, for example, nearly al-

Exhibit 3.   A Sample Review Statement

We have reviewed the accompanying balance sheet of ABC Company as of
December 31, 19XX and the related statements of income, retained earnings, and
changes in financial position for the year then ended, in accordance with standards
established by the American Institute of Certified Public Accountants. All
information included in these financial statements is the representation of the
management (the owners) of ABC Company.

A review consists principally of inquiries and analytical procedures applied
to financial data. It is substantially smaller in scope than an examination in
accordance with generally accepted auditing standards, the objective of which is
the expression of an opinion regarding the financial statements taken as a whole.

We are not aware of any material modifications that should be made to the
accompanying financial statements in order for them to be in conformity with
generally accepted accounting principles.

ways want a CPA's statement to this effect before they make a loan of any substantial size or complexity. By engaging a CPA to ascertain that its financial statements are in accord with GAAP, a company increases the attractiveness of its statements to outside users.

Accounting Procedures

The review is often the most cost-effective means of obtaining this assurance. When preparing a review, CPAs make enough analysis and inquiry to conclude that they "are not aware of any material modifications that should be made to the . . . financial statements in order for them to be in conformity with generally accepted accounting principles" (Exhibit 3).

This limited assurance contrasts with the absence of any opinion in a compilation and the quite positive statement in an audit, in which CPAs conclude that "in [their] opinion [the] financial statements . . . [are] in conformity with generally accepted accounting principles."

The level of analysis CPAs do is commensurate with the extent of responsibility they assume. In a compilation, the CPA merely assembles a company's prepared data and expresses no opinion about the financial statements. This service is thus appropriate only for extremely small companies and personal financial statements. It adds little to financial statements prepared internally and costs up to 25% of an audit.

The generally accepted auditing standards adopted by the AICPA define the scope of the underlying examination. They require the auditor to conduct procedures to verify the performance of the accounting system, of certain transactions, and of the account balances. For example, the audit of receivables requires the CPA to examine the entire sales, billing, and collection system. Further, the auditor must correspond with customers to determine the accuracy of account balances. Before finishing these and other procedures, the auditor gathers a great deal of information.

All this information is the basis for the audit opinion. An audit can be extremely time consuming and can result in a fee that may total many thousands of dollars.

Elements of a Review

A review is similar to an audit in that it is meant to gather information about the accounting system, about representative transactions, and about account balances. The CPA doing a review, however, relies on a significantly smaller volume of both internal and external information than in an audit. Accordingly, the review examination is designed to uncover major deviations from GAAP. For example, a review of receivables involves analysis of balance-sheet items such as accounts receivable and allowance for bad debts and analysis of income statement items such as sales and expenses. It also includes analysis of turnover, aging data, and credit policies as well as information from company personnel.

The procedures for reviewing receivables are typical of those for other accounts and differ from the procedures of an audit primarily in that in general no attempt is made to gather external evidence, such as the confirmation of receivables. But if, during the course of a review, the CPA thinks that in particular areas such evidence is necessary—for instance, if analysis indicates a substantial change in the age of receivables from the prior period—he or she might send confirming letters to customers. Or those using a company's statements may think that the equivalent of an audit examination is necessary in certain areas only, such as receivables or inventory. An advantage of a review is that the CPA's analysis and subsequent report can be tailored to a company's needs.

Which Service?

When you choose between an audit and a review, the key issue is whether a review adequately satisfies your objectives. In many cases, it does. The CPA doing the review can become sufficiently familiar with the company, its accounting system, and the industry it's in to conclude that no major GAAP violations exist. This conclusion should assure you that your company's financial system and information are reliable for making decisions. Moreover, many bankers in our study have indicated that, in support of a loan application, they would accept a review in place of an audit.

It should be noted at this point, though, that not all bankers will immediately accept reviews. They may be unfamiliar with the service and resist it, or they may confuse the reviews with the compilations and assume that no assurance is involved. If faced with either situation, you should ask your CPA for assistance in informing the banker of the nature of the review. You should also offer a copy of your CPA's engagement letter, for it specifies the service to be performed. If your banker objects to a review out of fear that it will result in a distant involvement of the CPA with your company, explain that a review requires about half the effort of an audit and assure the banker that the CPA becomes quite involved with the company.

Besides the comfort a review usually gives, it costs much less than an audit. The CPAs in our study indicated that for an existing client a review on average costs about 44% of an audit, and for a prospective client about 49%. The difference is due largely to start-up expenses for new engagements.

For the small company that has usually relied on audits (such as the electronic components manufacturer mentioned at the beginning of the article) and that clearly has a properly functioning accounting system, a review should, at considerably less expense than an audit, provide the assurance that no new problems exist. The company can, of course, always use the funds freed by the decision elsewhere.

Finally, if your company has previously engaged a CPA for tax or consulting services only, he or she may have become familiar enough with the company and its accounting system to provide a review for only a small incremental fee.

Other Considerations

Of course, in some circumstances an audit is more appropriate than a review. A company contemplating going public should have a history of audited financial statements. A company hoping to be acquired may find that audited financial statements facilitate the process. And for a company with serious doubts about the integrity of its accounting system or employees, a detailed audit may be worth the extra cost. Finally, a regulatory authority may require audited financial statements.

The bottom line is that engaging a CPA should provide the comfort that your financial statements conform with GAAP. In many cases a review is the most cost-effective way of achieving this objective.

PART
FOUR
BEST USE OF OUTSIDE
RESOURCES
AN OVERVIEW

Because small companies are usually operating extremely close to the bone—
in terms of number of employees and amount of cash available—they can't
afford much more than to produce their main products and services. To
effectively plan ahead, though, does require more. It entails having information about the marketplace, advice about managerial options, and cash
for additional facilities and capacity.

Fortunately for young ventures, there's been an explosion in the availability of outside resources especially tailored to the needs of small businesses. These resources fall into two main categories: first, educational-
consulting resources, which mainly provide information and managerial advice, and second, financial resources, which provide cash in the form of
loans and investments. These resources can also be divided broadly according to the kinds of business situations they cater to; some specialize
primarily in assisting would-be entrepreneurs and new businesses while
others specialize primarily in helping well-established ventures.

Sometimes the best resources are books and magazines. The last few
years have seen tremendous increases in the volume and quality of printed
material directed at both would-be and existing entrepreneurs, as this volume's editor chronicles in "Entrepreneurship: A New Literature Begins."
The author evaluates the most significant magazines and books according
to their usefulness to entrepreneurs.

When business owners go looking for advice and financing, the individuals they turn to most frequently are bankers, consultants, and accountants. Probably the most important point made by the authors of the articles

221

related to choosing such outsiders is that within each category important differences exist in the quality and type of services provided.

Thus, James McNeill Stancill in "Getting the Most from Your Banking Relationship" advises business owners to carefully survey a variety of banks and evaluate such factors as restrictiveness of loan covenants and rapport with loan officers. After all, he cautions, the banking relationship must be viewed as a long-term one.

The question posed by Harvey C. Krentzman and John N. Samaras "Can Small Businesses Use Consultants?" is answered affirmatively, provided owners can overcome certain fears they tend to have about consultants. Among the fears: that using a consultant will be prohibitively expensive and constitutes an admission of failure.

"Choosing and Evaluating Your Accountant," by Neil C. Churchill and Louis A. Werbaneth Jr., counsels business owners on important differences between small and large accounting firms. It also explains the alternatives among available accounting services.

Among financing sources, probably the most glamorous is venture capital. Its glamor also makes it seem unreachable, but as Jeffry A. Timmons and I point out in "Discard Many Old Rules About Getting Venture Capital," important changes are occurring. Among the changes: start-up situations are being viewed with increasing favor and non-high-technology businesses are obtaining funds from venture capitalists.

Various sorts of outside specialists can be extremely helpful in performing important tasks with long-term ramifications. One sort can help in developing foreign markets, as John J. Brasch describes in "Using Export Specialists to Develop Overseas Sales." Another sort can be invaluable in finding the best place to build a new plant or headquarters, according to Ted M. Levine in "Outsiders Can Ease the Site Selection Process."

And for owners willing to make the commitment to having an assortment of business experts available on a regular, long-term basis, there is the option of assembling some sort of board, either with or without legal powers. The challenges of choosing, compensating, and making use of directors are considered by S. Kumar Jain in "Look to Outsiders to Strengthen Small Business Boards" and Judy Ford Stokes in "Involving New Directors in Small Company Management." Harold W. Fox considers the advantages of directors without legal authority in "Quasi-Boards: Useful Small Business Confidants."

22

Entrepreneurship: A New Literature Begins

DAVID E. GUMPERT

Despite all the talk of recession and a hostile business climate, interest in entrepreneurship has never been keener. The number of business incorporations has more than doubled since 1975, all levels of government have devised special programs to assist entrepreneurs, and hundreds of colleges now offer courses on operating small businesses.

Heeding the call for more and better information, publishers have rushed to press with new books, magazines, and features devoted to starting and operating small businesses. Here David Gumpert describes and critiques some information sources that are helping to define entrepreneurship as a distinct discipline.

Suddenly entrepreneurship is in vogue. Despite burdensome interest rates and a stagnant economy, the number of business incorporations, as recorded by Dun & Bradstreet, rose to more than 500,000 in 1980 from 220,000 in 1975. And it's become fashionable for politicians and other policymakers to extol the innovativeness and job-creation potential of small businesses.

Recognizing this trend, a variety of organizations have recently extended support to entrepreneurs. In amounts unheard of since the late 1960s, venture capitalists are pouring money into new and existing small businesses. City, state, and federal agencies, which have traditionally been partial to the financing and labor needs of large corporations but realize that small businesses have a great potential for providing new employment, have devised financing and other assistance programs to encourage entrepreneurs.[1] Several hundred colleges and universities—versus only a handful a decade ago—offer courses on starting and operating small businesses. And dozens of small-business organizations, many of them offshoots of established chambers of commerce, have sprung up in cities around the country.

In response to the growing demand, publishers of all sorts have rushed to supply reading material on various aspects of starting and managing small businesses. In fact, during the last four years, they have published well over 50 books on entrepreneurship. Three new magazines aimed at would-be and existing entrepreneurs—*Venture, In Business,* and *INC.*—have been started during the same time span. They joined a fourth, *Entrepreneur,* started in 1972. Two established magazines—*Forbes* and *HBR*—have added regular features directed to small business owners. And the *Wall Street Journal* has added a weekly column about small business.

This outpouring of information can help make entrepreneurs more competitive. Advice about financial, managerial, and other developments fills a void for entrepreneurs, most of whom can't afford large staffs of specialists and expensive outside consultants. Although they might still choose the wrong business option, at least the entrepreneurs can know what their options are.

The new publications, with their many profiles and case histories of both successful and unsuccessful ventures, serve another purpose for entrepreneurs as well: they help relieve the loneliness and sense of isolation inherent in starting and running a small business. Simply knowing that others are facing the same problems can help reduce psychological stress. And learning how others have either succeeded or failed in solving their problems can give entrepreneurs insight into solving their own problems.

Finally, the bevy of new publications suggests that entrepreneurship is attaining respectability as a distinct academic discipline. In the past, universities have ranked entrepreneurship low in importance among business disciplines; understandably, instructors and professors interested in advancement ignored the subject.

But in recent years researchers have undertaken important studies and reported on them at a number of academic conferences devoted to the topic of entrepreneurship. One impressive conference was held at Babson College in Wellesley, Massachusetts in the spring of 1981. It featured research papers exploring the family backgrounds and attitudes of entrepreneurs, informal sources of financing, and investment approaches of venture capitalists, among other small business concern.[2]

All this is not to say that the new publications and research efforts fill the information and education gap that existed; the fact is that they don't. Researchers have done little to identify the most suitable strategies and planning approaches for small businesses. And while they have given much consideration to financial management, business policy, marketing, production, and organizational behavior in large corporations, they have given scant attention to these disciplines as they apply to small enterprises. When writing about small businesses, most academics and consultants merely simplify the theory and practice large companies use.

Given this lack of emphasis on planning and strategy, it is not surprising, then, that the publications tend to be strongest in their consideration of short-term managerial and legal problems; they are weakest in helping entrepreneurs formulate long-term strategies. Few present especially exciting or original points of view. Many adopt the attitude that, with persistence and common sense, entrepreneurial skills are easy to learn. Their formulas for success are usually based on familiar, primerish business concepts.

In addition, the publications deal extensively with some business disciplines and overlook others. Publisher interest has been strong in the areas of financing, control, and general management but weak in marketing and organizational behavior.

The literature also gives certain kinds of opportunity for entrepreneurs more attention than others. Writers have generated a great deal of information on financing sources, franchising, and government procurement but generally neglect exporting and consulting for small businesses.

Similarly, several books and magazines address the special problems women entrepreneurs face, but few are available that explore the problems of minority entrepreneurs (beyond the useful and highly respected 13-year-old magazine *Black Enterprise*).[3]

Despite their weaknesses, the new publications begin to answer an important educational need, and they hold the promise that researchers will fill the remaining gaps as interest in entrepreneurship as an academic area continues to grow. The publications divide most easily according to their focus toward would-be entrepreneurs or practicing small business managers, although some are appropriate for both groups. Here I will consider publications according to this breakdown.

Start-Up Information

For would-be entrepreneurs the commodity available in largest quantities from the new publications is the raw information that is important when starting a small business. *Venture* magazine, for one, provides a regular flow of information on the types of businesses attracting large numbers of entrepreneurs and reports on entrepreneurs' experiences in glamorous fields, such as alternative energy sources and computers, along with those in more mundane areas like food retailing and banking.[4] In a regular feature, the editors follow up on entrepreneurs months after they originally profiled them; not surprisingly, in that time many of the businesses have folded or the original partners have disbanded, sometimes winding up on opposite sides of courtrooms.

Venture also provides information on attractive or innovative financing options available to start-up entrepreneurs. It has issued articles on the growing popularity of leveraged buyouts and on the new financing opportunities available to minorities. And it publishes extensive information on the activities of venture capital firms.

The effect of this coverage is to leave regular readers with impressions about both the attractions and difficulties of starting or acquiring small businesses. Learning about other start-ups and their aftermaths or about financing devices that are beginning to catch on can kindle the imaginations of would-be entrepreneurs and can also help potential entrepreneurs avoid serious mistakes.

Where *Venture* perhaps falls short is in its failure to turn the general impressions from its articles into prescriptions that readers could apply to their own situations. The magazine certainly captures the excitement of entrepreneurship, but it does not fully exploit its potential as a useful learning tool for serious readers.

The magazine *Entrepreneur* also provides information about business areas attracting entrepreneurs but in less useful fashion than *Venture*.[5] *Entrepreneur* tends to focus on faddish new businesses like skateboard parks and suntanning centers and emphasizes the ease of entry without noting the long-term risks.

The Franchise Option

One area of new business start-ups about which writers and editors have provided extensive information is franchising. The reason for the publisher interest is that franchising has offered steadily expanding opportunities for would-be entrepreneurs. In recent years, between 100 and 300 companies annually have moved into franchising, bringing the number of franchisers to approximately 2,000. They account for more than 400,000 franchised outlets doing some $300 billion in annual sales.

Of the many how-to books on franchising, *Your Fortune in Franchising,* by Richard P. Finn, stands out as a worthwile introductory text for prospective franchise owners.[6] It describes how to investigate opportunities and explains such things as franchiser rights, site selection, training, promotion, financial management, and special opportunities for minority and female owners.

In recent years, a number of new franchise directories have appeared, yet the best one remains a long-published annual survey from the U.S. government, *Franchise Opportunities Handbook.*[7] It probably has the most extensive information about individual franchises of any publication and includes information on the number of franchise outlets, length of time the franchiser has been in business, start-up capital required, and assistance franchisers give to franchise owners.

Emphasis on Mechanics

For overviews of the information and techniques they require to start new businesses, would-be entrepreneurs have a variety of choices. In his book *How to Become Financially Successful by Owning Your Own Business,* Albert J. Lowry provides much useful advice on cash flow, legal structure of businesses, tax considerations, and buying existing businesses.[8]

Similarly, *How to Prosper in Your Own Business,* by Brian R. Smith, includes practical advice on financial ratios, inventory control, the role of computers in small businesses, and the availability of outside information sources.[9] His chapter on writing a business plan is thorough and thoughtful.

Where these and many of the other how-to books for starting businesses falter is in their considerations of the personality, career, and other human factors that help determine whether and how people should start small businesses. In discussing the career choice of entrepreneurship, Smith concludes, "The only questions to be answered are, 'Do you want to do it? If someone could give it to you, would you take it?'"[10] The implication in this and other books is that anyone can be a successful entrepreneur if only he or she follows the mechanical guidelines described in such detail by the authors.

Indeed, only a few books appear to give the human considerations the attention they deserve. One such book is Karl H. Vesper's *New Venture Strategies*.[11] He devotes approximately the first third of his book to considering such things as the psychological and sociological factors motivating entrepreneurs, the career stages at which entrepreneurship is most attractive, and the advantages and disadvantages of starting businesses with partners. Vesper presents convincing research using cases of business start-ups to back his points. The rest of the book advises would-be entrepreneurs on evaluating new venture ideas and competition and on acquiring a business.

Another book that explores the personal characteristics and skills necessary for entrepreneurial success is *New Venture Creation*, by Jeffry A. Timmons, Leonard E. Smollen, and Alexander L. M. Dingee.[12] The book, which is a college workbook–textbook, encourages readers to thoroughly assess their own strengths and weaknesses and to seek feedback from trusted friends and associates. It also encourages the partnership rather than the single-person venture as a means of improving chances for success, and it provides guidance on how patterns can best work together.

And finally, *Micro-Management*, by William A. Delaney, contains some useful caveats on forming partnerships, motivating employees, and marketing products.[13] Though heavy on anecdotes and light on analysis, the book has a realistic approach to preparing would-be entrepreneurs for the inevitable conflicts that arise among partners and the difficulties in motivating new employees. Delaney considers problems typical of new ventures, such as personal entanglements with employees, deciding on appropriate means of selling products, and growing too fast.

Managing Ongoing Businesses

Perhaps because experienced entrepreneurs have more savvy than would-be venturists, publications directed to the former group are generally more sophisticated and thoughtful than those written for the latter.

Two magazines catering to the needs of owners and managers in distinct segments of small business are *INC*.[14] and *In Business*.[15] *INC*. focuses on growth-minded businesses with more than $1 million in annual sales. Its staff of several dozen editors and writers keeps track of regulatory, tax, and political developments affecting small businesses. In an effort to identify effective managerial approaches for small businesses, the magazine profiles mostly successful (as opposed to troubled) small companies. It sometimes relies on consultants to write articles on various aspects of financial and organizational management.

While many of the articles in the initial issues of *INC.*, which first appeared in early 1979, seemed shallow and unfocused, the magazine appears to have matured of late. It has featured in-depth articles on the problems of growth and productivity facing small companies and has published fascinating accounts of success strategies used by such fast-growing small companies as Genentech and Air Florida.

Perhaps *INC.*'s most important contribution to small business literature has come from its consideration of marketing and organizational–personnel strategies that are most appropriate to entrepreneurs. Recent marketing articles have advised readers on how to sell to large corporations, how to remain a leader in a new and fast-changing market, and how to use demographics in market research.[16]

Even more impressive have been *INC.*'s articles on organizational and personnel issues. Several articles have dealt with attracting key managers, motivating employees, providing day-care facilities, and delegating authority. Most of these articles use company profiles that both illustrate their points and make interesting reading.[17]

In Business is directed to owners of smaller-scale businesses of under $1 million annual volume who are concerned about the impact their businesses have on their communities and life-styles. It tends to profile small alternative energy, craft, and natural food businesses and explores how owners of such businesses deal with their customers, suppliers, and community organizations.

The magazine's concern with the more prosaic and intangible aspects of small business ownership doesn't mean it is naive about the importance of business mechanics. Its articles on financing and marketing mainly stress the importance of the fundamentals of proper capitalization, market research, and other small business essentials. *In Business* also provides information on government and commercial financing programs available to small businesses.

The magazine's dual focus on social and business issues is refreshing. One gets the feeling that the editors are both sensitive and pragmatic, and these attributes are reflected in the magazine—a rare combination in any business publication.

Specialized Supplemental Sources

In addition to the steady flow of information and guidance from periodicals like *INC.* and *In Business,* various recently published books offer detailed information on specific techniques to assist small business managers. Also, a number of books give information on resources for entrepreneurs, most notably in the areas of financing, government procurement, computers, and the special needs of women entrepreneurs.

One that attempts to be all-inclusive in describing outside resources available to small business owners, along with guidance on using the resources, is *The Insider's Guide to Small Business Resources,* by Jeffry A. Timmons and me.[18] The book lists and describes small business resources in areas including education, consulting, international trade, government procurement, and financing.

Financing

The largest single category of specialization is financing of small businesses. Most of the books on financing attempt to cover all of the options—bank loans, government loans, venture capital, and so on. One particularly readable overview is *The Small Business Guide to Borrowing Money,* by Richard L. Rubin and Philip Goldberg.[19] It discusses all the major forms of financing, along with the advantages and disadvantages of each, and offers guidance for approaching financing sources. Rick Stephan Hayes's book, *Business Loans,* is another useful, though somewhat less readable, overview.[20] A more strategy-oriented guide to obtaining financing is Thomas J. Martin's *Financing the Growing Business;* it offers guidance on which types of financing are best for which types of companies and how to negotiate and evaluate loan agreements.[21]

For business owners considering selling franchises as a way of financing expansion, several information and guidance sources exist. The International Franchise Association in Washington publishes magazines and booklets that keep readers up on the latest franchising trends and regulations.[22] And two books by consultants ably compare franchising to other expansion approaches and offer step-by-step guidance on how to franchise businesses.[23]

Procurement and Computers

Books about government procurement and small business computers are particularly appropriate for small business owners and managers, many of whom are intimidated by the subjects.

The need for information on federal procurement becomes apparent when one considers that small businesses fill only about 25% of federal purchases while accounting for about half the nation's jobs and gross national product. Two books that make worthwhile attempts to demystify the procurement process are *The $100 Billion Market: How to Do Business with the Government,* by Herman Holtz,[24] and *How to Sell to the Government,* by William A. Cohen.[25] While both are useful, the Holtz book is the more readable and concise of the two.

The growth in computer models for personal and small business use and the drop in computer prices have made computerization of many tasks a realistic alternative for businesses of nearly any size. Shelves in retail bookstores are crowded with books about these business and personal computers. Two useful introductory texts are Brian R. Smith's *The Small Computer in Small Business*[26] and Jules A. Cohen's *How to Computerize Your Small Business.*[27]

Women

The number of books aimed at female business owners reflects a developing interest in entrepreneurship among women. (In 1978 a federal task force stated that the increase in self-employed women from 1972 to 1977 was three times that of self-employed men.) The books are useful in discussing ways women can overcome discrimination from bankers, suppliers, and others. One idea that many of the books promote is a women's network of business contacts; most of the books discuss and list organizations around the country that can place female business owners in contact with local networks. One of the most thoughtful and clearly written of these books is Charlotte Taylor's *Women and the Business Game: Strategies for Successful Ownership.*[28] Others worth noting are *Women's Networks*, by Carol Kleiman,[29] and *The New Entrepreneurs*, by Terri P. Tepper and Nona Dawe Tepper.[30]

Managerial Approaches

As do books directed to start-up entrepreneurs, books for owners of small businesses tend to concentrate on the mechanical aspects of operating companies. One that does a thorough job of exploring the important mechanical approaches is by John A. Welsh and Jerry F. White, *Administering the Closely Held Company.*[31]

The book convincingly argues that small businesses must closely monitor their cash flow and accounts receivable to avoid financial difficulties. Extensive tables and graphs show how to set up monitoring systems. *Administering the Closely Held Company* also provides useful information on reducing business taxes, measuring and improving productivity, deciding between LIFO and FIFO methods of valuing inventory, and managing inventory. Unlike most other books directed to small business owners, the Welsh–White book gives at least passing consideration to differences between the needs of small and big companies in such areas as inventory and financial controls.

A second worthwhile addition to the small business management literature is *Successful Management Strategies for Small Business*, by Harvey Krentzman, a management consultant.[32] The book is more a checklist of managerial chores and approaches for owners of small businesses than a complete how-to text on the order of the Welsh–White book. Krentzman's book makes good use of cases to explore the basics of marketing, production, inventory management, receivables, and accounting.

While Krentzman's book is concise and covers important aspects of small business management, it often stops just short of providing in-depth analysis and prescription and instead resorts to the obvious or banal. "The alert and interested owner-manager can overcome the obstacles to change through the desire to grow," he states at one point.[33]

Both the Welsh–White volume and the Krentzman book give little attention to the organizational and personnel problems confronting small businesses, not to mention long-range planning issues.

Planning and Strategy

While primers covering organization and personnel issues specifically applicable to small business are rare, at least one new book examines long-term planning and strategy from a small business perspective; that is *Strategic Planning in Emerging Companies,* by Steven C. Brandt, a faculty member at Stanford Business School.[34]

Brandt's book is addressed to owners of companies experiencing fast growth who need a rationale and perspective for planning. The book begins by tracing the stages of growth and typical management styles of small companies and then attempts to demystify the notion of strategic planning. In setting up a framework for managers to begin formulating long-term strategy, Brandt reassures owners of small businesses that attention to the future is worth the effort.

As a follow-up to the guidance on strategic planning, Brandt offers useful analysis of the key elements necessary for achieving competitive advantage and an overview of the elements of a corporate culture. In all, Brandt is thoughtful and not overly theoretical, though perhaps a bit idealistic. Near the end of the book he concludes: the term strategic management suggests a state of affairs in which all the members of dynamic organizations move as one in response to plans made, opportunities, and threats—like a flock of migrating birds winging a twisting course across the sky in what appears to be perfectly synchronous, almost effortless motion.[35]

Looking Ahead

The literature available to entrepreneurs has grown significantly in recent years. Instead of having to depend on publications directed to the general business community—usually meaning large corporations—small business owners can select publications that address their particular needs.

While the literature is still in a developmental stage, it offers the promise of helping transform entrepreneurship into a distinct business discipline, or possibly several business disciplines, with its own set of principles and concepts. The increased awareness and new information should help small business owners do a better job of managing and add realism to the dreams of prospective entrepreneurs.

Notes

1. See the following two sources: David E. Gumpert and Jeffry A. Timmons, "Introduction," *The Insider's Guide to Small Business Resources* (Garden City, N.Y.: Doubleday, 1982) and "Small Companies: America's Hope for the 80s," *INC.*, April 1981, p. 34.

2. For proceedings of the conference, contact Entrepreneurial Studies Program, Babson College, Wellesley, Mass. 02157.

3. *Black Enterprise,* available by subscription for $10 a year from Earl G. Graves Publishing Co., Inc., 295 Madison Avenue, New York, N.Y. 10017.

4. *Venture,* available by subscription for $18 a year from Venture Magazine Inc., 35 West 45th Street, New York, N.Y. 10036.

5. *Entrepreneur,* available by subscription for $24.50 a year from Entrepreneur Magazine, 2311 Pontius Avenue, Los Angeles, Calif. 90064.

6. Richard P. Finn, *Your Fortune in Franchising* (Chicago: Contemporary Books, 1979).

7. *Franchise Opportunities Handbook,* (Washington, D.C.: U.S. Department of Commerce, 1979).

8. Albert J. Lowry, *How to Become Financially Successful by Owning Your Own Business* (New York: Simon & Schuster, 1981).

9. Brian R. Smith, *How to Prosper in Your Own Business* (Brattleboro, Vt.: Stephen Greene Press, 1981).

10. Brian R. Smith, p. 20.

11. Karl H. Vesper, *New Venture Strategies* (Englewood Cliffs, N.J.: Prentice-Hall, 1980).

12. Jeffry A. Timmons, Leonard E. Smollen, and Alexander L. M. Dingee, *New Venture Creation* (Homewood, Ill.: Richard D. Irwin, 1977).

13. William A. Delaney *Micro-Management* (New York: AMACOM, 1981).

14. *INC.,* available by subscription for $18 a year from INC. Magazine, 38 Commercial Wharf, Boston, Mass. 02110.

15. *In Business,* available by subscription for $14 a year from The JG Press, Inc., Box 323, 18 South Seventh Street, Emmaus, Penn. 18049.

16. David Post, "How to Sell to Big Companies," *INC.*, March 1981, p. 66; Cathryn Jakobson, "The Hazards of Being a Trendsetter," *INC.*, March 1981, p. 80; Daniel Finlay, "Get to Know Your Customers Better," *INC.*, June 1981, p. 142.

17. James Fawcett, "Money Alone Can't Buy Top Talent," *INC.*, March 1981, p. 92; Sharon Frederick, "Why John and Mary Won't Work," *INC.*, April 1981, p. 70; Andrea Fooner, "The Bottom Line on Day Care," *INC.*, May 1981, p. 94; David De Long, "They All Said Bill Sauey Couldn't Let Go," *INC.*, May 1981, p. 89.

18. Gumpert and Timmons, *The Insider's Guide* (New York: Doubleday, 1982).

19. Richard L. Rubin and Philip Goldberg, *The Small Business Guide to Borrowing Money* (New York: McGraw-Hill, 1980).

20. Rick Stephan Hayes, *Business Loans,* 2d edition (Boston: CBI Publishing, 1980).

21. Thomas J. Martin, *Financing the Growing Business* (New York: Holt, Rinehart and Winston, 1980).

22. International Franchise Association, 1025 Connecticut Avenue, N.W., Suite 1005, Washington, D.C. 20036.

23. DeBanks M. Henward, III and William Ginalski, *The Franchise Option* (Phoenix: Franchise Group Publishers, 1979); and David Seltz, *Franchising: Proven Techniques for Rapid Company Expansion and Market Dominance* (New York: McGraw-Hill, 1980).

24. Herman Holtz, *The $100 Billion Market: How to Do Business with the U.S. Government* (New York: AMACOM, 1980).

25. William A. Cohen, *How to Sell to the Government* (New York: John Wiley & Sons, 1981).

26. Brian R. Smith, *The Small Computer in Small Business* (Brattleboro, Vt.: Stephen Greene Press, 1981).

27. Jules A. Cohen, *How to Computerize Your Small Business* (Englewood Cliffs, N.J.: Prentice-Hall, 1980)

28. Charlotte Taylor, *Women and the Business Game: Strategies for Successful Ownership* (New York: Cornerstone Library, 1980).

29. Carol Kleiman, *Women's Networks* (New York: Lippincott & Crowell, 1980).

30. Terri P. Tepper and Nona Dawe Tepper, *The New Entrepreneurs* (New York: Universe Books, 1980).

31. John A. Welsh and Jerry F. White, *Administering the Closely Held Company* (Englewood Cliffs, N.J.: Prentice-Hall, 1980).

32. Harvey Krentzman, *Successful Management Strategies for Small Business* (Englewood Cliffs, N.J.: Prentice-Hall, 1981).

33. Krentzman, *Successful Management Strategies,* p. 9.

34. Steven C. Brandt, *Strategic Planning in Emerging Companies* (Reading Mass.: Addison-Wesley, 1981).

35. Brandt, *Strategic Planning in Emerging Companies,* pp. 86–87.

23
Getting the Most from Your Banking Relationship

JAMES McNEILL STANCILL

Because banking relationships are based so heavily on trust, businesses should establish a relationship with a particular bank and a banker within the bank before the need arises, James McNeill Stancill advises. While a bank's lending rates are important, its services and familiarity with various industries should also be examined, he says.

Choosing a bank is one of the most important business decisions confronting the developing firm. Too often, though, the decision is made on the basis of the bank's convenient location.

Because the banking relationship plays such a significant role in determining company costs and even a company's survival during difficult times, the choice of a bank should involve a more systematic and detailed approach. This article will examine some of the basic considerations that should go into that decision.

The first thing to keep in mind is that banks vary substantially in the services they offer and in the expertise of their staffs. Banks can be broadly classified as retail banks, wholesale banks, and combination banks.

Retail banks specialize in personal loans, car loans, and home improvement loans, along with personal checking accounts. Wholesale banks specialize in business loans, and their personnel are trained to understand

Author's Note: I wish to express my thanks for helpful suggestions to Stephen A. Ferris, vice president, Bank of America, London office; and Leonard Weil, president, Manufacturers Bank, Los Angeles.

financial statements and are familiar with various financing approaches. Combination banks deal in both personal and business financing. Usually, though, certain branches of combination banks are designated as retail- and others as wholesale-oriented branches; feel free to inqure if the specialization of a particular branch isn't clear.

One of the best ways to find a suitable wholesale bank is to examine those in industrial or commercial centers. Though some retail branches are located in such areas to provide checking and other services to workers, you can usually avoid a retail office by paying attention to the name of the bank or bank branch.

In other areas, such as in regional shopping centers or downtown city areas, the distinction between wholesale and retail banks may not be clear unless the bank's name is indicative. Manufacturers, Farmers and Merchants, Commerce, and similar bank names are a good—albeit not a certain—way of locating a business-oriented bank. Asking businesses similar to yours where they do their banking is also helpful.

Because banking has become so much more competitive during the past ten years, business-oriented banks aggressively seek accounts from businesses of all sizes. When business development officers—the bankers seeking your account—approach you, receive them willingly to learn what they have to offer. Compare their offers to your existing bank's services. But be leery of the bank that seems to be offering only a lower rate on current borrowing. Rate breaks have a way of being retracted as time goes by and conditions change.

Evaluating Subtle Factors

Once you have identified several wholesale-oriented banks or branches, you must next narrow down the field. This can be done by considering points that banks ordinarily avoid discussing.

For example, some business-oriented banks have had a surfeit of losses or delinquent loans to real estate investment trusts (REITs) in recent years. Such experiences typically make banks quite conservative in their loan policies. They tend to shy away from loans to developing small companies and instead give preference to large industrial companies or even to auto or home improvement loans.

If the bank you are investigating or the one you use falls into such a category, major problems could develop if your company is the least bit marginal as a borrower—and how many developing businesses aren't?

Even if the prospective bank isn't trying to cleanse itself of REITs and other similar problems, it might just have a very high loan-to-asset ratio, which indicates a rather loaned-up position. Again, this will diminish the zeal with which a bank will respond to your needs. So, in the course of the initial interview with the bank's representative, ask about this point. (In today's business environment, a ratio of 85% of loans to assets would be considered rather high).

If the ratio of the bank in question is high, new and marginally profitable customers could easily get squeezed or rationed out of a loan request when money becomes tight.[1]

Varying Loan Policies

Another possibly important factor differentiating one wholesale-oriented bank from another is the bank's willingness to make intermediate or longer term loans. To some banks such loans are anathema, but to other banks they are a most useful way to serve the needs of customers. And even if a company does not immediately need a loan longer than one year's duration, the company might need such a loan at a future date.

Inquiring about such loans also provides a clue as to the bank's overall attitude. "Old school" banks will probably hold firm to the adage that banks should match the maturity of their loans to the maturity of their liabilities, or deposits. While this makes good sense financially, in general, it can be taken too literally, to the detriment of developing firms that need help.

A prospective bank or branch should also be screened with respect to the types of business loans it makes. Will the bank make an unsecured or signature loan? (I have always thought the term "unsecured" to be a bit ironic. The bank asks for personal guarantees of all principal stockholders and, as a general creditor, the bank is entitled to a claim on everything not otherwise secured. This is after the bank exercises its right of "offset," which means that the bank seizes any money the company has on deposit with the bank and applies it against the amount owed.)

Will the bank consider establishing—verbally or in writing—a line of credit for your company so that borrowing can be done when needed? If the bank feels that the company's needs are too large or its statements too weak for a signature loan, what sort of loan will it make against receivables?

A bank's flexibility within its official policies is important as well. Some banks have only one way to make a receivables loan and that is for a specified percentage (80% would be a progressive bank's target limit). A two-step procedure is followed.

First, the information is put on file with the secretary of state, making public knowledge the fact that the bank has a claim on accounts receivable, inventory, and, possibly, equipment. Following this, the company can borrow by sending to the bank a list of all eligible accounts receivable, which are usually those that are not more than 90 days old.

This process is not overly restrictive, but if a bank wished to be accommodating to its customer, it might not require a separate listing of all accounts receivable each time the company needed money. Instead, with an eye toward the amount of accounts receivable the firm normally has, the bank might establish an upper dollar limit against which the firm could borrow on request. Then the bank might check on the firm occasionally, say, every six months.

For example, if the firm normally has about $1 million in receivables, the bank would allow loans up to $800,000 at any one time. This arrangement would be obviously less cumbersome and less expensive to administer, particularly if a lot of small value receivables were involved. Therefore, if the bank exercises minimal supervision over the account (rather than very strict supervision), this would be a sign that the bank considers the customer a good overall risk. So, if everything else is equal and you are selecting a new bank, look for differences in arrangements that are potentially helpful to your company.

A bank's approach to accounts receivable financing can also provide an important warning signal that that bank is not the right bank for the business firm. If the bank representative says the bank handles accounts receivable financing but that that end of the business is handled "downtown," the implication is that this popular form of business loan is over the head of the personnel in the bank branch.

How then can this branch be a truly wholesale-oriented branch of the type that businesses need? Also, that approach suggests a distinctly more impersonal attitude toward such lending. If the agreement calls for 80% of the eligible receivables, that's all that will be lent. But such an approach fails to recognize an important fact of business life, which is that every firm needs an occasional accommodation—like loans of 90%, 100%, or 120% of the receivables. If this happens only occasionally, and not every other week, many banks try to accommodate their customers.

How about inventory loans? To some banks this, too, is a problem area. "Finance companies are asset lenders—we are not," they say. But in today's banking and business environment, a loan on inventory of, say, 50% to 70% makes reasonable business sense. Again, such a loan may not be needed by your company, but its availability is indicative of a more progressive wholesale bank.

Bank Services and Experience

After discussing the types of loans that are available, ask about the different types of services the bank can offer. Inquire if the bank offers such services as payroll check preparation, preparation of letters of credit, lockbox facilities, credit reference checks, international services, money market securities sales and purchases, and possible services for you personally.

Again, even though your company may not need all such services immediately, your business could well need them in the future. And the range and depth of services indicates the progressive nature of a bank.

If you can use letters of credit (LCs) in your business—and many businesses could use LCs if they and their banks would explore the possibilities—what is the attitude of the bank toward LCs? Some banks view them simply as a loan and count them against a customer's line of credit and debt capacity. Other banks take a more enlightened attitude and, while they don't issue LCs recklessly, they may do so much less restrictively.

A bank that is imaginative with regard to the services it offers is likely to be imaginative when your firm has a problem.

You also should expect to be able to negotiate the matter of compensating balances. Frequently they can be avoided entirely if the bank wants your business badly. Remember that compensating balances are a means of bolstering bank earnings on your account and are not intended as a source of collateral.

Somewhere in this screening process, inquire about the bank's experience with firms in your industry and of similar size. If a bank has a good deal of such experience, it will be more knowledgeable about the idiosyncrasies of your business. (And with knowledge and understanding goes confidence, a vital ingredient in the loan-granting process.)

You may find that the bank to which you are talking does specialize in your industry, but in a different branch. If the bank branch that specializes in your line of business is not conveniently located near your company, it may still be advantageous to use that office as the point of contact even though you make check deposits at a more convenient branch.

Finally, the question of bank size should be dealt with. How big should your bank be? This is, indeed, a difficult question. The bank should certainly be big enough, which means that loans to your business will not be more than 10% of the bank's capital. And in this regard, keep in mind the near-term growth of your company. It would be unfortunate to overlook this point and in a few years find that you have outgrown your bank just when you need an old friend.

The principle that I believe should govern the size dilemma is this: go with a bank that is big enough as outlined previously, that has the lending philosophy and services you need, and that *wants* your business, irrespective of size. A smaller bank that wants your business and can fulfill your needs makes a lot better sense than a larger bank that is relatively indifferent to your business. In fact, it may be to the company's distinct disadvantage to be too high up, so to speak, in a big bank's hierarchy.

Unless there is a very strong business reason or a very close personal relationship, being a little fish in the proverbial big pond might result in service problems that could be quite detrimental to your company's best interest. If you need some personal attention to your business problems at a time when your banker is involved in a much bigger account, you will wish you had more clout.

Choosing Your Banker

When a business manager has a financial emergency and has to literally introduce himself or herself to a banker, the odds of getting that bank's help are slim at best. Why? Because banks lend money to people they know, not to strangers. And the longer a banker knows someone, the more likely he or she is to accommodate a loan request.

A common mistake, especially by managers of developing companies, is to wait until the need arises to meet the bank manager. As we all know, the worst time to ask for a loan is when you need it. At that time, a firm's financial statements are likely to look their worst.

But another salient reason such timing is inadvisable is that a banker considers the firm's managerial talent before making a loan. True, collateral is important, especially for developing businesses, but if the banker does not have confidence in the managerial ability of the parties concerned, then the bank is unlikely to accommodate a loan request. (This contrasts with finance companies, which usually think first of collateral value.) Failure to anticipate a cash shortage is one of the earmarks of an inept manager.

How, then, do you ask for a loan before you need it? By getting to know your banker and allowing your banker to get to know you and your plans as the manager of a developing business.

First, you must choose the right banker. Usually the bank assigns an account officer on the basis of the size and importance of the account to the bank. Banks usually assign small businesses to the most junior lending-staff member, who may not even be a bank officer. (The lowest officer rank is usually assistant vice-president.)

But the business firm is not without a say in this selection—or at least it should have a right to indicate a preference. The principles to keep in minde are, first, to get a banker with sufficient clout in the bank (usually the person with the highest title) and, second, to seek compatibility.

If the firm feels it has been assigned an account executive lacking in influence, this may be a symptom that the bank or the office of the bank under consideration is too big for the company. Perhaps another branch has someone with the combination of experience and authority needed by businesses of your type. When your loan is being discussed in a loan committee meeting, it is comforting to know that your banker has the confidence of the group. If the committee is wary because of your banker's lack of experience, then its consideration of your firm as a loan candidate will be all the more difficult.

Seeking compatibility with the loan officer is almost as important as seeking someone with the requisite clout. For instance, you should probably avoid a banker who is substantially older than you, especially if the banker is near retirement, because all the rapport and confidence you build with the banker over the course of time will retire when the banker leaves.

Conversely, if you are fortunate enough to choose a standout banker who is moving up rapidly in the bank's organization structure, how do you protect yourself from losing the relationship to a promotion? Becoming familiar with other bankers in the same office, including your banker's superior, will hedge this possibility.

Other bases of compatibility include residence in the same neighborhood, joint community interests, athletic interests, and, of course, being graduates of the same school. Compatibility can obviously be established without such common interests, but they often provide the head start necessary to establish the degree of confidence and trust desirable in your relations with your banker.

Building a Relationship

With the bank and banker chosen, the interesting job of establishing rapport with your banker begins. Start this process by inviting your banker to visit your business. Don't worry that your business isn't larger than it is, but make every effort to put forth a good show. A dirty plant, for instance, is often a sign of either inept management or a manager who is too busy to worry about details. One rule of thumb is to pretend that the banker is an insurance or fire inspector and to have the plant ready for scrutiny.

Arrange to have your company's financial statements—usually quarterly statements are sufficient—sent to the banker without being asked. Some businesses slip up on this point. Revealing the financial health (or lack of it) to a banker who is a virtual stranger is apt to be quite distasteful.

But this information will have to be provided if a loan is requested, so why not start immediately? In fact, providing your banker with quarterly statements without being prodded is possibly the single most important thing that a manager can do to build rapport with the banker.

You might even go beyond simply providing quarterly statements by also providing your banker with a quarterly briefing on your business—what happened during the last quarter and what is expected to happen during the upcoming quarter or year. The most important element in such a briefing is a cash flow statement. If you can demonstrate that you know what you are doing and that you have been accurate in your previous forecasts, you will find that the banker is more receptive to requests for future loans. This is really the essence of asking a bank for a loan before you need it.

In deciding how best to keep your banker informed about your company, keep one rule in mind: *never* surprise your banker in an adverse way. Bad surprises mean risk and uncertainty, but more important, they mean a management that is not in control.

If you know that you are going to be unable to meet a payment, let your banker know ahead of time. If there are dark clouds gathering in your industry, talk about them before they become serious storms. Don't go out of your way to scare your banker, but candid appraisals of adverse events as well as potential trouble spots will go a long way toward building the confidence that bankers need to have in their customers.

How Important Are Interest Rates?

If the firm has done a good job of establishing rapport with its banker, the manager and the banker will find themselves able to discuss rates in a calm and reasonable way. Managers should be aware, though, of how unpleasant it is for the banker to be continually hassled over rates. True, you don't want to pay more than is reasonably necessary, but rate haggling will likely reveal a lack of the mutual trust necessary for a good business firm–bank relationship. During a financial pinch you need a loan, not a bargain interest rate. Do not jeopardize the loan itself by haggling over a slightly better rate. (Banks, as opposed to some other lenders, usually will not make a loan just because the customer offers to pay a higher interest rate.)

Banks sometimes grant a special interest rate to businesses in their difficult early-growth period. Without explicitly saying so, however, banks want to be able later to charge at least a normal rate or even a slight premium. Forgetting the help that the bank provided when the company needed it most will go a long way toward destroying the rapport it takes so long to establish.

And in the process of nurturing the relationship with your banker, keep in mind that you should never, but never, talk off the record with your banker. If your banker is doing the job, he or she will be continually on the lookout for symptoms of trouble, together with evidence of character and managerial skill. When discussing your company before a loan committee, your banker must show no hesitation or reservation. Anything short of this is likely to lead to second thoughts by all concerned at the bank.

Concluding Comments

Once you have chosen a bank and built a relationship with a banker, what expectations are reasonable in the area of loyalty? Simply stated, banks have the right to expect that a customer stick with them over a period of years and not be constantly flitting around town looking for a better interest rate. At the same time, companies have the right to expect that the bank will stick with them by providing needed capital, especially during times of crisis when vacillating can be particularly dangerous.

And how do you finally measure the bank's performance? You really need to review the relationship over time. Whether the bank has provided the necessary funds is the major measuring stick, but what of all the other services a business-oriented bank can and should provide? Are your deposited checks being processed promptly? Is the bank helpful and constructive in your cash management? Does the bank perform other services, such as the purchase and sale of money market securities, with a pleasantness and degree of competence bespeaking a first-class business-oriented bank?

If the answers are yes, congratulations. You have done a good job selecting the right bank, choosing the right banker, and establishing appropriate rapport. If not, consider doing some shopping.

Notes

1. An excellent article on the problem of credit rationing for smaller firms is "Private Credit Rationing," by Paul S. Anderson and James R. Ostas, *New England Economic Review*, May/June 1977, p. 24.

24
Can Small Businesses Use Consultants?

HARVEY C. KRENTZMAN and JOHN N. SAMARAS

Managing a small business is a way of life, and those who engage in it are likely to feel that the usual kinds of problem solving are not for them. But that does not mean that their long-range problems are not pressing, or that their time and ability are not absorbed by daily affairs.

In Los Angeles, the owner of a small electronics distributing firm sits at his desk, lonely and perplexed because his business is in trouble. "But nothing should be wrong," he thinks to himself. "We've doubled our sales, yet the very fact that we have so many orders is ruining me. We can't even make deliveries on time, anymore. And now the bookkeeper tells me we have a pile of bills that can't be met. With all these sales, where has the cash gone? What have I done wrong?"

In New York City, a small clothing manufacturer returns from her first vacation in ten years to find that her plant manager has died during her absence. "There go my vacations for the next ten years," she thinks. "Whom should I train to take his place? Ben? Sara? Maybe even Harry? And should I appoint someone now, or should I wait six months or so and see who shows the most promise? But in six months this place could become a hotbed of politicking. I've got to decide now, but what is the right decision?"

To people like these, beset by constant problems, the use of a management consultant becomes a possibility which they, at some point in their careers, must consider. But even this decision is not an easy one.

"Are consultants really useful to the smaller firm?" one person wonders. "Is the consultant's approach only suitable for big businesses? I'm not General Motors, you know." Another thinks of the complaints he has heard about how much consultants charge, but then he remembers some of his business acquaintances reporting that they would have been happy to pay twice the fee for the services rendered to their company by a consultant. Still another wonders secretly if hiring a consultant would be an admission that she is no longer able to manage her business. Imagine, the business she built up with her own hands, and now she has to turn to an outsider for help!

Issues like these, generally discussed only on a person-to-person basis—if at all—are much in need of being impartially and thoughtfully met. For this reason, we conducted a survey of 700 managers of small businesses located in every state, employing a questionnaire that not only inquired into their experiences with consultants but probed their apprehensions as to the usefulness of outside help.

Since readers know that the information a questionnaire turns up must be evaluated and presented, it might be important for us to state quite frankly our qualifications for doing this. One of the authors speaks from ten years of experience in consulting exclusively with small businesses; the other wrote a doctoral thesis on the relationship between small businessmen and consultants. Thus it should be noted that in presenting the survey results we have made use of insights gained from personal experiences with managers of small businesses on their problems, as well as facts collected directly from the businesspeople themselves.

As an indication of the interest the owners of small businesses have in this question, over 30% of those surveyed filled out and returned our questionnaire. We hope that this report of the attitudes expressed by the more than 200 respondents will dispel much of the confusion surrounding this important issue. We hope further:

1. That it will indicate to small business executives the areas in which some of their fellow businesspeople have found consultants to be of use, and at the same time help some other managers of small enterprises to understand their own attitudes which keep them from taking advantage of the possible services of outside specialists.

2. That the results will reveal to consultants the reason why small business contributes only $2 million of the estimated $400 million spent annually in the United States for consulting—because there are serious weaknesses in the programs they make available to small enterprise.

After a brief outline of the size of the dilemma in which small business executives find themselves, we shall report our findings. Not surprisingly, the actual statistics are less revealing than the implications drawn from the respondents' detailed comments. To cut through a number of conflicting definitions, our concept of a small business is one that is directly operated by an owner-manager or, if not so operated, does not have more than 500 employees.

Dimensions of the Dilemma

One might well ask, at this point, why there is any reason to worry about whether or not small companies use consultants. The answer is twofold: (a) the small business executive has a host of problems, and (b) consultants represent a *potential* source of help.

On the first point, witness these figures on business failures which shown undeniably that this section of our economy has had more than its share of troubles:

☐ Postwar failures of individual firms reached their peak in 1958, when the figure hit 1,495 for a single month (March) and 14,964 for the 12-month period. Since then the picture has improved, but the rate of demise still runs as high as 1,100 to 1,200 in an average month.

☐ Current trends, furthermore, indicate that out of every 10,000 firms existing today, 54 will fail during the course of the year, and, according to the Small Business Administration, business bankruptcies are increasing.[1]

But the number of enterprises that actually go under calls attention only to part of the story. When we remember that during periods of economic distress the net profits of small firms decline far out of proportion to those of their larger brothers, we cannot help wondering how many of them manage to survive, on a day-to-day basis, hoping against hope for continued national prosperity.

Common as it is to blame mergers, taxes, politicians, unions, and many other external conditions as the source of all ills, the facts of the case, as several observers have pointed out,[2] do not support such scapegoatism.

A Dun & Bradstreet study indicates that "inexperience and incompetence" accounted for 92% of the business failures in 1958![3] Does this mean, necessarily, that there are fewer competent people in small companies than in large? Of course not—but it does show that the margin for error is much narrower and managerial resources are much thinner.

The heads of small firms, constantly under fire, face a daily barrage of operating problems. More often than not they stand alone, with staff assistance at a minimum, and with virtually no reserves in time or money. Any number of unforeseen events can tip them over the edge.

For example, many small enterprises run into sudden crises for reasons like these, which a larger competitor can take in stride:

1 A major customer demands lower prices or cancels his account.
2 A competitor puts a new product or service into the field.
3 An important employee becomes ill or leaves.
4 The union requests a new contract.

5 The owner's family pressures him into spending less time "at the office."

For the executive of a small business, solving business problems is a matter of the gravest personal concern. But beyond the question of individual lives and a handful of families is the need to make this sector of our economy dynamic and progressive. We often forget that in the United States today there are more than 4.3 million small companies which account for 96% of the going businesses in the country and 50% of total economic activity. At a time when we need growth as never before, the health of these enterprises should be of substantial concern to all.

Sources of Help

We should point out here that many small businesses do accept aid from outside agencies, although management consultants as such may not be called in. For example:

☐ A number of firms try to find literature which they hope will contain suggestions relating to their particular situations. But lack of time to digest this material (coupled with the irrelevance of much of it to their specific problems) limits its usefulness.

☐ Many executives of small businesses turn to friends to help them with their operating dilemmas. As sound-thinking and well-meaning as these people may be, they seldom possess the salient facts in regard to the company or industry involved, or the varied experience necessary to give much solid help—particularly in a specific situation.

☐ A firm's banker, lawyer, and accountant are often called on to serve in what is essentially a consulting capacity. Of course these men have much to offer, but, except by chance of circumstance, they lack the rounded view possessed by consultants who, perforce, are experienced in a range of problems. One thing the manager of a small company particularly needs is to identify his problems in the first place.

☐ For some executives, the board of directors represents a real resource. One manager was saved thousands of dollars because a member of his board suggested a new insurance procedure just before a fire occurred which wiped out a large section of his shop. A well-informed, hard-working, practical-minded outside board can be a precious asset, although it is true that its members often do not have the time to help the manager in executing their good suggestions. Securing such board members is no easy task, of course, since they are rare among small companies.

☐ Still another outside source of help was described by Louis E. Newman in a recent issue of *HBR*.[4] Newman has established what he calls an "Advisor-Board" of specialists in functional areas that are important to his firm. These people, highly competent as specialists but equally experienced in general management problems, meet about once a month to criticize and advise the president. In this way they prevent him from developing what Newman calls a "god complex," and help him to maintain objectivity.

There is much to be said for this plan. It tends to force the president to act on a long-range basis because the advisers, since they do not live with the day-to-day dilemmas, consider the company's operations in broader terms. They bring fresh points of view to bear, and push the president into a position where he has to defend his decisions. In a case like Newman's, where the owner and the manager are different people, the suggestions and opinions of the Advisor-Board can help the manager sell the boss on sound projects.

On the other hand, for all its help it does not provide the whole answer. Given the fact that the president himself selects the members of the Advisor-Board, objectivity on larger issues may suffer somewhat. Particularly, in the usual situation in which the owner and manager are the same person, the effectiveness of the group will be lessened since the independent power of the president is greater. And most important—as we shall see later on— many small business executives need operating assistance as much as or more than they need a sounding board or good advice.

Even if the Advisor-Board does meet with key executives from time to time, it is almost impossible for such a board to appreciate fully the situation in which the manager operates. Its advice, without the opportunity or responsibility for follow-through, may constitute merely an additional pressure on the president. At best, it can only provide ideas, not much-needed executive talent for improving the "shop."

Finally, there is the Small Business Administration (SBA) which can help the smaller concern to gain access to adequate capital and credit, obtain a fair share of government procurement, and develop management training programs. The SBA also supplies some technical and production advice and gives aid during periods of disaster. But, useful as it is in its sphere, the SBA neither attempts nor pretends to do a specific consulting job in relation to the problems of a particular firm.

What Consultants Offer

In pointing out the limitations of these several sources of aid, we do not mean to ignore their considerable strengths. Certainly, many firms have been materially helped by their continuing contacts with accountants, bankers, directors, the SBA, and other agencies or individuals beyond the four walls of the company office. Each of these sources offers help in certain areas, and in effect emphasizes the potential gain that can come from outside assistance. The question that small business management has to answer is whether or not the consultant, with a more varied background and experience, represents a more practical source of assistance.

The executives of small businesses are probably far better informed about the specifics of *their own industries* than are most advisers. What they need is not only creative advice but on-the-job assistance (even if part-time) in carrying out projects such as these:

☐ Development of new and scientific methods of organization and operation.

☐ Introduction of new methods of producing or marketing existing and new products.

☐ Improvement of personnel recruitment, selection, and training.

☐ Resolution of immediate crisis situations and establishment of long-range planning techniques that will minimize future crises and maximize future opportunities.

Finally, although it is difficult to tell whether the chicken or the egg comes first, it does seem that the Association of Consulting Management Engineers, Inc. (ACME) has a valid point when it states:

> It is interesting to note that the most frequent users of consultants are usually the most successful companies. This is to be expected, as the most progressive-minded managements are constantly seeking more effective ways of managing their businesses.[5]

Thus, outsiders *assuming that they are qualified,* offer a fresh point of view—a broad understanding of management as opposed to a technical knowledge of a specific industry. Also, they must have, and must be able to exercise, an objective, unbiased point of view. And this will depend not only on the attitudes they bring to the job but on the attitudes of those who receive them.

Businesspeople's Attitudes

The basic facts that emerge from the survey are that only 32% of the responding firms have ever used consulting services; and further, as shown in Exhibit 1, that the smaller the number of employees, the less use of consultants. At the top of our category—firms with 400 to 499 employees—the usage is 57%; at the bottom—firms with fewer than 100 employees—the figure drops to only 27%.

These results by no means imply that there has not been a considerable effort on the part of consulting firms to promote their wares. Some 93% of our respondents have received brochures from consultants, and 84% of them

Exhibit 1. Percentage of Companies in Various Size Categories That Use Consultants

NUMBER OF EMPLOYEES	
0 — 99	27%
100—199	35%
200—299	39%
300—399	50%
400—499	57%

have been approached directly. But, as Exhibit 2 shows, the success of these determined efforts on the part of consultants appears to have been largely abortive. While 77% of the nonusers had been contacted by both mail and personal call, only 6% reported that they had been or were involved in negotiations with a consulting firm.

How adequate is this 6% return? Does it represent the limits of the market for consultants among small businesses? Hardly, for as Exhibit 3 illustrates, as many as 42% of nonusers of consultants have contemplated using a consultant, and 65% would consider using one who understood the nature of their firms' problems and operations.

Reasons for Rejection

Given this picture, and the evidence it provides of a potentially substantial but undeveloped source of management advice for these businesspeople, let

Exhibit 2. Success of Consultants in Soliciting Nonusers

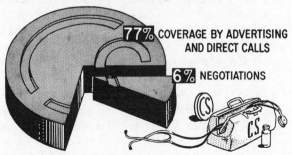

77% COVERAGE BY ADVERTISING AND DIRECT CALLS

6% NEGOTIATIONS

Exhibit 3.   The Market for Consultants Among Nonusers, on the Basis of Their Own Statements

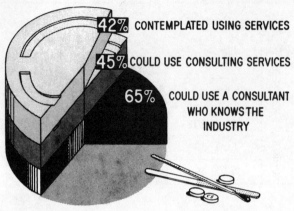

42% CONTEMPLATED USING SERVICES

45% COULD USE CONSULTING SERVICES

65% COULD USE A CONSULTANT
WHO KNOWS THE
INDUSTRY

us take a more searching look at some of the possible reasons for the latter's rejection of such help.

Fee Fears

One problem with consulting, as small business executives see it, is the size of the fee charged. How real is this barrier? Interestingly enough, as Exhibit 4 shows, while 87% of the nonusers claimed that the fee was of significant concern to them, only 24% of those using consultants stated that cost was an important consideration.

It seems clear that the idea of high fees scares off many managers who might be potential users of consultants. This fear is especially inhibiting to the owner-managers of small businesses, of course, because their dollars are customarily in short supply, and they are vitally interested in making the best possible use of their limited capital. The decision to hire a consultant is in competition with decisions concerning the purchase of a new machine or expanding the advertising campaign—the decision being based, of course, on what they consider the most productive way to employ available funds.

Presumably those who use consultants seem less concerned about the size of the fee because their companies have already received certain benefits. One user reported, "Our concept of fair charges would vary with the kind of information we desire. A fee of $250 a day might be inexpensive but, on the other hand, $50 a day might be extremely costly."

What is the fee which most respondents consider to be fair? Both users and nonusers generally agree on a charge of $100 per day. Once again, though, the conservatism of the nonusers is shown in the following figures as to what is considered a fair fee for one day's consulting service:

	Users	Nonusers
$ 25	2%	11%
50	12	26
75	7	12
100	50	44
125	23	4
150	6	3
	100%	100%

Exhibit 4.   Factors Influencing Decisions on Using Consulting Services

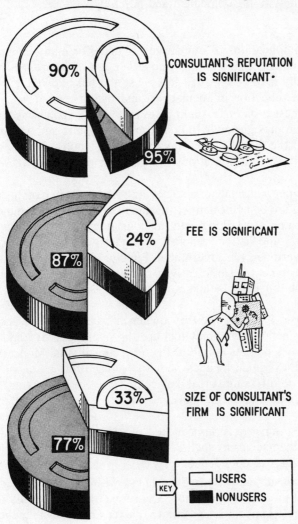

90%

CONSULTANT'S REPUTATION
IS SIGNIFICANT.

95%

87%

24%

FEE IS SIGNIFICANT

33%

SIZE OF CONSULTANT'S
FIRM IS SIGNIFICANT

77%

KEY

☐ USERS
■ NONUSERS

In short, the complaint about high fees expresses skepticism about the worth of the results expected rather than about the money charge as such.

Many of these fears as to the size of the consultant's fee could be alleviated if the owner-managers were not required to sign a formal contract; in other words, if they were able to fire the consultant should they feel progress is not being made. Moreover, if the consultant were paid weekly, as part of the regular payroll, it would accomplish two things:

1 It would establish the image of the consultant as an integral part of the business.
2 It would make it easier for the owner to compare his out-of-pocket costs with his immediate and potential savings.

Failure Fears

One of the implications of our survey is that, for many chief executives, calling on a consultant symbolizes an admission of failure. Such people are so emotionally involved in their business, and has allowed it to become so completely a reflection of themselves and their personal worth, that they see *its* weaknesses as *their* weaknesses and feel its agonies as their own. To such a person, asking for help is like calling it quits and accepting defeat. Facing up to the fact that their company is in trouble forces them to look squarely at their own limitations; so they put off the day of reckoning as long as they can.

One owner of a small manufacturing concern started off his relationship with a consultant by being actively ashamed of having him around. If anyone came in when he was talking with the consultant, he would slip him out the side entrance, and act, in general, as if they were a pair of conspirators plotting to overthrow the government. Finally, after many months of working together, the owner felt sufficiently at ease with the consultant as to introduce him to some business acquaintances—not as a consultant, but as an "associate"!

The basic insecurity felt by owner-managers may be aggravated by what many smaller companies feel are the overaggressive and sometimes misleading sales pitches tossed at them by consultants. Modest about their own capabilities, small businesspeople are resentful and suspicious of the consultant who offers universal panaceas. Here are three typical comments made by respondents to our survey:

☐ "We have been approached by many consultants. All have presented themselves as such experts in all fields that they did not inspire any feelings of confidence."

☐ "Consultants seem to be faced with the problem of having to oversell in order to get a job. Consequently their results cannot fully come up to expectations. A more relaxed approach . . . would improve their popularity and results."

☐ "I feel that it would be very desirable for the small businessman to be able to obtain competent consultation in this field at fees that a small business could afford, but when large organizations use high-pressure methods and charge exorbitant fees for incompetent service, it is my opinion that the business consultation service will suffer as a result."

Perhaps these fears on the part of the owner-manager account for the fact (shown in Exhibit 4) that 77% of the nonusers of consultants revealed a definite preference to be served by a small consulting firm. While this may reflect an opinion that the small consulting company would charge a lower fee than would the larger consultant, it may also indicate that small businesspeople do believe that their problems will be handled with more understanding and sympathy by another small company.

Wrong Man Fear

Closely related to this reaction is the apparently growing suspicion that the salesperson whom one meets and the consultant who does the job will turn out to be altogether different people. The former may be a most impressive young person who seems to size up your problem quickly and shows all the signs of being able to tackle the job with vigor and skill. But then, on the appointed day, a far less impressive specimen may appear to take the assignment.

Chief executives feel cheated by this procedure, which is apparently so widespread today that it actually deters some companies from hiring management help—as witness these strongly worded comments from the survey:

☐ "Regardless of his *firm's* reputation, it is the *man* himself who makes or breaks the job. And that is the prime thing so often disfavoring the use of consultants. The field analyst selling the consulting firm's services may be an excellent man, capable of discerning what must be done for the client, but so often the resident consultant sent in to do the job leaves much to be desired. Poor man, poor job, and another cynic added to the 'displeased client' list."

☐ "The greatest single problem on consultants is that they rarely let you meet the man who is going to do the consulting work before you hire him."

Competitive Fear

Small business owners are also fearful of an exchange of information. They are often afraid to talk over the specifics of their firm with a consultant for fear that their competitors might find out something useful from him. Unless they are familiar with consultants and how they work—and have confidence in the reputation of the consulting firm—they suspect consultants of being possible leaks to other firms. It is interesting to note, in this regard, that 90% of users and 95% of nonusers of consultants agree that the reputation of the consulting firm represents a most significant factor in the process of consultant selection (Exhibit 4).

Lost Time Fear

Another factor that makes it difficult for executives to get just the right person is a shortage of time, a typical attribute of the small company manager. This time shortage discourages them in at least two ways. In the first place, it is not easy for them to find the hours necessary to spot the person they need. Said one respondent, "Locating the right consulting firm, at the right price, and arranging to work together efficiently to further the company's financial and business interests, seems to be the stumbling block that many times postpones action."

Secondly, they are afraid that they will have to spend a great deal of valuable time talking with the outsider once the hiring takes place. A dramatization of a typical remark reported in the survey would show the businessperson saying to the consultant: "Look, I can't take the time to talk with you, and my people can't either. We just lost a worker on our production line, and we have to replace him. Maybe later." But of course there is never a "later" because there is always some new crisis to meet.

Wants and Needs

Behind these reasons seems to exist a lack of appreciation of what a good consultant might have to offer. Many managers feel they have been "burned," while others have heard stories about friends who feel they have been "abused." Some feel they are "too small"; others labor under the illusion that their particular problems are "unique"; and still others view the outsider's job as limited to narrow, current operating issues. "Our particular business," reported one manager, "is undergoing a rapid and drastic change which necessitates anticipating the future rather than correcting current problems"; therefore, he concluded, he did not need help. It may be that consulting firms need to reevaluate the advertising and informational material they are beaming to small companies.

The survey shows, also, that small firms are interested in hard facts rather than promises of some vague, future benefits. Nearly 50% of the nonusers are seeking evidence of success a given consulting firm has had in the past, so that they may relate this experience to their own situations, and, in turn, select the consulting organization that will be best for them.

By and large, the evidence of our survey indicates that small business managers believe that it is necessary to find just the right consultant for their needs if the relationship is to be fruitful. But they are not sure just where to find one, how to judge one, how to use one, and what yardstick to hold up to their performance. (Our own experience indicates, however, that a consultant to small business need not know the specifics of any one trade or industry; in fact, the real value of a consultant lies in their ability to make the general principles of good management work in specific companies.)

Over the long run this insecurity turns into complacency—another facet of the small business–consultant problem. This complacency is illustrated in Exhibit 5. Of the group using consultants, 76% reported that they felt they could define their problem before the consultant was hired; yet 70% of the same group admitted that other problem areas had, in fact, been discovered during the period of the consultant's efforts! Thus, speculation arises as to how many problem areas remain hidden from the sight of the complacent manager who feels in complete control of all phases of the operation.

Such a manager ought to consider how our respondents appraise the performance of their consultants. As Exhibit 6 shows, as many as 81% rate the consultants' performance as good or as better than expected. Apparently, also, expectations were fairly realistic, because the proportion of users reporting satisfaction with their consultants' performance is only slightly lower, 78%.

Hostile Hosts

It is true, of course, that consultants have often taken the wrong tack in their solicitation of small company clients. But it is equally true that some of the latter show attitudes of hostility that are so extreme as to be obviously distorted. Some of the comments elicited by our questionnaire fall into this class:

☐ "We could use a business consultant, but do we need one? I hope not!"

☐ "If they are so smart, why aren't they running their own business instead of working for peanuts? They're industrial parasites working on a fixed formula."

Exhibit 5. Extent to Which Consultants Discovered Unsuspected Problems

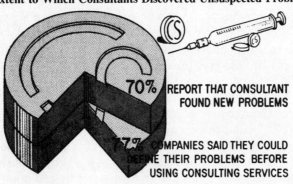

70% REPORT THAT CONSULTANT FOUND NEW PROBLEMS

77% COMPANIES SAID THEY COULD DEFINE THEIR PROBLEMS BEFORE USING CONSULTING SERVICES

Exhibit 6. Users' Evaluation of Consultants' Performance as a Result of Their Experience

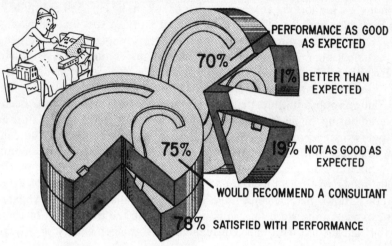

PERFORMANCE AS GOOD AS EXPECTED — 70%

BETTER THAN EXPECTED — 11%

NOT AS GOOD AS EXPECTED — 19%

WOULD RECOMMEND A CONSULTANT — 75%

SATISFIED WITH PERFORMANCE — 78%

☐ "I've been with firms that have used consultants; our firm used them prior to my regime. I have never seem them achieve a single constructive purpose. If consultants knew what they were doing, they'd be running a company themselves."

Often preconceived prejudices like these will prevent the business manager from turning to a consultant for help, when that obviously is the wise thing to do. A number of sudden changes may occur even in the apparently successful small firm which can cause serious dislocations. For instance:

☐ A firm may begin to experience trouble with delivery dates because it has become unresponsive to customer needs.

☐ An unexpectedly large order from an important customer may throw an inflexible company into complete confusion.

☐ As the chief executive grows older and retirement approaches, he may well find himself without a successor ready to take over.

☐ Internal dislocations, like the misassignment of personnel, may inhibit growth and may prevent an enterprise from recognizing its full potential.

Too Late, Cinderella

The "Cinderella" companies may be the most glaring examples. Here the chances are that the top decision maker—who is often a scientist or production expert rather than a manager as such—has become busier and busier with immediate problems, and that over-all systems and controls have not been adjusted to cope with the new dimensions of the company. Possibly the organization has piled one system on top of another instead or redesigning the whole operation, and the manager may not even be aware of it. The manager may look over production or sales figures, hope they are accurate, and go on from there.

The manager may be vaguely conscious of waste, but not particuarly worried since the company is growing and making money. But employees are becoming accustomed to laxity; profits are being thrown away; and one day the machinery will start slipping and stuttering. Then there will be trouble. Twelve o'clock will strike; it will be too late for management development or procedure revision. A big shake-up will be the only way out.

Challenge to Consultants

Thus, there seems to be considerable evidence that many small businesses ought to reconsider their attitudes toward consultants. But there is an even heavier obligation on the consulting industry to do some careful thinking about the services it offers.

We are convinced that many well-respected consulting firms are simply not set up to provide maximum service to small business today, nor are they prepared to overcome the many points of resistance which the owner-manager is maintaining. Based on the evidence we have uncovered, it would seem that only a handful of consultants have thought through the unique problems of the small businesspeople and geared their operations accordingly. Unless management engineers prepare themselves to work with these companies, they cannot expect to attract their support and their business.

We do not mean to imply that all the existing consulting firms either should or could readjust themselves to work with small business. For a large, highly specialized agency, it maybe economically unsound to solicit companies with less than 250 employees. Rather, the point is that this is a special kind of market, and a great many management engineering organizations could serve it *if* they wanted to gear themselves for it. Up to now they do not seem to have taken full advantage of the opportunities for service to small businesses and to the economy as a whole.

Specific Recommendations

What do consulting firms need to do in order to be of service to—and obtain the confidence of—the small business manager? Fundamentally, they have to understand his special problems and recognize the reasons for his aloofness. A key to such understanding can be found in the explanations small businessmen give for resisting the blandishments of the consultant:

1. Small business managers are sensitive about meeting and knowing the consultants who are actually going to do the work for them; the person who solicits should be the person who performs the service.

2.   Executives are often unfamiliar with the operation of consulting and are anxious about it. Therefore, a firm must see to it that the manager and the consultant establish a relationship of real confidence from the start. Without this rapport, there is little hope of success. Here is an actual example:

> A manufacturer of screw-machine products owned a large plant with modern equipment, but was unable to staff the plant properly. Both a perfectionist and irrascible, he was unable to trust or work with anybody over any length of time. To solve his problems, he called in a consultant who interviewed personnel and set up a going staff. Two months later, however, when the consultant returned, he found the organization once more completely demoralized, thanks to the personality of the owner who was constitutionally unable to trust even the consultant. Here the consultant had done all the right things, except the most important one: gaining the confidence of his client.

3.   A close working association is built on the recognition that often the manager's greatest need is for the help and companionship of top executive manpower. Too often the consulting method does not recognize this fact; a common approach is for the consultant to study the situation, write a long report, present it to the board and top management, and return to headquarters to receive his next assignment. Such a practice often leads to a fruitless relationship as in this instance:

> A rubber products converter called on the services of an outside consultant who spent a month going over all phases of his organization. At the end of the month, the manufacturer received a report which was two inches thick and which cost him slightly over $10,000. So much of the time of key people in the organization had been taken up in helping the consultant that, when the report was received, they were head over heels in back work which had to be done—so the report lay idle.
>
> By the time the report was read, other problems had developed and the report was almost completely dated. Here the technique was wrong—for it is impossible to do a lot of things fast with the small company. The key people in such organizations (from inventory clerks, production foremen, and bookkeepers, all the way up to plant manager and owner) simply cannot absorb new information presented in a lump. And the rate of their absorption equals the rate of progress the company is going to make as a result of any consultant's advice.

4.   Because small business managers are so deeply and emotionally involved in their companies, the consultant may find that he has to be patient and spend a considerable amount of time reassuring people all up and down the line, and explaining his function and his program. A good working relationship with top management alone is not enough.

5.   Since executive time is at a premium, the consultant should make sure that he is well prepared for his appointments with the manager, that

conferences are brief, and that they are set at times which are convenient for his client. In connection with this, we might add that exactly half of our respondent-users reported that their consultants caused a moderate to mild disruption of their organization.

6.   Owner-managers typically are jealous of their operating figures and sensitive about their mistakes. Consequently, consultants should avoid referring to the experiences of other clients or using examples from other firms. One of the fears revealed in our survey was evident in this comment: "I wonder if the consultant discusses *my* situation during his next appointment?" Perhaps this fear has some bearing on the fact that in our survey only 75% of users would recommend their consultants to another firm. See Exhibit 4.

7.   High-pressure sales methods and overblown claims and promises have only served to scare small business managers. Such exaggerations are not needed, and should be completely abstained from. It is significant that respondents feel their consultants performed as well as expected in 70% of the instances, and better than expected in 11%. On the basis of this evidence, most consultants are not promising more than they can and do deliver.

8.   Since, to nonusers, the cost aspect tends to be prohibitive, the consultant should be flexible in his fee arrangements, keep costs at a minimum, spread his billing out over a long period of time, and concentrate on quickly producing some results which yield visible savings. Charging monthly or by entire projects can place an undue burden on the client, and heavy, one-shot fees end many a small businessman's interest in consultants.

9.   Intimately related to the matter of the fee is the consultant's own overhead. In these days of rapidly expanding operations, it seems reactionary to recommend that the advisers to small business management keep their own operations small and flexible. But low travel costs, minimal office expenses, and a leanly staffed operation represent savings for the client which he will greatly appreciate. Furthermore, such economies ease the burden on the consultant who is under great pressure to produce tangible results quickly that justify the outlay being made by the client.

The Compleat Consultant

Earlier we examined the qualities of the ideal management consultant. Are different qualities required of the ideal *small business* consultant? Let us see if we can construct, from our evidence and experience, a general impression of what these attributes would be.

Shirt-Sleeves Approach
Most importantly, the perfect consultant must rid himself of the idea that he is *just* an adviser. He must get out on the firing line. He must supply the talent, the experience, the "generalist" background that his client needs.

His job, as we see it, is to study and recommend, and then once he has the manager's approval, to move out into the shop and help execute the plan. A consultant is the additional executive help the company needs, a part-time manager who makes himself available in a way that the firm can afford and absorb.

That last point is important, and is particularly significant in distinguishing the small business consultant. We should make clear that by "executing the plan" we do not necessarily mean actually moving the machinery into a better layout in the plant—though that may happen! What we do recommend is that the consultant be willing and able to take up the burden of recruiting, informing, and training the purchasing staff, the quality control people, foremen, workers, clerks, and all the others who are going to put his program into action, once that plan has been approved by the company's chief executive.

This means that he should not spend more than a day or so a week with the firm, for it is important that people be given the opportunity to absorb new lessons, to try out new ideas, without the "teacher" peering over their shoulders. But the consultant should return on a regular basis, perhaps weekly, to check on progress, help straighten out kinks, and provide the impetus for the next step.

When he does come to the plant, he should arrive early, stay late, and act like what he is—a part-time member of the staff. He should spend the bulk of his time out in the shop, not closeted in with the owner. His success will depend in large part on his ability to develop close working relationships with the manager and all his employees. How he conducts himself is almost as important as his ideas, since he is in the position, not of an "outside expert," but of a regular, responsible member of the management group.

After the particular problems are dealt with, he should be willing to maintain some connections with the company—if they wish him to do so. For example, he might serve on the board of directors or on the policy committee. When some special situation arises, he should be available for a quick consultation or for actual participation in the solution if his services are needed. Knowing the "nuts and bolts" problems of the company and its personnel, he can move in on a problem with speed and accuracy. Thus he stands in a continuing association with the firm much as its lawyer or accountant does, equipped to offer his special talent and know-how as it is required.

Two comments made in response to our questionnarie clearly indicate that this kind of shirt-sleeves consulting is what small business often seems to need:

☐ "We think a consultant can furnish the extra ability to a small company which cannot afford to pay for such talent in its executive staff."

☐ "Ours is a small firm, owned in its entirety by two men who have been with it since the start. Each is extremely active and each is well aware of our weak points; we don't need anyone to tell us what is wrong or needed. Our need is for part-time management assistance to implement what we already know should be done."

Further, we must add that after ten years of experience with the shirt-sleeves approach, it has had substantially good results for the small business managers involved.

Conclusion

What are the salient points in our investigation of the small business–consultant problem? While it is evident, from Exhibit 6, that most users of consultants (78%) are reasonably pleased with the services rendered them, there is still an unfilled need, both with them and, even more, with those not now using consulting services. To help fill this need, the qualities possessed by the ideal small business consulting firm would be:

☐ A shirt-sleeves approach to the owner-manager's problems.

☐ An understanding attitude toward the feelings of the manager and his subordinates.

☐ A modest and truthful offer of services, and an ability to produce results.

☐ A reasonable and realistic charge for services.

☐ A willingness to maintain a continuous relationship.

Such an ideal management specialist can certainly make a major contribution to the health and vigor of an important sector of our economy.[6] But if he is to do so, many small business managers must get over their fears and prejudices, face up to their problems, and recognize more precisely the areas in which they should be investing their limited time and funds.

Just as the consultant has to learn to work with the small business-person, the latter must learn to work with the consultant.

Notes

1. *Tenth Semi-Annual Report October 1958* (Washington, D.C.), pp. 9–10.

2. See Paul Donham, "Whither Small Business?" *HBR* March–April 1957, p. 73, and W. Arnold Hosmer, "Small Manufacturing Enterprises," *HBR* November–December 1957, p. 111.

3. *Management Review*, October 1957, p. 28.

4. "Advice for Small Company Presidents," *HBR* November–December 1959, p. 69.

5. *Directory of Membership and Services 1959* (New York), p. 4.

6. For the purposes of improving standards of management consulting services to small business and establishing a Code of Ethics, the Association of Management Consultants, Inc., has been formed. The group's address is 1223 Connecticut Avenue, N.W., Washington, D.C., 20036.

25
Choosing and Evaluating Your Accountant

NEIL C. CHURCHILL and LOUIS A. WERBANETH, JR.

The quality of a company's accounting advice directly affects its taxes, balance sheet, and management decisions. For a multinational corporation, choosing an outside accountant is usually a rather straightforward affair, because such companies tend to limit themselves to one of a handful of international accounting firms. Also, a multinational corporation can rely on expert internal advice to select its accounting firm and to oversee the relationship afterwards. For a smaller company, however, there are many more choices than international accounting firms. And the smaller company has limited internal resources to help make the choice and later evaluate the accountant's performance. In this article, the authors present to smaller companies a guide for choosing, evaluating, and working with all types of accounting firms.

Does your accountant always seem to take the government's side when computing your taxes? Does he or she have ready answers to your complex financial accounting questions and never need to look anything up? Does he or she appear either uninterested or uninformed when you ask for advice on issues not related to financial reporting, such as management control, product-line profitability analysis, and antiinflation measures?

If so, you may not be getting the accounting services you need and are entitled to.

As a smaller company owner, you need accounting information and advice as much as your counterpart in a large corporation. You may even need an opinion audit to satisfy lending requirements, to build a track record for possible future financial actions, or to satisfy concerns about management accountability.

Yet you are more likely than your large corporation counterpart to encounter difficulties in choosing and managing an accountant. That is partly because you probably lack the internal resources necessary to select such services adequately. You and your key associates most likely have the broadest background in sales, production, or engineering and the weakest preparation in finance and accounting.

Just to complicate the situation further, you have a wider range of options than your corporate counterpart. As a practical matter, large corporations are pretty much limited to national and international CPA firms. Yet your choices include international, national, regional, and local CPA firms and, for some accounting services, other types of firms.

Thus, as a smaller company manager, you have the widest possible choice of accounting firms, and you must make the selection with less understanding and insight than you might wish. This article is intended to help you make the right choice and then to manage the relationship with your accountant to increase the value of accounting services to you.

Choosing a CPA

How do you go about selecting a CPA firm? First, decide what services you are seeking and how they might best be performed. Consider whether you need write-up work, assistance in closing your books to prepare for completing financial statements, or an opinion audit. By the way, if you need write-up work, you may be better off using an accounting–data processing service of some kind and limiting the accountant to more creative tasks, such as preparing your taxes and offering management advice.

There may be specific areas you know need attention, such as more frequent financial statements, inventory costing and control systems, financial projections, or an opinion audit of financial statements. And there may be needs you are not even aware of—a better structuring of cost centers for more accurate product costing, a standard cost system, or a more current product-pricing system to help deal with inflation. You want to pick an accountant who will scrutinize your operations; give you financial, managerial, and accounting advice; and generally serve as a positive force in your business.

You may even consider using two firms. But split up the duties with care to avoid overlapping responsibilities. Confusion and ruffled feelings can easily result if one accountant prepares your financial statements and another performs audits and gives management advice, because the two accountants may have different opinions about what your numbers mean. A more workable approach is to have one accountant preparing taxes and another handling all the remaining accounting responsibilities. That allows for a clearer delineation of duties. It is safer, however, to go with one firm.

Most sizable cities have all or almost all of the Big Eight[1] firms represented and four to eight other national and regional organizations. There are also many smaller firms; some emphasize particular areas such as taxes, audits, and management advice and services.

Basic to picking an accountant is deciding whether to go with a small local or regional firm or a large national one. Five courses of action before choosing between a large and a small firm are:

1. Evaluate the levels of service and attention offered. The chances are they will be higher in a small firm than a large one; thus the likelihood is that a small firm is preferable to a large one in this respect.

2. Match your developing needs against the CPA firm's competence. A large firm, with its more extensive resources, is usually best equipped to handle highly complex or technical problems. A smaller one may be preferable for general management advice and assistance, because the firm's principals are more likely to be involved in handling the account.

3. Consider cost. Large firms usually charge more than small ones. A partner in a large firm will charge, on the average, about $95 an hour, while a smaller firm partner will bill closer to $55 an hour (add $5 an hour for each year after 1979 to account for inflation). Of course, either type of organization may cut its rates to lure a client felt to be particularly attractive.

4. Think about developing a track record for eventually going public. For this purpose, you might want a series of audits by a larger firm, since investment houses like well-known names.

5. Perhaps most important, be aware of the chemistry factor. Whether you choose a large firm or a small one, you are really choosing a person who will work with you and, within professional boundaries, for your best interests. You should hire someone who is going to be independent and stand up to you, while still understanding accounting, management, and tax problems from your particular point of view; someone concerned and knowledgeable about your business and what you want to do; and someone who will spend enough time studying your business to be of real help.

There are some accountants who don't like tight financial situations such as highly leveraged companies experiencing losses. Other accountants find such situations quite challenging. A frank discussion with a prospective accountant of your business's condition, goals, and problems will usually clarify whether the CPA is your kind of person.

What About a Small Firm?

In selecting among small accounting firms, consider the following:

Reputation with Bankers and Lawyers. Banks have accounting favorites chosen on the basis of the firm's toughness, stability, financial responsibility, insurance, and so on. In addition, lawyers are quick to identify the most expert CPAs, especially those who can be helpful in negotiating with the IRS.

Reputation and Involvement in the Accounting Profession.   Another way to assess the quality of a local firm is to ascertain how the profession regards the firm. For example, even if it doesn't have representatives on the taxation committee of the state or national CPA societies, the firm doesn't necessarily lack good tax people, but if the firm has a partner or a staff member on a state or American Institute of Certified Public Accountants tax committee, it means colleagues have recognized the firm's tax talent.

Quality of Practice.   The American Institute of CPAs has two sections for CPA firms to join—one for firms with clients registered with the Securities and Exchange Commission and one for firms that primarily have private companies as clients. Both sections have quality-control requirements, reviews by peers, and the like. All the large firms belong to the SEC section, but not all smaller firms have joined one of the two sections. Ask the firm you are considering if it is a member of either section. Being a member doesn't ensure a firm's quality but does tend to indicate it.

Professional Development.   Are the partners in the firm and their staff involved in continuing professional development and professional education? Ask them how many courses they have taken or seminars they have attended in the past two years over and above what might be required by their state. (CPAs are required by 26 states to take a certain amount of ongoing instruction each year to retain their licenses to practice and by the two AICPA divisions to continue their professional education.)

Overall Impression.   You must evaluate an accountant much as you do a doctor—on the way they act and handle themselves and how well you like them.

Or a Large Firm?

Not all large CPA firms are identical. Some are tough while others are less stringent. Some focus on large corporations and others seem most interested in growing, smaller clients. Considerations in choosing a large firm are:

The Local Office.   A critical consideration is the quality of the large firm's office in your area. Offices within firms can vary as much or more than the firms. Ask the local office for a list of area clients and then talk with some of them. This can be an excellent source of information.

Specialization.   One test of how well a large CPA firm is able to serve you is its knowledge of your industry. Ask a potential accounting firm for a list of clients in your industry, particularly those served by the office you are considering. Also, find out which of its members the firm considers specialists in your problems, where they are located, and how much access you can have to them. In some firms, groups of CPAs specialize in serving smaller companies. While not essential, this kind of specialization can be valuable.

Your Audit Partner. Perhaps most important, who is going to be in charge of your engagement? In almost every case, this will be a partner of the firm. He may do little of the actual accounting work or supervision; these will be the responsibility of a lower-level CPA. You should meet both individuals, though. If you like them and the right chemistry flows back and forth, obtain a guarantee that the partner will retain responsbility for your engagement for a certain period of time and that the in-charge accountant will also remain for at least the first two to three years.

Continuity of Staff. Although considerably less important than the partner and the in-charge accountant, staff stability is a legitimate concern. You can't expect that the staff will remain the same year after year—and you don't want it to, because bills will run up as individuals get promoted—but you don't want a completely new crew each year, learning its business at your expense. If you require more than one person on your engagement team, get a written guarantee of some reasonable level of continuity.

Consider an Opinion Audit

Regardless of whether you choose a large or a small firm, you should think about the possibility of an opinion audit. Though many owner-managers of small, closely held corporations tend to view audits as big-company procedures, convincing arguments can be made for a small business audit.

While an audit is not necessary for such internal considerations as tax planning, an audit can facilitate dealings with outsiders, such as banks and customers. Also, if your company has grown so much that you can't personally oversee all its activities and you would like some reassurance on how things are going, an audit can serve to avoid risk and provide peace of mind.

You may want someone completely independent of your organization to assess your financial and accounting situation and offer objective insights and criticism. Thus an audit can be a basis for management advice. In addition, an audit can be useful in future actions you might take, such as applying for a loan, selling your business, or going public.

There are, of course, arguments for not having an audit. For one thing, it is expensive; an audit of a $5,000,000- to $20,000,000-volume company can run between $12,000 and $40,000. Your business might benefit more by spending the same money for accounting systems, management advice, or planning information. The audit might be worthwhile, but at some stages of a business's life, other things take higher priority.

And while bank requirements are a major reason for small company opinion audits, you can make the following alternative proposal to your loan officer: "My CPA firm will give my financial statements a limited review quarterly. In addition, it will provide you, Mr. Banker, with a statement on loan covenants and with forecasts of the balance sheet and operating statement. Wouldn't you rather see where the business is going than where it has been?" If the banker buys the proposal, you have saved some money and obtained much more useful information for your purposes.

Finally, there is a midpoint between an opinion audit and no audit at all. That is to have the accountant prepare the unaudited statements and do all the preparation for an annual audit, such as observing the inventory. All that will save time and money if you decide to go ahead with an audit the following year. It won't cost much more than the normal accounting services and is a way station of sorts on the road of financial progress that might be considered if you have been seriously contemplating an audit.

If you have an opinion audit, you should recognize that its primary purpose is to allow the auditor to express an opinion about your financial statements, not to uncover fraud. If fraud exists, the odds are that audits performed over a period of time will uncover it, although not necessarily in any particular year. Auditors try to make clear to their clients that the discovery of fraud occurs not because the auditor searches it out but because the perpetrator gets so careless or greedy that the fraud becomes material enough to distort the financial figures. The auditor will review your internal controls as part of his engagement, however, and make recommendations that will at least minimize possibilities of major fraud.

If you alert the CPA that you suspect fraud, he can usually find it. To do that, however, he will use a diferent auditing procedure incorporating involved and expensive analysis and testing procedures known as discovery techniques. They are too expensive to be used in every auditing situation.

Another point about auditing that should be kept in mind is that the auditor, in rendering an opinion, is responsible not only to you, his client, but to others who read and rely on the audited statements. This responsibility has been vividly impressed on the profession as several of the Big Eight firms have reached multimillion-dollar liability settlements to dispose of cases brought by individuals who claimed to have been misled by erroneous auditing statements.

So be aware that while you are checking out the auditing firms, they will be doing their own checking to determine whether you have been convicted of fraud, have gone through bankruptcy, or are otherwise tainted. Their concern is simple: are you going to add to their legal burdens? Some firms will turn down clients who only want an opinion audit and want to buy it at the cheapest price. Their belief is that if the client doesn't want the firm but only its opinion, the firm will be better off without such a client in today's legal environment.

Overseeing the Relationship

As a unique sort of professional, an accountant can't be managed like most employees. But there are specific things you can do to enhance the relationship and ensure that you get appropriate service.

One advisable step is to use an engagement letter, which is written before the CPA firm starts working, and which sets forth the services to be performed for a company. For instance, the letter can indicate special areas in a company's operations that an audit should concentrate on and those things, such as searching for employee fraud or embezzlement, that may not be done. It also details charges for the work.

Many small accounting firms have begun to use engagement letters only in the past few years. Their function is to bring about a better understanding of the scope, terms, and objectives of the accounting and auditing engagement on the part of both the client and the accounting firm. Incidentally, one complaint heard from clients frequently is that engagement letters don't allow clients a fee reduction for training the CPA firm's recently hired personnel.

Another means of effectively directing the accountant–client relationship is to use an audit committee. Much has been written recently about the use of audit committees composed of outside directors in large, publicly held corporations. Such committees provide direct communication between the accountant and the board, thus providing a means by which the board can oversee the auditing effort. Most small companies don't need a formal audit committee, but if you have outside board members, it might be useful to assign them such a role. They can help manage the accountant–client relationship and possibly even become aware of findings that might otherwise be overlooked, such as weaknesses in financial controls.

If you form an audit committee, it should be in contact with the accountants prior to the start of the audit or to the finalization of the engagement letter to ascertain if the committee wants particular matters investigated, such as internal controls or even the president's expense account. Whether an audit committee exists, the president and the executive committee should also consider particular areas for the audit's attention before the engagement letter is signed.

Assessing the Relationship

Your outside accountant will reveal some personal characteristics that can help you judge his capabilities and influence his performance. Some things to look for include:

The Immediate Answer. If your accountant gives immediate answers to your questions without having to look anything up, be careful—it is almost impossible for anyone to do that, even a real specialist.

The Positive Approach.   Does your accountant try to get the job done the way you want, or does he try to run his own show? It is very important to have a CPA firm that works with you on your problems and needs. You don't want a consultant who acts like he is on the government's side every time he sees a tax problem. You want to know the territory and make your own decisions.

A Concern for Your Use of Information.   If the CPA gives you your financial statements only to observe you throw them in the desk without giving them any attention, he should be concerned. If he is any good, he will try to get you to read them and he will try to change them if you have objections. He should be interested in the way you use the numbers in making business decisions, and he should aid in maximizing their usefulness. Further, if the financial reports he has prepared haven't changed in the past few years and your business has, be careful. The statements should reflect organizational and product changes—such as product line or divisional P & Ls.

Advice and Choices.   Beyond performing the tax and accounting necessities, the CPA should be evaluating your operations, making recommendations, and suggesting other courses of action. You make the decisions, but he should tell you the choices. If he hasn't given you any advice, consider a change in accountants.

Businesses using small CPA firms should also consider the following questions in evaluating the relationship:

☐   Is the partner doing extra work because of lack of staff? If so, why pay for it?

☐   Is he available during tax season if you have a problem?

☐   Does he change the subject when computers and other technical-sounding subjects are brought up? One problem facing some small CPA firms is that their people aren't current in certain aspects of accounting service—computers; SEC and FASB pronouncements; ESOPs and ERISAs; IRS and other regulatory reporting needs; management and cost accounting; and so forth. That doesn't mean small CPA firms can't provide the range of services you need, but this matter should be checked.

☐   How specialized is the firm, and where is it heading in this respect? Some CPA firms don't want anything to do with companies registered with the SEC, while others shy away from real estate investment trusts. Discuss with your CPA the type of practice he wishes to develop; you might find you are heading in different directions.

Companies using large CPA firms should ask themselves the following questions:

☐ Do you see a constant rotation of new faces on your job? There should be some continuity.

☐ Do all the accountants meet your personal hiring standards? If not, why are they on your job?

☐ Do you have satisfactory communication with the partner in charge of your job and do you see him often? Further, do you have access to the top people in the accounting firm when you need them?

The final point to keep in mind about the accounting–client relationship is that it is a two-party relationship. You must communicate and cooperate with your accountant and he with you. Be prepared to pay for his services, and expect to get your money's worth. Hold him to a high set of expectations. If he doesn't come through, find someone who will, in the same firm or, if need be, a different one.

If your company feels its accounting needs aren't being properly met, then you should search for a replacement, keeping in mind that it is much easier for accountants seeking business to make grandiose promises than to deliver. Everyone has a tendency to be more interested in a new opportunity and to forget a little about old ones.

Taxes and Your Accountant

The most immediately relevant part of the accountant's work will likely be preparing your company's taxes. One common belief is that if you have certain firms or individuals prepare your return, you will not be audited by the IRS; the IRS, not surprisingly, disputes the claim. Yet this assertion continues to generate much discussion among business owners. Whether the claim is true or not, a legitimate question can be raised about what role the CPA should play in tax return preparation.

In England, when the chartered accountant signs a return, the government usually won't dispute it. In fact, some English small business owners complain that chartered accountants, by rigidly interpreting tax laws, act as an arm of government.

Things are different here, of course. Strange as it sounds, if a CPA firm builds its reputation with tax returns that are so scrupulously prepared that the IRS never finds flaws, it may not be doing a good job. A good CPA will favor its client when there is doubt.

Thus it isn't unreasonable for you to expect your CPA to comply when you tell him, "If there is anything questionable, don't deduct it or add it in. We don't want the IRS to find a nickel more than we owe." If you carry the matter farther, into gray areas, your CPA may become more cautious. You should expect him to explain the arguments on both sides and then, if he can accommodate you without breaking the law or violating his code of ethics, do what you ask.

Keep in mind that tax evasion and tax avoidance differ substantially. Tax evasion can mean going to jail; tax avoidance is strictly legal. For instance, failure to report income is considered fraud while overclaiming expenses may or may not be. Thus, in preparing a tax return or considering a tax position, your CPA should identify those transactions with options and explain fully possible outcomes on occasion even quoting you odds.

On any tax return, a number of gray areas will exist. Some are determined by decisions made last year, while others stem from new situations. The final disposition of those gray areas is your decision. CPAs, for their part, often measure their performance by IRS response to tax returns. As one CPA put it:

> I usually expect questions from the IRS. If a return comes back with no change, then I'd say that either it had a less-than-thorough review or I really didn't give the client all the possible decision-making options. The last thing I want is for the taxpayer to have a refund. Everyone, including the IRS, hates to give money back; refund may result in closer IRS scrutiny.

If an IRS agent pays you a visit, be sure your CPA is present. The agent should be given good working conditions, such as a private office where it will be possible to work efficiently and be minimally disruptive to your ongoing business activities; you should also free a corporate staff person to provide the agent with all necessary records and documents. Responsible management personnel should be made available. Your accountant should also maintain contact with the agent and discuss with him any IRS questions on your taxes before final decisions are made.

Concluding Note

The certified public accountant is a trained professional. The small business owner is a manager—either by training or by experience. The two of you should work together, questioning each other, challenging each other, and recognizing each other's strengths and weaknesses. The association can thus become a learning experience of sorts. The more that happens, the more each of you benefits personally, professionally, and financially.

Notes

1. In alphabetical order: Arthur Andersen; Coopers & Lybrand; Deloitte, Haskins & Sells; Ernst & Whinney; Peat, Marwick & Mitchell; Touche Ross; Price Waterhouse; and Arthur Young.

26
Discard Many Old Rules About Getting Venture Capital

JEFFRY A. TIMMONS and DAVID E. GUMPERT

Start-up entrepreneurs are finding loans from traditional sources more difficult and expensive to get than ever. On the other hand, their prospects of getting a positive reply from investors in start-up situations have actually gotten better. So conclude these authors on the basis of their survey of 51 venture-capital firms. Also, owners of businesses not in high technology can obtain venture capital more easily now, and having special contacts is not as important as it's often made out to be.

Of course, some ground rules still hold: venture capitalists are highly selective about which enterprises they fund, and they do prefer applicants with sound business plans in hand. This article is adapted from *Insider's Guide to Small Business Resources* (Doubleday) by Jeffry A. Timmons and David E. Gumpert.

Of all the sources of financing available to entrepreneurs, venture capital is probably the most glamorous. After all, the professional investors who run venture-capital firms put capital in those companies that they believe have the best chances of becoming the next IBMs, Xeroxes, and Polaroids.

Glamor, though, is often accompanied by mystique and misconceptions, and so it is with venture capital. Entrepreneurs tend to stereotype the 600 or so firms that comprise the venture-capital industry according to what

Author's Note: We are grateful to Mary Ellen Durning for major assistance with this article and to the Northeastern University School of Management for its support of our research. We thank also Linda Marcellino, Jeffrey Goodman, and especially Stanley Pratt, editor and publisher of the *Venture Capital Journal*.

273

type of business, stage of development, and percentage of ownership they seek. Misconceptions abound about how to seek venture capital and about the amount of time required to obtain it.

When added up, these preconceptions paint an unflattering picture of venture capitalists: they are uninterested in start-up ventures and completely biased toward high-technology companies; they try for majority ownership in their investments; and they take an unreasonably long time to make decisions. In sum, many entrepreneurs believe that most of these investors are less venturesome and more greedy than they let on.

Such stereotypes held little significance during the early and middle 1970s, when only very small amounts of venture capital were available to entrepreneurs. In fact, some of the preconceptions no doubt developed because entrepreneurs encountered extreme difficulty obtaining such capital. Today, however, such stereotyping serves the entrepreneur poorly because more risk capital has become available than at any time since the volatile go-go days of the late 1960s.

Thanks to a reduction in 1978 in the capital gains tax rates and a resurgence in the new-issues segment of the stock market, such investor groups as wealthy families, insurance companies, and pension funds have become interested in small enterprises. During 1980 nearly $1 billion of new funds flowed into venture-capital firms for such investments, while five years earlier less that $100 million had been available (according to publications that track the industry).

What criteria are venture capitalists using to invest all that money? And what can entrepreneurs do to increase their odds of obtaining some of it? With bank and other commercial loans either unavailable or offered to small businesses only at the prime interest rate plus 3% to 4%, these questions are important.

In an effort to understand better the investment practices of venture-capital firms, we surveyed 51 of the largest and most active firms around the country in late 1980 and early 1981. (See Exhibit 1 for a list of them.) Included were representatives of the three major categories of venture-capital organizations—private firms, corporate venture-capital groups, and small-business investment companies. (See Exhibit 2.)

We identified the 51 primarily on the basis of recommendations provided by Stanley Pratt, editor and publisher of the *Venture Capital Journal*, a monthly publication that reports on news and trends in the industry. We telephoned each of the 51 to interview a principal about the firm's investment goals and criteria.

Many of our findings contradict the more popular stereotypes about venture capital. Some of our findings, however, validate common perceptions. We have arranged our key findings according to (1) those that dispel popular notions and (2) those that support them. Finally, we offer advice for making intelligent use of the venture-capital market.

Exhibit 1.   Venture-Capital Firms in Our Survey

R.W. Allsop & Associates	DSV Associates	Carl Marks & Company, Inc.	Sprout Capital Groups
Adler & Company	First Capital Corporation of Boston	Massachusetts Capital Corporation	Sutter Hill Ventures
Allstate Insurance Company	First Capital Corporation of Chicago	Mayfield III	T.A. Associates
American Research and Development	First Dallas Capital Corporation	Narragansett Capital Corporation	Technology Venture Investors
BankAmerica Capital Corporation	Golder, Thoma & Company	Northwest Growth Fund	Texas Capital Corporation
Bessemer Venture Partners L.P.	Greylock Management Corporation	Oak Investment Partners	Venrock Associates
Brentwood Associates	Hambrecht & Quist	The Palmer Organization	Wells Fargo Investment Company
Burr, Egan, Deleage & Company	Harrison Capital, Inc.	Pathfinder Venture Capital Fund	Welsh, Carson, Anderson & Stowe
Business Development Services, Inc.	Heizer Corporation	Alan Patricoff Associates, Inc.	West Coast Venture Capital
Capital Southwest Corporation	Hixon Venture Company	Pioneer Group of Companies	WestVen
The Charles River Partnership	InnoVen Capital Corporation	Republic Venture Group, Inc.	J.H. Whitney & Company
Citicorp Venture Capital, Ltd.	Interwest Partners	Research and Science Investors, Inc.	
Continental Illinois Equity Corporation	Kleiner, Perkins, Caufield & Byers	Schooner Capital Corporation	
	Lubrizol Enterprises		

Dispelling the Myths

Myth 1 Most venture capitalists avoid start-up situations and seek established endeavors with good track records.

A dramatic turnaround has occurred over the past two years in the attitude of venture managers toward start-ups, according to our survey. As recently as 1975, says a National Venture Capital Association study, only 14% of investments were in start-ups. In contrast, nearly half of the investors we interviewed in 1980–1981 said 30% or more of their investments were in start-up ventures. Furthermore, 90% of the firms reported that they would consider start-ups. Leading this trend were eight venture-capital firms that specialize in start-ups and very early stage ventures; they reported that half or more of their investments were in start-up companies. Never before have so many investors been interested in start-up ventures, and this trend is expected to continue during 1982.

Exhibit 2. Overview of Venture-Capital Sources

	Private venture-capital firms	Small business investment companies	Corporate industrial venture capitalists
Estimated number—1981	200–250	305 +	Perhaps 50 in business
Principal objectives and motives	Capital gains 25%–40% compounded aftertax per year, five to ten times original investment in five to ten years; potential for public stock offering downstream	Similar to private firms	Acquired windows on technology; tap new talent; acquire new markets; spawn new suppliers; and for diversification, public relations, use of surplus cash, phil-anthropy, and capital gains
Typical size and range of average investment	$300,000 to $4 million; survey average: $813,000	Similar to private firms	$10–$15 million not unusual
State of ventures sought	All stages; 25%–35% start-ups more common	Similar to private firms	Later stages; rarely start-ups; seeking $100–$200 + million
Must business ask approval of its decisions from venture capitalist?	Unusual, required by perhaps 10%–12% of firms	Similar to private firms	Very common, 75% of decisions; review boards and directors

> *Myth 2 Venture-capital firms are interested only in high-tech-ology businesses.*

Computers, electronics, energy, medical products, and communications continue to lead the list of businesses these firms prefer to invest in. Over half our respondents confirmed that they prefer such high-technology enterprises.

At the same time, however, 41% indicated no preference at all. Thus there is still a great deal of receptivity to a wide range of other ventures. Recently funded, for instance, were the Sesame Street Touring Company as well as a chain of Mexican food restaurants.

Clearly, venture-capital investors are more open than ever to assisting nontechnological endeavors.

Myth 3 It's whom you know that counts.

Of all the stereotypes about venture capital, one of the most pervasive concerns the tightness of the investor network. The notion is widespread that the venture capitalist family is extremely close-knit. Entrepreneurs new to the process of raising capital often think that investors are difficult to reach without an introduction.

Our survey suggests that the opposite is true. An overwhelming 83% of our respondents said that how they are approached isn't very important— a letter, phone call, or personal visit will do. The vast majority of investors are in search of substance, not form, and entrepreneurs are likely to find them surprisingly accessible. An introduction through your banker or a business associate is certainly helpful but isn't necessary.

Myth 4 Normally it takes months, sometimes a year or more, to raise money.

Our survey indicates that the time required between the initial approach and actually raising the money averages two-and-a-half months. The slowest ten firms in the group claimed they take only three or four months. If the entrepreneur is well prepared with a business plan and realistic financial projection, he or she can sometimes get funding even more quickly. In fact, two firms reported that they had done an investment in one day!

Myth 5 Venture capitalists require complete management teams that meet strenuous criteria.

Certainly the quality and capacity of the management team are key concerns of venture capitalists. Several years ago, when few ventures were being funded, an entrepreneur with an inspiration but without a team stood little chance of getting money. That scenario has changed significantly in two ways. First, firms today often overlook the absence of an established team (only one-third of those we spoke to require one). Second, firms are often willing to help shape management (over half of our respondents indicated a willingness to do so).

In some cases, venture-capital firms even seek out experienced entrepreneurs to start new companies. Sutter Hill Ventures in 1980 asked Bill Poduska, a founder of Prime Computer, to form a new computer company. Sutter Hill offered Poduska both the freedom to pick a management team and $1.5 million in funding; he has since formed Apollo Computer.

Myth 6 Most firms seek a majority interest in their investments.

Entrepreneurs who haven't had outside directors as investors are understandably concerned about who will legally control their enterprise. Many suspect that investors are principally concerned with gaining control of 51% of the voting stock.

Our findings suggest this fear is unfounded: only 10% of the venture capitalists reported that they require a majority interest in their investments. And, as would be expected, such investments are usually in risky start-up or very early stage ventures that require a larger ownership position to offest the uncertainties. Experienced investors know that control through 51% ownership is an illusion. The growth and soundness of the venture rest with the quality of the founding team, not with the technicality of majority ownership.

Reinforcing Some Old Rules

Not surprisingly, we found that some of the preconceptions about venture investing have substance. The more valid notions include:

> *Venture capitalists are highly selective and fund relatively few proposals.*

Even though funding activity has increased dramatically during the past two years, investors remain extremely selective. One-third of our respondents reported that they funded 1% or less of the 500-plus proposals they received in 1980. And 94% said they funded 5% or less.

> *A complete business plan is the best way to gain the investor's attention and consideration.*

It's what you're going to do with the money that counts, not whom you know. The best mechanism for communicating ambitions, strategy, and competence is the business plan.[1] Nearly nine out of ten respondents said they require a plan or that they would help develop one; only 14% said a plan was not required.

> *Investors seek a substantial aftertax return on their capital— usually 25% or more annually over a five- to ten-year period.*

While most investors insisted that they use no rigid return-on-investment (ROI) formula, they generally quoted 25% to 40% compounded annually over a five- to ten-year period as desirable (or five to ten times the original investment in as many years). Moreover, these guidelines seem to have held over the past decade. As Exhibit 3 shows, they can also be quite helpful in estimating the percentage of ownership venture capitalists deem necessary to justify an investment.

> *Investors are willing to advance substantial funds once they decide to participate.*

The average value of the 305 investments that our respondents reported making over the previous year was $813,000. The investments ranged from a surprisingly low $17,000 to a high of $10 million. The investments we categorized as large averaged $2.2 million (apparently these were later-stage investments). Those we labeled small averaged $338,000 and included many

Exhibit 3.   Valuation of the Capital Investment for a Start-Up Venture

Assumptions	
ROI sought	$= 10x^s$ in five to ten years
Industry P–E estimate in year seven	$= 10$
Aftertax earnings (ATE) in year seven	$= \$2$ million
Sales in year seven	$= \$15$ million
Initial investment (II)	$= \$800,000$
Calculation	
Total return sought (ROI × II)	$= \$8$ million
Company value P–E × ATE	$= \$20$ million $= 10 \times \$2$ million
Share of ownership sought to justify $800,000 investment	$= \dfrac{\text{total return}}{\text{company value}} =$ $\dfrac{\$8 \text{ million}}{\$20 \text{ million}} =$ 40% of common stock

start-ups. The overriding criterion for the size of the initial investment was what the venture needed to succeed while attaining the investor's ROI.

Optimistic Outlook

The patterns that emerge from our survey are highly favorable for ambitious entrepreneurs seeking outside equity partners. Many venture-capital firms report an increase in the flow of proposals as business people respond to an improved economic climate. The terms, conditions, and structure of investments are reasonably flexible and can usually be tailored to fit the enterprise.

If, as an entrepreneur, you are rejected by one firm (and you easily could be), you should certainly try other firms. If you are willing to learn from rejection, you may get a more positive answer later on.

A word of caution about shopping for investment funds is in order. The primary consideration should not be the price obtained for your stock. Probably more important are the amount of time you consume seeking capital and the amount of technical and management know-how the investor brings to the venture. Wise entrepreneurs select an equity partner because of the experience, contacts, professionalism, and management competence that the investor can provide. Through a fruitful partnership you can get help refining your strategy and marketing focus, finding management team members, structuring the financial character of your business, and establishing a good reputation with creditors, suppliers, and customers.

Like most stereotypes, those about venture capitalists are only partially true. Perhaps the most important message from our survey is that venture capitalists are flexible, highly selective investors seeking the best possible returns on their investments. In this respect, they aren't much different from investors of other sorts.

Notes

1. See Jeffry A. Timmons's article, "A Business Plan Is More Than a Financing Device," *HBR* March–April 1980, p. 28.

27
Using Export Specialists to Develop Overseas Sales

JOHN J. BRASCH

John J. Brasch considers the usefulness of small companies developing overseas markets of the intermediaries that are known as export management companies.

Several years ago a midwestern manufacturer of medical equipment decided that exporting offered an opportunity to significantly expand sales. Although small, the company was the dominant supplier of its specialty product to the U.S. nursing home market, and it had prospered from sales to Canada as well. Also encouraging were numerous unsolicited inquiries the company had received from other countries.

But while exporting looked promising, the company knew that success in developing overseas markets would take time. It had had a slow and difficult start in U.S. markets, and there was no reason to expect foreign markets to be any different. Moreover, the company's management, already stretched thin, would probably have difficulty devoting sufficient time and effort to these new markets.

At about the same time, a manufacturer of hand tools was trying to figure out how to increase sales through its exclusive representative in Europe. The representative had visited the company's U.S. plant many times and had developed a warm relationship with company officials. During the prior five years, sales to Europe had been $100,000 or more annually.

Although it appreciated this export business, the manufacturer felt that its European sales should be much higher. As in the case of the medical equipment manufacturer, management had neither the time nor the expertise to try to increase sales on its own.

Both the medical equipment and the hand tool manufacturer have since solved their exporting dilemmas by hiring export management companies (EMCs). Export management companies are manufactuers' representatives that sell in world markets. The 800 or so U.S. EMCs tend to be one-person or small-group organizations. They account for approximately 10% of all U.S. export sales of manufactured goods.

The medical equipment company now has exclusive distributors in most European countries and in some Pacific, Latin American, and Middle Eastern countries as well. Its export operations have been profitable for the past two years, and the growth of its export sales has exceeded 50% annually for the past three years.

The hand tool company found an export management company that was capable of managing a distribution system in the entire European hardware industry. The EMC reorganized European distribution sales channels in such a way as to maintain the initial distributor's income as a token of appreciation for his past efforts. The hand tool company nearly immediately increased sales eightfold.

In both cases, the export management companies provided marketing management that the manufacturer had been unable to provide.

It is important to note that, in contracting with an EMC, neither company was admitting to any management deficiency. Each decided to focus its internal efforts on domestic markets and to leave the challenge to obtaining and expanding exports to outsiders.

Filling a Small Business Need

Indeed, small companies seldom have the internal capacity for export marketing management. This capacity requires the work of skilled and experienced export managers who have strings of contacts in various countries. Export managers understand foreign cultures. They are up to date on international politics, logistics, taxation, and legal problems. EMCs help fill this small company management deficiency on a contractual basis.

Many EMCs prefer to operate as contract export departments for the manufacturers they represent. Some even use the letterheads of clients as a way to encourage sales since foreign buyers prefer to deal directly with manufacturers and not with third parties. Other EMCs, wary of legal complications, operate under their names only.

EMCs operate as contract export departments by performing all the functions of such departments—doing research and planning; implementing promotional plans by, for instance, attending trade shows and placing advertising; creating distribution channels, which may include the appointment of foreign agents or dealers; processing orders; and reporting to management. In addition, some EMCs assume financial risk in dealing with foreign buyers by guaranteeing payment to their clients or by taking title to goods and collecting independently from customers.

Most EMCs specialize both by geographic area and by industry. For example, a number of EMCs owned by former Cuban nationals are very active and successful in Latin America. In contrast, few EMCs are active in Communist bloc countries, Canada, or the South Pacific. Usually EMCs prefer to represent several businesses within each of their specialty industries, which might include machine tools, medical equipment, or computers.

EMCs get compensation either from commissions or from discounts on goods they buy for resale overseas. These commissions and discounts vary according to the extent of service provided and the difficulty of the marketing task. For simple brokering, commissions may be 10% or less; but for developing unique channels of distribution, commissions and discounts may range to 30% or even 40% on occasion. Some EMCs also require that certain start-up expenses be paid; these expenses can range from $5,000 to as much as $50,000.

Locating an Appropriate EMC

Finding the right EMC is no easy task. Several associations of EMCs publish lists of their members, but these lists include only a small percentage of all EMCs since many good firms refuse to involve themselves in groups of competitors. For a list of EMC associations, see the appendix. Such lists provide only scant information for screening EMC candidates.

As a consequence, manufacturers usually choose EMCs on the basis of a brief search and minimal analysis. That is not to say that thorough assessment of EMC candidates is impossible.

Ideally, every small company that wishes to should be able to find an EMC that does the following: specializes in its product type, has in place a well-organized and controlled worldwide distribution system, is well financed and managed, and is willing and eager to devote significant amounts of managerial effort and money to launching a client's products. Such EMCs really do exist, particularly for heavy export industries such as medical products, telephone products, computers, and hand tools.

Initial Contacts

Finding EMCs that specialize in certain industries is usually not difficult. Friendly coexhibitors at trade shows may have suggestions. Some representatives advertise in trade journals. A company can contact an EMC candidate by letter, asking if the agent believes it has something to offer the company.

Initial replies from EMCs will likely be brief, but an EMC that expresses interest warrants at least a phone call and possibly a visit. If in this process the company finds a good match, things will happen fast. An EMC which sees that the manufacturer's product can be easily and cheaply distributed through EMC channels that already exist will aggressively seek a contract and begin distribution. In this situation, little more may be expected from the manufacturer than a contract and the production and shipping of orders.

Unfortunately, things do not usually proceed so smoothly. More often than not, EMCs must assume risks and invest funds to adequately develop export markets.

For example, a medical equipment product line such as the one mentioned at the beginning of this article requires testing in several countries. There may be problems of conversion to metric measure or to 220 voltage. Since new medical equipment must be thoroughly described and explained to potential buyers, advertising and displaying at foreign exhibitions are usually necessary.

Thus, many good EMCs are likely to be cautious about taking on new clients.

Differences Among EMCs

EMCs vary widely in the services they offer clients. For instance, some will accept all credit and collection risks in export transactions, while others will not pay for goods until they are reimbursed.

Some EMCs are traders and some are marketers. Traders are effective at getting orders quickly. They make deals on the basis of contacts—sometimes family relationships—and they operate best in Third World countries, where much business is done on a very personal basis. EMCs that are professional marketers usually seek to carefully define and implement long-term marketing strategies. Rather than make deals, they try to establish stable channels of distribution. While such marketing efforts take longer than simple trading, manufacturers end up with stable markets.

A manufacturer should thus ask a prospective EMC how it expects to obtain orders. A trader will answer that it "has contacts"; a marketer will discuss a long-term plan for selling the product.

EMCs also vary widely in size. They can be new one-person operations, or they can be very large firms with decades of experience. While large, experienced firms may seem to be better choices, small EMCs can often offer more personalized service than large firms, which must often cope with high employee turnover and large client loads.

Small EMCs seem to have different sorts of problems. Because it is so easy to set up EMCs, many are run by entrepreneurs with questionable qualifications in exporting. And like many new ventures, young EMCs have a high mortality rate.

Indeed, the gestation period for an EMC is much longer than for most service businesses—usually it struggles for at least three years before a regular income flow materializes. Weak firms usually fold within the first year or two.

Before entering into an agreement for export representation with a new EMC, then, a manufacturer should closely question the owners about their revenues and expenses as well as the managers about their personal incomes to determine their ability to weather the early storms. A manufacturer should also check with other clients and banks to determine financial stability.

As noted previously, EMCs tend to specialize in geographic areas and product groupings, though a few large, experienced EMCs offer representation in all parts of the world and in many product lines. Such product specialization is an advantage for manufacturers with traditional products but a problem for makers of products that are not sold through standard channels. Makers of products that do not easily fit into the specialties of EMCs may have to make special financial concessions to gain an EMC's commitment to a new effort.

What to Expect

From the EMC's viewpoint, either of the following situations can mean disaster:

1   Sales fail to materialize even though significant manpower and dollars are invested in market development.
2   Sales levels reach such heights that the client takes over the export function in order to save the commissions.

Given this double risk, a manufacturer should not expect an EMC to undertake a massive marketing development investment. For products that complement an EMC's product line, costly marketing efforts are usually not needed. But for products that demand special attention, manufacturers should frankly discuss the market development needs with a potential EMC. If some front-end investment is required, the small company should consider advancing part or all of the amount because whatever market acceptance is gained becomes the manufacturer's asset.

Small business owners should also seek to obtain a specific market development plan from the agent. Like many small ventures, EMCs try to avoid structured planning. If the prospective client wants to know the plan, he or she must ask, perhaps repeatedly.

The plan that is finally acceptable should begin with market targets. While some EMCs might talk about introducing products worldwide immediately, they are better off choosing specific markets.

Finally, small companies should keep in mind that an EMC is really much like a new regional sales manager. To be effective, the EMC must be trained and then supervised. Management needs to manage this resource as it would any other. Small business owners and their subordinates are thus well advised to travel with EMC representatives on some early trips and perhaps attend one or two trade shows with the representatives during the first months of operation. The EMC representatives can learn much from the manufacturers about promoting and selling products.

In hiring EMCs, small companies must be careful not to have unrealistic expectations. The export development process can be quite costly and difficult. Understanding this process can aid small companies in working with EMCs.

Appendix

EMC Associations
National Export Company
Gilbert Weinstein, President
65 Liberty Street
New York, New York 10005
212-766-1343

Export Managers Association of California
Stanley Epstein, President
Executive Offices
10919 Van Owens Street
North Hollywood, California 91605
213-935-3500

Overseas Sales and Marketing
Association of America
Peter Reinhard, President
5715 North Lincoln Avenue
Chicago, Illinois 60659
312-334-1502

Export Management Association of the Northwest
A.W. Bildsoe, President
815 Oregon Bank Building
319 Southwest Washington
Portland, Oregon 97204
503-223-1323

28

Outsiders Can Ease the Site Selection Process

TED M. LEVINE

Mr. Levine describes the assortment of agencies available for providing free, expert assistance in assessing expansion and relocation sites. He also offers guidelines for finding and using these agencies.

For sizable multinational companies, selecting expansion and relocation sites is easy. Their top managements, often aided by in-house facilities planners and outside consultants, continually review the relative cost-effectiveness of various production and distribution units around the country and the world and regularly examine alternative locales. Despite difficulties and frustrations, large corporations usually have both the experience and the personnel for a wide variety of site selection activities.

Not so for the smaller, more entrepreneurial organization. Deciding whether to move or expand is usually a one-time decision that no one in the company is equipped to handle. As a consequence, management may repeatedly postpone the move or expansion possibility from month to month and then from year to year. Or else someone within the company, usually the production manager, is designated to explore a new location on a special-assignment, "when you get time" basis. Often this person interprets the assignment (usually correctly) as being a matter of second-guessing the chief executive's preferences rather than coming up with an original and sensible recommendation. Not surprisingly, such assignments are frequently delayed indefinitely.

But most commonly the chief executive assumes control and makes the location decision on the basis of either friends and associates' experience or the possibility of combining a pleasant recreational activity with a new business site. In one instance, the head of a small, profitable high-technology company decided, after assessing various logical but not very exciting site possibilities, to move her headquarters to northern New England. The reason? She wanted to fulfill her new passion for skiing.

An Alternative Approach

Small companies can obtain outside assistance in site selection decisions that is not only competent but also free. Approximately 7,500 professional area development groups now operating in the United States, usually under the control or direction of a state development agency, are willing and able "to serve as the smaller company's whole site team," the head of one group told me recently.

Area development groups can be divided into three types: groups sponsored by state, city, or county governments that are pursuing economic development as a matter of public policy; civic organizations, such as chambers of commerce, industrial development corporations, and citizens' foundations that are promoting community business interests; and private organizations set up by industrial real estate agents, banks, utilities, and railroads, which usually benefit directly from the sale of their services and properties.

How interested are these groups in attracting and encouraging the small-scale business? In preparing this article, I surveyed about 20 professional developers across the country, and they agreed unanimously that assisting small business development has become a top priority in their communities over the past decade or so.

The following comment by Jack Hutchison, general manager of the newly established Greater Chattanooga Area Economic Development Council, is typical of the professionals I surveyed:

> When a smaller company is considering expansion or relocation, we find that the chief executive is often the person who gathers the facts and does the work. But the CEO can only spread himself so thin, so our staff is prepared to assist in handling the details of the contacts, in fact, in whatever the company official will let us do. For the smaller company, our staff can serve as a client's whole real estate department, and we charge nothing for this service.

Consider the testimony of David A. Edwards, executive director of the Fairfax County Economic Development Authority in Virginia:

> We have learned from analyzing our past efforts that at least 85% of industry in our country is small business. In fact, this pattern has developed to the degree that we are establishing a special position in our marketing section to work with small businesses. We believe this will benefit both the county's future growth and the business community.

A Range of Services

Exactly what services do area development groups offer the small but growing company seeking site selection assistance? First, the groups offer such information as wage and tax rates and utility availability. Second, they offer contacts with people who can cut red tape by, for example, running interference with various regulatory agencies. Finally, they offer financial assistance in such ways as arranging for loans, grants, and industrial bond issues.

A situation recalled by John Foltz, executive director of the Louisiana Office of Commerce & Industry, illustrates the range and sophistication of aids that may be available to alert small business owners:

> When Olympic Fastening Systems of California decided to expand, one phone call they placed was to our office. We learned from them that Vice President of Manufacturing H. L. Williamson and President Frank Nance would be in Little Rock, Arkansas on another matter; we arranged to pick them up in a state airplane, fly them to Louisiana, and show them the type of site they were seeking in two towns, both of which provided a program of speculative industrial building.
>
> They ultimately selected the town of Vivian. In addition to briefing the company, we also advised the two towns as to what the company was seeking, assisted town leaders in presenting their advantages and, perhaps most important, helped town leaders construct their already planned speculative buildings to Olympic's specifications.
>
> Overall, we were able to arrange it so that Olympic received not only a tailor-made speculative building program but also a free start-up training program and a full 10-year tax exemption in a town that was able to prove without any doubt that the company was wanted there.

Obtaining Federal Assistance

For a rather different series of services focusing on financing, consider the experience described by Judith Mahoney of the Minnesota Department of Economic Development:

> Juno Enterprises, Inc., in Coon Rapids, a suburb of Minneapolis–St. Paul, was a young company with excellent growth potential. But it was too small to qualify for industrial revenue bonds. Under the guidance of the department, the city of Coon Rapids applied for a Community Development Block Grant through the federal Department of Housing and Urban Development. The community's local development corporation was able to use the HUD grant to leverage Small Business Administration loan funds to make up the total package needed to construct a new building for Juno and to provide it to the company through a lease purchase agreement.
>
> As a result, Juno doubled its employment to 110 and was able to increase annual sales by 50%.

Juno's president, Beckwith Horton, said, "Little guys don't know how to run the maze. They have a business to keep in operation. The Minnesota Department of Economic Development crystallized and precipitated events for us, pulled people together, and ramrodded the thing through."

Exploiting State Resources

If area development agencies can be a hidden resource for growing companies, what are some ways to make this resource pay off in both the short and the long term? To develop successful relationships with experienced area developers, I would advise small business owners to:

Start at the Top Level. All 50 states now have state development departments or their equivalents, and most are well staffed and well budgeted. For both economic and political reasons, the states cannot favor one region, city, or site, so officials will most often offer honest appraisals of the suitability of various potential sites. More than half the states now have the computer capacity to identify sites and situations that meet client specifications: this capacity alone can mean an enormous saving of time and effort.

Ordinarily, state development departments screen and handle the initial business inquiry and try to advise the prospect about a variety of sites and communities that may meet its particular requirements. The "sale" is usually made at the community level, either directly by the on-site development group or through an industrial real estate agent.

Two central professional organizations can be contacted for names and addresses of appropriate state development agencies:

National Association of State
Development Agencies
Hall of States, Suite 116
444 North Capitol Street, N.W.
Washington, D.C. 20001

American Economic Development Council
1207 Grand Avenue, Suite 845
Kansas City, Missouri 64108

Assess the Credibility of the Development Group. Although state development agencies have become increasingly professional in recent years, some still cling to traditions and practices that can be dangerous to small companies. Here are several danger signals to watch for:

☐ Strictly political leadership. In a few states, the development director's job is a political reward and has the function of dispensing patronage. If such is the case, the smaller company might be wise to seek out the professional in the department who holds the title of deputy director or something similar and has long experience in the field.

☐ Regional favoritism. Some state development groups tend to favor particular regions within their states, especially regions that surround capital cities or that exert great political and economic leverage. In such instances, a company would be wise to examine regions and communities that have not been recommended but that seem to make sense when one examines surface criteria.

☐ Overemphasis on high unemployment areas. Most states exert strong political pressure to attract outside prospects to depressed areas by emphasizing their attractiveness. This may be described as a "worst first" policy. These states usually offer special economic incentives for development in such areas, but they should be viewed skeptically because in many cases the disadvantages of locating in an economically depressed area can seldom be entirely offset by even the most enticing inducements.

Provide the Economic Developer with Your Own Set of Priorities. Economic development specialists have isolated more than 1,000 site selection factors that may make a difference in picking a spot for expansion or relocation. Most important for the small business owner is to specify to the state what factors are vital to the business so that the development official can present the most attractive and cost-effective package. Unfortunately, this initial specification of priorities is not always made.

If in Doubt, Insist on Confidentiality. There are often good reasons for keeping a site investigation sub rosa—for example, to avoid labor problems in a facility being moved or to keep land prices from increasing once a business's interest is known. If asked, most area developers will be happy to work with businesses in absolute secrecy. They can even go further, actually serving as agents to business without revealing their clients.

A case in point: some years ago the state of Rhode Island, on behalf of an investor prospect, handled the acquisition and assembling of more than 120 contiguous parcels of property into a large industrial park without a word ever getting out to the media. Most professional developers can tell similar stories of property parcels in which their behind-the-scenes efforts prevented the escalation of costs.

Request a Current Inventory of Sites and Buildings. Most state development groups can now provide a fairly complete listing of available sites, industrial parks, districts, and buildings as well as detailed drawings and technical information about them. Check with the development executive about which ones might meet at least some of your needs before you actually look around the community. If you want to move with some dispatch—most small business owners seem to want to—keep an eye out for new speculative buildings, which are often modular units that can be moved into almost immediately, as well as for older structures that may have recently come onto the market.

A related point should be noted here. Often you will have to or will want to deal through a local industrial development group. In such cases, I strongly advise dealing with one group rather than several.

Ask for Other Small Business References and Check Them Painstakingly. Even the best development professionals often have axes to grind; other small business owners usually don't. So ask your development contact for the names of at least three small businesses as much like your own business as possible that have worked with the development organization. Then go see the owners yourself. Among the questions that will likely reveal the most important information are:

☐ How did the performance of the development organization compare with its promises?

☐ What have been the unexpected problem areas (if any) at the company's new site?

☐ What is the attitude of other community organizations toward industrial expansion and business in general?

☐ Are there any major antigrowth forces, and if, so, how powerful are they?

☐ If you had it to do over again, would you still choose to expand here? Why?

Once You Establish a Facility, Keep Calling on Your Development Organization for Further Services. This may be the most important point of all to be aware of.

Some 20 years ago the motto of many area development organizations might have been "find 'em and forget 'em." That attitude has faded with the growing realization that existing business is the basis of most new growth virtually everywhere in this country. W. Clinton Rasberry, Jr., chairman of the Greater Shreveport Economic Development Foundation, has expressed this thought in a way that I think most other developers would agree with:

> We assume that about 80% of a community's growth comes from internal sources and about 20% from external sources. It therefore makes sense to us and other development groups to place a major emphasis on assisting the companies that are already here, and we do just that.

If you still have any lingering doubts about how interested your development groups are in attracting and assisting small businesses, consider this summary comment by Don A. Newton, executive vice-president of the Birmingham Area Chamber of Commerce:

As far as the role of small business in economic development is concerned, my feeling is that this represents the guts of any successful development program. Too many programs fail as a direct result of the continuing attempt only to attract the major manufacturing companies.

My premise is that the community is much better served if it can attract 10 companies with 10 employees each rather than one company with 100 employees. The smaller companies are easier to attract and assist since generally their development expertise is limited and they are in greater need and more appreciative of personalized direct service.

A large network of area development agencies has been established. These agencies can help you answer most site selection questions with intelligence and authority. Moreover, their services won't cost you a thing.

29
Look to Outsiders to Strengthen Small Business Boards

S. KUMAR JAIN

Mr. Jain argues in favor of extensive employment of outsiders, citing as evidence previous analyses of the subject as well as his own research. He contends that outside directors can make up for the lack of important staff and management personnel that is often a problem in small companies. He also offers guidance for making the most effective use of outside directors.

Small companies frequently lack the staff and management expertise to do quantitative analysis, research, and long-range planning on the same scale as their large corporate competitors.

Hiring sophisticated consultants or permanent professionals to fill the void is usually prohibitively expensive. Such hiring, even on a limited basis, can also create internal problems because founding investors and managers may view consultants or professionals as a threat to their authority.

One way for small companies to tap some of the same resources that large corporations tap is to recruit outside experts to serve on their boards of directors. These outsiders should have expertise that compensates for small companies' managerial deficiencies. The challenge is to locate skilled people and then persuade them to accept directorships.

Large corporations, under the prodding of government regulators and shareholders, have in recent years been relying increasingly on outside directors. But small corporations have by and large failed to recognize the remarkable benefits available from appropriately qualified outside directors. Adding such directors to the board represents an opportunity to provide sorely needed guidance and counsel.

   This article will use the wide variety of articles and books devoted to the subject of corporate boards to offer advice to small companies interested in making use of outside directors. In addition, a list of articles and books is included for those readers wishing to explore the subject further.

Breaking Old Habits

Small company chief executives frequently feel more comfortable and secure having insiders—outright insiders, quasi-insiders, and just plain buddies—on their boards. Sometimes such board members give the appearance of being aggressive and independent while in reality they are passive. For instance, they may be excessively dependent financially on the companies' principal investors and thus deny their companies the benefits of objective judgment.

   Jeremy Bacon and James K. Brown, in their book *The Board of Directors: Perspectives and Practices in Nine Countries,* list the following causes of board ineffectiveness: "lack [of] objectivity and independence"; "lack [of] true authority over management"; "lack [of] a grasp of what is going on in the company"; and "not work[ing] hard enough."[1] Having too many insiders aggravates all of these problems.

   Managers of small corporations must, in effect, break away from the traditional procedure of placing family members and friends on the board. According to Louis W. Cabot, "These individuals loyally passed boilerplate votes and enjoyed each other's company for lunch but rarely considered in any depth the serious issues facing their companies."[2] Carefully selected outside directors—particularly those who have expertise in areas in which management is weak—can correct such deficiencies. Marvin Chandler—former CEO of Northern Illinois Gas Company—says, "It is almost ridiculous to have to justify the importance of a strong majority of outside directors."[3]

Choosing the Best Directors . . .

Persuading the most appropriate people to join boards is easier said than done. Knowledgeable professionals usually have many commitments. But managers at middle and higher levels of large and medium-size, technologically complex corporations can often be persuaded to accept opportunities to contribute to small corporations.[4] They gain prestige from being members or chairmen of the boards of even small companies.

   Research scientists and other technically trained personnel with large, well-known corporations frequently discover that their job assignments fail to make use of all their talents. They relish the challenges of small company directorships as fresh opportunities to display their technical versatility and gain recognition. Such potential board members also welcome the opportunity to obtain high-level managerial experience. Other potential outside director candidates are university professors in business schools, institutional administrators, retired executives, and management consultants.

Although consultants might be viewed as having inherent conflicts of interest as outside directors, attorney Robert M. Estes strongly supports management consultants on small corporation boards. He writes:

> I have attended conferences where management consultants who have gone on corporate boards describe their attack on management information systems, how they overhaul accounting procedures, how they review each decision on accounting options, and how they analyze marketing strategies and force changes to be made. This activity by an outside director could be an invaluable aid to a small business.[5]

. . . and Compensating Them

How much should smaller company directors be paid? No easy answer exists to that question. I surveyed 120 small and medium-size midwestern companies by mail and telephone late last year and discovered a wide variety of approaches to paying inside and outside directors:

☐ Interestingly, 45% of the responding companies offered *no compensation* to their board members.

☐ Board members were paid *retainers* ranging from $600 to $5,000 annually, or an average of $2,000 by 15% of the companies.

☐ Another 15% paid board members an *annual retainer and an additional meeting fee*. The annual retainer ranged between $600 and $5,000 annually, or an average of $1,900, and meeting fees ranged between $35 and $500 per meeting, with an average of $275 per meeting.

☐ The remaining 25% of the responding companies paid *only meeting fees,* which ranged from $25 to $500, with the average being $210 per meeting (see Exhibits 1 and 2).

☐ Some companies also made *additional payments*. About 20% paid board members for attending board committee meetings. These payments ranged between $75 and $650 per meeting, with an average of $300. A small proportion (5%) also paid additional amounts for consulting and advisory services. Such one-on-one consultation services provided fees from between $275 and $500 per day, the average being $350.

Outside directors tended to receive higher fees than inside directors. Only 4% of the responding companies provided an annual retainer to company officers serving also as inside board members. This contrasts sharply with the 26% providing annual retainers to outside board members.

Exhibit 1. How Small Corporations Compensate Board Members

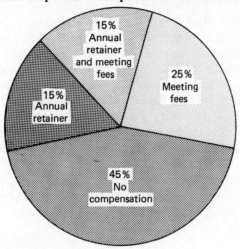

Exhibit 2. Compensation by Type of Small Company

	Family-owned companies	Companies owned by a small group	Companies owned by a larger group	All companies
No compensation	57%	35%	30%	45%
Annual retainer only	20%	7%	7%	15%
Retainer amount (range)	$600–3,600	$2,100–5,000	$600–3,600	$600–5,000
(average)	$1,650	$3,500	$1,800	$2,000
Annual retainer and board meeting fees	5%	5%	42%	15%
Annual retainer (range)	$600–1,600	$2,000–5,000	$600–3,600	$600–5,000
(average)	$1,000	$3,500	$1,600	$1,900
Per-meeting fee (range)	$250	$35–400	$200–500	$35–500
(average)	$250	$200	$300	$275
Board meeting fees only	18%	53%	21%	25%
Per-meeting fee (range)	$100–250	$25–500	$150–500	$25–500
(average)	$160	$200	$325	$210

Notes: Twenty percent of the companies paid for committee meetings of the board. Per-committee meeting fee ranged from $75 to $650, and the average was $300.

Five percent of the companies paid for consulting or advisory services or extra-time assignments for members of the board. Per-day fee ranged from $275 to $500, and the average was $350.

The range for such payments also differed. For inside directors, payments ranged from $1,000 to $2,400; for outside directors, payments ranged from $600 to $3,600. And only 7% paid meeting fees, ranging between $25 and $250 per meeting, to inside directors. This again contrasts with the 43% paying meeting fees—in the range of $35 to $500—to outside directors.

Only 19% of all companies responding said they carried directors' liability insurance. And the same proportion reimbursed board members for their out-of-pocket expenses for attending meetings of the board.

Differences and contrasts exist, too, between companies owned by families and those owned by small and large groups. (Small-group owned companies are defined in the survey as those with fewer than 50 stockholders, and larger-group owned companies have more than 50 stockholders.) While 57% of family-owned companies paid no compensation to board members, stockholder-owned companies were more generous; about two-thirds of these businesses offered compensation. (See Exhibit 2.)

Consultant Role of Directors

How should small companies use their outside directors? Once outside directors have been added, a redefinition of board operating policy is usually in order. "The [directors] must serve as consultants to the CEO and, with his approval, to others in the company," J. M. Juran and J. Keith Louden advised some years ago.[6] Obviously, the benefits of having outside directors can be realized only if the board becomes active rather than remaining passive.

The board must be assertive in forming and guiding company policy and in confronting management with fresh perspectives, new directions, and innovative targets. In this vein, it may be helpful to review some of the traditional—and often passive—functions of the board and then to note a few of the present and future challenges.

The basic function of the board is to represent the stockholders. It must guide the company toward desired goals, such as targeted profits, while also being mindful of its social responsibilities. Profits are usually linked to sales and cost control. If the company is to realize its growth potential, the board should be strong, independent, and unhesitating about probing, querying, taking issue—and even rejecting management proposals. But, as stressed earlier, the board must above all be able to appraise the CEO and senior members of the management team. Myles L. Mace emphasizes that the board must "identify successors for CEOs and other top executives, and . . . assure orderly succession when top executives depart."[7]

The Conference Board research study that compared board practices in nine countries concluded that "the director's job tends to center around the same areas of responsibility, whatever the country: (a) Long-range corporate objectives; (b) Corporate strategies or long-range plans for meeting objectives; (c) Allocation of major resources; (d) Major financial decisions, including changes in capitalization and capital investment programs; (e) Mergers, acquisitions, divestments; (f) Top management performance appraisal, succession, compensation."[8]

The opportunity for an independent and authoritative audit of the CEO's performance can be improved if the chairman of the board is an outsider. Too often the board chairman and the CEO are close friends who have developed a mutual interest in stability, control, and maintaining the status quo. This may have pernicious consequences because both may become more interested in appearance than substance; they may try too hard to avoid the risks inherent in the swirling stream of competitive realities.

But an outside chairman of the board is much more likely to place on the agenda appropriate and difficult items. One highly experienced attorney counsels: "Outside directors and the chief executive officer do not have totally identical interests and responsibilities relative to a particular enterprise, and recent developments have tended to accentuate differences in these roles."[9] Therefore, issues can be illuminated even if the CEO will be overly sensitive or feel uncomfortable about them. A board chairman who becomes dependent on or acquiescent to the CEO—for instance, a chairman who lets the CEO prepare the agenda and manipulate the issues—may well ruin the board's potential. [10]

According to Peter F. Drucker, companies and society need the kind of board member who also "makes sure that there is effective top management; who makes sure that management thinks and plans; who serves as the 'conscience' of the institution; as the counsel, the advisor, and informed critic of top management."[11]

Helping Handle Regulation

Besides helping evaluate company and management performance, outside directors can be of invaluable assistance in another area—dealing with the outpouring of federal regulations. Complying with such regulations costs American business an estimated $100 billion to $200 billion annually. Needless to say, the small corporation has not avoided being ensnarled in the regulatory net. By all accounts, the current wave of guidelines, reports, edicts, threats, and exhortations is a fresh burden on the vitality of many small corporations.

For large corporations, the obligation to divert, say 12% of their capital formation—otherwise available for product or process innovation to improve their competitive positions—to add to employment contributes to a drag on both production and productivity. But for small companies, such a regulatory burden may do more than hamper existence—it may extinguish existence. Small corporations must therefore be able to meet the regulatory challenge through systems of internal controls, reports, and reallocation of resources— formulated with the help of outside directors.

A Link to the Public

Outside directors can also aid small companies in their relations with non-managers and public shareholders as well as with the public at large. While the ethical behavior of small corporations has by and large escaped media attention, one cannot necessarily infer that all small businesses operate ethically. Operating executives, without outside directors to question them, may rationalize unethical or illegal behavior as being in the best interest of the company. Outside directors, through steadfast questioning, can help guide them in more appropriate directions.

Drucker seconds such reasoning by observing:

> An institution needs a "conscience." It needs a keeper of human and moral values and a court of appeal against tyranny and caprice or the equally harmful indifference of bureaucratic routine. It needs someone outside the daily work and the daily relationships who is concerned with what the institution stands for, what its values are, what it considers "right" or "wrong" . . . . The chief executive officer is rarely able to play this role, if only because he may have to support his management associates even when he thinks them sloppy, wrong, or callous.[12]

Buffer Zone

Additionally, outside directors can be invaluable in mediating a wide range of internal issues, including the following:

☐ Determining policy, regulations, and operating procedures.
☐ Selecting and dismissing executives.
☐ Caring for and maintaining property and assets.
☐ Controlling operating budgets, financial plans, and insurance programs.

Outside board members can play key roles in mediating conflicts and preventing emotional outbursts, particularly in companies in which there is more than one major investor or in companies in which some of the principal investors are also officers. In some small corporations, power struggles between key executives and important investors, ignited by a series of friction-causing events, have a way of erupting at crucial points in the development or expansion of businesses. If uncontrolled or unresolved, these conflicts can easily destroy companies—so the buffer zone provided by outsiders is critical.

Other Areas of Assistance

Outside directors can provide guidance in a variety of other ways as well. Every small corporation is threatened at least once with bankruptcy or with acquisition by another company. Unfortunately, few executives or directors have experience dealing with merger and takeover challenges. Of course, if outside directors have that experience, it can be extremely valuable. But even directors without such experience can provide views more independent than insiders' and thus offer a higher degree of stability and balance to company responses.

Planning is the weakest area in most small companies. Many executives, left to themselves, would prefer to deal with situations as they develop or on a contingent basis. Purposeful planning can be frustrating and painful. Outside directors can help the board give planning the importance it deserves. They can insist on and even lead the process, helping prevent the lack of planning and of financial controls that often contributes to the failure of small corporations.

Finally, outside directors can play key roles in the areas of research, development, and technological growth. Operating executives are sometimes so close to their areas of interest that they are hypnotized by the prospect of a glamorous technological breakthrough. They may overinvest or overcommit resources in unproved areas. Outside directors can help control sporadic outbursts of overoptimism through a process of strategic reevaluation of plans and programs.

Thus, in all of these ways, carefully chosen outside directors with appropriate areas of specialization can boost a small business's chances of survival and long-term growth.

Additional Reading

The following articles and publications may be of interest to readers who wish to pursue the subject of boards of directors further:

☐ Richard D. Hannan lists items to review when deciding whether to become a board member in "Board Membership– Accept or Decline?" (*From the Boardroom*), *HBR*, May–June 1976, p. 24.

☐ The Conference Board held a conference on November 18, 1971 to discuss new issues and priorities for boards of directors. The proceedings were published in 1972 in *The Board of Directors: New Challenges, New Directions* (New York:The Conference Board), 73 pages.

☐ For a stimulating discussion on functions of the board, see Myles L. Mace, "Designing a Plan for the Ideal Board" (*From the Boardroom*), *HBR*, November–December 1976, p.20.

☐   Milton C. Lauenstein discusses ways of emasculating board authority in "Preserving the Impotence of the Board" (*From the Boardroom*), *HBR*, July–August 1977, p.36.

For an excellent discussion of the social challenge and the relationship of the corporation to government and the community from the British viewpoint, see Sir Walter Puckey, *The Board-Room: A Guide to the Role and Functions of Directors* (London:Hutchison, 1969), Chapters 2 and 3.

Notes

1.   Jeremy Bacon and James K. Brown, *The Board of Directors: Perspectives and Practices in Nine Countries* (New York:The Conference Board, 1977), p.13.

2.   "Louis W. Cabot on an Effective Board" (*From the Boardroom*), edited by Myles L. Mace, *HBR*, September–October 1976, p.40.

3.   Marvin Chandler, "It's Time to Clean Up the Boardroom," *HBR*, September– October 1975, p. 73).

4.   Donald S. Perkins, "What the CEO and Board Expect of Each Other" (*From the Boardroom*), *HBR, March–April 1979, p. 24*

5.   Robert M. Estes, "The Case for Counsel to Outside Directors," *HBR*, July–August 1976, p. 129.

6.   J. M. Juran and J. Keith Louden, *The Corporate Director* (New York: American Management Associations, 1966), p. 27.

7.   Myles L. Mace, "The Board and the New CEO" (*From the Boardroom*), *HBR*, March–April 1977, p. 16.

8.   Bacon and Brown, *The Board of Directors*, p. 17.

9.   Estes, "The Case for Counsel to Outside Directors," p. 127.

10.   Robert Kirk Mueller, chairman of the board of Arthur D. Little, Inc., discusses this situation in "The Hidden Agenda," *HBR*, September–October 1977, p. 40.

11.   Peter F. Drucker, "The Bored Board," *Wharton Magazine*, Fall 1976, p. 25.

12.   Drucker, "The Bored Board," p. 23.

30

Involving New Directors in Small Company Management

JUDY FORD STOKES

Ms. Stokes suggests guidelines for choosing outside directors and for integrating them into companies' management organizations.

Once smaller companies decide to appoint outside directors, the companies must make some important tactical and policy decisions.

How can the best and most appropriate outside directors be selected? How many outside directors should be chosen? And, perhaps most important, how can the outside directors best be integrated into the companies' decision-making processes?

As the previous article by S. Kumar Jain suggests, outside directors can aid small companies in various important ways. But successfully grappling with these questions will improve the quality of the assistance the outside directors provide. This article, then, will attempt to answer them. It will also touch briefly on some issues affecting inside directors.

Avoiding Conflicts of Interest

When selecting outside directors, small companies should look for candidates with expertise in management and other critical areas. One place to begin the search is to ask for suggestions from the company's own attorneys, bankers, and accountants. However, the temptation to use these professionals themselves as outside directors should be avoided; sometimes these professionals feel inhibited about offering advice or making decisions for fear of jeopardizing their professional relationships with the company. In other words, they have built-in conflicts of interest. They can, however, be useful as occasional guests at board meetings.

There are ways to get around conflicts of interest. For instance, the chief executive of one small manufacturing company handled the problem in the following way: early in the company's history, he appointed its attorney, accountant, and banker to the board. When the comany reached the stage of needing an audit, the accountant voluntarily resigned as a director so he would not violate the accounting profession's ethical standards, which prohibit auditors from having official ties with companies being audited.

Some years later, when the company reached $6 million in annual sales, the chief executive decided that the banker and lawyer should not have professional relationships with the company while they were serving as directors. He highly valued them in both their professional and directorship roles but felt that the professional roles could be more easily assumed by others. So he asked both men to stay on as outside directors and give up their professional relationships with the company. Because both respected the chief executive and his decision and also felt loyal to the company, they agreed to the arrangement.

Number of Outside Directors

No absolute rule exists for deciding how many outside directors to appoint. One index is to include as many or nearly as many outside directors as inside directors in order to achieve at least numerical equality between the two forces. Another index, employed by many publicly held companies, is to use a ratio of three outside directors for each insider, though such a ratio may rely too heavily on outsiders to suit most small companies. There should be enough insiders to allow outside directors to obtain answers about a range of management problems on an ongoing basis; such interchanges let outsiders get a good perspective on companies' operations.

Indeed, inside directors can be of more help to small companies than is often realized. The argument that inside directors will resist upsetting or defying CEOs is not as valid as it once was, what with today's increased emphasis on the accountability of individual directors—including the threat of liability lawsuits. So insiders are now more likely to speak up and even to take action to discharge CEOs if necessary. Plus insiders are more likely than outsiders to be aware that companies are in serious trouble. In addition, inside directors can convey board policy and direction to other managers throughout the organization. They are thus extremely well equipped to act as two-way conduits of useful information.

In the case of one medium-sized manufacturing company, inside directors were instrumental in helping reverse a deteriorating profit situation that developed after the CEO moved 250 miles away from the company's headquarters and reduced her role in the company's day-to-day operations. Left in the hands of untested managers, the company experienced manufacturing problems and declining sales and, after a couple of years, was precariously close to bankruptcy. Only the insistence of several inside directors convinced the CEO how serious the situation had become; she moved her family back near the company and resumed full-time management. The company is now flourishing again after two years of diligent rebuilding efforts.

Making the Most of Outsiders

Once the outside directors have been selected and have taken their seats on the board, small company CEOs face the task of integrating the new members into the company's management. The CEO must familiarize them with company operations, keep them informed of present activities and future plans, and send them regular communications. After all, outside directors are dependent on this information to make important decisions and offer critical advice.

New directors should be briefed on company operations and finances before the first board meeting so that valuable time isn't lost orienting them. Prior orientation also allows the new members to feel comfortable and, possibly, to make specific contributions at the first meeting.

Another worthwhile practice is to arrange periodic briefings and exchange sessions between managers and directors. One innovative CEO arranged for his company's board to visit plant sites and offices and to meet with the staff over a three-day period. The staff, too, benefited from its contact with board members.

The results, although positive, were not quite what the CEO had in mind. The visit represented the first occasion some of the newer directors had spent so much time with fellow board members. New peer relationships were established during and after the formal presentation schedule. Directors began sharing pertinent concerns and apprehensions about delicate subjects, such as board renewal, management succession, and the company's strategic direction.

At previous board meetings the formal atmosphere and the time constraints had never permitted these subjects to be explored. In contrast, the informal circumstances provided a fertile field for such discussion, and the net result was positive for the corporation. Although the CEO was unprepared for the various issues the board raised at the end of the three-day program, he helped take specific steps to come up with answers to directors' concerns. The company now provides such informal exchanges regularly to help tune the board in to important corporate issues.

The key to making directors effective is to involve them in company affairs. They should be assigned specific responsibilities, such as assembling needed data on executive compensation and production or serving on the more traditional audit, nominating, or compensation committees.

Other devices can be used to involve directors. Some small companies have begun to employ what is known as a board book to retain pertinent information. These books can be divided into two sections—current and permanent. The current section normally includes the meeting agenda, minutes of previous meetings, reports to the president and chief financial officer, adjustments to plans, issues to be voted on, and presentations by management. The permanent section includes the board meeting schedule, committee memberships, corporate structure, organization charts, and curricula vitae of directors. Usually the board book is delivered at least a week before the meeting and collected at the end of the meeting to be updated.

At the very least, board members should receive the correct agenda for board meetings at least one week in advance. The agenda should include pertinent notes and specific questions that may require preparation. A brief monthly newsletter circulated to board members that discusses pertinent company affairs can be a real asset. Other attempts to intertwine the board and the company, such as frequent telephone communication and plant site visits, are well worth the effort. For directors to provide the services of which they are capable, they must be properly integrated into the company structure. They can then begin to pay their own special kinds of dividends.

Editor's Observations

The preceding articles by Jain and Stokes set forth compelling arguments for the use of outside directors by small companies. They do that not only by pointing out the benefits of the experience of outside directors but by citing the dangers of too-heavy reliance on partners, relatives, subordinates, and other insiders.

Yet, as both authors suggest, the subject of outside directors is a much easier one to theorize and preach about than it is to do something about. And, as they also imply, the decision to make use of outside directors involves subtle but important underlying issues.

Members of long-established boards in large companies, which characteristically consist of a majority of outsiders, may never have encountered such sensitive issues or may have long since left them behind. But chairmen of companies first introducing outsiders will wish to move carefully.

The simple act of deciding to include outsiders on boards that formerly had only insiders can be threatening from several viewpoints. For strong-willed, successful entrepreneurs the decision represents an admission of sorts that their companies need help and guidance in some form or another. The decision also raises the issue of trust, because bringing in outsiders means having to share with them information known previously only to insiders.

It also usually means facing up to the fact that the company has reached a new plateau of growth and success, for the need for outside directors frequently arises from the need to deal with increasing complexity. As welcome as the new plateau may be, certain side effects—such as having to ease longtime loyal associates off the board—may be less welcome.

Perhaps the most threatening aspect of the decision is the prospect of giving up authority and control to outsiders. Yet the simple act of including outside directors on boards does not mean the outsiders have substantive decision-making powers, particularly if the outsiders remain in the minority and if companies are closely held. Indeed, the whole decision about appointing outsiders might be easier if viewed as an effort to recruit new sources of expertise rather than as exposure to new sources of conflict.

Properly implementing the decision, though less threatening than making it, can be difficult. This kind of decision is all too easy to implement carelessly. For instance, it is tempting to select outsiders on the basis of their fame or wealth rather than to consider their expertise, conscientiousness, and compatibility with inside directors.

Some company presidents try to get outsiders to serve on a voluntary basis, especially because their exact contributions and benefits cannot be known in advance and in any case usually aren't evident immediately. One surprising finding Jain made was that nearly half of the 120 companies he questioned about use of directors didn't pay their directors. (About three-fourths of nonpaying companies used outside directors.) As interesting as small companies might be, as charismatic as their CEOs might be, or as wealthy as outside directors might be, there's no getting away from the fact that most people work harder and more effectively if they are being paid.

If carefully implemented, the decision to appoint outside directors can be a productive one for both sides. Small companies gain from the infusion of new ideas and insights. And the outside directors, whoever they may be, also stand to gain. If they are consultants, they gain experience that will help in advising clients. If they are executives of large or small companies, they develop ideas to use in running their own businesses. Such interchanges, multiplied many times, can benefit both the small business community and the executive education process.

31
Quasi-Boards
Useful Small Business Confidants

HAROLD W. FOX

To whom can small company owners turn for objective and informed feedback about their major business problems? The most obvious sources—lawyers, accountants, consultants, directors—usually have limitations that prevent them from being either candid or helpful enough. Owners of small businesses willing to make the necessary recruiting effort, though, can form quasi-boards of directors to assist in their companies' decision making. Ironically, because they lack official power and are detached from companies' day-to-day operations, quasi-boards can have both owners' confidence and important strategic influence.

Running a successful small business can be a lonely task, thanks largely to the entrepreneur's natural tendency to be secretive.

Secrecy seems necessary partly because of a fear of competition. Most small businesses are easy to start and simple to operate, given the proper financing. They are also, of course, highly susceptible to failure. But the successful entrepreneur has demonstrated the viability of the business and fears that others with a similar specialty, a minimum of financing, and a knowledge of the company's operations could replace it in the marketplace.

At the same time, the owner feels that "my business is different"— and does not, therefore, see the need to share with others the challenges of planning strategies and operations.

In addition, the owner-manager frequently fears being targeted by relatives and others seeking various kinds of favors. The less they know, the owner assumes, the less they will pressure me to give unemployed son-in-law Louis a job, buy office supplies from some nice young striver, or extend favorable credit terms to an acquaintance of my mother's bridge partner.

Ironically, it's when a small business finally becomes profitable that the need for an entrepreneur to confide in others becomes acute. After a new business has weathered a shakedown period of round-the-clock schedules, daily crises, and quick-witted improvisation, a daily routine evolves. Now subordinates perform the tasks that the founder and associates used to do. The founder is the boss; the founder's original associates are called managers. Overlapping responsibilities and cramped quarters inevitably lead to bickering. And, with time, the camaraderie from jointly surmounting obstacles gives way to a climate of underlying tension.

Yesteryear's conquering heroes stay on for lack of equally remunerative and impressive employment alternatives; the owner retains them from a sense of obligation. But procedures stifle the managers' impulses, and the boss's secrecy impedes their effectiveness. The boss and many of the managers are in over their heads.

To whom can owner-managers turn for the special advice and assistance they need? The usual sounding boards—the company's public accountant or lawyer—apply their particular professional viewpoints, often without coming to grips with important administrative or operational issues.

Consultants may also be inappropriate, if only because the owner-manager's administrative problems are not just a matter of one-time assignments. Rather, the problems are ongoing and require some permanent provisions for dialogue and participation with outsiders respected as peers.

The board of directors, in theory, offers entrepreneurs a source of guidance, but in practice small company boards are often either an arena for battling family and shareholder interests or a nominal body to ratify the owner's proposals. Because the directors have significant authority owners are usually reluctant to place too many outsiders on their boards; conversely, outsiders may be reluctant to get involved because they dislike quarrels and legal entanglements.

Alternative Approach

Small companies can enlist expert advice at low cost, however, through a few independent overseers who might be referred to as a quasi-board of directors, an advisory board, or an advisory council. Quasi-boards perform many of the functions that conventional boards dominated by outsiders do (or should do) in publicly held corporations, but without the latter's legal power and accountability. (See Exhibit 1 for a comparison between conventional boards and quasi-boards.)

A quasi-board probes deeply into matters of policy and operation. It critiques management's actions, raises new questions, and offers suggestions to strengthen the company. An advisory board's effectiveness depends on the proprietor's voluntary decision to respect its advice. And because the quasi-board has no legal power, the owner does not feel threatened when it exposes problems, worries and ideas. In cases of family squabbles or disagreements among partners, the quasi-board offers a detached and neutral viewpoint and can often arbitrate settlements.

Exhibit 1.   Conventional Boards vs. Quasi-Boards

	Conventional[a]	Quasi
1	Accountable to numerous interests for corporate product.	Not accountable.
2	Have or need directors' liability insurance.	No such need.
3	Required to make certain public disclosures.	No such requirements.
4	Spend an average of 122 hours annually on board duties (survey of 576 major companies).	Spend an average of 30 hours annually (survey of ten owner-managed companies).
5	Select or dismiss the president.	No such power.
6	Represent the stockholders.	No such representation.
7	Elected by stockholders for stated term.	Appointed by owner-manager who determines tenure.
8	Nominated because of respected position in the business world, pliability, or being a symbol of hitherto unrepresented group, as well as prudence and diligence.	Selected for prudence and diligence.
9	Comply with legal requirements.	No special requirements.
10	Evaluate performance of CEO and key executives.	Yes, evaluate performance.
11	Review and approve major corporate objectives, policies, budgets, and strategies as initiated by CEO.	Yes, plus take some initiatives.
12	Monitor the company's financial structure.	Yes, monitor financial structure.
13	Monitor, review, and appraise management.	Provide opinion but lack authority.
14	Monitor, review, and appraise management's decisions and plans, management development, and employee relations.	Yes, monitor, review, and appraise.
15	Serve individually as advisers to the president and, with his or her approval, to others in the company.	Yes, advise.
16	Monitor the company's performance.	Yes, monitor company's performance.

Exhibit 1. (*Continued*)

	Conventional[a]	Quasi
17	Assume responsibility for management of the board.	No such responsibility.
18	Review document of board responsibilities periodically.	No such review.
19	Ensure company's compliance with all national, international, foreign, state, and local laws affecting the enterprise.	No such function.
20	Do not usually arbitrate quarrels.	Arbitrate quarrels that threaten company's existence.

[a]Adapted from Myles L. Mace, "Designing a Plan for the Ideal Board," *HBR*, November–December 1976, p. 21.

The Best Candidates

Organizaing a quasi-board need not be difficult. With the help of an attorney, the owner drafts a description of the board's function, emphasizing its advisory role and its exemption from legal responsibility toward the company's shareholders. Then the owner recruits a panel whose collective outlook and judgment he or she feels comfortable with.

Members of such boards usually receive far less pay than directors of large corporations. Typical fees range from $500 to $1,000 per session. The quasi-director's honorarium, besides being an expression of appreciation from the owner, balances two factors. It is high enough to establish an obligation of diligence. On the other hand, it is low enough to preserve the member's autonomy. Advisory boards offer neither the prestige nor the financial rewards sufficient to tie a member to a company with which he or she disagrees.

Appointments are based on ability and willingness to contribute. Advisory panels thrive only in an open-minded atmosphere, where all members can freely argue their convictions. The quasi-boards with which I am familiar have never taken a vote. Rather, after spirited exchanges of opinions, members always reach a consensus.

An advisory board functions best if it is small. Ordinarily, four or five members—the owner (chairperson) plus some outsiders with overlapping expertise—suffice. Members should have empathy for small business problems, care about the company's success, and work effectively with other board members.

Members can come from any number of backgrounds, including the following:

☐   Staff work in a giant corporation.

☐   Top-level responsibility in a bank or small noncompeting concern.

☐   Technical knowledge (e.g., chemical engineering) of the company's business.

☐   Consulting experience or professorial status in business administration.

☐   Contacts with regulators, vendors, or large buyers.

☐   Professional specialty such as practicing attorney or practicing psychologist.

☐   Broadly diversified business experience with a record of success.

The last-mentioned qualification is probably the most valuable. Over a period of time company objectives change, and the board's effectiveness increasingly depends on members who, together with the owner, can redefine the council's scope and objectives. If the outsiders have coped successfully with a wide variety of challenges, they will likely tackle the next change in direction as well.

Business owners are likeliest to meet prospective members at country clubs, executive seminars, and through acquaintances and recommendations. Prospects with the appropriate personal and technical endowments rarely refuse an owner's invitation to join. Why? Some feel underused in their own organizations. Many welcome a change of pace and a chance to prove or raise their potential.

While small business owners are limited in what they can pay members, they are free to demonstrate their appreciation in more imaginative ways. One proprietor rented a motion picture theater and invited all council members, top executives, and their spouses to an afternoon of movies and popcorn. A distributor who frequently runs sales contests gives quasi-board members rotating assignments to investigate the top prizes—fully paid vacations to exotic resorts. Another owner entertains the panel on her yacht. In these and other ways, shrewd business people are eager to show their thanks to those who help them.

Striking the Right Balance

Two to four formal meetings per year, preferably on weekends, usually keep a quasi-board current yet limit its role to matters of greatest significance to the company. Occasional ad hoc committees and private sessions with the owner-manager, as needed, supplement the regular schedule.

The purpose of the board may vary somewhat among companies. For example, a small bank in California organized an advisory council of local business and community leaders as a sounding board for keeping in touch with the community. At quarterly luncheon meetings under the chairmanship of the bank's president, officers took turns presenting to the board new developments and other matters for comment. Inauguration of a bank newsletter was one of the quasi-board's first projects.

Especially at the outset, an advisory council must avoid meddling in procedural details. Forbearance helps allay the apprehensions of department heads. As in any new relationship, the owner-manager, executives, and members of a fledgling board may be skeptical. Early successes and reassurances help dispel these misgivings. Ideally, the company's owner and executives handle the exigencies of the moment and look to the advisory board for guidance on basic, long-term challenges.

During its orientation stage, a newly constituted quasi-board learns the business and focuses on traditional management functions. A typical action is a recommendation for a logical organization design including, where needed, position descriptions for the top managers and organization charts. At several companies, these requests forced management to strengthen internal control, fill functional gaps, and eliminate overlaps. As byproducts, internal squabbling dies down and the need for policies in some operating areas (inventory control, insurance programs) becomes evident.

Gaining Acceptance

In several cases, executives' revelation of dishonesty by subordinates overcame the initial resistance within their companies to setting up a quasi-board. Each quasi-board recommended appropriate protective measures, which in turn paved the way for budgeting and long-term planning. Small business, after all, is not immune to white-collar crime.

Since some crisis—cutoff by a major supplier, reduction in sales, need for a loan—frequently triggers the board's start-up, the panel's initial encouragement or guidelines for a solution help it gain credibility.

The first meeting of one quasi-board, for example, touched on cost overruns, a slippage in margins, division of responsibility for producing and filling orders, shipping delays, and sales agents' dissatisfaction with commissions. A board member suggested a simple job order and project accountability system, which helped the executives resolve these and other problems as well. Several years later, the president still refers to this contribution as the one that confirmed his confidence in the quasi-board.

As its acceptance grows, so does the range of issues confronting the council. Often the issues aren't what they originally seemed to be. For example, one company was eager to commercialize three new products of seemingly high potential, but it lacked the marketing skill. After questioning the owner, the panel redefined this problem as imbalance in organizational design and haphazardness in selecting product ideas for development. The problem was now put in a perspective that company management could deal with.

Helping Map the Future

Sometimes councils can persuade owners to change their plans. When the owner of a seasonal business presented to her quasi-board a set of plans for geographic expansion, members noted that she had picked the locations arbitrarily and had no estimates of sales potential. Eventually, the owner shelved the plans. She and the board are looking for a contraseasonal business instead.

In another case, a seven-year-old diversified manufacturing company incurred its first deficit, which the owner-manager deemed an exception that further growth would rectify. Council members noted, however, that many distant operations were out of control and apparently unprofitable. They persuaded the owner to shrink his business by more than one-half. Almost immediately, the business began generating profits. From its reduced scale, growth resumed—this time soundly planned, financed, and controlled.

When the president of a prosperous small corporation decided to reward his employees with stock bonuses, he was taken aback when both his accountant and his lawyer advised him that a distribution to everybody on his list would total 35% of his shares. He mentioned his misgivings to a council member, who suggested that the president map out a series of distributions especially as rewards for extraordinary performance, instead of a single large gift. The member also recommended a 1000:1 stock split and the subsequent awarding of no more than 100 shares at a time. This solution pleased the president and provided incentives for eligible managers.

At a resin manufacturing company, the president asked the quasi-board to interview the finalist among candidates for a key position. An executive at a major corporation, this top candidate had previously exhibited self-assurance and demanded compensation that had overawed the president and his staff. Questioned closely by a board member, the candidate conceded that much of her vaunted experience was exaggerated, her job status at the major corporation terminal, and her expectations unreasonable. She did not join the company.

Boards can also provide valuable contacts, as the president of a specialty manufacturing company that dominated the local market found out when he sought national recognition as industry spokesman. He did not know how to proceed, so a council member, who was vice-president of public relations for a multibillion-dollar corporation, explained how to get media coverage and other exposure. The member then introduced the president to a public relations organization, which got the necessary publicity effort started.

Adopting Various Roles

Advisory boards can be particularly effective in resolving the conflicts so common in small companies. At a publishing company, the chief executive and the managing editor clashed about operating policies. The board interviewed each person separately and established an agenda for a one-on-one meeting in which the two individuals aired their views. This frank exchange saved the publisher an employee who would have been almost impossible to replace.

Another company's production manager revolted against the sales-minded executive vice-president, also the owner's son. Both parties threatened to quit and start rival businesses. The owner, unable to settle this dispute, empowered the quasi-board to decide the future of the company. The board was split on what to do. Finally it called the bluff of the two antagonists. Each was told he was free to leave but unlikely to earn elsewhere anything near his present income. If they stayed, they had to "cool it." Both men acquiesced. Harmony prevailed and, to the surprise of everybody, they became close friends.

Somewhat similar clashes occurred at two other businesses with advisory boards. At one of these, private interviews with top executives revealed that the superintendent of production and the manager of quality control were working at cross-purposes. Further probing indicated that poor communication, ambiguous assignments of responsibility, and vague standards were the main causes. The board explained to the owner-manager how to rectify these structural problems and recommended that she do so.

At the other company, the district managers ignored the general sales manager. The latter merited the owner's backing, in the quasi-board's opinion, and the owner agreed.

Perhaps the most delicate subject that reaches quasi-boards concerns managerial succession. One president without natural heirs wants the board to select and supervise his successor after his death. Thus far the members have resisted this sensitive assignment. But some quasi-boards have been drawn into this issue—where impatient fifty-year-olds are waiting for father to yield his place to them.

Be Demanding

When quasi-boards fail to live up to the business owner's expectations, a purge may be necessary. Members who are apathetic in meetings or skip many meetings should be asked to resign. One board requested the owner to nudge an absentee colleague who prolonged his nominal association with the group. In such a situation, prompt severance and replacement are appropriate.

Some members favor staggered turnover for continual self-renewal of the quasi-board. One quasi-board conducts an annual evaluation of its own performance.

In practice, no conflict exists between a board of directors and a quasi-board. The position of director is nominal in most closely held corporations; in proprietorships and partnerships it does not even exist.

Nor does the quasi-board usurp the role of consultants. It does not conduct detailed studies, install systems, formulate procedures, or implement special projects. It *is* concerned with important policies, questions of strategy, and decisions that promote a company's lasting prosperity. And successful quasi-boards contribute to the growth of not only the company but also the owner-manager, executives, and their own members.

PART FIVE

PLANNING FOR TOMORROW
AN OVERVIEW

Planning, whether for personal or business purposes, is invariably a difficult task. We're invariably reminded by insurance agents and accountants that we should systematically plan our personal financial portfolios and our estates, but how many of us do it formally and then update the plans regularly?

The same holds true for business planning. Actually, the situation may be worse for business owners simply because the meaning of planning as it applies to businesses isn't entirely clear. Planning can be viewed in simple terms, such as forecasting sales a year ahead and attempting to meet the projection. Or it can be seen as consciously trying to mesh personal-career objectives together with business objectives and analyzing the best ways of achieving the various goals.

The personal-career side of small business planning seems to get short-changed in the business literature. "Coping with Entrepreneurial Stress," by David P. Boyd and me, represents one of the first efforts to assess the emotional satisfactions and demands placed on owners. Our research suggests that business ownership is at once extremely satisfying and quite stressful; we recommend that owners seek to become more introspective than they tend to be, in an effort to cope effectively with such difficulties as loneliness, the delegation of responsibility, and relations with employees.

The business objectives of owners in the short term, if course, are to make the business as financially successful as possible. But looking further ahead, the owner is seeking to build equity in the business—to give it financial value to potential acquirers once the owner decides to retire. Toward that end, James McNeill Stancill argues in his article, "Does the Market Know Your Company's Real Worth?" that owners can influence the valuation eventually assigned to their companies. He advises owners to concentrate on such factors as the earnings pattern, dividend policy, and stock market listing.

To begin formal planning procedures, business owners must overcome the seemingly insurmountable barriers of finding both the right time and place (preferably quiet) to start assessing company strengths, weaknesses, and goals, maintains Roger A. Golde in "Practical Planning for Small Business." He concludes that once they begin the process, the tasks of analyzing both internal and external information in a systematic and constructive way become easier.

One task of any long-term plan must include management succession. Once owners have some idea of how they intend to deal with this issue, they can take steps to change the legalities of stock ownership and distribution so as to minimize their eventual tax obligations. One approach to handling this issue is described in "'Freeze' Assets to Lower Estate Taxes and Keep Control," by Wallace F. Forbes and Anthony C. Paddock.

The last three articles deal with what is often the final, and most traumatic, act of business ownership—selling out. Don Albert Grisanti details the turbulence that is frequently a part of selling one's stake in a business to close relatives in his article, "The Agony of Selling Out to Relatives." He has specific suggestions for reducing the trauma.

Even when relatives aren't buying the business, the experience is difficult, from the vantage points of both financial analysis and emotional stress. Michael G. Berolzheimer lets the reader in on pointers learned from his own experience selling a company in his article, "The Financial and Emotional Sides of Selling Your Company." I follow up that discussion with observations gleaned from a panel of commentators including a corporate acquisitions expert, a lawyer, and a business owner.

32

Coping with Entrepreneurial Stress

DAVID P. BOYD and DAVID E. GUMPERT

Succeeding at your own business is one of the great American dreams. It suggests that you've achieved some of the most valued goals in our society—independence, wealth, and satisfaction in a career. A recent study of 450 entrepreneurs done by these authors confirms that many successful entrepreneurs do indeed achieve these goals and that small business ownership is one of the most satisfying career experiences available in American life. But the study also shows that entrepreneurs pay an extremely high cost for such satisfaction—at least once a week 55% to 65% of those surveyed have back problems, indigestion, insomnia, or headaches. To keep getting the satisfaction entrepreneurship brings, though, they appear willing to tolerate such evidence of stress.

As a result of their research, the authors question whether a high level of stress is an inevitable by-product of small business ownership. In this article, they show several entrepreneurs describing the changes they have made to reduce the stress their work causes and offer additional approaches for coping with such stress.

Much of what has been written about entrepreneuship concerns how to start a business and what produces financial success. Here we see something new to the literature—an inquiry into the emotional and physiological effects of owning a business.

The summer of 1980 was a trying time for Roger B. and his metal-finishing company, which had reached an annual volume of $4 million. "I was going through some major plant personnel problems and changes," he recalls.

Roger especially remembers a day in August:

Authors' Note: We wish to thank Lewis Shattuok, executive vice president of the Smaller Business Association of New England, for his invaluable assistance in making our research possible. We are also grateful to Northeastern University's Research and Scholarship Development Fund, to the dean's office of its College of Business Administration, and to *Harvard Business Review* for making available the resources necessary for this research.

I was in the plant at 8:30 that morning with a salesman who was trying to justify his existence in the company. At the same time I was covering for another guy by answering telephones. Suddenly, I began to slur my words and had this eerie feeling go through me. I asked for a glass of water. It didn't help. My secretary drove me to the emergency room. When I arrived, my blood pressure was 175 over 145.

Roger had had a slight stroke. Although he recovered, he still occasionally feels his blood pressure soaring during tense moments at the office. He continues to work more than 60 hours a week, though, and insists he enjoys it. Within a few years, he hopes he will reach his business goal of having $10 million in annual sales.

Joe T. is a distributor for bearing and transmission manufacturers. He began the company with his father and brother more than 30 years ago. It has been profitable from the start and now has more than 100 employees. Almost every day, though, Joe has indigestion. He tries to relieve it by taking antacids, but they are not totally effective, and many nights he sleeps sitting up.

Joe says, however, that he could not be happier with his work: "I can do what I choose. I don't have to answer to anyone. I can leave, I can retire, and I can take money out of the company. It's a beautiful way to live, and I don't see why everybody doesn't do it."

Marie S. owns a fast-growing abrasives manufacturing company with annual sales of $30 million. About five nights a week, she suffers from insomnia. "It's common for me to wake up at 3 A.M.—I can almost set my watch by it. Then I'll stay awake for a couple of hours. I sit and read until I get sleepy and then go back to bed."

Despite insomnia, Marie would not consider working anywhere else. "We've had offers to buy us out. The business is not for sale. I wouldn't sell my kids and husband and dog, and I won't sell my business, whether it's succeeding or failing. It's a commitment."

As these vignettes suggest, a small business can be both trying and satisfying. Financial risk is inherent in the decisions entrepreneurs must make, yet substantial profits are possible when their decisions are right. Anxiety and exhilaration run neck and neck through the small business experience. The degree to which these extremes of emotion occur has not been thoroughly studied. So far, the research has concentrated on the backgrounds and attributes of persons who are entrepreneurs rather than on the psychological and physiological fallout from running small companies.

In late 1981 and early 1982, we undertook a research project to identify situations, issues, and occurrences that can cause entrepreneurs stress, on the one hand, and satisfaction, on the other. We mailed a survey with both specific-answer and open-ended questions on it to 1,000 chief executives of established small companies in New England and got 450 completed questionnaires back. From the 64% who signed the form and expressed willingness to be interviewed, we chose 7 to talk with individually.

What left the strongest impression on us was the depth and range of difficulties that entrepreneurs encounter on a daily basis and, paradoxically, the amount of pleasure they derive from this experience. They enjoy the career they have chosen and have few regrets about staying in it. Only 2 out of 450 disagreed with our statement that a career in small business brings satisfaction and self-fulfillment, and none strongly disagreed. Indeed, 21% agreed with it and 79% strongly agreed.

In view of the romanticized notion of small business ownership—connoting as it does independence and financial comfort—the satisfaction entrepreneurs express is not surprising. What is surprising is the price they are willing to pay for it. At least once a week, 57% have back problems, 57% impaired digestion, 62% insomnia, and 64% headaches. One-third of the respondents have one or more of these symptoms at least twice a week, and more than one-third have chest pains once a week.

Yet out of 450, only 12 mentioned damage to physical health as a cost of owning a business. Just 7 perceived a need to reduce their level of stress. In answer to our questions about the costs and rewards of small business management, our subjects concentrated on psychological satisfactions rather than physiological costs. Joe T. may sleep sitting up with indigestion each night, but he still wonders why everyone else doesn't see what a "beautiful" life he has.

With all their problems, why do these people find so much fulfillment in their jobs? And why are they willing to sacrifice so much for it? We sought their answers.

The Benefits of Ownership

For entrepreneurs who survive the start-up stage, the financial and psychological rewards can be great. Our respondents have been with their companies an average of 14 years. Nearly two-thirds founded the companies they manage. Their responses indicate two quite positive aspects of business ownership.

Entrepreneurship Can Be Lucrative

Nearly three-fourths of the respondents earn more than $40,000 annually, 59% over $50,000, and 20% over $100,000. Of the benefits cited in the open-ended questions, financial rewards and perquisites rank high on the list. An entrepreneur expressed his satisfaction this way: "To my delight and glee, I am making more money than I ever thought possible. This is something I still pinch myself about."

Small business offers an opportunity to create substantial and profitable financial enterprises. Two-thirds of the companies in our survey have annual sales exceeding $1 million. In 1981, two-thirds had returns on equity of 10% or more, and more than one-fourth had returns above 25%.

Entrepreneurship Has Important Psychic Returns

Independence and freedom of decision making were among the benefits the entrepreneurs we investigated mentioned most frequently. Owning a small business allows "as much control of your own future and fortune as is possible in today's world," declared one business owner. "I'm not worrying about being accepted by the in group—about promotions made by being a yes man to a Godfather." "Since no committee or consensus is necessary," observed another, "you have elasticity in managing."

Joe T., owner of the bearing company, agrees:

> I like the opportunity I have to implement ideas. How many people do you run into who say, "Boy, I wish I could do this"? Then they present it to a board or somebody, and they shoot him down. They can't do that with me. If I'm wrong, I'm wrong, but I can go ahead and do anything I want to.

Being accountable only to oneself was another treasured benefit that our respondents spoke of. There is no sign-off hierarchy for owners. As one owner said, "You can only be fired by failure."

Many respondents also mentioned a sense of achievement. Entrepreneurs have the satisfaction of getting results promptly. "I can bring my own ideas to fruition and measure my own achievement," one respondent explained.

In response to a question on what these entrepreneurs would do differently if they were beginning again, the most recurring answer was that they would have formed their businesses earlier if they had known how satisfying running them was going to be.

The Costs of Success

The entrepreneurs in our sample might seem to be on Easy Street, since 90% of their businesses show a profit. They should be able to take extended vacations, pursue outside interests, and regulate their work pace. Yet our findings bring into question their notion that they have control over their activities. Our survey shows that the stress of our respondents is not significantly related to the size or profitability of their companies. The owners of the struggling companies are no more likely to exhibit medical problems of stress than are the owners of the more thriving companies.

Stress, after all, is not exclusively a reaction to unpleasant experiences, nor does it stop being a problem after one achieves financial success. It seems to be part of entrepreneurship. The entrepreneur must carefully weigh long hours and personal deprivation against sizable—but elusive—rewards. Such wide ranges of hardship and satisfaction lead inevitably to stress.

Contrary to popular belief, stress is not entirely bad. As other research has indicated, stressful events, at least initially, can spur efficiency and improve performance. Stress becomes a life-threatening problem only when it is unrelenting. If not kept within constructive bounds—and those bounds vary from person to person—it wears down the body's defense against illness.[1] While research has not conclusively established the precise role of stress in causing disease, stress has been linked to coronary arteriosclerosis and hypertension. Unfortunately, our respondents seem to be prime candidates for such serious illnesses.

Sources of Stress

Through our interviews, we identified four causes of stress:

Loneliness

Though entrepreneurs are usually surrounded by others—employees, customers, accountants, and lawyers—they are isolated from persons in whom they can confide. "You can't go to anybody who could really help you because they're competing with you," explained one manufacturer. Long hours at work prevent entrepreneurs from seeking the comfort and counsel of friends and family members. Another respondent said he keenly feels "the lack of support from a large organization and lack of recognition from the community."

Isolation means loneliness. The independence and freedom of entrepreneurs' positions may obscure their loneliness. On the questionnaire, many respondents pointed out the advantage of having no bureaucracy, but few mentioned loneliness. During our interviews, however, they raised the issue often.

After discussing the advantages of small business ownership, Joe T., for instance, confided that, "Loneliness is my biggest problem. With whom do you talk? I'm supposed to talk with my accountant, I'm supposed to talk with my banker, with my lawyer. Well, I can and I do, but they can't be objective. They all have an axe to grind because they work for me in one way or another."

More often, what these small company owners said only implied loneliness or expressed it indirectly. They all complained of spending so much time on business that they have little left for family and friends. Indeed, in some cases, confusion existed in their minds about where their business lives end and their personal lives begin. Shelby L., owner of a container distributorship with $4 million annual sales, indicated on the questionnaire that he works between 40 and 49 hours weekly. But during the interview, he said that he often spends three or four evenings a week at trade association meetings and suppliers' shows.

While Shelby noted that his wife definitely considers the shows and meetings to be work (she refers to herself as "the widow L."), he does not, because these activities are different from "sitting behind a desk or making sales calls." Such functions serve a tenuous and uneasy combination of business and social activities: "I meet people, but then I'm thinking that I'm not getting any business benefit out of it. I still go, probably on account of the camaraderie, beers, dinner, and so on." Yet Shelby acknowledges that he can't entirely let his guard down because of the competitive relationships among the participants. The get-togethers, then, not only take time but leave him confused about their real value.

Immersion in Business

The small business owners we interviewed expressed pride in their financial accomplishments. Their earnings are signs of achievement and give them the freedom to choose a variety of leisure activities.

They also find their financial rewards to be a source of frustration, however. It's one thing to be unable to take an exotic vacation because you can't afford it. It's another to be able to afford the trip but feel unable to take it because business won't allow your absence. Said Joe T., "It's an advantage that I can get away, but I'm not doing it." Half the respondents in our survey take two weeks or less for vacation per year; 60% work more than 50 hours a week, and nearly 25% work more than 60 hours. Almost two-thirds work on weeknights, and 55% usually work on Saturday.

Because entrepreneurs work long hours, they have little time for civic organizations, recreation, or further education. Two frequently cited costs of business ownership were the overwhelming dominance of professional life and the personal sacrifices it entails.

Roger B., owner of the metal-finishing company, indicated the ambivalence entrepreneurs feel about extracurricular activities: "I would love to go to lunch and not rush back to the plant. I eat most lunches on the premises. I felt the only way to become less involved in the day-to-day business was to make the company grow larger. I knew if I stayed small I'd be operating out of my pockets."

Roger succeeded in expanding, but it did not bring the salutary results he had expected.

> I have three children, but I don't spend much time with them. There was a time when we all went to Florida for a month. That was back when the company wasn't growing. Those were good times. Last year we arranged to go to the Virgin Islands. I should not have gone, but the trip was prepaid and the money not returnable. It turned out to be the best vacation I'd ever had. It was like being away for six weeks, though it was only six days. That helped me get through last year.

Small business owners often feel that their businesses deprive them of outside activities. Tom O., owner of a chain of automotive supply stores, said, "I've always regretted the fact that I didn't finish college. If I had no other concerns, I could return to get a degree. It would be interesting, exciting, and different."

If Tom hadn't been so busy running his company, he "probably would have had more fun," he said.

Up until a couple of years ago, I worked every Saturday. One more day out of seven is a lot if you can spend it with your kids. But I don't know anyone who's successful in his own business who did not start out by working at least 60 hours a week. And I've done that for many years.

People Problems

About 60% of our respondents had had experience working for large companies. They left secure but often sedentary posts in search of greater financial reward and the chance to be decision makers.

Complete independence in decision making is illusory, though, since business owners must depend on partners, employees, customers, and suppliers for judgments. The complaint we heard most often from those we interviewed concerned the frustration and disappointment they experienced in their relationships with partners and subordinates. Approximately 30% had gone into business with partners; more than two-thirds of this group had dissolved their partnerships by the time we sent out our questionnaire. A third of them did so because of the conflict they had had.

When asked what they might do to make their work more satisfying, the most frequent response of these managers was to "devote more attention to management-employee issues." In some cases, conflict with their partners had arisen over how to supervise subordinates. Dick H., owner of a heating products company, was strongly opposed to the permissive management style of his older brother.

With eight employees, you can operate in a very open, amiable way. With 20, it's a different game, and with 40 it's different again. You cannot do things as you used to when you were really small. It's very difficult for me—a good old boy from Alabama—because I want to be liked by everybody. But you can't be that way.

Successful entrepreneurs usually know precisely how they want their companies to function; the problem is getting employees to make it happen. One owner ruefully concluded that "the sense of responsbility and obligation for the well-being of the company cannot be delegated."

Listen to the lament of Roger B.:

I grew, but the organization didn't grow with me. And God knows, I tried. I made 61 management changes from November 1978 through December 1981. As a matter of fact, I keep a list. My secretary's updating it now, because we're switching department heads. It's incredible. In the best of times, it's a pressure business. I give the responsibility, but most people do not want to work hard. And all you need is one weak link. If you don't discover it, you're going to ruin the strong links.

The entrepreneurs complained that they were doing detail work that should be delegated. As one owner expressed it, "The company has 60 employees, and while there are functional managers, there's no vice-president. They all report to me, and they report to me on trivial stuff. If I could find a good strong general manager, he or she could sit here and handle all these problems and I could go out and do creative things." One entrepreneur voiced a desire he had in common with the others when he said he longed "to gamble with other ventures and to oversee rather than administer."

Even those who think they have a handle on the delegation process admit to frustration. Marie S., owner of the abrasives company, contends that "it doesn't really worry me to farm things out because I know in advance other people are going to disappoint me. If you don't expect too much from them, then you're delighted, you're surprised, if by chance they do well."

Later in the interview, though, Marie commented on the cost of patience:

> I like to be involved in the mechanical process of making our product, and I know how to do it. If something's wrong in the process, I can fix it. What isn't so easy for me is to fix someone's thinking. When they're doing something that they shouldn't be doing, I've got to change their thinking. And that's hard for me. To sit down and reason with them is time-consuming.
>
> I could leave my desk and fix the problem in less time. On the other hand, there are too many guys out there. I can't do all their jobs. I've got to make them see the process the same way that the company sees it.

Allowing employees to mature in the midst of frenzied activities can be "very frustrating," but Marie added, "it can be satisfying too."

The Need to Achieve

To survive and prosper as a business owner, one must be a hard driver— an achiever. Achievement brings satisfaction, as the overwhelming number of respondents who expressed happiness about their careers demonstrates.

In the course of the interviews, though, it became clear that a fine line exists between attempting to achieve too much and failing to achieve enough. More often than not, the business owners appeared to us to be trying to accomplish too much. One entrepreneur betrayed the reason for his competitive drive when he noted that "company growth is a reflection of your overall ability." Dick H., the heating products distributor, typifies the harried high achiever: "I'm not a bullet—I'm a shotgun. When I come to work, I try to be four things at once and talk on the phone and push papers. I don't like being that way." Dick maintains this pace even though he doesn't need the money. "I could make more money cutting back, believe me."

His most satisfying challenge, he added, is negotiating acquisitions of companies, but it also creates the most stress.

> My insomnia is usually when I'm in the middle of a deal. I'm rehearsing it and saying, "Well, what am I going to do? What are the boundaries of the negotiation? Where will I yield?" I'm never satisfied that I've done the job I should. And I suppose I should be satisfied. I should be willing to sit back and say "Gee, you're a smart son-of-a-gun for having put that deal together with such a little bit of equity."

I'm sure that if I continue the way I'm going, I will have health problems in five or ten years. What worries me is the geometric progression in my business activities. The stress is directly proportional to the activity. I realize how to succeed, and I'm doing it. And that's all wonderful, as long as I don't kill myself in the process.

Tom O., owner of the auto supply stores, also realizes the dangers of unbridled ambition. He is trying to temper his achievement need and often reminds himself that "They're not going to take all this business and put it in my casket. The Egyptians tried it with their pharaohs, but they never seemed to come back and get it."

The other side of the achievement coin is Shelby L., the owner of the company distributing glass and metal containers. His company has arrived at a sales plateau, and the halt in growth is frustrating. Shelby finds "coasting for a year inconceivable." This is how he explains his reactions:

I don't think anyone can feel comfortable in business. There's always some other monkey like myself ready to tear up your back. I really feel if I stop, they're going to shoot me. But it's difficult to catch a moving target. Whether it's moving up and down or left to right, at least it's moving.

Increasing Awareness

How can entrepreneurs improve the quality of their business and personal lives to counter their high levels of stress? There are no pat answers. Stress is a serious problem in our society, whether or not one owns a business.

Given the causes we have identified, though, entrepreneurs can combat excessive stress by first, acknowledging its existence, second, developing coping mechanisms, and third, probing their unacknowledged needs.

The first step in controlling stress is to become aware of how destructive it can be to the physical and psychological patterns of one's life. While many of the entrepreneurs we surveyed seemed vaguely aware of these dangers, they were reluctant to delve deeply into the problem. Said Roger B., "I don't say anything about the problems. That's part of what's bothering me. I don't blow my stack, so it just eats away inside."

Edmund N., president of an engineering equipment company, said much the same: "People problems upset me, but I don't show my concern. Then one day I fibrillated and spent three weeks in the hospital."

Why the reluctance to consider the problem? One reason is that these executives believe they are having so much fun: virtually 100% agreed with the statement that a small business career brings satisfaction and self-fulfillment.

Since they are enjoying themselves, entrepreneurs tend to ignore their high stress level. For every sleepless night or bout of indigestion, there is the exhilaration of making a major sale or solving an intricate production problem. Entrepreneurs are much more likely to anticipate the challenges and successes of their work than to face its stress-related difficulties.

But there is a more subtle and pervasive aspect—the implicit threat that if owners acknowledge the dangers of stress, they will in some way rock the boat. If the stress disappears, so might the fun.

A more practical answer might be offered for this reluctance to view the stress as an important issue. Despite their financial success, the small business owners we surveyed see themselves in a constant struggle for survival. It is easy to pass this stress off as an inevitable part of the struggle and to regard it as an unnecessary distraction from their work.

Entrepreneurs should see not only that stress is damaging to health but also that relieving it does not necessarily diminish the satisfaction of owning a business. By reducing stress-related symptoms, they could enhance the quality of both their personal and their business lives.

Coping Mechanisms

When entrepreneurs acknowledge that stress is a problem to face, they can begin to do something about it. One approach is to use stress-reduction techniques accepted in the medical community, such as transcendental meditation, biofeedback, muscle relaxation, and regular exercise.[2] Since these techniques have received much attention in the press, we shall not describe them further here.

Another step business owners can take is to clarify the causes of their stress. When they do so, solutions often surface. The search for causes might begin with the four areas of vulnerability our survey uncovered—loneliness, business immersion, people problems, and obsessiveness about the need to achieve. Of course, additional factors may be at work, including family conflicts and financial difficulties.

How does one cope with these causes? None of the business owners we interviewed claimed to have an easy solution, but most described approaches they had found at least somewhat helpful. These include:

Networking
One way to relieve the inevitable loneliness of operating a business is to share experiences with other business owners. The objectivity gained from hearing about the triumphs and errors of others is itself therapeutic.

Several executives paid tribute to the discussion groups sponsored by the Smaller Business Association of New England. One entrepreneur remarked that he felt relaxed in the "noncompetitive" atmosphere and found his loneliness abated. Some said they got a similar effect from serving as directors of other small businesses. Roger B., for instance, said, "That is the greatest relaxation I can possibly ask for."

Getting Away from It All
The best antidote to immersion in business, said those interviewed, is a good holiday. Many spoke longingly of vacations but admitted they seldom took

them. For some, there was the dread of oppressive work piling up in their absence. For a few, another unstated aspect was worrisome: suppose the business ran well without them?

Those who took the plunge, however, nearly always found the experience worthwhile. Joe T., the business owner with chronic indigestion, saw his symptoms disappear during a vacation in Germany. "I ate German food, I drank beer, I had schnapps. But I didn't take one antacid pill until I was in the Frankfurt airport boarding a plane to come home."

If vacation days or weeks are limited by valid business constraints, short breaks may still be possible. Tom O. goes to the town library to sort out his ideas in quiet. "I put a pad down and write as the thoughts come. No one interrupts to ask, 'What do I do about this?'" Such interludes allow a measure of self-renewal. Executives in small businesses can interpose gaps between commitments to help lessen the harmful effects of stress.

Communication with Subordinates

Because small companies usually cannot offer the same financial and advancement opportunities to employees as large corporations, entrepreneurs often assume that people problems are insolvable.

In fact, being small enables companies to offer certain advantages to employees. Owners are in close contact with subordinates and can readily assess the concerns of their staffs. The personal touches often unavailable in large corporations, such as company-wide outings, flexible hours, and small loans to tide workers over until payday, are possible. Some entrepreneurs argue that their employees are often more individually productive than their counterparts in large organizations.[3]

Only one entrepreneur we interviewed felt comfortable and satisfied in his relationships with subordinates. His approach may be instructive: Edmund N. makes a point of walking through the plant to talk with employees. He has conversations about work and personal matters with each employee at least once a week and thus is close to problems on the floor. "There's little bitterness," he says. "We don't allow it to develop." When he must lay employees off, he tries to place them in other companies.

Edmund focuses on the personal growth and development of the people at the plant—his foremen, for instance. "I have tried to give them stature," he says. "Now workers aspire to be foremen. They see that distinction is available for effort." In these efforts to establish rapport, Edmund has found relief from his own stress.

Find Satisfaction Outside the Company

Countering obsessiveness in the need to achieve can be difficult, since the entrepreneur's personality is inextricably bound up in the fabric of the company. If entrepreneurs can step aside from their work occasionally and become more passionate about life itself, they may gain some emotional perspective that is very helpful.

Some of the need to achieve can be fulfilled outside the workplace. To relieve tension, Shelby L. goes antiquing, for instance, and Edmund N. researches a Revolutionary War general. Edmund says his research is a "refuge" from work and an "avenue" for his achievement need.

Delegating

All these coping techniques require time, of course, to implement. Many entrepreneurs said frankly that the only way they could find the time was to delegate tasks, but they added that delegating is much easier said than done.

Shelby L., for example, concedes:

My temptation is to check every invoice and make sure that we got 15 drums or 50 drums or 500 drums and that we paid the right price. I could spend seven hours a week doing it, and I wouldn't find $300 worth of damage, if I found that. So it really isn't worth it. But it's very difficult to keep your fingers out of things that you did as you built up the business.

Marie S. has reluctantly decided to delegate export sales, which she built from nothing to $8 million. "I'm sorry to let it go. It won't be done as well as I did it years ago. But it will be done better than I've done it for the last two years. If you're involved in a growth situation, you must prune your areas of activity."

If delegation is to save time and thus relieve stress, the appropriate delegates must be found. They must then be trained for task accomplishment. Delegation represents a preliminary sacrifice of time in the hope of long-term savings. "If I spend three solid months with someone," Roger B. reflects, "I can train him. But where can I find three solid months? Still, I should have done it. If I had, I'd be ahead today. I might be on the beach in Florida right now."

Probing More Deeply

Useful as the previously listed approaches are in moderating stress, the business owners in our survey had difficulty implementing them. Shortage of time is certainly a factor, but that cannot be the only reason. Because of their independence, owners have more control over their time than most people.

By involving themselves so totally in their vocations, entrepreneurs may be seeking to fulfill some deep but undefined psychological need. Perhaps the sort of satisfaction they receive from the business appears unobtainable elsewhere.

We did not find the business owners we interviewed much inclined toward introspection. Most said that the hour and a half or two they had spent on our interviews were the longest periods they could remember sitting still and reflecting about themselves. After the sessions, all of them commented that the time had been well spent. A few said that the interview had given them new insights and helped them rearrange their priorities.

A small but significant segment of our respondents—nearly 12%—have sought psychiatric counseling. We don't know how successful this experience has been, but from our interviews with those who went through counseling, we do know that it works best when business owners seek it independently. It is less efficacious when spouses or well-meaning friends prod them into going.

From our study, we learned that entrepreneurship is abundantly satisfying, on the one hand, but eminently stressful on the other. If small business managers come to terms with stress, they can enhance their careers and lengthen their lives.

Notes

1. See, for example, John M. Ivancevich and Michael T. Matteson, *Stress and Work: A Managerial Perspective* (Glenview, Ill.: Scott, Foresman, 1980), pp. 75–100.

2. See for instance, Arthur P. Bnet, Randall S. Schuler, and Mary Van Sell, *Managing Job Stress* (Boston: Little, Brown, 1981), pp. 102–109.

3. See Thomas H. Melohn, "How to Build Employee Trust and Productivity," *HBR*, January–February 1983, p. 56, for evidence.

33

Does the Market Know Your Company's Real Worth?

JAMES McNEILL STANCILL

Stock prices for publicly held companies and sale prices for private companies are determined entirely by market forces beyond the manager's control. Or are they? Can managers of smaller companies exert any control over the valuations assigned their companies? This depends on whether the factors used to determine value are subject to easy interpretation and application.

   While acknowledging that some factors are easily interpreted and applied, and that they are in this sense objective, Mr. Stancill argues that many of the financial criteria can be interpreted quite subjectively, particularly those for small companies. They tend to receive less attention from securities analysts and others than do large corporations. He contends further that entrepreneurs can exert some degree of control over how analysts apply these financial criteria and perceive their companies. Among the issues that he maintains are most susceptible to influence are a company's industry assignment, its earnings pattern, its stock market listing, and its dividend policy.

Not long ago I asked the officer of a regional investment banking firm why the price–earnings ratio for a small publicly held company was so low. "After

Author's Note: I wish to thank the following for their suggestions: Russell Diehl of Peterson, Diehl, Speyer & Brown, Inc.; William R. Zimmerman of Zimmerman Holdings, Inc.; and Bruce P. Emmeluth of Seidler, Arnett & Spillane, Inc.

all," I said, "this company has the potential to grow since it's in the dental equipment industry. It seems to me it warrants a high ratio."

"Don't you know," my friend replied, somewhat puzzled," that that company is mainly a machine shop? That puts it into a low-growth industry classification."

Why is it that even companies in the same industry have markedly different P–E ratios? And how can investors arrive at appropriate P–E ratios when they are confused about which industry a company belongs in?

To wonder about such things in an era when respected finance textbooks refer to the "efficient capital market hypothesis" seems to be the height of irreverence. Isn't the P–E up to the forces of the market—a market whose participants are all knowing? How does one account for the wide differences in companies' P–E ratios—even in businesses within the same industry classification? In the Moody's *Industry Review* of January 15, 1982, under the 1981 rankings for "Textiles—Miscellaneous," 28 companies are listed. One of the companies, Guilford Mills, the sixth largest, is first in operating profit margin and first in return on capital but only twelfth in P–E ratio (its below-average rank is 6.7:1). In fact, for 23 of the 28 companies that made a profit in their last fiscal year in this category, the range of the P–E ratios was from 47.5:1 to 1.6:1.

The latest industry grouping for restaurants (dated February 26, 1982) includes 42 companies. The smallest company listed, Florida Capital Corporation, is third in operating profit margin and fourth in return on capital yet last in the P–E ranking for the 37 companies that reported a profit.

The list could go on and on. And what about the hundreds of thousands of closely held businesses? If shareholder wealth is a function of both a company's earnings and its P–E multiple, can anything be done to raise the P–E?

I believe management can do a number of things to influence its P–E multiple—too many, perhaps, to include in one article. Nevertheless, in the following pages, I attempt to identify the most important financial issues for management to consider.

For instance, why is a company classified in one industry instead of another? What can a company do about being classified in a poorly valued industry? And what does a company's pattern of earnings tell a prospective buyer or the stock market? Can normally intelligent, reasonable people discern the profitability of a company, or is it so hidden that it can be observed only after tedious examination? And if the company shows an unfavorable earnings pattern to those making valuations, are there favorable patterns that it might look for?

Should a developing company seek listing on an exchange or remain in the over-the-counter market? How should management deal with stock market movement? And what about dividends for the developing company? Can they improve the market value of the business, or do they send out the wrong signals about the company's stock? Finally, of what importance is a company's debt–equity ratio in the subjective appraisal of share value for publicly held companies or the company's overall valuation if the business is closely held?

While there are other subjective factors—largely nonfinancial—that might influence the value of a developing company, I believe these are the most important of the subjective financial factors.

My main concern is the developing business. The owners of the privately held company should be at least thinking about eventually going public. Most of the strategies I discuss in the next pages are inappropriate for the privately held business that never intends to go public.

Determining the Industry

Which industry is your company in? That question sounds simple, but it is not easy to answer. I recall working with a person who was quite experienced in corporate acquisition. Together we were examining a small publicly held concern that made electrical products. At least that was the way the company was presented to us. One man held majority ownership, so the acquisition would not be unduly complicated. But a line of not very exciting electrical products? Why bother? Then it occurred to this person that this company really made test equipment, which was much more financially attractive than electrical products.

What's in a name? Quite a lot, I think. Calling the company a manufacturer of testing equipment rather than a maker of mundane electrical components might make a huge difference in its overall financial attractiveness. A company's industry classification tends to set the range of its P–E ratio, especially if the business is closely held. We rank such businesses by classifying them as "growth industries," "services," "job shops," or "run of the mill businesses." Aftertax multiples for closely held businesses may be six to eight times the earnings for a low-technology type of company and more for a high-technology concern or one with fast growth prospects.

Once publicly held developing businesses become identified with a particular industry, changing their identification to another P–E industry category is difficult. When Milan Panic established International Chemical and Nuclear, Inc., it was quite apparent that he had his eye on at least two industries with strong investor appeal. In the mid-1970s, the company was renamed ICN Pharmaceuticals, presumably to avoid the negative connotation of *nuclear* on the one hand and to gain the positive connotation of *pharmaceuticals* on the other.

Why a concern comes to be identified with a specific industry in the first place is perplexing. Failing to realize the importance of the P–E ratio can easily lead one to say, "What difference does it make?" But if you look at two businesses with the same sales and earnings and one is valued at ten times aftertax earnings and one at five—well, there is no need to pursue the obvious.

The case at the start of this article is an interesting example of a company failing to adequately address the question of industry classification. If the company had spun off the higher P–E dental products division (as a stock dividend), the two publicly held businesses thereby created would probably have had a *combined* total value greater than the one that was viewed as "just a job shop." Speaking of job shops, one good way to change that classification is to add a proprietary product line. If successful, the business might then be classified as a "proprietary product company" and command a higher valuation than it would as a job shop.

By either starting companies or making acquisitions in more attractive industries, a company can take off in a whole new direction. In looking to the long run, however, management must be careful not to redirect the company into a voguish sort of industry.

What's the Earnings Pattern?

In textbook finance, a company is worth the present value of its future earnings. To put meaning into this statement, however, one has to ask, What future earnings? And at what discount rate? Whether managers like it or not, the future is forecast from the past. What pattern of earnings has the business established? Furthermore, the people doing the forecasting—whether they be analysts for investment firms, bankers for closely held concerns, or people trying to evaluate the company for the purpose of buying it—are not clairvoyant. I believe that businesses with patterns of earnings that are easy to forecast and analyze will get the highest valuations. Consider the following examples.

The 'Where Are You Going?' Syndrome

The company described in Exhibit 1 has created a pattern of earnings that makes predicting future earnings difficult. The trend seems to be downward,

Exhibit 1. **Failing to Set A Trend**

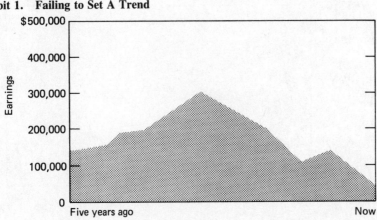

but it's anyone's guess whether that will prove out. Of course, perceptive observers will ask pointed questions about such things as R & D investments for future growth and on that basis try to forecast earnings beyond "time now." But suppose the person making the forecast is not very clever and imaginative. Suppose, for example, the person doing the forecasting is a junior analyst only obeying instructions to use the past as a basis for projection.

The conclusion to draw from such a pattern is that the fortunes of the company are sinking and that the cash flow to provide a return to investors or to service a loan for a leveraged buyout is not there.

The company's owners might have "saved" some of the earnings from the earlier period. If they had concluded that future earnings could not keep up with current results, earnings might have been held back by write-downs of otherwise questionable assets—inventory, receivables, or even fixed assets. Thus, future periods would be relieved of these charges against income. The trend might appear level or even upward, but certainly not downward, as it does the exhibit.

The Turnaround That Doesn't Turn

Then there is the manager who is too eager to get out of the red and doesn't "clean house," a situation that is described in Exhibit 2. Instead of writing off "all the sins of the past," management allows earnings to turn positive, only to see them sink into the red again. If analysts perceived that the turnaround was complete after two years and accordingly recommended the stock of this company, imagine how upset they would be (not to mention the people who had bought the stock on the recommendation of these analysts) if earnings fell back into the red. The analysts would probably feel they had been misled and that the only way they would ever recommend the stock again would be if the chief executive deemed responsible was dismissed or left the company.

Exhibit 2. Failing to "Clean House"

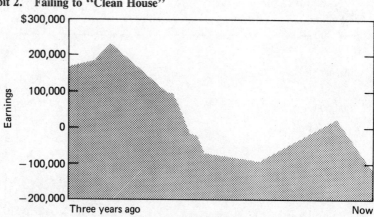

It is not necessarily investment analysts who are misled. Consider how a banker would feel if his own customer fell into this circumstance, especially after a leveraged buyout in which the turnaround had supposedly been completed. Here, the most appropriate strategy would be to allow losses to continue until all the losing projects were written off and the way was cleared for earnings to rise—that is, if the equity section of the balance sheet would support such a move, for you don't want a negative net worth.

The 'We Never Pay Taxes' Syndrome

How many managers have said that the best way to run a closely held business is not to pay taxes? Too many, I'm afraid. Don't get me wrong. I'm not saying that businesses should seek to pay as much tax as they can. On the contrary. But how do you value a company that makes no money? If the concern is closely held, it might be possible to minimize earnings by paying a salary or a bonus to the owner-manager and thereby reduce or eliminate taxable income. The problem is that the Internal Revenue Service will consider the reasonableness of such payments when it examines them for tax deduction. If, for the size of the company in question, the IRS decides the remuneration is excessive, it will disallow or reduce the tax deduction.

Since many owners know that the IRS might disallow such a deduction, they often resort to "creative ways" of burying the remuneration to reduce taxes. It is at this point that short-run goals like minimizing taxes can interfere with long-run goals—like selling the business. If the "creativity" is so imaginative that others (potential buyers, for example) can't find where the remuneration and "goodies" are hidden, the creativity becomes counterproductive.

The Ideal Pattern

A pattern should be easy to understand and should slope upward. Consider the examples in Exhibit 3.

The example on the top shows an unbroken trend of rising earnings, so projecting future earnings is quite easy. (Whether reaching such a conclusion from an extrapolation of such data is correct is another question.) The example on the bottom shows that in one year the company had a loss but that earnings rebounded quite well and are apparently continuing the upward trend. I think that most analysts or prospective purchasers would "forgive" the concern for the loss year if the cause of the loss had been eliminated.

Per Share Earnings and Stock Price

What would an "appropriate" earnings per share (EPS) for a developing business be? This is another way of asking how many shares to leave outstanding and what stock price range to seek.

Exhibit 3.   Charting an Ideal Course

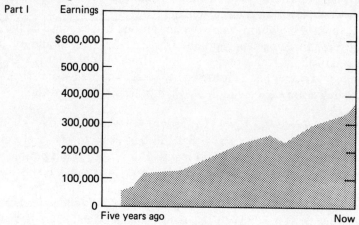

Part I

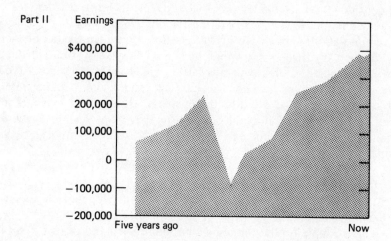

Part II

We might say that stock prices fall into four categories—penny stock (which sells for less than $1.00), low price ($1.00 up to $10), medium price ($10 up to, say, $75) and high price (more than $75). Which of these is appropriate for a developing company?

Penny stocks are usually thought of as being strictly speculative. Mining stocks and oil exploration stocks are examples. Most developing concerns would want to avoid this image if possible. I use the word *image* advisedly, for I remember a conversation with a man who was trying to sell his closely held business and retire—he was about 70. He said he had been approached by a large company whose president he knew. The owner-manager had looked up the price of the public company's stock in the newspaper and observed that "it only costs 75 cents. I don't think that's very good, do you?'' I was tempted to explain that the public company could have changed its stock price upward simply by having a reverse split of its stock, but the owner-manager's mind was made up. That was a ''cheapo'' stock, and he wanted nothing to do with that company. In business, *it's not so much what you are as what people think you are that counts.*

For most developing companies, an EPS that will put the stock— because of the P–E ratio—into the low-price range would seem to be appropriate. In this range you can buy round lots (100 shares) for less than $1,000; most people prefer to buy in round lots, not just because the commission is lower for round lots but also because people feel ''wealthier'' buying round lots than they may actually be. With more potential buyers rather than fewer, the market expands.

Using this same line of reasoning, an entrepreneur who had started a medical equipment business was selling his stock to any physician, surgeon, or dentist who would buy it for $2.00 a share. He began doing so when the company was formed and did so as long as it remained unregistered, that is, nonpublic. Only once did anyone ask him what P–E the price represented, although it had ranged widely during the two or three years before the company had gone public. His reasoning was simple: How much can you lose on $2.00 a share? The situation was rather like placing a bet at the race track, but the strategy worked.

Another reason for a developing company to avoid a high stock price is that some advisory services regularly review and recommend low-price stocks. A growing small company that is out of the low-price category risks being overlooked by such analysts and may fail to attract shareholders. Incidentally, if the company's stock price goes above the desired price range, a stock split may lead to a slightly higher P–E if, after the split, the price is slightly higher than the split indicates. Of course, some spectacular stock offerings like Genentech start out at a substantial price and go on up from there. But few stocks are like Genentech's.

As simple as it seems, stock repurchase for publicly held concerns is another way for management to affect the earnings per share. True, the earnings report contains a footnote ''on fewer number of shares,'' but the impact is still there.

Acquiring another business for a lower P–E than the acquiring company enjoys also raises earnings per share—the so-called ''pop in earnings.'' Of course, the reverse will cause an EPS dilution. Another factor that might reduce earnings per share is the ''treasury stock'' method of reporting earnings. If ''stock equivalents'' exceed 20% of the outstanding stock, then the earnings must be reported not as ''primary and fully diluted'' but only one way according to this method. Stock equivalents are convertibles, warrants, and stock options. I remember one developing company that issued too many warrants when it made its initial public offering of stock and a year later found that it needed an 85% increase in absolute earnings to obtain the 15% increase in earnings per share it desired.

Listed Versus OTC Stock

Which is better for stockholders' wealth—to be listed on the American Stock Exchange or to be in one of the various groupings of the over-the-counter (OTC) market? On the positive side, being a listed company carries prestige and, as a possible consequence, some additional liquidity, especially when a stockholder uses the stock as collateral for a loan. Also, in a merger proposal, a listed stock may be more attractive than an unlisted one. A strong point in favor of an exchange listing is that the latest price quotations are available in any daily newspaper that carries stock listings. If a company is OTC, the stock price may be carried only in newspapers within the company's region.

On the negative side is the potential problem of an undercapitalized specialist handling the company's stock on the exchange. Of course, all the specialists admitted to participation in an exchange meet its minimum capital requirement, but that doesn't amount to much.

Listing on an exchange also subjects the valuation of a stock much more to the opinion of a single party than if it were OTC with a number of market makers. I remember the open disagreement one developing company's president had with his Amex specialist about ten years ago. It became so heated that the president withdrew his company from the Amex and returned to the "security" of the OTC.

If a company is OTC—and there are numerous categories of the OTC, such as NASDAQ listings (National Association of Securities Dealers' Automated Quotations) and regional OTC—a market for its stock will be made by one or more brokerage firms. For some lightly traded stocks, only one or two brokerage houses will "make a market" in the stock. For others, there may be two or three dozen market makers spread across the country. This arrangement is rather like having two or three dozen mothers watching out for your well-being, but whether it will benefit the P–E ratio—and thus the wealth of your stockholders—is moot.

It is logical to assume that the research department of a brokerage firm making a market in a company's stock will, from time to time, report the progress of the developing company to its customers. These reports can do a lot to bring the developing concern to the attention of investors. If a number of brokerage firms are making a market in the company's stock, there should be a number of such research reports. And, just as in any form of merchandising, the more buyers who see your product, the better sales will probably be. At least you should have a better chance of getting a higher price for a given quantity.

State of the Stock Market

From time to time, some industrial groupings get hot in the market and as a group find that their P–E ratios are well above their prior levels. For example, from mid-1970 to early 1972, stocks in the recreation industry category soared to three times what they had been selling for and what they have been traded for since. Real estate stocks, which lagged badly for much of the 1970s, saw a run-up in their stock prices in the early 1980s. Pollution control stocks have also gone through a big price rise in the last four or five years. And the list goes on.

When these upswings occur, what should management do? How do you distinguish a fad in stock price movement from an ordinary shift in P–E ratios? Again, a complete discussion of this question is too detailed for this article, but the important point is that management should take advantage of such swings and not just sit back and say, "Isn't this nice." It should use this period of ebullience in the stock market to further the growth plans of the company, perhaps by offering a new issue of stock to raise funds for expansion or even for acquiring another company.

Many companies are swimming against the current. "Don't waste good earnings on a bad market" is an old saying with more than a modicum of common sense. If the market for stocks in general or for just a particular industry grouping is in the doldrums, the wisest course may be to move earnings sideways for a period rather than trying to buck the trend (assuming, of course, that you can do so legally and ethically).

What Price Dividends?

Every student of finance knows Durand's formula for the capitalization rate for a company's equity: $D/P + g,$ where D/P is the dividend yield and g is the expected growth rate in dividends. And who can deny that dividends are important in the valuation of stocks of large corporations? But what about the smaller publicly held company? What if it pays no dividend and is not expected to in the forseeable future? Of course, we could substitute earnings for dividends in the formula and, to get a share price, let g be expected growth in earnings, but we would still not be addressing the question of how important dividends are in the stock valuation.

By definition, the developing concern is growing and presumably has a way to go before its growth rate diminishes. If such a business were to inaugurate a dividend, wouldn't analysts ask questions about the reasons behind the action? Can't the company make better use of such funds? Furthermore, since dividends are taxed as ordinary income, wouldn't most stockholders of developing companies like to see capital gains rather than ordinary income? Why, then, should a developing company pay a dividend?

When a growth company declares a cash dividend, it signals that its growth is slowing down. Is this what the developing business wants to convey to the investing public? Even if the payout is small, would it help the price of the stock? I doubt it. If this dividend signaled a slowdown in growth, the company might be transmitting what is called negative information.

Well, if cash dividends are ill advised, what about stock dividends, which are theoretically used as a way of sharing profits while conserving cash? This way, stockholders can increase their shares in the company or sell the dividend stock and can often get capital gains treatment.

As I see it, the trouble with this approach is that shares outstanding increase at a compound rate. It's a 5% stock dividend this year, but next year it's 5% of 105%, and so forth. This pattern holds down growth in earnings per share.

You can argue with some assurance that if the company's stock price drops less than the value of the stock dividend does, the P–E ratio has actually risen. The only apparent reason for such an occurrence is that the market perceives a stock dividend as a harbinger of continued growth. To the extent that there is growth, modest stock dividends are indicated for growth stocks.

Falling Chips

This article is an answer to those who argue that a company shouldn't worry about its P–E ratio because it lies outside company control. "Just keep cutting the wood and let the chips fall where they may!" Indeed, current financial theory speak of "risk classes" and discount rates "appropriate" to a given risk class, as though such a determination is as easy as adding two and two. For most developing companies, I question the efficient market hypothesis. Instead, I see many investor decisions being made on the basis of subjective impressions as well as objective data. It is up to the smaller company to do all it can to put its best foot forward.

34
Practical Planning for Small Business

ROGER A. GOLDE

Guidelines for the action-oriented manager who hasn't the time, or inclination, to look very far into his company's future.

What are the barriers to planning in a small business? How can the small businessperson get the planning habit? Small businesspeople want to know—and answers are not easy to find.

Very little has been written on planning in a small business. A recent bibliography on planning lists some 150 books, articles, and pamphlets.[1] Yet only one entry appears to deal specifically with small business problems.[2] Moreover, not much of the little that has been written about small business planning copes with the particularities of the planning process in the small business setting; much that has been said could just as well have been said about Standard & Poor's top 500 corporations.

In this article I hope to go a step beyond the existing literature. I will direct my discussion at the small business executive who is already convinced that planning is a good thing. This executive may even have read about breakeven analysis, pro forma balance sheets, and sales forecasting. But it is *very* unlikely that he is really doing much rigorous planning. In fact, he may not even be sure about what he ought to be doing. Further, he probably feels a bit guilty about his confusion and lack of planning.

It is important that the chief executive of a small firm become more sophisticated about planning—for, by and large, it is he, and he alone, who plans. Since he often is the founder of his company, it is natural that he chart the future of his enterprise. Lack of funds and manpower mitigate against establishment of a separate planning department as is done in many large companies. Whatever planning is done tends to stay locked up in the chief executive's head. Certainly the informal nature of the planning process adds to the difficulty of communicating about the plan.

Often a small business executive will claim that secrecy is a reason for not discussing his plans with anyone. He feels that utmost secrecy gives his company a competitive jump on larger companies, which are compelled to make extensive reports and submit to various regulations. Whether this secrecy really applies to dissemination of all planning information is another question. Sometimes an executive also fears discussing plans which may not materialize and so may create discouragement within the company.

But how do we break down the barriers to planning in small businesses? First, we must take a close look at the key characteristics of a small business. Next, we must examine how these characteristics inhibit the planning process in the small company. And finally, we must consider some methods of removing (or at least lowering) the barriers to planning that exist in small businesses. This sequence of analysis will be followed in this article.

Key Characteristics

In small businesses the amount of management time available for planning is at a premium. Small business management must handle almost all of the functional areas which exist in large organizations. Yet the size of a small company does not permit hiring even one person for each function. It is rare to find a small firm with top management fat in it.

Furthermore, the chances are that top management has had little training in planning. A primary reason for this is that the top managers of a small company are frequently the founders. The skills needed to start a small company do not necessarily include planning ability. Rather, a flair for sales or promotion—or, in the case of technologically oriented companies, certain engineering or technical skills—is often the key. Rarely are small business presidents selected because of their planning abilities. Yet in a large company top managers are quite often chosen just because of their planning acumen.

In a small company a great deal of management activity is taken up with the handling of day-to-day "brush fires." In large companies layers of management keep most of the brush fires from consuming top-management time.

In a small business, moreover, the impact of short-run problems is heightened by the usual tightness of money. Now that the easy capital markets of the early 1960's are over, few small companies find themselves overcapitalized. In essence, the financial limitations of a small company pose a severe problem of resource allocation—and this includes management time and talent.

This allocation of time depends on the small firm's attitude toward the future. This is important to our subject, particularly since planning so deeply involves consideration of the future. And here the small business' attitudes are somewhat paradoxical.

On one hand, the small business manager has much incentive to concentrate on the future of the company. In most cases, it is the long-run future which will bring the significant material rewards. Few small businesses are immensely profitable until many years after their inception. Profits also correlate somewhat with growth, and likewise take time.

On the other hand, the growth of a small business is likely to be a pretty painful process, with many setbacks occurring along the way. The chances for success, when rationally appraised, may not be very high. The small businessperson typically feels at the whim of the market, unable to exert any control over future events in the industry. In a young company, lack of extensive operating history adds to the great feeling of uncertainty about the future.

So, deep down, even though it may exude great optimism, the small firm is uneasy about the future.

Planning Tendencies

It is easy to see how these characteristics affect the planning typically done (or *not* done) by small companies. The basic tendency of small business is to shy away from planning. To the small firm, planning means grappling with tremendous uncertainties over which it seems to have little control. Naturally, such planning is done in the shadow of an inherent fear that the conclusions which may emerge will be rather dismal.

There are other, more tangible restraints to planning. We have seen how the struggle for day-to-day survival in small companies saps the amount of attention which can be devoted to planning. But without planning the danger is that the firm will overestimate the attention required by immediate crises. Thus the lack of planning will in itself precipitate an ever-continuing series of brush fires which might otherwise have been avoided.

Insofar as a small firm does plan, the keynote is informality. Details are fuzzy and not pinned down. For example, most small companies have little written communication and use word of mouth instead. Control procedures are usually informal and ad hoc. Part of the leaning toward informality is explained simply by the fact that writing things down and figuring out details take time, time which may be well worth expending in the long run, but which can appear extravagant in the short run.

Somewhat related to this informality is the lack of mathematical techniques in small business planning. Rather, the emphasis is on subjective thought. Numbers seem to represent a preciseness against which the small business planner consciously or unconsciously tends to fight. Of course, the planner may also lack the necessary numbers know-how.

Naturally, the small business chief executive is likely to describe this whole situation differently. He will first point out that his company is, after all, quite small, and the operations are not really complex. Thus it is pretty easy to keep things in one's head. He will claim that numbers can never replace intuition or judgment. He overlooks the possibility that numbers might be an aid to judgment. In any case, one important result of all this informality and lack of numbers is that planning frequently does not cover all parts of the firm nor does it treat them as an integral whole.

Another tendency of small business planning is that it concerns itself with the short run. Both the fear of planning and its informality contribute to this, of course. And it is true in many small companies that change does occur so rapidly and extensively that it may not really be fruitful to plan carefully more than two or three years ahead. Perhaps the frequency of planning should be increased in a small company rather than increasing the time span covered by the planning. It may be more important to review the firm's plans every three or six months for two years ahead than to review plans once a year for five years ahead.

But, as things stand, planning is typically used to get a small enterprise out of a current bind rather than to prevent future troubles. This naturally adds to the shorter run nature of the planning time scale in a small business.

Overcoming Barriers

Our discussion of planning, so far, has been in the abstract. Yet if small business managers are to profit from what is offered here, our observations and suggestions have to be brought down to earth, made specific and concrete. Perhaps this can be achieved best if we use a hypothetical case history—that of Enner Price, a typical chief executive of a small business, in this case a small firm making aircraft instrumentation.*

Business periodicals, management seminars, and executive friends from large corporations have all convinced Price that planning, along with motherhood and democracy, is a good thing. On New Year's Day, Price resolved to really try and use planning in his business. In fact, he decided to start that very day. Consequently, he sent his wife out to a movie and sat down to do some planning.

As he heard his wife start up the car and drive away, Enner Price suddenly realized this was really the first time he had sat down in peace and quiet to think hard about what was going on in his business. His mind glided easily enough into business thoughts. There was that new piece of equipment on which a purchasing decision was needed. . . . Perhaps a stock option program should be installed this year. . . . Oh yes, two secretaries were leaving next week. . . . What about that new piece of equipment?. . . Would

---

*A small firm is defined here as a manufacturing firm with 500 or less employees (roughly in line with the definition used by the Small Business Administration). This is somewhat arbitrary, and much of what is said in this article may well apply to nonmanufacturing or other companies which are larger or otherwise do not fit our definition.

For purposes of this article, planning will refer to the process of systematically thinking about the future of an enterprise as an integrated whole. This process is likely to involve consideration of objectives, forecasting of both external and internal change, analysis of the effects of that change on the firm, and actions or decisions determined on the basis of the analysis.

that big contract come in? . . . The plant needed some paint. . . . And thus Price's thoughts rambled for several hours.

Time and Place

Actually, Price had made an excellent start in overcoming one key planning barrier: namely, lack of time and place. Otherwise, with the premium on management time and the importance of day-to-day crises (if events are left to themselves), there would be simply no periods of peace and quiet when Price could sit back to reflect on the over-all position of his firm and plan for the future. More than likely, an executive like Price would not even have a private office at the plant.

Very often, finding the proper time to plan takes care of the space problem and vice versa. One research company president set up every other Wednesday night as a planning evening when everything was quiet at the office. Sometimes she used Sunday afternoon for the same purpose. The chairman of the board of a small tool company in Detroit took the reverse approach. He set up an office for himself at the opposite end of town from his plant and found that this provided effective insulation from employees' barging in with questions.

Master Planning Form

The New Year's Day ruminations of Price led him to discover that it was hard to get a handle on this planning thing. He had glanced at a few books, but they were pretty abstract, and he did not really have the time to plow through them. Nor did Price feel he could take time off to attend some advanced management program. And when his wife's car pulled in the driveway, he was still muttering about the need for a way to get started—an automatic starter like the ones developed for automobiles to overcome the frustrations of the hand cranks used in the early 1900's. As a matter of fact, Price was not even sure he was at the hand-crank stage. (Nor was Price alone in his quandary. According to a survey of 106 small manufacturers in Minnesota, "the hardest part of planning seems to be getting started.")[3]

In some limited sense, pencil and paper can provide a sort of hand crank for planning. Pencil and paper help to channel the mind which tends to go off on a string of associations. But very often the decision to write down ideas requires a great deal of conscious effort. Many of the tendencies discussed previously (such as informality, fear of precision, and the like) militate even against the use of pencil and paper.

However, once an executive is at the pencil and paper stage, it is possible to introduce other planning aids as starters of a more automatic nature. Specifically, the use of printed forms or outlines can be most helpful. Exhibit 1 presents a possible master planning form, as well as instructions

Exhibit 1.   Master Planning Form

| | Change | | |
Item	NY	YAN	Comment
Research & Development			
Products			
Product mix			
Service			
Supplies			
Suppliers			
Inventory			
Subcontracts			
Storage & Handling			
Quality control			
Space			
Leasehold improvements			
Equipment			
Employees			
Fringe benefits			
Customers			
Sales outlets			
Terms of sale			
Pricing			
Transportation			
Advertising			
Promotion			
Packaging			
Market research			
Financing			
Insurance			
Investments			
Management reports			
Management procedures			
Management organization			
Governmental environment			
Economic environment			
Industrial environment			

Exhibit 1. (*Continued*)

| Item | Change | | Comment |
	NY	YAN	
Competition			
Community environment			

Instructions: NY = next year; YAN = year after next. All changes are estimated in relation to the preceding year. If a quantitative change is anticipated—i.e., change in size or amount— use the following symbols: L = large, M = medium, and S = small. Quantitative changes are assumed to be increases unless preceded by a minus sign.

If a qualitative change is anticipated, use the following symbols: l = large, m = medium, s = small.

Note that the notions of small, medium, and large changes are obviously subjective and will vary with the person using the form.

In general, a small change denotes some sort of minimum level of change which is thought important enough to make note of. Most of the expected changes will probably fall in the medium category, indicating significant change of some magnitude. The large category will usually be reserved for unusual changes of striking impact.

The notion of qualitative changes may need some clarification. This category of change would cover such items as a change in customer mix (which might or might not result in an increased number of customers). Using a new source of supply for raw materials and changing the media allocation of the advertising budget would also be examples of qualitative changes.

for using it. By no stretch of the imagination should completion of this form be considered as the whole of the planning process. The master planning form simply embodies some characteristics which have been found useful in starting the planning wheels turning.

No numerical estimates are required in order to fill out the form, so that executives who have not engaged in rigorous planning before do not need to feel uncomfortable about predicting the future in exact numerical terms. This should reassure them that exact numbers are not needed to start planning. In fact, devoting attention to the details of precise figures may take attention away from other important parts of the planning process.

On several occasions I have used a list of bookkeeping accounts with some success. But I noticed that while the procedure worked fairly well with department heads, the top executives had trouble keeping in mind all the accounts which sprawled over four pages or more. Furthermore, top managers really seemed to think in terms of physical happenings, rather than accounting categories—for example, increased space rather than rent or utilities, changing price rather than increasing net sales and accounts receivable. Lastly, many planning areas have no direct accounting counterpart—for instance, changed management procedures or improved services.

Accordingly, this master planning form is purposely designed to fit on a single page so that the executive may keep all his thinking about the company in full view. He can then ponder the various interrelationships among the parts of his company both now and in the future.

Price, being an adventurous soul, decided one day to fill out a master planning form. He found it was a little harder than he had anticipated. He had to keep going back to erase answers, modifying them on the basis of new thoughts and interrelationships. For instance, Enner Price's company was thinking about starting work on a new altimeter for use in private executive aircraft. A master planning form partly filled out, in regard to the new altimeter only, is shown in Exhibit 2.

While the form Price used had space only for thinking two years ahead, it would be easy to extend it for any number of years. Planning needs differ from company to company and industry to industry. If a firm really knows how to plan rigorously two or three years ahead, then it can decide for itself whether to extend the process. This is not to say that planning five or ten years ahead is the same as planning two or three years ahead. Different techniques must be used and different problems will be encountered, but the basic planning process is much the same.

Price discovered that when he had finally filled out the form (in fact, he used several), he had something down in black and white that he could discuss with other members of his management team. The filled-out form was not really self-explanatory, but it highlighted the areas for discussion and allowed other executives to contribute their advice and opinions about the various topics included. Moreover, for the first time other top managers could get a feel for where the company was heading and the various problems to be dealt with. The planning was no longer completely locked up in the chief executive's head. And at the same time, the form could be prepared in a way to minimize the problems of secrecy.

Chain Reaction

Use of the form leads into certain other aspects of planning by:

- ☐ Pointing up the need for specific information
- ☐ Raising questions
- ☐ Encouraging the start of goal and policy formulation.

For example, filling out the master planning form forced Price to realize that he would need to obtain a specific schedule of equipment and production space from his head of manufacturing. His sales manager would have to come up with some detailed cost figures related to the use of sales representatives, trade shows, and so forth. Also Price found it hard to put any coding for change down for some categories, such as inventory, because he was uncertain about the present situation. So he was forced to search out some data on present operating conditions, a most important part of the planning process.

Exhibit 2. Hypothetical Completed Master Planning Form

Item	Change NY	YAN	Comment
Research & Development	Mm	− S	Start development of new altimeter for executive planes.
Products		Ss	First sales of new altimeter.
Product mix			
Service		s	Slightly different for private planes.
Supplies		s	Needed for new altimeter.
Suppliers			
Inventory			
Subcontracts		S	Most of subassemblies will be subcontracted.
Storage & handling			
Quality control			
Space		S	Little bit of production space for new altimeter.
Leasehold improvements	M		Need for dust-free area.
Equipment	S		New test equipment.
Employees	S		Couple of technicians for development work.
Fringe benefits			
Customers		sS	Plan to hit owners of executive planes.
Sales outlets		Mm	Will need more sales representatives rather than own sales force.
Terms of sale			
Pricing			
Transportation			
Advertising		− M	Not so effective to private owners.
Promotion		m	Will switch to more demonstrations and trade shows.
Packaging			
Market research	S		Informal poll of private owners known by company.
Financing	S		Additional working capital for production.

Exhibit 2. *(Continued)*

Item	Change NY	Change YAN	Comment
Insurance			
Investments			
Management reports		l	Need for simple product costing system.
Management procedures			
Management organization		m	Will have to reorganize production department.
Governmental environment		s	CAB regulations more favorable to our device.
Economic environment			
Industrial environment	Mm	Mm	Tremendous growth in private executive plane field.
Competition			
Community environment			

Price also found himself pondering new questions and areas, such as appraising just how different the private commercial airplane market was from the military and public airline markets. He wondered whether he would have to keep introducing new products every year. Some of the categories on the master form, such as "governmental environment" or "management procedures," were areas that Price had not considered explicitly prior to this. Thinking about them raised new issues.

Lastly, Price began to get a glimmering of what was meant by goals, policies, and strategies. He began to understand how planning puts together competitive conditions, customer needs, company resources, and management desires. These kinds of notions are, of course, at the heart of planning, as most articles on the subject insist. The point is that most approaches to planning suggest starting with analysis of goals and objectives in order to derive a strategy and policies. But goals and objectives are fairly abstract concepts. While they provide a nice, tidy place to start the planning process, unfortunately this is not a very practical beginning point for many small business executives. This is not to deny the importance of dealing concretely with goals and objectives at some point in the planning process.

The mention of planning forms also brings to mind the use of a cash flow form or, perhaps, a pro forma balance sheet form. Certainly, these kinds of forms can be extremely helpful in the planning process, but they are not really good starting points. If an executive can draw up a sensible projected cash flow or pro forma balance sheet, he must have done a great deal of solid planning beforehand. In other words, these forms can be filled out only by somehow performing a series of planning exercises and then reducing them to dollar terms. (Note that the master planning form contains many items which never appear in accounting records, although they may greatly affect the final figures for a particular account. For a useful collection of various cash flow forms, the reader is referred to Appendix A of the book *Cash Planning in Small Manufacturing Companies*[4] which presents over 20 examples.)

Outside Advice

As Enner Price moved further along in his planning efforts, he felt an ever greater need to talk with others. In the first place he realized that he might not think of everything and wanted somebody else to check on his thinking. Secondly, Price hoped that other people might have some specific planning experience or knowledge from which he could benefit. As in many small companies, however, Price did not feel there was anybody else in the firm to whom he could turn for such help. So he began thinking of who outside his company might be of assistance.

Outside people may be very valuable aids to planning. Company directors, accountants, lawyers, bankers, or advertising agencies frequently prove helpful. In most cases, the help these people can provide is more in developing the planning approach than in actually doing major chunks of the company planning. The cost of such outside help is likely to be minimal or nonexistent if these people are already servicing the company in some fashion. If more concrete help of a sizable nature is required, it is always possible to call in an outside management consultant.

Formal use of an outsider in planning has one other helpful effect. As discussed previously, the pressures on a small company executive are immense, and the executive typically responds to the strongest pressures—a customer screams for an order, a supplier yells about getting paid, or the production man demands a new jig. But nobody is pounding on the executive to do his ''planning.'' An outside person can become the one who continually gives firm reminders that time must be spent on planning.

Internal Information

Price now began to go to his office one Saturday a month to plan. He had filled out a master planning form, revised it several times, and added a few items of his own, plus coding in some other information. He set up periodic meetings for planning discussions with one of his directors and the executive of the bank where the company kept its account. What Price now found he needed as much as anything else was information, and lots of it, so that he could pin down details and work up some figures. He needed information both on the internal operations of the company and on many outside areas.

In general, no sweeping collection of special internal data need be made—no complicated market studies with statistical samples. So far as internal operations are concerned, a top executive usually has a pretty good idea of how to find the information needed, especially since the size of operations is small. The bottleneck comes from the fact that in planning one usually takes a more comprehensive look at things than in the short run.

Planning thus involves developing new data from existing data, or recasting information in different ways. This can be time consuming, particularly if the small company wishes to re-plan frequently. One way to minimize this problem is to make the format of short-term reports relevant to their ultimate use for long-term planning.

For example, one small clothing manufacturer was very interested in knowing something about his sales by geographical area for planning purposes. Since the company sold to a huge number of outlets each month, it would have been quite a job to report sales geographically each month. Besides, management was most immediately interested in sales by product, which is the way accounts were grouped on the monthly reports. It was decided that time and money would not permit issuing a second monthly report grouped by geographical areas.

What occurred, however, was that instead of just listing the name of an account each month, the geographical area was listed as well. Thus when the sales summary by geographical area was needed for planning purposes, it could be collated from the monthly reports quite quickly. Subsequently, it was discovered that little extra time was required each month to arrange the account listings under each product by geographical area. This saved even more time in preparing the data needed for planning.

In another case, a rapidly growing electronic products company found itself with a great number of product lines. In planning decisions, the analysis of cost, price, and volume relationships were of key importance. This firm decided to shift to a direct costing type of reporting where fixed costs were given separately on the short-run reports. This greatly aided the use of these reports for planning purposes, though for short-run control and reporting purposes the regular overhead allocation system had been quite satisfactory.

External Sources

When it comes to finding information on areas external to the company, the problem is somewhat different. The real trick is to know what *source* of information is reasonable, accessible, and inexpensive. One such source is people, sometimes the very people who are so close at hand that they may be easily overlooked.

The persons closest at hand in a company are its employees. Often an

employee may have a relative or friend who can be a good source of information. Talking to employees is often done informally in most small businesses, but it is rare that a blanket appeal for information is made to all
employees. It may be the seemingly least-likely employee who has the proper
contact.

Where customer reactions and interests are the issue, the sales outlets
for the small company may have a wealth of information and ideas. Furthermore, it may be possible to use these sales outlets to collect specific
information that is desired. In one case a small food company requested its
jobbers to ask a few simple questions of the grocery store managers on their
next visit. The questions related to a potential new product line. On the
basis of the information collected, the company decided to go ahead with
limited production of the new item.

Suppliers are another commonly overlooked source of information.
They can be particularly helpful on problems concerning competition in the
industry. A supplier often sells to more than one company in the same
industry, or else he talks from time to time with other suppliers of the same
industry. One manufacturer of shiny metallic discs for use in outdoor advertising signs questioned the firm which supplied him with coated raw
material. While on a business trip, he also contacted other suppliers with
whom he indicated he might at some future time do business. Through
judicious questioning, he discovered exactly what coated materials his competitors were using and even got an idea of his competitors' sales volumes.

As a matter of fact, useful information can often be gleaned from talking
directly with one's competition. Somehow this approach seems like anathema to many small businessmen. Yet a competitor may have worthwhile
information on industry conditions which he considers to be common problems facing both firms. Of course, trade associations are set up to help with
just this kind of information. Many small companies are not aware of the
information to be had in written form or, even more importantly, from talking
with their trade associations.

Naturally, since few competitors are really exact duplicates of each
other, it is often possible to exchange information or ideas, particularly in
areas where the two companies do not really overlap. Sometimes these
consultations with competitors lead to pleasant surprises.

For example, the president of a small metal-working job shop visited
a competitor in hopes of checking up on some of the new machines he
understood were being used by the competitor. During the conversation it
became apparent that both companies had some unique equipment which
had been built in-house to do particular jobs. The two presidents exchanged
information on certain machines and talked about working out a cross-license
arrangement on two other pieces of equipment.

If one primary source of outside information is people, then the other
main source is written material. The wealth of statistical and descriptive
data on many business problems is enormous. Because large companies often

have planning staffs, it is possible for them to plow through a heap of written material to find what they are looking for. In the process they become somewhat acquainted with what kinds of information are available and where.

Since a smaller company cannot afford this kind of program, the use of written information is often ignored altogether, even when a written document exists containing the exact information desired. The problem is that the executive may have no idea that such a written document exists. For example, planning a long-run advertising program might require substantial data on various media rates. If the executive involved had not worked extensively in advertising, he might be unaware that Standard Rate & Data Service would solve his problem.

Ideally, what is needed is a reference book of reference books. Unfortunately that does not seem to exist. Of course, there are bibliographies on various business subjects, but all too often they list only the titles of the books. Unless the titles are clearly descriptive, the various kinds of information they contain remain concealed.

(One source of such information is "Where to Find Marketing Facts."[5] This article contains a sizable list of reference books in the marketing field with a reasonable amount of detail on what each book contains.)

Small companies seldom make full use of library facilities at their disposal. In contrast, large companies often develop one or more specialized libraries with appropriate source materials, including a librarian. Naturally, most small companies cannot afford this kind of luxury. Yet access may frequently be had to these large-company libraries on request. Furthermore, there are many other public and private library facilities which are usually near at hand. For instance, in Boston the list of business libraries belonging to the Special Libraries Association to which the public may request access includes these:

- [ ] One public library branch devoted exclusively to business.
- [ ] Six university libraries.
- [ ] Six libraries maintained by banks or investment bankers.
- [ ] Eight libraries maintained by insurance firms.
- [ ] Twenty-six libraries maintained by research and manufacturing firms in a number of fields.

There also seems to be little contact between executives of small businesses and teachers of business administration. A good way to find out what printed information is available in a certain field is to talk with a business professor whose field of specialty includes the company's area of interest. In many cases a personal acquaintance with the professor involved is not mandatory. Most professors welcome the contact with business executives, especially if it is courteously handled by preceding any phone call with a letter.

To complete this list of obvious but overlooked sources of information of use in planning, mention should be made of the Small Business Administration. Besides the wealth of statistics and printed information produced, it also has wide associations in the community. Consequently, it can be of help in directing a small company executive to a ready source of information.

Key Questions

Price continued to spend his one Saturday a month on planning, but naturally he did not spend all his time on a master planning form. Usually he put his feet up on his desk and tried to do some thinking. Some Saturdays he had no trouble at all in getting into some important aspects of his future plans. But on other days there did not seem to be any way of provoking thought. It seemed to him that it might be useful to have a list of provocative questions to stimulate thought.

An exhaustive list of questions would be an impossibility, for, naturally, each company will have its own special questions. Nevertheless, in Exhibit 3 I have put together at least the beginning of such a list of questions in hopes that each reader can add to it. Of course, each functional area could have its separate list of questions, but Exhibit 3 has concentrated on indicating more general types of questions which could apply to many functional areas. All the questions in Exhibit 3 are ones I have asked or been asked in various company settings. And all have at one time or another led to new planning insights.

Conclusion

The premise of this article has been that there is more to helping a small company plan than convincing the top executives that "planning is a good thing." There are certain elements of a small business which make planning easier than in a large company. There are less data to gather, fewer layers of management through which information must pass, and operations may be less spread out. In addition, the real profitability of a great majority of small companies lies in their future, a fact which forces management to have a motivation for planning. On the other hand, small companies face special problems and restrictions in their planning efforts.

The highlighting of some of these special situations should be helpful in itself. Realizing explicitly some of the barriers to planning may be the first step toward overcoming them. More is needed, however, and several specific aids to small business planning have been discussed.

The aids mentioned all have a common denominator—that of developing the executive habit of questioning and seeking information. We have seen that while no formal procedures are required, outlines and checklists can be helpful. Small businessmen must remember that developing the in-

Exhibit 3. Provocative Questions

New facts and new techniques of analysis
1. How do operating figures compare historically?
2. What is percentage distribution of costs? Of customers? Of management time? Of purchases?
3. What new ratios should be looked at (e.g., sales per employee, return on investment, profits per square foot)?
4. What new factors should be looked at (e.g., age of employees, age of facilities, product life, fixed versus variable costs)?
5. What sources of information do I use to find out about the company?

Spotlight rarely thought-about areas
1. What function do I expect from the board of directors?
2. Should I worry about my industrial security from theft? From espionage?
3. Does the company need some public relations work—for example, how many times did the company name appear in newspapers or trade journals last year?
4. What major decisions were made last year? By whom?

Specifically defining important areas
1. What companies compete with our company?
2. What products compete with our products?
3. What element of the economic environment affects our company the most?
4. What piece of information would I most like to have about the industry or the competition? What would I do with this information once I had it?

Negative approach
1. Who does not buy our products? Why not?
2. What should the company stop producing?
3. What am I doing that should be done by others or perhaps not at all?

Functional cross-relationships
1. How could purchasing help marketing?
2. How could marketing help production?
3. How could personnel policies help finances?

Suppositions
1. Suppose I or a key employee has a serious accident today?
2. What if quality were reduced?
3. What if the company changed distribution channels?
4. What could the company make instead of buy, or vice versa?
5. What if we modified the product? Would it appeal to new customers?

formation habit does not necessarily mean hiring a large organization to do market research. It can mean nothing more than picking the phone up and talking to a few friends about what is new in the industry. Nor does a questioning attitude mean only a filling out of lengthy checklists. It can mean simply asking a few "whys" when an employee walks in with a comment about operations.

And, after all, are not questioning and information seeking as much the heart of the planning process as is setting goals, policies, and strategies?

Notes

1. Blair E. Olmstead, Editor, *Bibliography on Planning* (Pleasantville, New York: The College on Planning of the Institute of Management Sciences, 1960).

2. National Industrial Conference Board, *Budgeting Expenses in Small Companies*. Studies in Business Practices No. 58 (New York: NICB, 1952).

3. Delbert C. Hastings, *The Place of Forecasting in Basic Planning for Small Business* (Minneapolis: University of Minnesota Press, 1961), p. 23.

4. Joseph C. Schabacker (Washington, D.C.: Small Business Administration, 1960).

5. Steuart Henderson Britt and Irwin A. Shapiro (*Keeping Informed*), *HBR*, September–October 1962, p. 44.

35

"Freeze" Assets to Lower Estate Taxes and Keep Control

WALLACE F. FORBES and ANTHONY C. PADDOCK

Owners of successful small companies frequently face a dilemma when they want to do estate planning: how to maintain management control without imposing the burden of stiff estate taxes on those who eventually inherit ownership. One solution to consider, say these authors, is "freezing" assets. This entails applying one of three possible techniques of reorganizing ownership interests. When performed correctly, each procedure can pass on to future owners the benefits of the rising value of the company while permitting the existing owner to retain control.

Owners of successful privately owned companies must grapple with the dual problems of minimizing estate taxes and passing control of their businesses on to family members or employees (unless they want to sell out).

The tax law amendments enacted in 1981 help ameliorate the first problem somewhat by reducing estate taxes slightly and eliminating them when ownership passes to the owner's spouse. But the problems remain when the values of rapidly growing companies are high enough to be taxed and the companies are not being given over to the owner's spouse.

To minimize these problems, a number of sophisticated techniques, referred to collectively as "asset freezing," have evolved, which simultaneously:

☐ Minimize estate taxes.

☐ Minimize gift taxes during the life of the current owner.

☐ Help the current owner maintain control of the business during his or her lifetime.

☐   Provide continuing income protection to the current owner, his or her spouse, or beneficiaries who are not expected to be involved in the company's future management.

☐   Ensure that control passes to those the owner chooses as successors.

How does asset freezing accomplish all of these goals? By maintaining the owner's taxable interest in the company at or near its present value and bequeathing or selling the company's future value growth to those the owner wants as successors.

Three methods exist for carrying this out, each of which entails a reorganization of ownership interests:

1   Recapitalize the operating company itself so that the present owner receives preferred stock and successors receive common stock.
2   Place the owner's interests in a holding company, which in turn issues preferred stock to the present owner as well as common stock that can be given or sold to successors.
3   Establish a partnership in which the present owner receives a partnership interest with limits on its appreciation potential while successors receive general partnership interests, whose growth is unlimited.

The purpose of issuing preferred stock or a limited partnership interest is to give the current owner an interest that will not appreciate in value with subsequent growth of the organization and thus not become part of the current owner's taxable estate. The future growth in value would instead accrue to the common stockholders or other partners.

The rest of this article considers each of the three estate-freezing methods just listed. It concludes by examining common obstacles to implementation.

Recapitalize the Existing Company

This, the most common of the three techniques, usually involves an exchange of existing common stock for one or more classes of new preferred stock, as shown in Exhibit 1. The preferred stock can carry terms tailored to the holder's needs. These terms might, for example, ensure retention of voting control by the present controlling stockholder or continuation for life of dividend income for that person, his or her spouse, or other family members not in the business.

A recent example is the recapitalization of a rapidly growing agricultural company. The principal stockholder was a 62-year-old man who owned 70% of the company's common stock. The balance was held by one son (the only other family member active in the business) and two daughters. The company was recapitalized as follows. First, a Series A cumulative, nonvoting pre-

Exhibit 1.   Three Estate-Freezing Methods

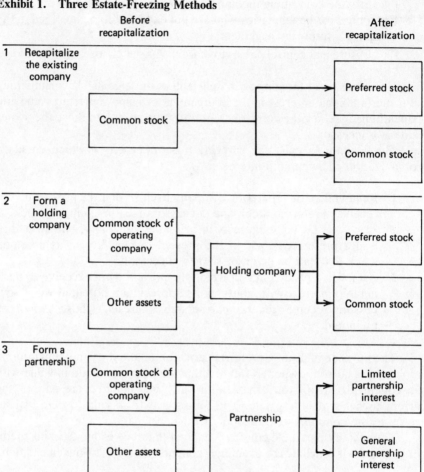

ferred stock was issued and exchanged for the common stock held by the
principal's two daughters. The holders would receive a continuous income
stream but have no say in the company's management.

Then Series B noncumulative voting preferred stock was issued and
exchanged for the principal's 70% interest in the company. The stock gave
him the power to determine management policies, including setting the payment of dividends on Series B stock; he could also direct the ultimate distribution of the stock by sale, gift, or will.

The son, who was expected to play an increasingly important role in
the company, retained his common stock interest, which would rise in value
as the company's earnings grew.

The dividend rate of the Series A preferred stock was set at a level that reflected its investment quality, which was determined through a comparative study of publicly traded preferred stocks. The Series B dividend was set at a lower rate than the Series A because the Series B stock carried with it control of the company.

Form a Holding Company

This approach entails exchanging the operating company's common stock for the common and preferred stock of a newly formed holding company. It is most appropriate when family wealth includes major assets other than the operating company (such as real estate, oil and gas leases, the stock of a public company), when several owners of large interests in the operating company remain, or when the owners do not want to disturb the capital structure of the operating company. Exhibit 1 illustrates the restructuring involved.

This technique allows the operating company's capital structure to remain free of additional classes of equity—a substantial benefit if the operating company wants to complete a private or public sale of its stock at some time in the future. Although the holding company technique means that preferred stock dividends will be taxed twice (once at the operating company level and once at the holding company level), this is usually only a minor drawback because of the 85% dividend exclusion available to the holding company.

If the IRS regards the new company as a *personal* holding company, a tax liability may result. However, if the operating company's dividend payments to the holding company can be limited to the amount necessary to pay the latter's preferred dividends and if all holding company earnings are paid out as dividends, the tax exposure will be slight.

A recent example of the advantages of the holding company approach involved a privately held retail chain, which had numerous store locations that were built and then leased back to the operating company by various family-held realty corporations. The strong growth of the operating company and the proliferating number of store locations pointed to a need to freeze the value of all the companies.

Since the family members' ownership interests in each company varied, a single holding company was formed to pull the corporate assets together under one umbrella. In exchange for new preferred and common stocks tailored to meet the needs of individual family members (continuous income for some members and growth but little income for others), all the common stock of the operating company and of the realty companies was put into the holding company. The new preferreds were structured so that their dividends would not drain the organization of funds needed to finance future growth.

Form a Partnership

Estate tax planners have given increased attention in recent years to the partnership structure for freezing value, partly because partnerships offer benefits in current income tax planning as well as in estate tax planning. These benefits result because partnership income (or loss) is directly taxable to the partner. When interests other than a closely held company (such as real estate or oil and gas) are contributed to the partnership, the partners may be able to take advantage of personal income tax benefits, which are passed through to them individually. These benefits may include tax-shelter losses, for example, or the allocation of taxable income to partners in lower tax brackets.

In the partnership approach, the use of limited partnership interests has the same effect as the issuance of preferred stock in either the direct corporate recapitalization or the holding company approach (see Exhibit 1).

In the typical family partnership situation, the family members who are nearer retirement receive partnership interests that, like preferred stock, have limited ownership rights. These interests provide specified claims on profits and preferential treatment respecting claims on partnership assets. Younger family members receive either limited or general partnership interests, with the latter involving potentially greater financial risks and rewards. Although the general partners exercise control, limited partners in many cases can dissolve their interests and at any time receive the value of their initial contributions to the partnership.

Distributions to the partners are usually tiered so that the limited partners receive preferential payout of earnings over the other partners up to a specified dollar limit and a very small share of any additional distributions. This limits the overall return on the limited partnership.

Two partners in their sixties who owned a major shopping center in the Southeast recently used this approach. A real estate appraiser determined the value of each 50% interest and each partner then established his own separate family partnership, contributing his 50% interest on a limited partnership basis with another family member as the general partner. Each limited partnership received 95% of the first tier of cash flow coming into his family partnership (cash flow being defined as the then current annual level of cash flow). He would, however, receive only 10% of the additional income resulting from the growth of the shopping center, while the general partner of the new partnership would receive 90%. Each limited partner had the right to withdraw at any time and be paid cash and notes by the partnership in an amount equal to the initial value of his share of the shopping center.

The general partner of the family partnership contributed other assets worth approximately 20% of the value of the limited partner's contribution. This was sufficient to provide a cushion for the limited partner in case the total value of the family partnership diminished—an unlikely occurrence in view of the rapidly rising real estate values in the area.

Freezing Dangers

One of the most challenging aspects of recapitalization is determining the correct values of each security or partnership interest. The tax benefits can be negated if, on challenge by the IRS, the "before" and "after" values of the assets and securities used in the exchange cannot be shown to have been approximately equal at the time of the estate freeze. In general, a shareholder who gives away more in value than he or she receives in the exchange is subject to a gift tax on the difference; a shareholder who receives more in value is subject to an income tax on the difference.

One instance of the difficulties that can ensue if the valuation issue is not approached soundly occurred several years ago, when the principal in a large, closely held corporation, recapitalized his company by exchanging the company's existing common stock for existing preferred stock and new common stock on the basis of their book values. He gave the new common stock to his heirs as a gift. The value of the gifts was determined by subtracting the total book value (par) of the preferred stock from the total book value of the old common stock. However, based on the values of similar preferred stocks that were publicly available at the time of the recapitalization, the company's preferred stock was not worth par, and therefore the value of the common stock was actually higher than was calculated.

Four years later, the principal died. An independent valuation of the preferred stock, prepared for his estate taxes, indicated a value of only 25% to 30% of par. The IRS noted this and charged that the preferred stock had never been worth par and that either the value of the gifts or the value of the common stock in the estate had been underestimated. The result was a substantial and unexpected tax bill.

To avoid such pitfalls, keep in mind a few basic rules regarding valuation factors when considering an estate-freeze plan:

1.   The fair market value of the preferred stock or partnership interest exchanged for the common stock will not equal its par or stated value unless its provisions are consistent with preferred stocks of similar quality trading at par in the marketplace. In other words, if a 6% rate is placed on a preferred at a time when 12% is the going rate, its market value won't equal par unless some other features justify its 6% rate. Par or stated value has no bearing on the market value of preferred stocks.

2.   The valuation of a company's common stock is primarily based on the company's future earning capacity. As a consequence, even if all of the company's current earnings are used up in paying the dividend on a preferred stock, the common stock will still have value as long as the company is expected to grow.

3.   The value of the company's common stock after a recapitalization cannot be computed by simply subtracting the par or market value of the new preferred stock from the total value of shareholders' equity before the exchange. The postrecapitalization common stock must be valued in light

of the effect that the preferred stock will have on the earnings of the common stock. The total value of shareholders' equity after recapitalization (common stock plus new preferred stock) will usually not be the same as the value of shareholders' common equity prior to the recapitalization.

4. *Book value* is an accounting term. It represents the accounts of the company stated primarily on a historical-cost basis. Since the fair market value of most nonfinancial companies' common stock is based primarily on earning capacity rather than on the value of assets, book value of the common stock will only by coincidence equal its fair market value.

A Sophisticated Mechanism

The estate-freeze approach to estate planning is a sophisticated mechanism. Properly designed, it is a flexible tool that can offer substantial benefits. Poorly designed, it can bring unexpected liabilities.

The key consideration is whether one of the three techniques can help the owner meet his or her estate-planning goals. If a freeze seems appropriate, valuation becomes one of the most important elements in structuring a plan that will withstand a challenge by the IRS. Many factors must be considered, such as the values of the assets being contributed and the terms of the ownership interests issued. Of course, anyone considering an estate freeze is well advised to consult tax and legal counsel from the start. When done correctly, asset freezing can ease the concerns business owners feel as their business careers wind down.

36

The Agony of Selling Out to Relatives

DON ALBERT GRISANTI

Selling a business, or an interest in a business, is a trying event under the best of circumstances. The seller must negotiate such purely business matters as price and terms of payment and then must deal with the traumas of giving up the "baby" and deciding what to do next. Add to these routine difficulties the circumstance of selling out to a relative and you've got the makings of a horror show. Such issues as sibling rivalries and family distrust inevitably complicate the already complex divestiture in such areas as determiniing price, getting outside valuations, and hiring attorneys. The author recently went through the experience of selling his share of a family restaurant business to his younger brother. He recalls the agony of a nearly four-year process that left him much wiser than when he started.

As a paralyzing blizzard swirled through Louisville one day in January 1978, I sat quietly in my home and tried to resolve the conflict swirling through my mind. Should I wage a major battle with my younger brother for control of our family restaurant business or simply sell it to him?

Since the death of our father in 1974, I had been president of the business and had seen sales quadruple through the successful opening of a second restaurant. A third operation would open soon. I should have been looking forward to continuing dynamic growth along with critical accolades from local, national, and industry media, but I wasn't. Instead, I faced a number of disturbing personal and business dilemmas that made me think seriously about selling my interest in the family business. But I wouldn't be selling to just anyone. I would be selling to my brother.

Thus, in addition to the usual questions one has when selling a business—for example, about taxes and legalities—I had some special ones. Could a classic sibling rivalry of some 30 years be overcome, or would the struggle carry over into the negotiations and into our personal relationship?

Did my brother indeed have what it takes to run the business? Were we both willing to sell the entire business to outsiders if we couldn't agree on the price? Should the business be sold for what it's really worth, or should its value be discounted to keep it in the family?

Before I describe how I went about trying to answer these and other questions, some history is in order.

Grisanti Inc.'s Birth and Growth

Casa Grisanti was started in 1959 by my father, uncle, and cousin. It was a modest Italian restaurant located in an old factory building in the Phoenix Hill section of Louisville, where these same three partners had operated a plaster piggy bank factory. The restaurant was successful from the beginning, thanks to the joint efforts of the three partners. Responsibilities were divided according to abilities and interests. All went smoothly until, in the late 1960s, the status quo was disrupted by strong pressure for growth. No forum existed for airing difficulties, and eventually the partnership began to dissolve. Between 1970 and 1974, the company was passed via a number of stock transactions from the first to the second generation.

Immediately after graduation from St. Louis University in 1970 with a B.S. in psychology, I went to work in the family business. My younger brother, Michael, joined me in 1973 after receiving a degree in restaurant management from the University of Denver. Our father died in January 1974, and because I had been at the helm during his prolonged illness, I was elected president at the age of 26. From the time I took over company leadership we had had a board of directors, including several outsiders, which met regularly. The company had a written plan to develop the Casa Grisanti into one of the top restaurants in the country and to develop a group of family-style Italian restaurants.

In 1975 we transformed the Casa Grisanti from an everyday restaurant into a first-class dining experience. Tuxedoed captains and waiters served northern Italian cuisine, with many specialties flambéed tableside. Fresh flowers, double damask linens, and family-crested silver adorned tables, and dancing flames from the tableside cookery reflected off a 75-foot-long floor-to-ceiling solid brass wall. The Casa Grisanti received local and national critical acclaim for its culinary successes. Accomplished fine artists displayed their work there and turned the restaurant into a gallery forum for artistic talent as well.

Recognizing the need for additional managerial talent, we recruited a manager in 1975, who proved to be very valuable to the business. In 1977, the company opened its second operation, a suburban restaurant featuring country-style Italian cooking in a casual atmosphere. Mamma Grisanti's was designed as a turn-of-the-century grandmother's home with four dining rooms: the parlor, library, kitchen, and bedroom, with the attic as the bar. The restaurant was filled with family memorabilia, and the atmosphere was relaxed and comfortable. We prepared pasta in full view of the guests and grated fresh Parmesan cheese over it. The average customer spent $12 at Mamma Grisanti's and $35 at the Casa Grisanti.

Michael and I were confident that the difficulties that had troubled my father and uncle in the start-up of the business would surely not plague us. Their airing of business disagreements openly in front of customers and employees had been painful to me and other family members.

My brother and I established guidelines to avoid such difficulties. For instance, we would not discuss business at family dinners, and we would use outside directors and other impartial parties to mediate and help us get along.

That approach worked for a while, but then things began to change. In 1978, the manager we had hired three years earlier was allowed to purchase 10% of the company's stock. What was once a 50–50 relationship between two brothers became a 45–45–10 relationship between two brothers and an unrelated, though very talented, manager.

Much can be said about the inappropriateness of granting such a powerful position to a minority stockholder. It complicated not only ongoing management decision making but also any efforts I might make to sell my holding. Inexperience on my part as well as bad legal counsel was largely to blame for that poor decision. Nevertheless, the decision was made, and 1978 became a turning point in both my life and that of the company.

Personal Choices

The same year the outside manager gained an ownership stake, I realized that I was at a personal crossroads of sorts. I had traveled extensively since I was young and knew I wanted to live in a more cosmopolitan area than Louisville. I saw the business as a possible vehicle for accomplishing that by opening new restaurants in major cities. But my two partners wanted to confine any expansion to the Louisville market.

Still single and just 30, I also wanted to take some time off to pursue other interests. I might live in New York and study art history, architecture, and Italian. Or spend a winter skiing in Aspen and a summer on the beaches of southern California. I wanted time for myself. I wanted to explore other career opportunities like writing, or being an art dealer, or engaging in real estate development. I might have tried some of these things just after college if I hadn't felt pressured to work in the family business right away.

In addition, I had to face up to what was probably the major underlying issue in our company—the sibling rivalry between my brother and me. Michael and I simply did not communicate well. We never openly battled with each other but instead waged a cold war by skirting or disagreeing on major issues that needed to be handled. An unstated reason for allowing an outsider to become a third partner was to mediate peace agreements in our undeclared war.

The underlying conflicts were classic. As the older brother, I was frequently seen as being the big bad guy—too aggressive, insensitive, and a bully. At a family dinner once, my brother even reminisced about our childhood days when I locked him out of the house. As the younger brother, he appeared to get his way by playing the role of the cunning and devious fox.

These roles were no doubt exaggerated in our minds. Yet in the context of a disagreement over control of the business, I sensed a danger in my seeming to be the bully pushing my brother around and in his appearing to cleverly take what wasn't rightfully his.

Business Problems

Aggravating the personal difficulties were a number of vexing management problems. For one thing, the board of directors, which had never achieved the importance I anticipated, lost even the limited value it had. The two outside members, who apparently felt dominated by the three owners who also sat on the board, left their positions. While their influence had been limited because they'd felt inhibited from speaking out, their departure removed even the semblance of outsider input. My partners had never been enthusiastic about the presence of outsiders, so the chances of reconstructing the board were slim.

Simultaneously, the business plan I had put together as a way of encouraging long-range planning lost its credibility. After all, the outside board members were at least symbolically associated with the idea of long-range planning; their departure seemed to suggest to my partners that such a long-term view was no longer necessary, and the focus shifted to short-term matters. Because my business plan, which had been adopted by the board, stressed the development of new restaurants outside Louisville, my partners were all the more eager to ignore it.

As if all these problems weren't enough, Michael and the minority holder were frequently at odds over operational matters.

My Decision

In January 1978, I resolved to sell my shares to the corporation. I didn't have the desire or the business stomach to do battle for control of the company. Little did I know that my decision to reach an amicable end to my participation in the business was only the first step in what was to develop into a four-year emotional roller coaster ride.

As a first step, I relinquished all my civic, charitable, and industry roles to allow Michael to become accustomed to filling them. Because his wife was opening a practice as a dentist, the transition to a more visible role in the community was expected to come fairly naturally. Meanwhile, I was single and was enjoying the increasing amount of time I spent away from Louisville.

I soon found out, though, that selling my shares to the corporation was going to be neither routine nor enjoyable.

We had a formal buy–sell agreement that provided a formula for the purchase of shares from a deceased stockholder's estate. However, no formula existed for the redemption of the stock from a living shareholder. The procedure outlined in the agreement called for the offering of the stock first to the corporation, then to an individual stockholder, then to anyone. I offered my shares for sale to the company for the first time in January 1978. There was much discussion and, after some time, it became clear that Michael was not yet ready to buy me out and run the business. Something was missing.

In the summer of 1978, I offered to buy my brother's shares in the family business. He expressed interest and took three months to talk to prospective employers in the Louisville area. But after carefully examining this option, he decided he wanted to stay put.

Now at least I was convinced that he was committed to the business. So the issue I had to begin grappling with was how serious I really was about leaving the company. I put the issue out of my mind as we made any number of market studies about expanding the business outside of Louisville. Always present, however, was a lack of serious commitment by my partners to these projects. It eventually became apparent that the only way for the company to expand its scope was to open another Louisville restaurant.

I had my pulse on the Louisville dining market and thought that a first-class restaurant featuring charcoal-grilled fresh seafood and American regional cooking would be a great success. I negotiated a superb lease for an 1880s-vintage iron-front warehouse, which I hoped to restore. It was located across from the site of the planned new Kentucky Center for the Arts. I arranged industrial revenue bond financing, which made the project very attractive.

We signed the lease on the Sixth Avenue Restaurant in the fall of 1979. Soaring interest rates during that period necessitated interrupting construction for about six months during the spring and summer of 1979; that meant a delay in opening the restaurant.

It was during this lull in activity that I once again resolved to leave the company. In May 1980, I handed my partners a handwritten letter of resignation. This time I was firmly committed to leaving. I agreed to stay on only through the construction of the Sixth Avenue Restaurant and for six months after its opening.

My two partners still did not really believe that I intended to leave. In addition, they still had bothersome conflicts between them. But I concluded that I had done all I could to encourage my brother. It seemed that I should now step away. I left for eight weeks during the summer lull in construction, and when I returned, things were quite different.

Finally, a Resolution

When I returned, I found that Michael had a much more positive attitude toward himself, the company, and his responsibilities. He clearly had begun to act very aggressively. He rejected the notion of my staying on through the opening of the new restaurant. He was no longer willing to take a back seat to big brother. He wanted to do all the work and get all the recognition.

In September 1980 we began negotiations on the sale and had reached a tentative agreement in principle by October 1. On that date, I resigned as president and became chairman of the board for one year. For cash flow reasons and for the convenience of the buyers, the closing was scheduled for a year later, October 1, 1981.

Timing was quite important to both of us. While a mutual trust in such transactions should develop, one should never assume that a deal is a deal until all the papers are signed. In early October, I suggested that both parties meet concurrently with counsel to hammer out the details of the agreement. We set a goal for completing the agreement by December 24, 1980. These months might seem long enough to work out the contractual details, but I could not get my brother and his lawyer to meet with me and my lawyer to complete this final stage of the negotiations process by the intended date.

Seller's Doubt

The third restaurant was to open in late January 1981, but my heart was not in it. On the other hand, I realized that the new operation would double the company's revenues. Thus, I continued to press for the signing of the agreement, but at the same time I recognized a lack of confidence on the part of my younger sibling in this major undertaking.

Negotiations on interest rates and other terms continued through the spring while I was in New York and Michael was in Louisville running the business. Meanwhile, I continued to research the potential value of the company.

A period of seller's doubt set in. We had no impartial valuation of the business, so I began to fear I had sold my interest for too little. Additional resentments accumulated for other reasons. The Casa Grisanti Restaurant was due to receive a major industry award in May 1981, and I wanted to attend the black-tie affair at the National Restaurant Association Convention in Chicago. I felt I had been a major component of the success for which the restaurant was being honored. I didn't think it was too much to ask. But my brother didn't want me near that awards ceremony.

I stayed away but resolved that it would be a costly bit of self-indulgence on his part. In June, I revised our agreement of the previous fall, raising my selling price and calling for payment of the noncompete agreement over five years instead of ten. I signed it and sent it to my brother via counsel. He rejected it and said that something else would have to be worked out.

Finally, the two of us met in Los Angeles in August 1981 and concluded that we would sell the entire company to outsiders!

I contacted various brokers to list the company nationally and renewed industry contacts to sell off one or two operations individually. When I returned to Louisville in late August to formalize this agreement to sell the company, Michael presented me with the agreement that I had signed in June, only now he had signed it and agreed to buy my stake. I had been forced to take three steps forward and two steps backward in order to be one step ahead.

Hard Lessons

After going through four years of sometimes intense and sometimes relaxed negotiations, I have developed several principles that I believe would be useful to anyone contemplating selling a business interest to a relative:

Stay Away from the Business. Expect long-standing difficulties, such as sibling rivalries, to continue and perhaps even intensify. As familiarity breeds contempt, distance can keep tempers from flaring.

Hold all negotiating sessions away from the business. Some neutral area will keep both parties from feeling threatened. By keeping a physical distance from the business, the seller can also help ease the period of self-doubt and ebbing self-confidence that inevitably follows the decision to sell.

Give the Buyers Control and Confidence During the Negotiating Process. Relatives usually don't have enough respect for each other's abilities. But to make a successful transition, the buyers must feel at ease with their new-found power and additional responsibilities in controlling the company.

While the buyers are gaining power and confidence, you the seller will gain a new sense of respect and admiration for their managerial abilities. This occurred in my situation, and I really wish there had been some way to increase my confidence in my brother's abilities before I had decided to sell out. Events might have progressed differently.

Expect That Selling Your Interest to a Relative Will Be a Drawn-Out Process. Plan for as long as three to five years between the decision to sell and the final closing. In our case, the time from the first offering of my shares for sale in January 1978 to the closing in October 1981 was almost four years.

This period can be reduced if both parties are truly serious. Once a *real* decision to buy and an equally real decision to sell have been made, the documentation can be handled in a matter of weeks.

The period from the letter of intent to the final closing can be horrendous. Both parties are likely to have second thoughts and everything may seem to be falling apart at critical moments.

I recommend that buyers and sellers, with their respective legal counsel, get together to hammer out the final document. Several intense sessions may fray some nerves but will expedite the final stage of the process and in the end cost everyone less aggravation, time, and money.

Seek Valuation of the Company.   This is perhaps the most difficult problem to handle in a sale among relatives. After all, relatives are supposed to be able to trust each other and not need interference of this sort.

An appraisal will determine the fair market value of the business. If the professional appraiser is chosen for his or her honesty, integrity, and expertise, both parties should have confidence in the opinion. If there is disagreement over the opinion, then a second, and even third, opinion or review can be requested.

The appraisal should give both parties the confidence necessary to complete the negotiations.

The exact method for this appraisal should be outlined in a buy–sell agreement. Our agreement was very specific in the event of a shareholder's death but did not even touch on an evaluation procedure for a lifetime transfer of stock.

I couldn't get the buyers to agree to professional valuation because of their insecurity about outsiders. The company's audit firm was my source of advice on valuation of the business and, more important, on the company's ability to handle the cash flow requirements of the long-term buyout. But this was an awkward situation because these accountants also continued to counsel the buyers. One might rightly argue that a serious conflict of interests existed here. As the seller, I eventually had to rely more on my own instincts and the current market and less on the financial adviser's opinion.

Entertain Other Potential Suitors.   Even when it has been agreed that the buyer will be a relative in the company, plan on investigating other potential purchasers in the event the relative gets cold feet. I pursued two avenues: national real estate brokers, who could market the whole company if that became necessary, and a large publicly traded food service company, for which I was doing some consulting work. Although it never became necessary to negotiate with either party, this process gave me some other perspectives on the company's value.

Make All Agreements Formal and Legal.   There is a temptation among relatives to assume that since they should be able to trust each other, many aspects of the negotiations can be kept informal and unwritten. Unfortunately, misunderstandings can easily arise—*especially* among relatives. Thus, with a long-term buyout, be sure that your legal counsel drafts mutual releases to be signed by both buyer and seller. The corporation and the buyers individually release any claims against the seller for actions or omissions in his or her capacity as an officer or director of the corporation. The seller does the same for the buyers and the corporation.

Also, seek protection from default. In my case, if payment is not received within 15 days of the due date, the buyers are in default and I can call the full amount due and payable. The buyers personally pledged the common stock to guarantee payment.

Finally, hire the best legal counsel you can find and get the buyers to agree to pay the fees. This condition was important for me because it gave the buyers a financial incentive for expeditious handling of the documentation. It also solved another problem: the buyers wanted me to retain out-of-town counsel, apparently to provide a veil of secrecy over the proceedings. I objected because of the inconvenience to me, and my brother dropped the request. Evidently he didn't want to bear the extra expense.

Don't Expect Business Concessions to Improve Family Relations. I wanted to improve relations with my brother, not only because we had other jointly held investments but also because he is the only brother I have. But I also wanted the maximum possible for my share of the company; he wanted to continue the company's growth and yet gain complete control of the business.

I made a major concession in giving up a cash settlement and agreeing to a long-term payout in the hope of an improvement in fraternal relations. This turned out to be wishful thinking on my part. To expect one agreement to improve 30 years of sibling rivalry was a pipe dream.

In Retrospect

Selling an interest in a family business to a family member is a deeply emotional experience for both parties. In many respects, it is more like a divorce and child-custody settlement than a business transaction.

Both parties are interested in the well-being of the offspring (the business) yet want to protect their own interests. Now that I know the company is being well managed and has a bright future, I can plan my pursuits and nurture my interests.

Under my brother's leadership, the company is continuing to do exceptionally well. It is maintaining its preeminent local market position, and I have every reason to expect full payment from the company for my shares. Relations with my brother remain civil and very businesslike. I continue to expect more. Perhaps I'm too much of an idealist.

37

The Financial and Emotional Sides of Selling Your Company

MICHAEL G. BEROLZHEIMER

Because many large corporations are on a constant lookout to acquire fast-growing private companies, owners of such companies usually have frequent opportunities to sell out. Sometimes the owners have valid reasons for wanting to sell. These reasons can include changes in markets, technology, resources, capital requirements, and management loyalty. Of equal or greater importance are personal factors such as the owner's age, career aspirations, and marital situation, along with the existence of heirs to take over the business. Once a decision is made to sell, the owner faces a thorny problem: how to arrange the sale. Mr. Berolzheimer provides one company owner's personal account of the sale of his company. He explores first how he came to the decision to sell and then how he negotiated the sale.

Back in the spring of 1977, I seemed to have everything a man of 36 could possibly want. I was president and a principal shareholder of a company with about $25 million annual sales. Because the company was helping pioneer a new consumer product area, running the company was exciting and future prospects appeared bright.

I should have been looking forward to endlessly favorable growth curves, but I wasn't. Instead, I faced a number of disturbing business and personal problems that made me think seriously of selling the company. But that prospect suggested its own equally disturbing set of problems.

How would I go about finding serious bidders? Who could advise me? Should I have a business broker? What would I tell my employees? Should I talk to one potential buyer at a time or several?[1]

Since those anxiety-provoking days of 1977, much has changed in my life. I have successfully completed the task of selling my company, Duraflame Inc. I now have the unmistakable luxury of hindsight. My hope is that the advice I received, together with my actual experience, will aid others who face the deeply personal and emotional question of whether to sell their companies and, if so, how.

First, though, I should relate some history.

Duraflame's Birth and Growth

My brother and I founded Duraflame in 1969 in Stockton, California with a $20,000 investment. The company's business was to market fireplace logs made of a mixture of mostly sawdust and wax together with a small amount of coloring agents. The firelogs were made by a subcontractor with specialized skills in wood processing and a need to dispose of wood waste. Three competitors were already in the $1 million processed firelog market at the time of our entry.

Duraflame's objective was to develop quickly a national brand based on superior product quality, premium price, and extensive distribution so as to obtain a dominant market share. This effort would be supported with a modest advertising program, strong sales management, and rapid production expansion.

Nine years later, in 1978, Duraflame's sales were $28 million, representing over 50% of the total firelog market. Yet the company had operated profitably in only five of these years. Losses occurred during the season of 1974–1975 when sales declined sharply because of recession, in 1975–1976 because of our excessive carry-over inventory, and in 1976–1977 because of heavy competitive pressure from a market entry by Colgate-Palmolive.

The nine years of operation were a mixture of triumph and disappointment. The triumph stemmed from our extremely succesful marketing effort and fast sales growth. The disappointment was the result of the losses and also the occasional friction with my brother about Duraflame's policies and future directions.

For instance, I wanted to commit capital toward diversifying into new consumer products, but some family members argued—perhaps correctly—in favor of more conservative financial policies.

Business Considerations for Selling

In 1977, when I first thought seriously about selling Duraflame, the idea seemed to make good business sense. It would solve the problem of the internal disagreements over the company's future directions and also reward my brother and me quite handsomely on our original investment.

Selling the company would relieve me of several other business concerns, such as the risk of marketing a seasonal product, the product's sensitivity to economic conditions, increasing oil prices (wax is a byproduct of the manufacture of lubricating oil), and frequently shifting competitive pressures.

It all seemed reasonable provided an acquirer could be found who understood the fundamental value of the company in the future, who would pay for that value *today* (with no contingencies), and who would recognize the key factors in the business's success and not unwittingly destroy the Duraflame brand name. *Projected* net income justified close to $8 million in goodwill value alone, based on 20% pretax return objectives. But how would a potential buyer judge past performance?

Possibly more important, did I really want to sell the business—from a personal viewpoint? Answering that question meant doing some very intensive soul-searching.

Should I Sell My 'Baby'?

In retrospect, the soul-searching started in 1976, when I attended a regional conference of the Young Presidents' Organization in Washington, D.C. Having always been interested in politics, I thought the conference would be an opportunity to find out more about the national political scene. But what I learned at that conference had less to do with national or international issues than with what I learned about myself.

Wayne Dyer, author of a number of books and articles about personal psychology, was there to speak about feelings and choices. He said that *we* make choices as to how we feel and should not blame our grandfathers, fathers, mothers, sisters, children, or wives for our feelings. For some time I had been unhappy with the way I was feeling. The concept that I could do something about it—if I so chose—was simple but very powerful. I proceeded to write down a projection of where I would be in ten years if I continued on the path of the previous ten years. Here is what I saw:

☐ Continued difficulties in my marriage.

☐ Continued responsibilities for a group of separate family companies in the wood-processing business—of which Duraflame was one—without the authority to build and lead the enterprises. That situation evolved because my father, brother, and I had differing viewpoints of company goals.

☐ Increasing danger to the companies and their employees because of the family differences.

(As one small company, we could keep our differences in a single room. However, our group of companies had grown from less than $7 million sales in 1969 to more than $50 million in 1977–of which Duraflame was approximately one-half. No one appeared ready to sacrifice his or her own goals for someone else's, and our divergent viewpoints seemed likely to have an increasingly serious negative effect on profits and employee morale).

☐ A probable change in my role within the family businessess—from one of stimulating opportunities for creative business development to one of conservative financial custodianship for my relatives and my children.

☐ Ten years of continued personal illiquidity.

These details may bore the reader, but I believe company owners must understand their personal objectives before they decide to sell (or buy) a company. By April 1977 I had decided to develop a strategy for selling the company *if* I chose to do so. However, I had not yet actually reached the emotional decision to sell.

Specific Pointers

The Young Presidents' Organization conducts an annual week-long international seminar, which includes an idea exchange session. I was given the honor of organizing the idea exchange for the 1977 meeting at Vienna University. Not surprisingly, I included a discussion of strategies for selling your business. The following basic principles emerged during that idea exchange and in subsequent conversations I had with executives:

☐ You only sell your company once. Whoever is buying your company buys companies repeatedly. Therefore, you must prepare yourself very thoroughly and leave nothing to chance.

☐ Selling your company is a personal affair. You cannot delegate the responsibility to someone else, including a business broker. A family company is *you*. Therefore, you have to sell it. I discarded the notion of keeping myself distant—as I might in labor negotiations—as unworkable.

☐ Sell for cash if you want liquidity and if you do not want your assets tied up in someone else's company.

☐ Negotiate with two or more willing buyers at the same time. Do *not* deal with only one company. This was especially important advice for me because I had come to believe that to deal with two or more people at the same time was somehow unethical. However, I approached potential buyers very discreetly and thus avoided tainting the company with a shopped-around image.

☐ Do not tell your employees. This is another rule with ethical overtones that I found difficult to accept but I nevertheless followed. For nine months only one person at Duraflame knew I was trying to sell the company. Employees speculated about a possible sale, but I never answered them formally. Informally, I tried to give the impression of seeking to establish a positive value for Duraflame, in the eyes of the company's directors, by talking with potential buyers.

☐ Carefully select those companies that your company will appeal to most. This was easy advice to follow because of the numerous inquiries I had received over the years from companies wanting to acquire Duraflame. I had always rejected these inquiries—but not before courteously greeting the acquisition people to gauge the depth of their interest.

☐ After selecting the companies you would like to negotiate with, develop a substrategy for contacting them. That is, who will make the contacts, with whom, and what will be said? This is a delicate process that requires careful planning.

☐ Plan on 18 months to complete the sale. This should include one year to select the buyer, followed by 6 months of final negotiations. In fact, I took approximately one year to select the finalist but needed only 3 months for the final negotiations because both parties had tax considerations and other incentives for quickly completing the transaction.

☐ Once you negotiate the framework of the deal, select a lawyer who will negotiate the details in a style compatible with your own personality. A poor lawyer can disrupt the delicate negotiations and kill the deal.

☐ Organize your company so that you can spend 100% of your time on the sale process. The time should include rest and relaxation to keep sane and cool. Early on, I appointed our national sales and marketing manager as general manager to take care of Duraflame's day-to-day operations. Without his dedicated leadership during a most critical period, I would not have had the time and energy necessary for the task.

☐ Stay alert and healthy. In my experience, every day brought a potentially fatal new issue concerning the proposed transaction. You have to *will* the sale to happen. This takes a healthy mental attitude.

☐ Finally a company is not sold until the money is in your bank account. Horror stories abound about deals that have fallen through just before the closing papers were to be signed.

These principles eased my anxiety about *how* to sell the company. I knew the time had come to make the decision. And somehow—perhaps unconsciously—I came to the point one evening in April 1977 that, yes, the idea made sense. I consulted with other family members and directors and they agreed. I then settled on June 1978 as my target date for completing the sale.

Why June 1978? First, that would give me 14 months to go through the process and reach the final agreement.

Second, I thought the country would begin a recession by the fall of 1978, and I knew that most of our losses had occurred because of the 1974–1975 recession, when the firelog market dropped 40% after having doubled during each of the previous three years.

Third, I felt I would want liquidity by about mid-1978 if I decided to separate from my wife so as to maintain our previous individual standards of living.

Finally, why wait for another unforeseen event to create a new crisis in the business?

Now began the process of courtship—what a friend calls the Indian rain dance. This was a key part of the negotiations and perhaps the most delicate phase.

The Rain Dance

Over the years I had kept a file of all the prospective acquirers I had talked with as well as other possible candidates suggested by close friends familiar with leading consumer products companies. I then compiled a list of companies that would be logical acquirers of Duraflame.

Carefully selected intermediaries contacted a total of seven of these companies. All but two initial discussions were with the presidents or the executive vice-presidents of potential acquirers. All were large, cash-rich companies that were in consumer products businesses and had policies of diversification.

My objective during this process was to keep three companies on an active list of potential acquirers. When one dropped out, I added another.

Of the seven companies, two declined nearly immediately because Duraflame did not interest them for one reason or another. Two more declined when they realized I would accept only cash and would not commit myself to an earn-out agreement coupled with a long-term management contract.

That left three companies to go through the serious process of financial review, plant visits, and so forth. One company dropped out because it concluded it would "kill Duraflame with overhead" since Duraflame was, in one official's words, the most complicated small business to manage in that company's history of acquisition analysis. That left two companies— one of which was Kingsford Co., a subsidiary of Clorox Co.

Bargaining with Kingsford

Kingsford acquired Duraflame because Kingsford was the logical company to do so. Its management knew it and I knew it. The idea had made sense since 1973 when Clorox acquired Kingsford, a charcoal briquet maker. In 1974, Kingsford entered the firelog business but abandoned it in 1976 because of poor product quality.

Nonetheless, it was obvious that Kingsford and Duraflame should be married. The space in the supermarket occupied by charcoal briquets during the summer months is occupied by firelogs during the winter, and distribution patterns for the two products are similar.

Since our suitability for each other was so obvious, I had gradually come to know various officials at Clorox and Kingsford. However, despite this fact, I decided that the best way to approach them would be through a close friend who would explain that he felt I could be convinced to sell the company if they were interested.

The negotiation process was long and arduous. It was, at the same time, an intellectual, business, and emotional challenge. It was an important learning experience, and a few lessons stand out today as being particularly valuable.

Keep a Notebook on Your Desk.   Make notes of every conversation regarding the negotiations. These notes can become important when you or the potential buyer have memory lapses concerning previous understandings. I learned this lesson after such a lapse over a small detail cost us $40,000.

Negotiate to Keep the Escrow Amount as Low as Possible.   The escrow amount is a percentage of the sale price held back to protect the buyer from inventory and other variations discovered later. In our case, it was less than 3% of the nearly $14 million total purchase price. The escrow amount should be the *exclusive* remedy for inaccuracies in the transaction. The seller must be careful to protect his value of the transaction from unknown, unforeseen, or forgotten events which could impair the value.

Write Your Own Draft of the Letter of Intent or Memo of Understanding.   Do this at the conclusion of the initial negotiations, preferably during a quiet weekend so you can concentrate. It will guide your lawyer and serve as the document from which you and your team will negotiate the final contract. Include as much information as possible because details agreed on during the months of preliminary discussions tend to be forgotten during the final negotiations.

Including such items in the original memo of understanding will give the buyer less room to make subsequent changes. Remember that during the period following the handshake, many people will become involved who will want to show their business acumen by improving the deal for whichever party they represent.

Be Totally Honest and Candid About Your Business.   That does not mean you have to confess speculative concerns about the future, but avoid being devious. Include bad news as well as good news. Your forthrightness will improve your credibility with the buyer and also help put him or her more at ease.

Determine How the Buyer Intends to Allocate His Acquisition Price.   For example, high allocation to fixed assets gives the buyer a greater base of depreciation but raises the issue of income recapture for the seller. In my case, it was important to limit the buyer's valuation of the noncompete clause to avoid the possibility of that part of the transaction being taxed as ordinary income rather than capital gains.

Do Not Be Afraid to Reject an Offer.   Kingsford's first offer totaled $2 million in goodwill and required complicated restructuring of the company prior to the sale. It was rejected as an insult to the investment made to build Duraflame as the firelog industry leader. We parted company, and I continued the rain dance with another possible corporate suitor.

Then one day, about a month later, I received a call from a Clorox executive who thought we should meet because there had been "misunderstandings." We met for dinner and that night agreed to the central principle of the transaction. My insight into Clorox's objectives and its past analytical assumptions allowed me to tailor our discussions to its perspective.

As an example Clorox officials had assumed no price increase for the 1978–1979 season, but I explained we had just announced a 10% price increase to the trade, which meant their pretax profit estimates were significantly understated. I was therefore able to lend support to my price objective and also suggest that Clorox could reasonably expect to meet its return-on-investment objectives.

Be Assertive Regarding Your Own Worth.   This is important if you want to arrange a consulting agreement or continue employment with the company. I, for one, had no idea how much to seek from my employment contract, which covered half my time for one year. On the advice of several business friends, I selected the highest sum I had considered and told Clorox officials. They agreed.

Avoid Becoming Complacent About the Transaction.   After you have reached an agreement in principle, the hard work has really just begun—as the reader will see.

The Negotiating Team

I reached a preliminary agreement without assembling a negotiating team. The reason was simple: I did not know whether I could create the deal. My goals had been high from the outset, and I did not intend to deviate from them. But once a sale was in sight, the negotiations over the final contract needed to be properly managed.

My initial step was to hire the best lawyer I could find. I made my choice based on interviews and reference checks of two specialists in mergers and acquisitions. One of the lawyer's first actions was to obtain Kingsford's agreement to pay all our legal and accounting expenses—about $50,000—*if* it acquired Duraflame.

Apart from professional competence, I wanted the lawyer to be personally committed. My lawyer promised to play that role. He was always available—days, nights, weekends. He never visited my office nor I his. I discovered that nearly all meetings are unnecessary if one is willing to spend countless hours on the telephone and make use of a speedy mail delivery service.

The rest of the team was assembled after April 3, 1978, which was opening day of Duraflame's three-day sales meeting at Lake Tahoe. The meeting represented our kickoff for the 1978–1979 season. At 11:00 the previous evening, I telephoned the company's three key executives and asked them to meet me for breakfast at 7:30 A.M. Over breakfast I told them of the agreement.

Afterward, I had the dubious pleasure of being the leadoff speaker at our sales meeting and spent two hours explaining the sale and answering questions about it. Most of the answers had been worked out prior to the meeting through joint consultation with Kingsford. That afternoon we informed food brokers who sold our logs to retailers, and the following morning we issued a press release, which was relayed over various wire services. To the credit of our staff the sales meeting continued in a somber but professional manner.

I met with our key executives in the afternoon and asked the chief controller to participate with me during the final negotiating process. He indicated that he was unhappy at not having been included earlier in the negotiating process. While he was tremendously valuable during the final negotiating phases, I do not see what might have been gained by having him or other staff members involved in the early stages. He, our accountants, a second controller, and our lawyer made up the negotiating team.

We met about eight times over a three-month period at Clorox's headquarters in Oakland to negotiate the final agreement. Each company's staff attended all these meetings. Every word of the one-foot-high legal document was negotiated. Hundreds of thousands of dollars rode on the language. Tens of thousands were at stake in the placement of commas and periods. Each day my staff would alert me to some new item that had developed into a potential crisis.

This was the most emotionally difficult period for me. It seemed a time of constant crisis. I was extremely sensitive to anything and anyone who might kill the deal. A few examples will show the importance of maintaining your mental and physical health during this period of tremendous stress.

Emotional Trials

Six weeks into the final negotiations, a family member dropped by my office to complain that I was being too soft in the negotiations. He cited several examples to illustrate his point. Apart from his abrupt, critical manner, I was upset at being second-guessed when Duraflame was about to be sold for more than two-and-a-half times the value that the same family member would have sold Duraflame for ten months earlier.

Eight weeks into final negotiations, Kingsford representatives and I were at odds over the language of a clause regarding the firelog production plant. During a break from the formal negotiating sessions, I met privately with one of Kingsford's chief negotiators and suddenly found each of us accusing the other of being stubborn and cheap. About an hour later, we broke the bottleneck over the language issue. I raise this point because I feel both parties must get their feelings on the table and risk emotional crises in order to make progress.

I also felt extreme tension during the Duraflame shareholders' meeting called to review and approve the final transaction documents. This meeting was timed to occur approximately three or four days before the final signing—only when all the wording in the various documents had been carefully negotiated and typed in final form and approved by Clorox and my staff.

Present at that meeting in addition to the shareholders were four lawyers. During the six hours of discussion about the contract I feared that any revision would jeopardize the overall transaction.

Happily, the stockholders' questions and concerns were answered without any material changes being required in the various documents. With the meeting behind me, I went to Clorox's offices for the final signing. However, even that meeting consumed more than four hours of negotiations over such things as out-of-state income taxes and the wording of one press release. Finally, we had the signing ceremony!

The Aftermath

Selling your company is a deeply emotional experience. It is also a tough experience.

I have since been able to concentrate on my real love—nurturing new consumer products—by forming a venture-capital partnership devoted to backing consumer companies. The Early Stages Company's objective is to be the leading venture-capital firm specializing in consumer products; other venture-capital firms tend to invest in high-technology companies or lever-aged buyouts.

Selling Duraflame has thus given me a new career opportunity, personal liquidity, and a sense of freedom. And this last benefit is the most precious one of all.

Notes

1. A valuable book for those thinking of selling their business is Stanley M. Rubel's *Guide to Selling a Business* (Wellesley Hills, Mass.: Capital Publishing Corp., 1977).

38
Selling Your Company
Additional Perspectives

DAVID E. GUMPERT with comments by **DOUGLAS E. KELLOGG, JERRY W. LEVIN, KENNETH J. NOVACK, RICHARD M. HEXTER,** and **ARTHUR H. ROSENBLOOM**

Small company owners who decide to sell out are embarking on an obstacle-ridden and emotional journey. In the previous article, Michael G. Berolzheimer described his experience selling his processed firelog company and specified many of the difficulties he encountered and lessons he learned. In this article, five special commentators and a number of readers assess Berolzheimer's experience and pass along their own advice and observations about selling small companies. Following readers' and commentators' observations, the author adds some comments.

What is the best strategy for small company owners to follow when selling their companies? Or *is* there really a single best strategy to guide the sale of small companies?

Michael G. Berolzheimer tackled the first question in the preceding article, in which he detailed the strategy he used to sell his fast-growing company, Duraflame Inc., to a large conglomerate.

To recap briefly, Berolzheimer recounted how a combination of personal and financial problems, including marital difficulties, disagreements within his family about the future direction of the company, and personal illiquidity, convinced him to sell the company. He traced step by step the process of finding a buyer, negotiating a preliminary agreement, and ultimately, grinding out the complex final terms.

In the course of the 15-month sale process, Berolzheimer came to a number of conclusions about how best to sell small companies. He advised small business owners considering selling out to avoid using brokers or consultants to handle the negotiations, deal with two or more willing buyers simultaneously, refrain from telling employees about negotiations, develop a substrategy for contacting potential buyers, organize their companies so

387

as to be able to spend all their time on the sale process, and plan on 18 months to complete the sale.

He also offered advice about negotiating that included the following: keep notes of every conversation regarding the negotiations, keep the escrow amount as low as possible, draft a letter of intent or memo of understanding at the conclusion of initial negotiations, remain open about revealing unfavorable as well as favorable aspects of the business, firmly reject any offer seen as unfair, and avoid becoming complacent after reaching an agreement in principle.

The question of whether a single best strategy exists came up when *HBR* sought to broaden the discussion by inviting reactions from readers and from five commentators. The commentators and readers analyzed Berolzheimer's approach and, while agreeing with many of his suggestions, also offered alternative approaches.

The five commentators are involved in various aspects of selling small companies. Douglas E. Kellogg is president of a miniconglomerate that has acquired seven small manufacturing companies and sold two during the past 15 years. Jerry W. Levin helps direct Pillsbury's acquisition efforts and thus has a corporate perspective on small company sales and acquisitions. Kenneth J. Novack is a lawyer frequently involved in sales of small companies. Richard M. Hexter and Arthur H. Rosenbloom are consultants who often advise small companies considering selling out.

We asked the commentators to answer the following questions: How typical was Berolzheimer's overall experience and how would you evaluate his handling of the situation? Which of his suggestions were most universally relevant? Based on your experience, what might he have done differently?

Evaluating the Approach

Though the commentators tended to view Berolzheimer's experience as fairly unusual, in general they applauded his management of the sale process. "Each sale of a small company tends to be unique," said Kellogg. "Berolzheimer describes factors in his experience which seem to reflect his particular style of management and negotiation—his dedication of 100% of his time to the sale, his concern about every detail of the negotiations, and his carefully thought-out plan, together with a definite schedule. My impression is that Berolzheimer was a strong and determined negotiator and that the success of the sale of his company could be almost completely attributed to his skill."

To Kellogg, Berolzheimer's accomplishment was not insignificant. "The sale of a long-established successful business is probably the most wrenching experience in a business owner's career," he observed. "The satisfaction in starting and operating a successful business is one of life's most rewarding experiences and the loss or sale of the enterprise can be a fate worse than death."

Several commentators especially approved of Berolzheimer's overall assessment of his aspirations and role in selling the company. "Before Berolzheimer decided to sell or selected a buyer, he analyzed his goals, which included his desire to achieve financial liquidity and to free himself from business and other relationships he found difficult," said Novack. "His decision and strategy successfully realized those goals."

Hexter was impressed by Berolzheimer's "initiative" in "creating objective and specific criteria for the sale" and in "personally dominating the decision-making and selling process."

"Having participated as both principal and agent in dozens of such transactions, I find this is not a common occurrence," Hexter said. "Most sellers react rather than act. Few owners have the posture or attitude which permits them to perform so freely or individually. Few entrepreneurial businessmen are such purposeful goalsetters and are as focused in the pursuit of that goal. Most sellers make more use of others in the selling transaction."

A Special Perspective

One commentator was able to assess Berolzheimer's approach from an unusual viewpoint. Although we at *HBR* did not know it when we asked Levin to comment, Pillsbury was one of the three unnamed companies alluded to in the article that seriously considered acquiring Duraflame. Levin provided some background about Pillsbury's evaluation of Duraflame and its decision not to acquire Duraflame. This information sheds light on how large conglomerates view potential acquisitions:

"We had been very interested in Duraflame for years because of the high degree of convenience of the product, supermarket distribution, good price/value relationship (compared principally to firewood), and our perception that the product was primarily made of a waste product in ample abundance (sawdust).

"Our acquisition analysis confirmed our belief that artificial fireplace logs have a huge market potential. But we also learned that under Duraflame's technology the product is made principally from a petrochemical product in limited supply (wax) and a rather specialized type of sawdust. Though the problem might have been solved through research, Duraflame was actually shipping sawdust from the West Coast to the East Coast because the sawdust available on the East Coast wasn't working very well in the logs.

"Mike Berolzheimer also seemed to be a one-man show and we suspected that it would take much more than one individual to replace him. We finally decided that the expensive distribution and procurement system would lead to high administrative costs that would prevent us from earning a consistent and attractive return on our investment. So we declined to bid.

"I should add at this point that whatever the pluses and minuses of Mike's approach, he fully met his objectives. Given what we know about the company and our own acquisition and divestiture experiences, that was an extraordinary success on his part.''

Things to Emulate

The commentators felt that small business owners could learn several generally applicable principles from Berolzheimer's actions at each stage of the process. More than one thought his early consideration of his personal situation was particularly noteworthy.

"Perhaps the most universally applicable and important observation made, and effectively demonstrated, by Berolzheimer was that prospective sellers must understand their personal objectives before they decide to sell their companies,'' stated Novack. "Too frequently, principal stockholders and managers view a sale as the only viable solution to serious problems involving inadequate financing, lack of investor liquidity, management weaknesses, or other major personal or business problems. In many cases, such problems can be dealt with effectively by taking other steps, such as a public offering, a private placement, an acquisition, a spin-off of a division, elimination of a troublesome stockholder, or addition of new management.''

Hexter agreed: "Perhaps the most valuable part of Berolzheimer's chronicle is his repeated focus on the personal and emotional issues underlying the sale of a closely held business. Frequently, these issues end up dominating the negotiations and become more important than the more rational commercial and financial concerns.''

Some commentators also pointed to his overall control of the divestiture process as a useful model. "Berolzheimer is an excellent example of a businessman maintaining control of the process of selling his business,'' observed Novack. "Too frequently, sellers are uncertain because of their lack of experience and defer to investment bankers, lawyers, or others on major business decisions which they, the businessmen, should be making. Experts' advice is important and should be sought, but sellers should not abdicate responsibility for deals.''

Hexter observed, "His recognition that every deal requires a driver— whose will to succeed will overcome inevitable obstacles—is right on target.''

Berolzheimer's efforts to plan and schedule the acquisition process made sense despite the limitations of such efforts, according to Kellogg. "I agree with this strategy completely,'' he stated, "even though my experience has indicated that acquisitions seldom turn out the way they were originally planned and scheduled. But I don't know of any other way to start such a program. A plan and schedule can certainly start the program off in the right direction and with constant adjustment and correction can be useful means of control.''

Hexter and Levin similarly seconded the author's advice to oversee various strategic aspects of the sale process. "His method of screening and approaching possible candidates was excellent for a company of Duraflame's type and size," Hexter said. "His efforts to understand the ultimate potential buyer gave him an important advantage during the negotiating phases."

Levin recommended a number of the author's tactics in conducting the negotiations: "His decision to handle the negotiations himself and not delegate the responsibility to someone else was a wise one. Rarely can a third party represent a successful businessman as well as he can himself. Mike is a very articulate individual and it was a pleasure dealing with him.

"His decision to negotiate with more than one willing buyer was to his advantage. From a buyer's perspective, we would much rather be dealing with the company on an exclusive basis, since we feel it is in our interests to do so. In our own divestitures, we have been very uncomfortable with fewer than three interested parties but find it difficult to work with more than five.

"Mike's substrategy of carefully contacting selected prospective buyers is also well taken. We have a practice of writing down a telephone script and discussing it among members of our acquisition and divestiture department before making calls. We also think out who should be contacted.

"Mike had some worthwhile points for actually conducting the negotiations. Making notes of every conversation is important. Lapses of memory, usually favorable to oneself, always seem to occur, so the notes are valuable later on.

"His suggestion to be totally honest and candid about the business is very important. Because we keep notes on everything said and are carefully watching for contradictions in the material presented to us, we sooner or later seem to find out about sellers' problems. Being totally candid and honest at the very beginning enhances the probability of closing without a major adverse change in the transaction. We are usually willing to accept certain negative factors along with the positive ones in our acquisition candidates. We just hate to find out about them on our own.

"Selecting the negotiating team is more an issue of personal style and quality of people available. Mike hired the best lawyer he could find and got the buyer to agree to pay the legal expenses. That's optimum for the seller but, strangely, pretty good for the buyer also. We have always been able to work better with experienced professional lawyers. Negotiations are easier and more often concluded. Inexperienced lawyers are often reluctant to advise their clients to take any risks, whereas lawyers who have been through such negotiations a few times know what's reasonable."

Several commentators found that Berolzheimer's description of the intense pressures he felt after the agreement in principle and before the final agreement rang true. "The time between an agreement in principle and the closing is a critical period during which both buyer and seller have a vested interest in the business," observed Kellogg. "And those interests are quite different depending on whether the deal is a sale of assets or stock. Berolzheimer indicates that he had some trouble during this period and I suspect that, if he had it to do over again he would try to move more quickly from letter of intent to closing.''

The near-collapse of negotiations that Berolzheimer experienced during this period is fairly common, according to Rosenbloom. ''Our experience tells us that it's virtually a condition to closing that there be one or more points at which negotiations threaten to break off,'' he stated. ''Emotions on both sides should be vented. The deal can be put back on track if the parties exhibit flexibility, a give-and-take attitude, and the ability to horse-trade.''

Seeking Outsiders' Help

Most of the commentators saved their most detailed analyses for areas of disagreement with the author. They were nearly unanimous in differing with Berolzheimer over his decision to forgo using outside consultants in the negotiations until after he had reached an agreement in principle.

''In my opinion, sellers should not reach agreement in principle without the benefit of active assistance during the negotiations from experienced advisers,'' said Novack. ''Experienced lawyers specializing in purchases and sales of businesses can make major contributions to structuring such transactions. Lawyers should be able to more than pay for themselves if they get in early enough. They can help sellers negotiate the best possible letters of intent or memoranda of understanding because, at this stage, buyers are often still wooing; thus sellers have a golden opportunity to set the stage favorably for the final negotiation of many important issues, such as indemnification and escrow terms, allocation of purchase price, registration rights (if applicable), timing, payment of expenses, and closing conditions.

''Similarly, investment bankers can frequently suggest and arrange contacts with possible buyers which might not otherwise occur to sellers, such as potential foreign buyers; investment bankers can help rationalize higher prices and lend credibility to the negotiations. Accountants can make suggestions about current business decisions with accounting or tax implications which could affect the sale, develop formats presenting information to justify asking prices, or determine the tax implications of various deals to companies and their stockholders.''

Levin labels Berolzheimer's single-handed approach ''a dangerous practice. It is difficult to understand all of the tax, legal, and financial issues one can get tripped-up on; buyers have been through the procedure many times before and generally know how to move such issues in their favor. As an example, Mike recommends selling for cash to obtain liquidity. Mike's business had a huge amount of goodwill, so his preference for cash created a purchase transaction with heavy nontax-deductible write-offs.

''Few assets were involved, so the tax benefits of the nontaxable exchange were probably limited. If Mike had been willing to accept a stock transaction which could have met pooling requirements and provided him with liberal registration rights, he not only could have made the situation more attractive for most buyers but could have better managed his own tax situation. Proper advice early would probably have picked up this point.''

Similarly, Hexter saw various advantages to be gained from outside advisers. "Berolzheimer's narrative suggests he prefers to be the field general and operate alone," he said. "Over the years, I have seen the value of experienced intermediaries proved time and again. Clearly, no one can delegate the final decision-making responsibility to someone else, but good advisers, brokers, or investment bankers can shorten the selling procedure, simplify the screening procedures, patch together discussions after the inescapable breakdowns, and help bridge the emotional crises provoked by selling a company. When the seller does not himself have a personality such as that of the author, the broker can be the one with the will to see the deal through the obstacle course.''

Hexter also noted: "Berolzheimer could afford to take tough negotiating positions because he would not have to live with the new owners after the sale. Owners planning to stay on as managers often want a third party to play the 'black hat' role in negotiations to preserve ongoing relationships after the sale.''

Dealing with Employees

The commentators also disagreed sharply with Berolzheimer's decision to refrain from telling employees about the negotiations to sell Duraflame until after he reached an agreement in principle. Rosenbloom observed: "Given the activity of company rumor mills, which tend to paint the direst of pictures to employees, and the resulting risk of loss of fretful employees, the best approach seems to be as follows: advise employees about a possible deal once substantive negotiations are under way; describe the transaction's advantages to the seller company and its employees; and describe any understandings respecting employee retention.''

Novack offers another reason for informing at least some employees that negotiations are under way. "Many sellers find that the conduct of the business slips during the sale process because it is just not possible to give both the attention they require," he stated. "This can be especially damaging if the deal drags on and then falls through. Telling key, trusted employees early enough can offer the principal manager the coverage and the leverage he needs to manage both the business and the sale. In addition, sooner or later, employees usually learn what's going on. It may be desirable to run the risks of telling the key people early because, among other things, they might be able to help and they will appreciate hearing the news directly from the owner.''

Finally, the commentators disagreed with Berolzheimer's advice to sellers to devote all their time to the selling process. "Most owners continue to spend a significant amount of time running their businesses during negotiations in order to be able to make some last-minute operational or financial changes that may give them some eleventh-hour advantages," said Kellogg.

Levin was more emphatic about the importance of sellers keeping tabs on operations. "No time is more important, and perhaps more difficult, for keeping the business healthy than the time of sale," he said. "It is risky to make any major management change during this period. I don't think Mike needed to spend 100% of his time on the sale process, and he might have been better served delegating some of the sale process earlier and delegating a little less of the business operations matters."

Reader Comments

A number of readers related their own experiences with and lessons from buying and selling companies. We are unable to publish all the responses because of space limitations; the following are a sampling of the letters received:

"Michael G. Berolzheimer's article was very close to my heart. The doubts, the pain, and the indescribable joy at being free of the burden touched me deeply.

"In 1975, I had inherited the largest retail lumber operation in Texas. That was the good news. The bad news was an enormous overburden of debt combined with a vast change in the marketing of building materials that was squeezing out the independent owner in favor of timberland owners. With the help of a highly competent general manager who had previously been able to use his own head and the sale of some 'dead' assets, we were able to turn the monster around by the end of 1977. The realization that under the best circumstances the return on equity would equal a good certificate of deposit without the certificate's security precipitated our decision to sell.

"Unlike Berolzheimer, I stayed away from the discussions involving the sale. The rationale was that anything I said was the final word, whereas an intermediary could find reason to delay until some point was cleared with me in private. This method cost us several suitors but really paid off well with the final buyer, for it seemed to build up his anxiousness to conclude the negotiations. I would not recommend this strategy to others unless they have a very trustworthy party (such as my general manager) to handle the deliberations. Also, one should have an accountant who knows a great deal about the sale of a business.

"We did not advertise the sale to our employees, but we did answer any inquiries with the truth, because honesty is the best policy to stop ill-founded rumors. In no way did this policy put the sale of the business in jeopardy. In fact, the key employees worked harder than before to make a good impression on potential new bosses. Of course, a couple of 'bad apples,' hoping to get immediate promotions, tried to defame some others in the company. The new owners saw this clearly and promoted the rumor-mongers out of jobs.

"My family was supportive of the entire effort because the alternatives were stunted growth, high risk, and psychological tension. If push had come to shove, however, I had control of 85% of the stock.

"In April 1978, I met with the new owners-to-be for only the second time, and this time it was to sign the final papers and accept their check. I didn't know one could hold his breath for three hours!"

Lee Paulsel
President
Venture Capital Investments
Fort Worth, Texas

". . . Having started a company in 1957 which I merged with a larger corporation in 1961, I could readily identify with the financial and emotional factors which Berolzheimer brought out so vividly.

"While I and other shareholders were not nearly so well informed or sophisticated as the author and lacked some of his motives for wanting to make a sale, in retrospect we didn't do too badly from a financial standpoint. The one area in which we differed most dramatically from Berolzheimer was that we planned to continue working for the company after the merger. We naively believed, having been reassured by the acquiring company on this point many times during the negotiations, that things would be much the same after the merger as they were before. This turned out not to be the case at all, and neither party should ever have expected it to.

"My remuneration depended to a substantial degree on a bonus arrangement which was tied to the profit performance of the division I now managed. However, the acquiring corporation, of which the division was not a small part, severely restricted the kind and size of contracts it would take. Needless to say, I didn't remain very long, in spite of a five-year employment contract, and neither did a sizable number of the other key employees who had made the company an attractive candidate for merger in the first place.

"Within a couple of years, the acquiring company owned only the shell of what had been acquired, and there was more than enough unhappiness and discontent to go around. Even though we benefited financially from the merger, we were unhappy about what we perceived to be wasted opportunities for our technical and business expertise that should have increased the value of our stock. (Because it was 'letter' stock, we had to wait until we left the employ of the company before we could sell it.)

"In retrospect (and enough years have passed for most of the bitterness to have dissipated), all parties would have been better served if everyone had been completely candid about what postmerger conditions would be. We could have accepted reasonable changes without difficulty if they had been laid out for us and discussed during the merger negotiations.

"Similarly, the manager's remuneration formula should have been structured so that it would not be as adversely affected by postmerger conditions that were largely controlled by the acquiring party. Any 'sharp' dealings in this area are likely to be interpreted as evidence of bad faith and lead to serious demotivational consequences not just for the manager but for those who are influenced by him. If unforeseen changes become necessary for the overall welfare of the larger organization, they should be quickly and thoroughly explained to the affected manager, and steps should be taken to make him 'whole' again if his active cooperation and support are desired."

Donald G. O'Brien
President
D.G. O'Brien Inc.
Seabrook, New Hampshire

". . . The strong memory I have of my only acquisition is that it could not have happened if the seller didn't believe I would be the best caretaker of her 'baby.' Concluding the acquisition involved everything from my encouraging her to find a good lawyer (a real estate friend was her original agent) to bringing her a fresh red rose for the final signing.

"Last year, in a reversal of these roles (a large New York publisher was courting me), I had an opportunity to witness the worst possible approach to any seller. Only at the conclusion of my first meeting—a three-hour luncheon with their chairman, president, and corporate development official—did they ask the first question about how I had brought the company to its current attractive level. They never did get around to discussing whether I would be invited to stay on, the pangs of selling a company founded 65 years earlier by my grandfather, what mistakes or plans I had made for the company, and so on. Needless to say, that was also the last meeting with those folks!

"Especially in companies that have developed under the guidance of a small team or even one individual, the seller must be approached in a sincerely friendly way. It worked for me."

Richard Rosenthal
President
F & W Publishing Corp.
Cincinnati, Ohio

"... My company, in 1977, acquired a competitor that had been owned by four publishing companies. A few principles of my own emerged from the negotiations:

☐ Keep negotiations moving. We were in Massachusetts; all four publishers, in New York City. A major assignment given to our intermediary was to keep the ball rolling.

☐ Don't get stalled by minor details. Have the intermediary ready to ask the question: 'How important is this item on a scale of 0 to 10 in relation to the overall picture?'

☐ Constantly reassess the probability of a successful outcome. As Berolzheimer points out, selling (or buying) a company is nearly a full-time job for a small company president. If the probability slips below 50%, call it off. You have a business to run. You can always reopen the question later and start assessing the odds all over again. We did that with our acquisition. We were rebuffed in our first attempt and returned two years later and reopened negotiations.

☐ Keep a notebook on the acquisition negotiations to avoid future misunderstandings, and also write internal position papers and proposals to your intermediary, to any colleagues who are working with you on the negotiation, and to yourself. In the memos to yourself, address yourself not as if you were the president of the company but as if you were a vice-president of acquisitions preparing a proposal for the president. This approach revealed many factual gaps in our knowledge (which were filled) and led to a sounder strategy and decision. 'Memos to self' saved us thousands of dollars and hours of time; the memos wired colleagues into my thinking, served as a stimulus for input from those colleagues, and kept us unified.

☐ Ignore all of your ego needs except the need to pull off a profitable deal. That deal should generate enough ego satisfaction.

☐ Above all, keep in mind that the deal must benefit both the buyer and the seller. If the balance tips significantly from one to the other during the negotiations, then the likelihood of completing the transaction will drop. Keep trying to look at the picture from their viewpoint. If you do, then you can identify the real issues that have to be dealt with and anticipate standoffs.

☐ We paid our intermediary 5%. The deal was under $1 million. One rule of thumb is that intermediaries should be paid 5% on the first million dollars.''

Glenn H. Matthews
President
College Marketing Group Inc.
Winchester, Massachusetts

A Final Note

Berolzheimer's article and the preceding commentaries prompt several observations. One is that the seemingly forbidding act of selling closely held companies can and should be approached much like the host of other business decisions company owners must make. That is, overall goals must be determined and then the best strategies formulated to achieve those goals.

A second is that the significance of feelings and emotions cannot be ignored when making important business decisions. Such factors tend to get minimized or suppressed in many instances. Nevertheless, as Berolzheimer and the commentators emphasized, the assessment of personal aspirations and emotional needs can be the most important step not only in deciding whether to sell out but also in determining how to approach the negotiations. The buyer must also keep emotional considerations in mind if negotiations are to succeed.

Another conclusion is that seemingly innocuous negotiating techniques—what is said during the initial contact, how many potential buyers are involved, and so forth—may be quite important to achieving a successful and satisfying sale. While negotiating styles play a significant role in a sale, probably no one overall technique is best. Rather, sellers must choose the style that best suits both the situation at hand and themselves, keeping in mind that openness and candor should underlie any approach.

The original article and commentaries recurrently raised the question of the value of consultants. Berolzheimer carefully researched possible approaches to selling a company and successfully carried the ball to the agreement-in-principle stage without the help of consultants.

The commentators, three of whom have an obvious bias toward consultants, indicated that Berolzheimer was quite fortunate to have made it as far as he did without outside advisers. Maybe the most that can be said is the following: in Berolzheimer's case consultants were not required to carry out the sale of the company; however, persuasive arguments can certainly be put forth for using them.

Finally, note that one question was barely considered in either the article or the commentaries: How does a seller decide what price to seek and a buyer what price to offer? The fact that the subject received scant attention during the course of two substantive discussions about selling small companies may be testimony to the importance of such factors as personal feelings, various business trends, and negotiating techniques.

One might even deduce that these factors are of such overriding importance that they have more to do with setting prices than the quantitative evaluative techniques focused on in many textbooks. Or perhaps it can be argued that *HBR* should publish an article which considers in further detail that aspect of selling small companies. We are certainly open to the possibility.

About the Authors

Jerry L. Arnold is an associate professor in the School of Accounting at the University of Southern California and is the director of the USC School of Accounting's SEC and Financial Reporting Institute. He has a Ph.D. from the University of Michigan and teaches primarily in the M.B.A. program. His major research interests are in the areas of accounting policy setting and issues affecting smaller companies, and he has published numerous articles on these subjects. During the summer of 1981, he served as an Academic Fellow in the Office of the Chief Accountant of the Securities and Exchange Commission in Washington, D.C.

Michael G. Berolzheimer is the founder and president of P&M Cedar Products, Inc., and co-founder of The Early Stages Company, a venture capital firm specializing in early-stage, consumer-oriented investment opportunities. He is currently director of the The Wine Group (Franzia), Businessland, Eljenn International, Specialty Shelter, Sierra On-Line, Thomas E. Wolfe, Homestead Provisions, and P&M Cedar Products, Inc. Mr. Berolzheimer received his B.A. degree from Harvard College and an M.B.A from Harvard Business School.

John J. Brasch began a business career in 1979 after leaving a position as professor of international marketing at the University of Nebraska at Lincoln. He received his D.B.A. from Washington University in St. Louis in 1969. Mr. Brasch currently serves as the president of International Management Services, Inc., an export management company serving more than a dozen firms in nearly all major world markets. Mr. Brasch has published other articles in journals such as Journal of International Business Studies *and* Journal of Small Business Management.

Albert V. Bruno *received a B.S. (with Honors) from Purdue University. He earned a M.B.A. and Ph.D. from the Krannert School at Purdue. He has authored or co-authored more than 40 articles, monographs, research notes, and book chapters in a variety of professional journals. He has been the recipient of major grants from NASA and The National Science Foundation. In 1981 he received the President's Special Recognition Award at the University of Santa Clara. In 1982, he was one of 13 recipients nationwide of the Leavey Foundation Award. He currently holds the Glenn Klimek Chair at the University of Santa Clara where he teaches in the business school.*

Neil C. Churchill *is a distinguished professor of accounting and director of the Caruth Institute of Owner-Managed Business at Southern Methodist University where he teaches and does research into owner-managed enterprises and planning and accountability systems in entrepreneuring companies. Prior to joining SMU he was on the faculties of Harvard Business School and Carnegie Mellon University. Professor Churchill has been involved with consulting and management education in a number of companies in the United States and abroad. He is on the Board of Directors of several owner-managed companies, on the Policy Study Committee of the Heller Institute for the Advancement of Small Business Enterprises, and the Small Business Committee of the American Institute of CPA's.*

Michael A. Diamond *is a professor of accounting at California State University, Los Angeles.*

Stahrl Edmunds *is a professor of management in the Graduate School of Administration and director of the Dry Lands Research Institute at the University of California, Riverside. He is a former dean and vice-chancellor of the university where he has been since 1967. Mr. Edmunds also has 25 years of business experience as an executive with such enterprises as Hughes Aircraft Company, Ford Motor Company, McGraw-Hill, National City Bank of New York, and Northwestern National Life Insurance Company. He is the author of six books and 48 articles on business and public policy, economics, small business, and environmental problems.*

Wallace F. Forbes *is president of Standard Research Consultants, a New York City based firm that specializes in providing business valuation and related financial services for private and public companies. He is a graduate of Princeton University and Harvard Business School, a member of the New York Society of Security Analysts, and a chartered financial analyst. His articles have appeared in such publications as* Chief Executive, YPO Enterprises, The Monthly Digest of Tax Articles, *and* Business Horizons.

Don Albert Grisanti *is a food service management specialist and principal in the firm Grisanti Associates, Ltd. with offices in Tiburon, California. He has created, owned, and operated restaurants which have won the Insti-*

tutions Ivy Award, Travel/Holiday Fine Dining Awards, and Mobil Four Star Rating. He graduated from St. Louis University with a B.S. degree and completed the Smaller Company Management Program (SCMP) at the Harvard Business School.

David E. Gumpert *is an associate editor of the Harvard Business Review, who has responsibility for editing the magazine's "Growing Concerns" feature directed to owners and managers of small businesses. He is also the coauthor, with Jeffry A. Timmons, of* The Insider's Guide to Small Business Resources, *an extensive compilation and evaluation of managerial and financial sources available for entrepreneurs. Prior to joining the Havard Business Review in 1978, he was a staff reporter with The Wall Street Journal for nine years. Mr. Gumpert is a recent graduate of the Harvard Business School's Smaller Company Management Program. He received his B.A. in political science from the University of Chicago and his M.S. in journalism from Columbia University Graduate School of Journalism.*

John H. Hand *is professor of finance at Auburn University. He received a B.A. degree from Swarthmore College and a Ph.D. from Massachusetts Institute of Technology. His articles have appeared in* The National Tax Journal, Business Horizons, Journal of Financial Research, Journal of Risk and Insurance, Financial Management, *and other business and economic journals.*

Lore Harp (McGovern) *is co-founder, president, chairman, and chief executive officer of Vector Graphic, Inc., a Southern California-based manufacturer of small business computers. She moved from Germany to California in 1966. In 1976, with only $6,000, she founded Vector Graphic, Inc. in conjunction with Robert Harp and Carole Ely. Vector went public on October 13, 1981 and is currently traded over-the-counter with the symbol VCTR. Ms. Harp is able to use her entrepreneurial expertise and interest in high-growth companies for the benefit of other potential entrepreneurs as a director of the American Electronics Association. In addition, she is a director of Pacific Technology Ventures, Inc. and on advisory committees for Montgomery Ventures and the First Women's Bank, along with being a member of the Committee of 200 and the Trusteeship. She holds a B.A. and an M.B.A. Ms. Harp is married, has two children, and is an avid skier and tennis player.*

Robert Hershey *is professor of management and psychology at the U.S. Merchant Marine Academy.*

James Howard *founded Country Business Services, Inc., a business brokerage and consulting company located in Brattleboro, Vermont.*

S. Kumar Jain *is professor of management and international business at Southern Illinois University at Edwardsville. Dr. Jain has also owned and* *managed businesses and worked for the United States Government. He has an academic background in physics, mathematics, civil engineering, industrial engineering, and corporate finance. Dr. Jain also brings to small corporations, on whose boards he serves, and whose top management he counsels, extensive business experience from many parts of the world and an exposure to diverse problems from varied industries. He now lives in the St. Louis area.*

Herbert Kierulff occupies the Donald L. Snellman Endowed Chair in Entrepreneurship and Free Enterprise at Seattle Pacific University. Earlier, he taught at the University of Southern California, where he and a colleague founded the Entrepreneurship Program, a unique 16 unit business major which won the Justin Dart award for academic innovation. Kierulff/Associates (the management advisory firm he established in 1968) specializes in: (1) profit improvement planning and implementation, (2) turnaround management, (3) new venture startups and management, and (4) acquisitions and divestiture. He has acted as an advisor to the CEO's of over 100 start-up ventures and existing smaller companies. He has also consulted to larger firms and federal government agencies in his specialties, and directed and/or made presentations in over 50 major seminars and workshops for executives.

Harvey "Chet" Krentzman is president of Advanced Management Associates, Inc. and a successful consultant and coach to more than 75 manufacturing chief executives for over 25 years. He is also a professional corporate director of private and public enterprises. His dedication to the field of small business management includes the founding of the Score Program, Association of Management Consultants, The Institute of Management Consultants, and the Small Business Foundation of America. He has received national recognition for his book Managing for Profits, *published by the U.S. Small Business Administration. Mr. Krentzman's most recent book is* Successful Management Strategies for Small Business *(Prentice Hall, 1981). Mr. Krentzman has authored numerous articles, lectured throughout the United States, and has helped many small businesses and managers build their enterprises and prosper. He is also vice-chairman of the Boston Symphony Orchestra's Board of Overseers.*

Ted M. Levine founded Development Counsellors International, Ltd., a firm that specializes in economic development marketing, in 1960. He is a member of the American Economic Development Council and the National Association of State Development Agencies. Since 1960 he has served as consultant to over 70 major clients including 18 U.S. states. He has written numerous articles for professional journals and national publications and has spoken before business and trade associations on a dozen occasions. Mr. Levine received his B.A. and M.B.A. from Cornell University.

William P. Lloyd is the Liberty National Professor of Finance at Auburn University, where he has been on the faculty since 1979. Since receiving a D.B.A. degree from Indiana University, he has published widely in journals such as Journal of Finance, Journal of Financial and Quantitative Analysis, Harvard Business Review, and Journal of Financial Research. His recent interests have included the problems inherent in various ownership structures in small businesses, especially the problems faced by the minority stockholder in a closely held corporation. He is currently a board member in two such corporations.

Peter Mailandt is working as an independent management consultant in Dallas, with clients in the high-tech and energy-related industry, specializing on internal and external business development issues. Previously, Mr. Mailandt was director of planning and development at the Oilwell Division of U.S. Steel. Before that he worked at McKinsey & Company as a management consultant, assisting clients in the U.S. and Europe in solving a wide range of operational and strategic issues. Mr. Mailandt earned an M.S. and a Ph.D in nuclear physics and an M.B.A. from the University of Minnesota. He has published in journals as diverse as, Physical Review, Harvard Business Review, and Oil & Gas Journal among others.

Shelby McIntyre is an industrial engineer with an M.B.A. and a Ph.D. in marketing from Stanford University. He has published a number of articles on the potentials and difficulties of achieving innovation and successful new product development in high-technology firms. He has published in Management Science, Journal of Marketing Research, Organizational Behavior and Human Performance, Journal of Applied Psychology, Harvard Business Review, Business Horizons, Academy of Management Journal, Industrial Labor Relations Review, and Industrial Marketing Management.

Thomas H. Melohn is president and co-owner of North American Tool & Die, Inc. He graduated cum laude from Princeton University in 1952. Mr. Melohn has held executive positions with C&H Sugar, Swift and Company, Pet Milk, and the Leo Burnett Advertising Agency.

Anthony C. Paddock is vice president of Standard Research which he joined in 1978. Pror to joining SRC, he was vice president and director of the Corporate Finance Division of The Chase Manhattan Bank and a member of the Investment Banking Division of Merrill Lynch, Pierce, Fenner & Smith. He is a graduate of Harvard College, the Harvard Law School, and Columbia Business School. He has had extensive experience at SRC in dealing with the design of estate freezes.

Steven D. Popell is president of Popell, Inc., a management consulting firm specializing in small companies in the San Francisco Bay area. He has published in Community Property Journal and Business. He is also the *author of* Computer Time-Sharing—Dynamic Information Handling for Business *(Prentice-Hall, 1966), which was translated into French and Japanese. Mr. Popell graduated from Harvard College in 1960 with an A.B. and received an M.B.A. in 1965 from the Harvard Business School.*

Richard Raysman *is an attorney with the New York City law firm of Brown, Raysman & Millstein, and is chairman of the New York State Bar Association Computer Law Subcommittee. Mr. Raysman specializes in contract negotiation, litigation, protection of proprietary information, and other areas of law relating to computers. Mr. Raysman has written for* The New York Times *and co-authors a monthly column on Computer Law for the* New York Law Journal.

Robert B. Rogow, C.P.A., Ph.D., *is an associate professor of accounting and head of the department of accounting and finance at Auburn University in Auburn, Alabama. He is a graduate of the University of Arkansas and is a frequent contributor to both academic and professional accounting and finance journals. Mr. Rogow is a consultant to several small businesses and local governmental units. He is an active professional development seminar leader for certified public accounting societies and firms.*

James McNeill Stancill *is associate professor of finance at the Graduate School of Business, University of Southern California, and a principal in the consulting firm of Stancill & Associates. In his consulting, Mr. Stancill deals almost exclusively with what he calls the "developing firm," the type of financial management he teaches. Before joining USC, Mr. Stancill taught at the Wharton School, University of Pennsylvania where he received his Ph.D. in finance and economics.*

Judy Ford Stokes *is president of Judy Ford Stokes & Associates, Inc., a company that has grown to be one of the largest food management/design firms in the country, representing over 20 million meals a year. Ms. Stokes also serves as an outside director to several Boards of Directors, and she conducts corporate management seminars on strategic planning and inside value of outside directors throughout the country. Judy Ford Stokes is the author of the best selling book,* Cost Effective Quality Food Service, *publisher of* The Stokes Report, *a nationally acclaimed cost management newsletter for the foodservice industry, and the author of numerous articles for national publication.*

Jeffry A. Timmons *holds the Paul T. Babson Professorship in Entrepreneurial Studies at Babson College, Wellesley, Massachusetts. He is the first to occupy the Chair for two years (1982–3 and 1983–4). He is a graduate of Colgate University and has his M.B.A. and D.B.A. from Harvard University. Dr. Timmons is professor of management at Northeastern University (on leave), where he launched, in 1973, the first major in entrepreneurship and* *new ventures in the United States. He is lead author of* New Venture Creation, *(Irwin, 1977) and co-author of* The Insider's Guide to Small Business Resources, *(Doubleday, 1982). He has also written numerous articles on entrepreneurship and venture capital, including five in the* Harvard Business Review, *and was included in Pratt's 7th edition of* Guide to Venture Capital Sources. *He has served as a consultant to venture capital firms in the United States, United Kingdom, Sweden, and the Philippines; to organizations including The World Bank, Citicorp, Vlasic Foods, Monsanto, and General Electric; and to numerous start-up and rapid-growth ventures. He currently has funded research from the National Science Foundation to examine venture capital investing in high technology firms. His teaching and research interests focus on new ventures, venture capital, entrepreneurial management, and the application of microcomputer technology in these firms.*

Derek F. du Toit *is chairman of Classic Holdings (Pty.), Ltd. in Cape Town, South Africa. He has written many articles relating to his major sparetime interest, antique and classic cars.*

Tyzoon Tyebjee *has been teaching on the marketing faculty of the University of Santa Clara since 1977. Prior to that he taught at the Wharton School. Mr. Tyebjee has a Ph.D. and an M.B.A. from the University of California. He also has a master's degree in engineering from the Illinois Institute of Technology. Articles by Mr. Tyebjee have appeared in* Harvard Business Review, Journal of Marketing, Journal of Marketing Research, Management Decision, IEEE Transactions, Technovation, The Journal of Consumer Research, Journal of Marketing Science, *and* The Journal of Consumer Affairs. *Mr. Tyebjee is a principal investigator in research grants from the National Science Foundation and the Marketing Science Institute. He has investigated the venture capital market for high-technology startups, the performance of such embryonic firms, and the nature of the marketing function in rapidly growing firms.*

Karl H. Vesper *is a professor of business administration, a professor of mechanical engineering, and chairman of the management department at the University of Washington School of Business, where he has been on the faculty since 1969. His main academic interests are in entrepreneurship, technological innovation management, and strategic planning. The book on which this article is based is entitled* New Venture Strategies *and is available from Prentice-Hall. He is also the author of* Engineers at Work, *a casebook published by Houghton-Mifflin. Mr. Vesper earned his B.S.M.E., M.S.M.E., and PH.D from Stanford University. His M.B.A. is from the Harvard Business School.*

John A. Welsh, D.Sc., *was founder and chief executive of Flow Laboratories, Inc., which is now a major operating division of Flow General Inc. (NYSE).*

Prior to that he was treasurer of Thermo Electron, Inc. (NYSE) and president of Joseph Kaye & Co., Inc. In 1970 he became the founding director of the Caruth Institute of Owner-Managed Business at the Edwin L. Cox School of Business, Southern Methodist University. He received his education at Massachusetts Institute of Technology and taught engineering courses there for four years. He began his career as a pilot in World War II.

Louis A. Werbaneth, Jr., *deceased, was a partner with Touche Ross and Company.*

Jerry F. White *is a management consultant specializing in new, fast-growth businesses. He is also chairman of the Owner-Managed Business Center, Inc. in Dallas, Texas which produces and markets innovative management development programs for owner-managers. He is associate director of the Caruth Institute at Southern Methodist University. Mr. White has presented more than 300 seminars on Profit & Cash Flow Management throughout the United States and Canada to more than 5,000 entrepreneurs and owner-managers. During his earlier career he was associated with Westinghouse, IBM, and Collins Radio. Mr. White is co-author of two books:* Administering the Closely Held Company *(1980) and* The Entrepreneur's Master Planning Guide *(1983).*

Herbert N. Woodward *has served as president of International Science Industries, Inc., a Chicago based holding company for several smaller companies, and chairman of Intermatic, Inc.*

Author Index

Subject Index